THE
COMPLETE
SOFTWARE
DEVELOPER'S
CAREER GUIDE

JOHN SONMEZ

SIMPLE PROGRAMMER

For online information and ordering of this and other Simple Programmer books, please visit simpleprogrammer.com. For more information, please contact:

John Sonmez, Simple Programmer
john@simpleprogrammer.com
500 Westover Drive #7981
Sanford, NC 27330

Simple Programmer
500 Westover Drive #7981
Sanford, NC 27330

ISBN-13:978-0-9990814-1-9 (paperback)
ISBN-13:978-0-9990814-0-2 (electronic)

Printed in the United States of America

CONTENTS

SECTION 1
GETTING STARTED AS A SOFTWARE DEVELOPER   19

SECTION 2
GETTING A JOB   123

SECTION 3

WHAT YOU NEED TO KNOW ABOUT SOFTWARE DEVELOPMENT 275

SECTION 4

WORKING AS A DEVELOPER 455

SECTION 5

ADVANCING YOUR CAREER 617

PREFACE

I didn't expect to be writing a book so soon after writing my last book, *Soft Skills: The Software Developer's Life Manual*. (https://simpleprogrammer.com/cgp-softskills)

Well, I guess it hasn't been that short a period of time.

Soft Skills was released in December of 2014 and I began writing this book in the summer of 2016.

But, when you write a book, 1.5 years doesn't quite seem like enough of a break.

Writing a book is pretty hard work.

Sure, it's rewarding to have that book you wrote sitting on your bookshelf, but the process of getting it there is not always the most enjoyable.

So, you might be asking yourself, why then did I decide to write another book?

And why—by my standards at least—so relatively soon?

It's definitely not a matter of economics, because there are definitely more financially lucrative ways to spend your time other than writing a book.

And it's definitely not because I love writing.

While I do admit I enjoy it—at times—it's definitely a more painful than pleasurable experience.

Why then embark upon another journey, that isn't going to make me much money, is going to suck up a large amount of my time and at least be somewhat painful?

Well, mostly it's because I have to.

When I look at all the books written for software developers, I find there isn't a single book that tells software developers from A to Z how to not only start their career, but thrive in it and advance it and what exactly it is they need to know to be as successful as possible.

I get thousands of questions on my YouTube channel from software developers, young and old, experienced and new, male and female, from every country in the world asking about all kinds of "soft" topics related to software development.

Questions like:

How do I get started as a software developer?

How do I learn technical skills?

How do I negotiate my salary or pick between a contract job and salaried employment?

How do I deal with my boss, my coworkers, prejudice, women in tech, being a woman in tech?

What do I really need to know and how can I learn it?

College, boot camp, self-taught?

How do I find a job? What if I don't have any experience?

How do I pass an interview?

How should I dress?

How can I advance my career and take it to the next level?

I could go on and on.

The bad news is, I haven't found a single resource to point software developers to which answers all of these important questions.

The good news is, what you are holding now is that resource.

So, despite my reservations about writing another book—especially so soon, at least in my mind—I decided to write this book, not because I want to write another book necessarily—although I can't deny there was some itch of wanting to get back to writing—but because I firmly believe that when you see something that is needed you either find it or you create it.

I couldn't find it, so I'm creating it.

I hope you'll join me on this journey.

John

IS THIS BOOK FOR ME?

There you were, minding your own business when this book's awesome cover grabbed your attention and you just had to pick it up (or click on it.)

Now you are flipping through the pages asking yourself, "is this book for me?"

Don't worry, I can assure you I wrote this book just for you, even though I don't know anything about you.

How? You ask. After all, I don't even know that you can read.

Well, actually I do know you can read, because if you couldn't, my words wouldn't be magically vocalizing in your mind at this very moment.

I also know one other thing about you, which is that we share a keen sense of humor—or at the very least you can tolerate my humor—since you are still reading thus far.

Well, before I lose your interest permanently and you put this book back down on the shelf or click that other window in your browser, I suppose I should get a bit serious and get down to business.

All joking aside, no matter where you are in your software development career, this book has something to offer you.

For the scanners among us, allow me to quickly categorize you into one of three categories and you can read the category that is most relevant to you:

BEGINNER OR JUST INTERESTED IN LEARNING SOFTWARE DEVELOPMENT

If you are starting out and trying to learn software development / programming or you've learned a little, but haven't gotten your first job a software developer yet, you'll find the largest amount of value in the first two sections of this book where I talk about how to get started as a software developer and how to get your first job.

The rest of the book you'll find useful to fill in any knowledge gaps you'll need to succeed as a software developer, thrive in the workplace and advance your career.

You'll find relevant topics in this book that you won't find in any other book on software development (that I'm aware of) which will help you get rid of all the confusion with how to actually get your start, learn your first programming language and navigate the murky waters of college versus coding boot camps versus self-taught education.

MID-CAREER DEVELOPER

You'll likely find the most value in section three, "What you Need to Know About Software Development." This section fills in any knowledge gaps you may have and will help you to actively manage your career to succeed in the workplace.

But that doesn't mean you won't get any value out of the first section of the book, because even though you may already know how to program, you'll probably find it useful to learn how to further develop and pick up new technical skills, learn new programming languages, apply for jobs, craft a resume, and negotiate your salary.

And if you are interested in advancing your career—which you should be—you'll find the last section of this book, "Advancing Your Career," useful as well.

EXPERIENCED PROFESSIONAL

I know. I know you know all this stuff.

You don't need a basic book from some "hot-shot" on how to get started as a software developer. You don't need to learn what source control is or get insight on whether you should go to college or boot camp.

I get it—really, I do.

But, trust me on this one, this book is still for you. Here's why.

First of all, about half of this book is dedicated to working as a developer and advancing your career.

Even though you've been around for awhile and have likely been very successful—congrats by the way—you will probably find some benefit in learning how to better handle your coworkers and boss, sell your ideas, handle leadership and, heck, even get a raise or a promotion.

If you haven't already, you'll probably find yourself up against this "glass ceiling" in your software development career, where you don't feel like you can make much upward progress.

Been there, done that, got the t-shirt.

Fortunately, I also bashed my head right through that glass ceiling and I'll show you how to do it by telling you how to build a personal brand, speak at conferences, start a side-project and a whole lot more.

Finally, even though the beginning sections might seem a bit basic, you'll still likely find some value in the information about learning technologies, getting a high-paying job, negotiating your salary and choosing between contract and salaried employment.

Plus, you mentor other developers don't you?

Would be nice if you had some good advice written down to give them about starting out, wouldn't it?

So, yes. Yes, I say again, this book is for you, whoever you are.

I'll even venture so far out and be so bold as to say that even if you don't have the slightest interest in software development, you'll still probably get a bunch out of this book, because even though this book is specialized to software developers, it's really about managing your career and being as successful in it as possible.

And if you've made it this far, then this book is *really, really* for you, because obviously you like me—and you know what, I like you too. ;)

CHAPTER 1

HOW TO USE THIS BOOK

You've no doubt noticed this is a long book.

At last count I had this book at about 202,000 words.

That's a lot of words.

So, I thought I'd start off by telling you a little bit about **why this book has so many words**, and **how you can get the most out of this book.**

Depending on where you are in your career, whether you're just starting out, have a few years experience under your belt, or are a seasoned professional, you'll find that different sections will apply more or less to you and you may want to revisit some sections or chapters over time.

THE PURPOSE OF THIS BOOK

You might be wondering **why I decided to write this particular book.**

(I mentioned it briefly in the preface, but I want to rehash it a bit here.)

The most common questions I get from readers of my blog (https://simpleprogrammer.com /cg1-blog) and from my YouTube channel (https://simpleprogrammer.com/cg1-youtube) are about how to get started as a software developer and how to have a successful career.

I haven't been able to find a complete manual that teaches new—and experienced—developers how to really excel at their careers and how to deal with inevitable issues that come up when working in our industry.

I briefly touched on some of these topics in the careers section of *Soft Skills* (https://simpleprogrammer.com/cg1-softskills), but I felt like a more in-depth treatment of the subject was greatly needed.

So, while *Soft Skills* focused on a software developer's complete life—including one's career—**this new book is focused *only* on your career.**

It's also designed to be a standalone book, so you don't have to have read *Soft Skills* or any other book to get the most out of this book—or even have any experience with software development.

THE BOOK'S GOALS

First of all, I want to help new software developers learn all the important things they need to know to get started and jump into this sometimes tricky and complex field.

I want to give new software developers **a resource on all the important aspects of the field**, teach them what they need to know to get started, and show them the best way to get their first job.

In my mind, these are **the most important struggles** that new software developers face.

Next, I want to help existing software developers fill in the gaps of knowledge they may be missing — as far as their career is concerned — as well as provide them some guidance on how to survive as a working software developer.

I'll address problems concerning how to balance things like life and work, how to work on a team, how developers can sell their ideas and get raises and promotions, and how to deal with both leadership and prejudice.

Finally, I want to help software developers at any stage of their career **advance to the next level.**

I'll talk about how to build a reputation in the software development industry, the different career paths you can take, and books you should read. I'll cover side projects, conferences, and other topics that will help you **get to that next level** and become an **exceptional developer.**

Everything in this book could still be classified as soft skills since I'll be talking more about what you need to know and do theoretically rather than how to do it.

I believe this type of wisdom is still greatly lacking in our community and industry, and I strongly believe it is more valuable in the long term than learning a particular programming language or framework.

This book is broken down into five sections, each with small chapters—just like I did in *Soft Skills*.

- Getting Started as a Software Developer
- Getting a Job
- What You Need to Know About Software Development
- Working as a Developer
- Advancing Your Career

The big goal of this book is that no matter where you are in your software development career, you should be able to get something out of this book which will help you reach the next level in your development as a developer.

HOW TO USE THIS BOOK

It might seem pretty obvious how one should use a book.

The most practical manner in which to use a book, such as this one, is to pick it up and read it.

(Although, if you have the print version and it is thick enough, you may find some use in utilizing it to increase the height of your monitor on your desk.)

This book can of course be read cover-to-cover—and I'm assuming that is the way that most people will choose to consume this book, but **it can also be read section-to-section or chapter-to-chapter.**

Let's suppose you are just starting out in your software development career and you haven't even really learned to program yet.

In that case, it would be beneficial to start with the section "Getting Started as a Software Developer," which will be most relevant to you—and happens to be the first section anyway.

But, suppose you already have a job as a software developer and have been coding for a few years. You might want to jump right to "Working as a Developer" or perhaps "What You Need to Know About Software Development," to fill in any gaps.

Or maybe you are just interested—or immediately interested in—advancing your career.

In that case, you might find jumping straight to the "Advancing Your Career" section to be the most prudent course of action.

Similarly, with the chapters in this book, **each one is standalone.**

So, you can scan through the table of contents and pick which chapters apply to you or answer questions you have now or in the future.

The book was designed this way because I know situations and concerns change over a software developer's career.

When you are first starting out you want to know how to start out, but you might also want similar sort of advice if you are trying to learn a new programming language or new technology.

You might not need a job or need to negotiate a salary right now, or you might not be dealing with a nasty coworker or boss, but sometime in the future those chapters might be very relevant to your current situation.

I've always been frustrated when there were parts of a book that I wanted to go back to, but I couldn't remember where they were because they were buried in some chapter I remember reading.

So, **I tried to make this book read both straight through as well as act as a reference manual for your software development career.**

REPETITION AND ACTION

I'll say one last thing about how to use this book before we jump into the actual content in the next chapter.

First of all, **this book won't do you much good at all if you don't take action on what is written here.**

It's nice to read a book—and perhaps even agree wholeheartedly with the author—but, it doesn't come to much use if you don't apply what you are learning in your life.

Rather than burden you and tell you that you should really "do the exercises at the end of each chapter"—there aren't any—or tell you to take copious notes or make sure you apply one thing you've learned each day, I'm going to give you a much simpler solution—one that I employ myself.

REPETITION

If you really want to change your behaviors and adopt principles and best practices in your life, one of the best ways to do so is to **surround and immerse your brain in the ideas and concepts you want to integrate into your life.**

One of the best ways to do this is to utilize repetition.

It's a low-stress way of absorbing and applying information.

I do it myself all the time.

There are several books I've read over a dozen times, because they are so valuable to my career and my life and I really want to internalize the concepts and philosophies in those books.

So, **I'd highly encourage you to read and re-read the sections of this book which are most relevant to you** and perhaps even **put a reminder on your calendar** to go through the book again in a year or whatever interval you find most beneficial.

ACTION

All of the ideas and strategies I'm about to share with you won't do you or your career any good unless you start taking practical steps to put them into action.

To make this as easy as possible, I've put together a collection of resources that I'm calling The Complete Software Developer's Career Guide Digital Toolkit (https://simpleprogrammer.com /career-guide-toolkit).

The Toolkit includes my step-by-step process for finding a software developer job fast (even if you don't have any experience yet), a crash course on preparing for a software developer interview, a how-to guide on how you can dress at work to get more respect from your boss and coworkers, a "debuggers cheat sheet" to help you hunt and kill nasty bugs...

I'd conservatively value the resources in this Toolkit at $175, but they're included at no extra charge with your purchase of this book.

You can download your copy here (https://simpleprogrammer.com/career-guide-toolkit).

And as your career and life changes and grows, my sincere hope for you is that you continue to get value from this book.

Alright, so, let's get started...

SECTION 1

GETTING STARTED AS A SOFTWARE DEVELOPER

"If you have a dream, you can spend a lifetime studying, planning and getting ready for it. What you should be doing is getting started."
—Drew Houston

By far, the most common types of questions I get about software development are about how to get started.

In life, it seems the biggest obstacle to actually doing something and becoming what you want to become is getting started.

Whether it's starting a new workout regimen, training for a marathon, starting a business, writing a book, or—more specifically, in this case—programming, the most difficult part is always getting started.

It's easy—and tempting—to waste away countless hours debating what you should do.

It's much easier to read and study than to actually do.

It's much easier to think about taking a step and debate endlessly of what direction you should take that step, than it is to actually do it.

But, the secret is, you only need to take one step at a time.

You only need to summon all the courage and determination you can muster and say to yourself "I've debated enough, I've pontificated enough, I've got a plan—and it might not be the best one—but, I'm just going to do it anyway."

And, once you do that, you'll be on your way.

Before you know it, you'll look back and see the thousands of steps you've taken that have gotten you where you are, at the crest of the mountain instead of the base of it.

But, before you can do that, you do need to have a plan.

As many would-be software developers refuse to take a first step at all, there are an equal number of would-be software developers who act too brashly, without any information or plan and jump right in without knowing where they are going or where they want to end up.

In this first section of *The Complete Software Developer's Career Guide*, we'll go over the basics of getting started as a software developer.

We'll talk about how to put together a real plan for becoming a software developer, what technical skills you'll need to have to make it in the world of code, and how to develop those technical skills.

We'll also cover what programming language you should start with and the best way to learn that programming language, whether by teaching yourself, attending a coding boot camp or through the traditional route of going to college.

By the end of this section, my goal is for you to know enough to get started and to have an actual plan of how and when you are going to do it.

If you are already a software developer, you might still find this section useful, either to help you fill in any gaps you have, plan your future career better or decide how to continue your education in software development. (You might also find the information useful to pass on to someone you know who is struggling to enter the field and could use some guidance.)

Either way, you'll want to download the Software Developer Skills Assessment (https://simpleprogrammer.com/career-guide-toolkit) that's included with your purchase of this book. With this tool you can quickly find and fill gaps in your technical skills—and become a more confident developer.

I can give you all the advice and information in the world about software development and what path you should take, but nothing is going to happen until you step out in faith and put that first foot forward.

As I like to say, you have to "trust the process."

So, let's get started...

CHAPTER 2

HOW TO GET STARTED

When I first got started as a software developer, I had no idea what I was doing.

I was also frustrated. **Nothing seemed to make sense**, and I didn't think I'd ever "get it."

The reason I'm telling you this is that if you have picked up this book, you might feel that exact same way.

Don't worry, **this is normal. In fact, it's natural.**

And let me make one thing abundantly clear: **you don't have to be a genius** or even have **above average intelligence** to be a software developer.

When you first get started in the field of software development, if you don't feel overwhelmed (https://simpleprogrammer.com/cg2-overwhelmed) and like you just jumped into the deep end of a pool with weights tied to your ankles, you are probably either doing something wrong, or you're not human—maybe both.

Anyway, you should expect it to be difficult and confusing when you start out, but it's not always going to be that way—I promise.

HOW I STARTED OUT

I remember when I was first teaching myself to code. I didn't have all the resources we have today. In fact, **I didn't have any resources.**

I downloaded the source code from a popular MUD. (That's a Multi-User Dungeon. Think *World of Warcraft*, but no graphics—just text. Yes, this was in the "dial up to a BBS system using a modem" days.)

I didn't even know what I was looking at. All I knew was that I wanted to create my own version of a MUD and add my own features, and the key to doing it was buried somewhere in this pile of strange cryptic strings.

I started messing around. I changed variables to different values. I looked for some code that seemed to control the odds of getting a critical hit on an opponent. I changed it, recompiled the MUD, and saw what happened.

Sometimes it did what I wanted. **Sometimes it didn't even compile.** As I saw what worked and what didn't work, I learned.

I still didn't know what I was doing, but within a week or so of tinkering around with the code, I had managed to create a version of the MUD that actually had some of my "features" in it.

A long way from becoming a proficient programmer, but it was a start—we all need a start.

The reason why I am telling you this story is because, **more than picking up a textbook, more than going to college or a boot camp, more than anything else… I believe this is the way to get started programming.**

You have to tinker around and see what works and what doesn't. (I believe this is the best way to learn, period. See my section on Learning Quickly in *Soft Skills: The Software Developer's Life Manual* (http://simpleprogrammer.com/cg2-softskills)).

But **learning to code and learning how to get started in the world of software development are two very different things.**

Yes, you need to learn how to code, but there is much more to software development than just coding. This chapter is about the "more."

LEARNING ABOUT THE PROFESSION

First of all, you need to know something about developing software.

It's both easier and harder than you think.

A whole section of this book is dedicated to the idea of "What You Need to Know About Software Development," but I'm going to give you a quick overview here.

Software development isn't just programming. Programming is a large part of it, but just knowing how to code isn't going to take you very far—especially if you want to make a career out of this vocation.

The idea behind most software development projects is to **automate a manual process**, or to create a new automated way to do something that was too difficult to do manually.

Think about the word processing software I'm using right now. I happen to be typing this chapter using Google Docs.

Without Google Docs or other word processing programs, I'd have to either type this document on a typewriter or hand write it.

If I wanted to format the document to print it, I'd have to manually typeset the letters to be printed.

If I wanted to fix mistakes—especially spelling errors—I'd need to keep a bottle of whiteout nearby. (And probably a bottle of whiskey as well.)

Now it's not just Google Docs allowing me to do all this. There are a bunch of hardware and software programs involved that allow me to automate the manual process of typing or handwriting a book, but I think you get the point.

Therefore, let me emphasize to you a key concept that you should learn as early as possible as you embark on this journey to be a codeslinger.

You have to know how to manually do something *before* you can automate it.

UNDERSTANDING THE PROBLEM

Too many aspiring—and experienced—software developers try to write software without fully understanding what it is supposed to do. They want to just jump right in and code. (Which is fine for learning to code—as in my example with the MUD—but not for creating production software.)

Obviously, **you are smarter than that**, since you are reading this book.

The process of software development always begins by first understanding the problem to be solved. What are you automating?

Different software development methodologies do this in different ways, but that's not an important point right now. Right now, the point is that you have to, in some way, gather some kind of requirements and an understanding of the problem being solved before you can write any code.

This might be as simple as talking with a potential customer and discussing what needs to be built and how it should function, or it could be as formal a creating a fully documented specification.

DESIGN

Once you achieve that understanding, you then come up with some kind of design for how that problem is going to be solved in code—again, before any code is written.

Think of this as the architectural blueprint for your code. Once again, different software development methodologies handle this in many different ways, but what is important is that **you have some level of design before you jump in and start coding.**

This applies at the large scale and the small scale. Some developers who learn about Agile software development (we'll talk about that in a later chapter) think they don't need to design anything, that they can just start coding right away. While Agile development focuses on less up front design, **design is still necessary.**

You don't build a house by randomly just nailing two-by-fours together.

WRITING THE CODE

Once you have some idea of the design of the software, it will be time to either write some tests that will define what the software is supposed to do (also known as Test Driven Development or TDD), or it will be time to start coding. (We'll discuss TDD more in later chapters.)

Writing code is a discipline in itself, so we won't be getting into that here, but I'll recommend two great books on writing good code that you should definitely read.

First, I recommend *Code Complete* (https://simpleprogrammer.com/cg2-codecomplete) by Steve McConnell. This is a classic book every software developer should read.

The second is *Clean Code* (http://simpleprogrammer.com/cg2-cleancode) by Robert Martin, another classic book which will help you learn to write better code.

These books will help you learn how to structure your code and how to write code that is easy to understand and maintain.

Both of these books had a profound impact on my coding skills, especially in regards to clarity and design.

TESTING AND DEPLOYMENT

So, once code is written, we ship it, right?

Wrong. **Now comes the process of testing the code.** Again, different methodologies are going to handle this in different ways (https://simpleprogrammer.com/cg2-agile-testing), but in general, some kind of testing has to happen before the code is released to the end user.

For example in traditional, waterfall development projects, testing happens at the very end of a project, but in "agile" projects, testing happens during each iteration, which usually last about 2 weeks.

Once code is tested, it's ready for deployment, which may be a whole process in itself (https://simpleprogrammer.com/cg2-deployment).

We don't get into the details just yet—there will be a whole chapter on this topic—but deployment is the process of getting the finished software installed on a server, put into an app store, or made accessible in some other way to the users of that software. (And that process can be quite complex.)

Along the way, code may—ahem, should definitely—be **checked into source code repositories** where different versions of the code and its changes over time are stored.

In most complex applications that deal with any kind of volume and data, there is also **likely to be some kind of a database involved.**

The database typically will store user data for the application or configuration information and it may also need to be updated along with the source code.

Many software development teams use some form of continuous integration to build the code automatically when developers "check in" parts of it.

MORE TO WRITING CODE THAN JUST WRITING CODE

And finally, let's not forget debugging. As a developer, a large amount of your time is going to be spent figuring out why your code—or someone else's—doesn't work.

As you can see, there is a lot more to software development than just writing code.

You'll need to be aware of all this stuff before you can get a real job as a software developer. Hopefully, you'll have at least some experience and skills in a few of these other proficiencies as well.

But, fear not. **The purpose of this book is to prepare you for all that**—or at least spin you around and point you in the right direction. You might need to fill up the backpack with all the supplies you need for yourself, but I'll at least tell you what to pack.

HAVING A PLAN

Ok, John, I get that software development is more than just writing code and that I'm going to spend a lot of time debugging things, but you still haven't told me how to get started. What gives?

Ah, yes. I see your point, but guess what? Here is the good news:

You've already gotten started. Congratulations.

By picking up a book, like this one, and actually trying to understand that software development is much more than just writing code, you have **a better start than most software developers will ever have.**

Ok, yes, yes, I know that was a bit of feel-good fluff, but it's honestly true as well. Someday when you get to be a grouchy old software developer like me, you'll be preaching the same thing.

Now, on the more practical side... you need a plan.

Yes, a plan. A real, actual, no-BS plan for how you are going to go from knowing nothing or next to nothing about software development to a full-fledged software developer.

There are many roads you can take to get there—I'll be covering some of them in the upcoming chapters—but what's important isn't so much what road you take but rather that **you pick a road and stick to it.**

PUTTING TOGETHER THE PLAN

Let's talk about what your plan should entail.

First of all, you need an **honest assessment** of where you are right now and what things you are going to need to learn.

Do you have any programming experience?

Do you know any programming languages?

Have you ever built an application, or are you starting completely from the beginning?

What about all these other skills I talked about earlier?

Do you have any of them?

Do you know anything about databases, source control, TDD, testing, debugging, or software development methodologies?

Also, ask yourself what **kind of software development you want to do.**

Sure, everyone wants to be a game developer (https://simpleprogrammer.com/cg2-game-dev), but is that practical? And is that where you want to start? Are you willing to put in the long hours and fight with all the competition you'll face going down that long and lonely road?

So many people set off in a direction in life but don't think things completely through first.

Take some time to answer these questions, so you'll be able to come up with a good plan for getting started.

Don't get me wrong. I'm going to help you as much as possible in this book, but **I can only take you so far.**

I can give you all the information you need to become a good, even great software developer, but you are going to have to **organize it into an action plan** that is tailored to you. And then *you* are going to have to follow it.

CREATING THE PLAN

Once you've thought about these questions for a bit, it will be time to develop an actual plan.

The best way to develop your plan is to **work backwards from the goal you want to achieve.**

Rather than "learning to program" or "becoming a software developer," you should come up with **a specific goal of the kind of software developer you want to be.**

In the "What You Need to Know About Software Development" section of this book, I'll be covering the different kinds of software development roles or jobs you might want to consider, but you can also do some research on your own to determine what best fits you.

You want to be **as specific as possible**, so that you can know exactly what it is you need to learn, how you want to craft your resume and portfolio, what schools or programs you might want to enroll in, and even what jobs you want to apply for.

I know it's difficult to make a decision and make a commitment, but I can't stress enough just how important this is!

The more specific you are about what kind of software developer you want to become, **the easier EVERYTHING is going to be.**

You'll be able to clearly know what it is you need to learn and what you need to do for every step of the way.

WHO WANTS TO BE AN "ATHLETE?"

Think of it this way: suppose you wanted to be an "athlete."

That is pretty dang broad. How should you train to be an "athlete?"

Maybe you should lift weights and run, but maybe you should practice swimming. Maybe you should hit a ball with a tennis racket.

Better do all those things and more, so you are prepared for any sport that you might end up getting on a team to play.

See how ridiculous that sounds?

That is how ridiculous—in fact even more so—it sounds when someone expects to be a "software developer."

Instead, **pick your sport.**

Once you know the sport, you can know how to train for that sport and that will make your life much easier—trust me.

Start with the goal and works backwards to determine what you need to know and do in order to reach that goal.

Once you've done that, you can work out your plan.

The beginning of your plan should be all about what you need to learn. Figuring out the order of what you need to learn and how you are going to learn it is important.

Then, you should be figuring out what you will need to do to prepare for applying for jobs and getting your first job.

Finally, you need an actual plan for getting the job. Where are you going to look? What are you going to do? **What kinds of jobs are you going to apply for?**

I'd probably also add a plan for how you are going to continue your personal development and education after getting your first job.

A little overwhelming, I know, but don't worry. The reason I wrote this book is to **make all that easier for you.**

In the next few chapters, I'll be helping you figure out what you need to know and how to gain that knowledge, and in the following sections, I'm going to give you the details about how to get a job.

For now, you can start thinking about **what your plan is going to look like**, and try to figure out **what kind of developer you want to become.**

HEY JOHN

But what kind of developer do I want to become?

Good question. If you are just starting out, you might not even know what options are available to you—besides game developer.

Fortunately, this is not something difficult to figure out—although it may require a little bit of research.

Later in this book, I'll discuss some of the types of software developers. Mostly in the "What You Need to Know About Software Development" section, but you should also do your own research.

Ask software developers you know what kind of software development they do or what kind of developers they are.

Think about what kind of things you are interested in creating and research some of the associated technologies and programming languages.

There are a wide variety of technologies and sub-vocations you can focus on as a software developer.

Do you want to write web applications? Mobile applications? Do you want to write the code that makes a refrigerator regulate its temperature properly? Perhaps you want to write the code to send astronauts into space?

Think carefully and then research. If you ask the right questions, the answers are never hard to find.

A CONCRETE EXAMPLE

I always find real examples useful, so let's look at a realistic scenario for someone who wants to become a web developer utilizing Node.js as their primary technology:

Goal: Become a Node.js developer.

Plan:

LEARNING

- [ ] Learn the basics of JavaScript.
- [ ] Learn about web pages and web development technologies like HTML and CSS.
- [ ] Learn the basics of Node.js.
- [ ] Be able to write some kind of simple Node.js web application.
- [ ] Learn about the different frameworks and technologies developers use to develop Node.js applications.
  - [ ] Fill in some frameworks or technologies to use with Node.js from research above.
- [ ] Learn some kind of database technology to use with Node.js.
- [ ] Learn computer science basics:
  - [ ] Algorithms.
  - [ ] Data structures.
- [ ] Learn best practices for writing good code.
- [ ] Learn how to design the architecture of a Node.js app.

PREPARING FOR GETTING A JOB

☐ Start looking at job descriptions for a Node.js developer in my area and find out what skills employers want.
☐ Come up with a list of companies, locally, that I can likely get a job at.
☐ Start attending user groups in the area.
☐ Start networking with other local Node.js developers.
☐ Hire a resume writer to help me write a good resume.
☐ Practice coding interview questions.
☐ Practice mock interviews.
☐ Build a portfolio of a few apps to demo.

GETTING A JOB

☐ Contact all the people in my networks to let them know what value I can provide and what I am looking for.
☐ Start applying for junior-level jobs or internship programs.
☐ Plan to apply for at least two jobs each day.
☐ Debrief with myself after interview and decide what skills need to be worked on.

Your plan will be rough at first, but as you figure out more about what you need to learn and do, you can fill in more details.

Having some kind of plan in place is important. You can always change and adapt the plan, but if you don't have a plan to begin with, you'll be aimlessly floating in random directions and will probably get frustrated and be more likely to give up.

In the next chapter, I'll help you refine that plan further as we discuss the technical skills that you are going to need in order to become a software developer.

CHAPTER 3

THE TECHNICAL SKILLS YOU NEED TO HAVE

I'm a big supporter of helping software developers develop *Soft Skills* in addition to their technical skills—in fact, I wrote a complete book about it (http://simpleprogrammer.com /cg3-softskills)—but there is no denying: **technical skills are important.**

I mean, if you can't actually write code and develop software, all the soft skills you learn won't really do you much good. Perhaps you'd make a good manager or coach, but not a software developer.

But, if you are reading this section of the book, I'm assuming you are interested in becoming a software developer—or a better one—so let's talk about the technical skills you are going to need to know.

THE SKILLS THAT PAY THE BILLS

Now, this is a topic that tends to overwhelm many beginner software developers because it can feel like there is **so much to know**, and it can be difficult to even **know where to start.**

I'm going to try and break it down here into what the most **essential and beneficial** technical skills are that will benefit you the most in your **quest to become a software developer.**

This chapter is by no means meant to be an exhaustive list of all the technical skills you could possibly need as a software developer, but I've tried to list the essential ones and give you an overview of them here.

Fear not. In the section of this book titled "What You Need to Know About Software Development," **I'll be dedicating a chapter to pretty much every one of these skills**, and we'll take a much deeper dive.

I've also condensed this list down into a useful tool, the Software Developer Skills Assessment, which you can download free here (https://simpleprogrammer.com/career-guide-toolkit).

So, without further ado, here is a brief overview of the technical skills I find most important.

ONE PROGRAMMING LANGUAGE

I think it's best we start with this one, don't you?

Can't really be a programmer without knowing a programming language—you know what I mean, Vern? (See Ernest P. Worrell (https://simpleprogrammer.com/cg3-ernest) if you don't get that reference. Enjoy.)

We'll talk about selecting which programming language to learn in the chapter cleverly named "What Programming Language to Learn," **so don't stress out about that just yet.**

I will say very quickly, though, that **the choice of which programming language to learn** (https://simpleprogrammer.com/cg3-what-language) **is not as important as you may think it is.**

Instead, let's talk about why I'd suggest starting with just one programming language and not trying to learn everything there is under the sun.

Many beginner programmers try to hedge their bets by learning several programming languages at once before they try to take on their first job as a software developer.

While I think that you should eventually learn more than one programming language, **I would advise against doing it upfront** because it will just lead to confusion, and it will divert your energies from many of the other technical skills you are going to need to learn.

Instead, I'd advise you to **go deep and focus on learning the ins and outs of a single programming language,** so you can feel really confident in your ability to write code in that language.

Remember how we talked about being as specific as possible when deciding what kind of software developer you were going to become?

That's the idea here.

HOW TO STRUCTURE CODE

After learning a programming language—or preferably while learning it—I am a firm believer that the next thing you need to know is how to properly structure your code.

I've already given you an **excellent resource** to help you to learn this extremely valuable skill: *Code Complete* by Steven McConnell (https://simpleprogrammer.com/cg3-codecomplete).

What do I mean by structuring your code?

I mean to write **good, clear, understandable code that doesn't require a large amount of comments because the code itself is communicative.**

Many software developers go through their whole career without learning this skill, and it's unfortunate because this is the primary way I—and many others—judge the skill and competence of a software developer.

Good code structure shows a dedication to the craft beyond just getting the job done.

Structuring your code is really the art part of software development, but it's also critical because you and your co-workers have to work with your code and will spend considerably more time maintaining existing code rather than writing new code.

I'm not going to go into how to properly structure your code in this book since—like I said—I've already provided you with an excellent resource, but **you should strive to learn how to write good, clean code from the beginning** rather than learn this skill afterwards.

I can just about guarantee that, even if you are a beginner, if you can write good, clean, concise, and understandable code that expresses its meaning in the structure itself, just about any interviewer who sees your code is going to **assume you are an experienced professional.**

And to some degree you will be, or at least on the path to be, because you'll be treating this career as a profession, not just a job: a sign of a true craftsman.

OBJECT ORIENTED DESIGN

This one is debatable, especially if you are learning a program language that isn't object oriented (OO), but **enough of the software development world thinks in terms of OO design, so you need to make sure you understand it.**

Object oriented design is a way of designing complex programs that breaks them down into individual classes or objects (instantiations of classes), which encapsulate functionality and have specific roles and responsibilities.

In software development, **we are always trying to manage complexity.**

Thinking in terms of objects helps us do that because it allows us to define and design a complicated system out of a bunch of interacting components, rather than try to tackle the entire complexity as a whole.

There are plenty of functional programming languages out there today, but **the most popular languages and patterns you'll find in software development are still heavily, if not completely, influenced by object oriented design and analysis.**

You should have a good understanding of what a class is, what the different types of inheritance are—and when to use them—as well as understanding terms like polymorphism (https://simpleprogrammer.com/cg3-polymorph) and encapsulation.

ALGORITHMS AND DATA STRUCTURES

This is a large portion of what you will or would learn if you took a traditional college or university program to get a degree in computer science.

Algorithms are the common ways of solving various computer science / programming problems.

For example, there are several algorithms that are commonly used for sorting lists of things programmatically. Each of these sorting algorithms has a different set of properties regarding speed, memory size requirements, and the ideal kind of data it works on.

There are many of these algorithms in the field of computer science, and it is also **important to understand how to write your own variations** (https://simpleprogrammer.com/cg3-problems)

of these algorithms to solve the kind of tricky problems you might encounter when solving real programming problems.

Often, being good with algorithms can allow one developer to solve a problem in an hour that might take another developer several days to figure out.

Unless you are familiar and good with algorithms, **you won't even know an elegant solution already exists out there.** So, for this reason alone, I consider it a valuable skill to acquire.

Data structures fall into a similar category and work in conjunction with algorithms.

There are several data structures all software developers should be familiar with including:

- Arrays or vectors
- Linked lists
- Stacks
- Queues
- Trees
- Hashes
- Sets

By having a good grasp of data structures and algorithms, you can easily and elegantly solve many difficult programming problems.

When I first started programming, I was really bad at data structures and algorithms because I was mostly self-taught.

I didn't realize the true value of them until I started competing on a site called TopCoder (https://simpleprogrammer.com/cg3-topcoder) where knowing data structures and the algorithms that operate on them gave you a serious competitive edge.

Quickly, it became apparent how useful these skills were in the real programming world as I encountered problems that I previously had no idea how to solve, and which are now extremely easy—and fun.

In fact, **I consider this to be one of the most fun areas of software development.** It's really rewarding to work through a difficult problem and to utilize data structures and algorithms to develop a clean, elegant solution that performs really well.

The best resource, at the time of this writing at least, is by far Gayle Laakmann McDowell's excellent book, *Cracking the Coding Interview* (https://simpleprogrammer.com/cg3-cracking).

In this book, she goes over just about everything you need to know about algorithms and data structures.

It's a challenge to learn this stuff, but well worth it. This is one of those skillsets that can set you far above your peers. **A MAJORITY of software developers are pitifully ill-equipped in this area.**

And if you want to pass an interview at a company like Microsoft or Google, **you will definitely need to master this skillset.**

A DEVELOPMENT PLATFORM AND RELATED TECHNOLOGIES

You should have some experience and mastery of at least one development platform and the related technologies or frameworks that go with it.

What do I mean by platform?

Well, **generally it means operating system (OS)**, but it can also apply to other abstractions that act similar to operating systems.

For example, you could be a Mac developer or Windows developer focusing on the Mac or Windows operating systems, but you could also be a web developer focused on a specific web platform.

I don't want to pull this down into a discussion about what exactly a platform is—different people will have different opinions—but for the purpose of this discussion, **I'm going to define a platform as a specific environment that you develop for, which has its own ecosystem and particularities.**

Again, this is another one of those things where I don't think it's so important what you choose, so much as it is that you **choose something.**

Companies usually hire developers to develop for a specific platform or technology.

You'll have a much easier time getting a job as an iOS developer if you have expertise with that specific platform.

This means being familiar with the platform itself, as well as what development tools, idiomatic patterns, and common frameworks programmers typically use when developing for that platform.

You might think the choice of a programming language determines the platform, but that is actually rarely the case.

Take C# today. You can be a C# developer and write code for Windows, Mac, iOS, Android, Linux, and even embedded systems.

So don't just pick a language; pick a platform as well.

FRAMEWORK OR STACK

In addition to learning a specific programming language and platform, I'd also highly advise learning a framework or, better yet, a complete development stack that goes with it.

What is a framework?

What is a stack?

A framework is simply a set of libraries that are used to develop code on a particular platform or on multiple platforms. It usually makes common programming tasks on that platform easier.

Going back to the C# example. Most C# developers use the .NET Framework for writing C# applications. The .NET Framework consists of many libraries and classes that allow a C# developer to work at a higher level of abstraction since he doesn't have to completely reinvent the wheel every time he wants to do something.

For example, part of the .NET Framework contains code for manipulating images. This code would be extremely difficult to write from scratch, so the framework is a huge benefit for C# developers writing code that needs to manipulate images in some way.

A stack is a bit different. **A stack is a set of technologies, usually including a framework, that are commonly used together to create a full application.**

For example, there is a common stack called the MEAN stack. It stands for MongoDB, Express.js, AngularJS, and Node.js.

MongoDB is a database technology.

Express.js is a Node.js framework for creating web applications.

AngularJS is a front-end JavaScript framework for creating the user interfaces for web applications.

Finally, Node.js is a runtime environment for developing web-based applications in JavaScript.

It's not important that you understand all that—unless you are going to be a MEAN developer—but what is important to understand is that, if you know all those technologies and frameworks, you'll be able to develop an entire web application.

Stacks make it easier to create applications because they provide a common paradigm which many developers are using to develop applications, so knowledge can easily be shared and you can be sure that a particular set of technologies are proven to work together.

Learning a stack can be extremely valuable because it means you have all the required skills to develop a full application. Many companies that have an application which was developed using a particular stack will be looking for software developers that are familiar with that stack and can hit the ground running.

BASIC DATABASE KNOWLEDGE

Even though the landscape of databases has changed quite a bit in the last few years, I don't see databases going away anytime soon, so I think you probably should know a thing or two about them, don't you?

At the time of writing this book, **there are two main database technologies:** relational databases and document databases.

I would say that a developer today should at least be familiar with relational databases and probably should have some understanding of document databases as well.

In software development, databases are often used to store data for an application.

Some teams will, of course, have dedicated database developers or database administrators (DBAs), but that doesn't really excuse you from not knowing at least the basics of databases.

At the very least, you should know:

- How databases work
- How to perform basic queries to get data
- How to insert, update and delete data
- How to join datasets together

In addition, you are probably going to want to know how to **retrieve and store data program-matically from your code** with your chosen platform and / or framework.

Most developers are expected to be able to write code that can interact with a database.

SOURCE CONTROL

Source control is an integral part of any software development project.

Back in the day, before we used source control, we'd have a network share with all the files for a project on it, or we'd pass thumb drives back and forth with different versions of the software on them.

I'm ashamed to admit that I've participated in these shenanigans more than once.

But, **I was young. I was stupid. You don't have to be.**

Almost all professional developers today are expected to know how to use source control to check in code, check out code, and hopefully merge changes from multiple sources.

Source control at its most basic level allows you to keep a history of the changes made to different files in a software project.

It also allows for multiple developers to work on the same code at the same time and to merge those changes back together.

We won't go into the details here, but **you should know how to use at least one source control system very well**, and you should be familiar with most of the basic source control concepts.

Just about all professional software development teams will use some kind of source control in today's software development world.

BUILD AND DEPLOYMENT

Today, most software development projects have some kind of automated build and deployment system.

There are several different software applications out there that help teams to automate both of these tasks, which used to be manual and, for some teams, still are.

What is build and deployment, you ask?

Good question.

Well, you know how you write that code and check it into a source control system?

It would probably be a good idea to have some way to make sure that code actually works after you check it in.

That's where a build system comes in.

At the very least, a build system is going to compile all the code and make sure there are no compilation errors.

A sophisticated build system may also **run unit tests or user tests, run code quality checks, and provide some reporting** on the current state of the code base.

A deployment system will be responsible for deploying the code either to a production machine or perhaps to some kind of a test environment.

You don't have to be an absolute expert in these technologies, but **it's pretty important that you understand at least the basics of how these systems work**, and the process of building and deploying code.

Often, the actual responsibilities for creating and maintaining a build and deployment system will belong to a quickly growing field called DevOps (short for developer operations).

But, that doesn't excuse you from understanding at least the basics of how this process works.

TESTING

It used to be that developers didn't have to know much about testing.

It used to be that we'd write a bunch of code and "throw it over the wall" to a bunch of testers who would find all kinds of bugs in our code, we'd fix the bugs, and that was that.

Not anymore.

With so many software projects adopting what is called an Agile process, (we'll discuss this more when we get to methodologies), software developers and testers are having to work much more closely together (https://simpleprogrammer.com/cg3-agile-testing).

Quality has really become the responsibility of the entire team—I'd argue that it always has been.

With that said, you need to know something about testing.

You should at least be familiar with some basic terms like:

- Whitebox testing
- Blackbox testing
- Unit testing (not really testing)
- Boundary conditions
- Test automation (https://simpleprogrammer.com/cg3-bat)
- Acceptance testing

A good developer—and I'm assuming you want to at least become a good developer—tests their own code before giving it to someone else.

If you really want to be considered a professional and not just a hack, **this is non-negotiable.**

DEBUGGING

Ah, many a novice software developer has his dream smashed on the rocks of the debugger.

Everyone wants to write code, am I right?

But ain't nobody want to debug their code? Ya hear me?

Ya feel me?

Truth time.

You are going to spend perhaps 90% of your time as a software developer figuring out why the hell your code doesn't work (https://simpleprogrammer.com/cg3-debugger-mindset)**.**

I know this isn't glamorous. I know you just want to write new code all day, but the world just doesn't work that way.

If you apply a methodology like test-driven development, you'll probably spend a whole lot less time in the debugger, but regardless, whatever you do, no matter how you try and get around it, **you are going to have to learn how to debug your code** or someone else's.

So, rather than taking a haphazard approach to something you know you are going to have to do, you should just **bite the bullet and actually learn how to do it effectively.**

In the chapter on debugging, I'll talk more about this, but for now, just know, you gotta know how to do it.

METHODOLOGIES

Intimidated yet by the laundry list of things you need to know?

If not, here's one more—but I promise this is the last one.

While some software development teams just start writing code and get things done when they are done, **most teams have some kind of methodology they at least pretend to follow.**

(By the way, side note here: don't expect any team to actually really follow the software develop-ment methodology they profess to use (https://simpleprogrammer.com/cg3-waterfalls)*. I'm not trying to be cynical or point fingers here. I'm just a realist, and I happen to know there are a whole lot of people who say they are doing software development methodologies like Scrum just because they have a meeting where everyone stands up every day.)*

For this reason, it's critical that you are at least familiar with some of the basic ideas behind the most common software development methodologies.

Today, I would say those are **waterfall development** and **Agile development.**

Most teams will claim they are doing Agile. Agile itself is a pretty loose concept, but there are some practices and, dare I say, rituals that you should be aware of if you want to be able to talk the talk, so to speak, and fit in on an Agile team.

We'll talk about this more in depth in the chapter on software development methodologies.

OVERWHELMED? DON'T BE

I know this is quite a bit of stuff, and I've barely scratched the surface on most of these topics.

Right now you might be feeling a bit overwhelmed and like you don't understand most of what these technical skills are.

That's ok. You aren't supposed to yet—unless you are already a practicing software developer, in which case, shame on you! (Just kidding. I love you, but **you really better get your shit together**—really.)

Anyway, I'm going to be covering most of these topics in much more depth in the section of this book titled, "What You Need to Know About Software Development."

So, just chillax as they say.

Next, I'll be telling you how to learn technical skills in general, so by the time you get to the actual chapters on these technical skills, you'll be ready to go.

HEY JOHN

I noticed there are quite a few links in this book and you seem to be promoting a bunch of your other products and stuff... what gives man?

Ah, I'm glad you asked.

First, let's talk about the links.

Yes, there are quite a few links in this book. But, don't worry, you don't have to follow all of them.

Just click on, or go to the ones you are interested in.

I mostly tried to link to relevant or correlatory information that I produced in the past as much as possible, just in case you wanted to go deeper or find out more about a subject.

Most of the links will go to my blog posts or YouTube videos, where I usually have much more to say on a subject—or just because they are entertaining as hell.

(Also, if you click any of the links in this book—or type them into your web browser—you'll be taken to a page that has a list of ALL the links in the book organized by chapter.)

Oh, and for plugging my other products. Yes, you are right. I am definitely doing that.

It's called being smart.

Books are cheap. You don't make a lot of money writing a book.

In fact, if you write a book, you should really have another reason for writing it, rather than making money.

One reason why I wrote this book is to help promote some of my other products and "stuff" that I think you'll find valuable.

It's not meant to be "spammy" and you don't have to buy anything—this book is designed to be a huge value by itself with nearly 800 pages—but, it's there if you want it, and I'm going to promote it.

CHAPTER 4

HOW TO DEVELOP TECHNICAL SKILLS

Now that I've given you a nice long list of technical skills to develop, you might be wondering how you are going to develop all of those skills and how long it is going to take you.

Well, as for the length of time—don't worry—you'll be developing your technical skills as long as you are a software developer. **Think of it as a journey, not a destination.**

You will always be able to get better—if you choose to.

I've spent plenty of time developing my technical skills the wrong way (https://simpleprogrammer.com/cg4-learning-mistakes).

However, in my three years of creating over 50 highly-technical developer training courses on Pluralsight, I've also learned how to develop technical skills at a lightning fast speed while teaching others at the same time.

I used to think the best way to learn a technical skill was to take a big reference book and read it cover-to-cover.

Back then, I read too many 800+ page books to count and didn't benefit much from the exercise; although my arms might have grown from carrying around books of that size.

I don't want you to make the same mistakes I did, and if you already have, **I want to show you a better way.**

LEARNING HOW TO LEARN QUICKLY

Before we get into the specifics about learning technical skills, I think it's worth taking a second to talk about learning anything quickly and teaching yourself in general.

We'll go much more in-depth about the topic of teaching yourself in an upcoming chapter in this section, but I want to go over the basics here and talk about **a methodology I use to learn anything quickly.**

As I mentioned, I spent a large amount of time both learning and teaching various technologies.

I learned whole programming languages in a matter of weeks (https://simpleprogrammer.com /cg4-7-languages) and then turned around and taught courses on them.

During that process, I developed a **reliable system** for learning just about anything I needed to learn.

This wasn't so much a conscious effort as it was a necessity. I was trying to learn at such a rapid rate that I had to come up with efficient ways of doing things, and naturally, patterns of learning developed which helped me to become faster and faster.

I'm just going to cover the basics here, since you can find a whole course I put together on the subject at "10 Steps to Learn Anything Quickly" (https://simpleprogrammer.com/cg4-10-steps) or in a few chapters in my *Soft Skills* (http://simpleprogrammer.com/cg4-softskills) book.

THE BASIC PROCESS

The basic idea is pretty simple.

Essentially, you want to first **get a good idea of what you are learning and what the scope of it is.**

You need to get enough information about your subject to understand the big picture and narrow the subject down to a small enough scope that you can actually tackle it and wrap your head around it in a realistic amount of time.

Then, **you need a goal.** You need to establish what it is you are trying to learn and why and, most importantly, what metric you will use to know that you've learned it.

Far too many people set out to learn something but have no way to measure whether they have succeeded or not.

Equipped with that starting point, you can start to **gather some resources for learning.**

I recommend not just reading one book cover-to-cover but to instead gather multiple resources, which may include books, blogs, podcasts, magazines, video courses and tutorials, expert opinions, etc.

Then, you are going to use some of those resources to **create an actual plan for learning.**

You can do this by using the resources you've gathered to create a systematic, sequential set of steps for you to learn what you want to learn.

For example, you could utilize the table of contents of one of the books you found to help figure out what order you should try to learn things in and what is important.

You are basically going to figure out in what order to learn everything you need to know about your topic.

Then, you dive in. From your learning plan, start with each module you are going to learn about your subject. For each module, **learn enough to get started, play around** for a bit, and then go back and **answer any questions you had** while playing around.

You are basically going to focus on **learning by doing**, which we'll talk about in a second.

The key here is to not learn too much up front. Instead, utilize natural curiosity to drive your learning as you play around on your own. Then, go back and actually read the text or consume the content about your topic, with questions in your head and some experience which will **naturally guide you to seek out what is actually important.**

A big problem we face when learning by consuming a bunch of material is that we don't actually know what is important. By playing around first and forming your own questions, you solve that problem and what you learn actually sticks.

Finally, you **take what you learned and you teach it to someone else.**

It doesn't really matter the format and it doesn't matter who you teach it to. You could talk to your dog or the squirrels in your yard if you like. Doesn't really matter.

What matters is that you somehow reorganize the thoughts in your head in a way that communicates them to the outside world.

This is the place where learning changes from knowledge to understanding (https://simpleprogrammer.com/cg4-teach)

And that's it.

What we have here is a basic formula you can apply to **just about anything you want to learn quickly.**

If you'd like to see a more detailed example, complete with a workbook and videos that can help you master this process, you can find it here: "10 Steps to Learn Anything Quickly" (https://simpleprogrammer.com/cg4-10-steps).

Now, let's talk more specifically about learning and developing technical skills.

LEARN BY DOING

I believe **we all learn best by doing**, but when it comes to technical skills, this is paramount.

It is just not possible to learn most technical skills by simply reading a book or even watching a video tutorial.

You may get an idea of what is possible using a particular technology, programming language, or tool, but **until you've actually used it yourself, or solved problems with it, you are only going to have a surface level understanding.**

Just about everything I talked about in the last chapter is going to require more than book knowledge in order to gain any real level of competency.

This might be obvious for programming languages, but **can you really learn how to use source control from just reading about the syntax?**

If you've never made the mistake of merging a file into the wrong branch or checking out the wrong version of the source code, and you've never actually used a version history to figure out where a bug got introduced, you aren't really going to know how to use source control—you'll just think you do.

(Don't worry if you don't understand any of that yet.)

But didn't I promise to teach you all of those technical skills in a later section of this book?

Aren't you reading a book right now, hoping to learn something?

Yes, but the key is that the **learning doesn't stop there.**

You can read my words and gain a cursory understanding of a topic I'm talking about here, but at some point **you are going to need to put down this book and actually take some real action** (https://simpleprogrammer.com/cg4-taking-action) to actively learn what you are reading about by doing (at least for the technical skills we are talking about here).

HOW TO LEARN BY DOING

At the risk of regurgitating some information that might seem obvious, I'm going to tell you about how to actually learn by doing—**consider this as a reminder for something you already know.**

Whenever you are going to try and learn a technical skill, start by **figuring out what it is going to help you do.**

If you don't have an immediate need for the skill, you might even question whether you need to learn it at all. A large amount of time is wasted by learning technical skills we are never actually going to use in the real world. Believe me, I'm so guilty of doing this that it's not even funny.

You'll have a much easier time learning something if you have an immediate application for it—a real reason to learn it.

I guarantee you will be learning like you've never learned before if you are being instructed on how to skydive right before you fly up into the sky and jump from a plane.

But what if you don't have a pressing need? What if you are learning a technical skill because you want to be able to get a job where you'll need to use it?

In that case you need to manufacture a reason to use that skill. **Create a goal.**

AN EXAMPLE OF LEARNING BY DOING

Let's look at a real example.

Suppose you wanted to learn about relational databases and how to use them.

You could just try and read about a database and run some queries against it to play around with—and that might be somewhat effective.

What if instead your goal involved creating a database to store a collection of movies you owned?

What if your goal was to query this database, insert new movies, delete movies, update the titles, etc?

What if you wanted to create a simple application to let you access the database and do all this?

Now, you have a purpose and a way to learn by doing.

Now, you have something to do.

How do you approach learning about relational databases?

You crack open that book or you watch that video tutorial, looking for specific information you need to know to solve your actual problems.

Then, you **actually create and use a database** and not just as an exercise. You have a real goal.

Think about how much more information you'll retain when you work and learn in this way.

And won't it also be so much more fun?

HOW I TEACH TECHNICAL SKILLS

As I mentioned earlier, I have taught quite a few technical skills in a pretty large variety of technologies in my day.

Therefore, I thought you would benefit from seeing how I teach technical skills to make them easier to learn. That way, you can just apply this concept when teaching them to yourself.

Make sense?

When I teach technical skills, **I want to give people the biggest bang for their buck**, and I don't want to **bore them with a bunch of stuff they don't really need to know** or could learn on their own when they actually need to learn it.

Instead, I focus on teaching what will be **immediately valuable** and giving students the resources they need to practice what I call "just in time learning" when they need to go deeper on a topic.

There are three main things I try to teach someone when I am teaching a technical skill:

- The big picture: what can you do with the technology?
- How to get started.
- The 20% you need to know to be the most effective.

Let's break each of these things down.

THE BIG PICTURE: WHAT CAN YOU DO WITH THE TECHNOLOGY?

I always start with the big picture.

I believe in the power of Google to solve most of your problems, but **you can't Google something if you don't know what it is.**

Therefore, I first try to teach my students how big a particular technology is and **an overview of what it can do.**

This is at a very surface level. I'm not showing them or you how to do everything in a technology; I'm just giving you a quick tour and overview of all the points of interest on a map.

For a programming language, for instance, I might talk a bit about the **history of the language** and what it is mostly used for.

Then, I might jump in and show you **all the constructs of the language** and the **language features**—especially the unique ones.

Finally, I might introduce you to the **various libraries** that are a standard part of the language and give you an idea of what you can do with them and what they cover.

The idea here is to **give you the complete lay of the land without going into the details.**

You can always look up the details on your own for the things you are interested in.

At this step, **I want to eliminate the unknown unknowns.** I want to make sure that you establish what you don't have any knowledge about, so when you need to learn about it, you can know where to look.

My goal is that you don't say, "Oh, I didn't know X could do that," but instead say, "I know X can do it. I'm not sure how, but I can figure that out later."

Imagine trying to learn woodworking without knowing that such a thing as a dremel or router existed.

You don't have to know how to use those tools, but without knowing they exist, you would be severely handicapped.

HOW TO GET STARTED

The next thing I like to teach students is how to get started.

This is often the most difficult part of learning a technology—and it's the precursor to "doing"—so I try to make this as painless as possible.

I want to show a student how to download whatever they need to download, get it installed, create their first project, and compile their code.

Once a person is able to overcome this obstacle, they can start playing around and actually build things or work with the technology.

If this barrier to entry seems too high, someone is likely to just read a book or watch a tutorial and never actually get their hands dirty.

You can utilize this in your own studies by making sure you focus on discovering how to get started with a particular technical skill early on in your learning process.

Look for specific tutorials or guides that will show you how to get started, then you can take it from there.

YOU NEED TO KNOW 20% TO BE THE MOST EFFECTIVE

Finally, I try to teach students 20% of the information concerning the technology that they'll use 80% or more of the time.

Almost everything in life falls into what is called the Pareto principle, which basically states that 20% of something produces 80% of the results.

The key to learning a technical skill is figuring out what the 20% is.

What 20% can you learn that will be used in 80% of the work you do using that technical skill?

This is where it is really going to be critical to be doing rather than just reading.

Many books and even tutorials are written like reference manuals, not giving particular emphasis to the 20% of the technology that is most important to know.

If you are actively working with a technology, you'll quickly discover what you use the most because it will be extremely painful to not know it.

Let's look at the relational database example again.

Most likely, if you learn about relational databases, you'll find that writing select statements is pretty squarely in that 20% area.

If you just read a book on SQL, you might find equal weight given to selecting, inserting, updating, deleting, indexing, and various other database functions.

However, if you actually try and create a database and use it, you are going to be doing a whole lot of select statements. You'll also quickly realize that you need to learn how to join tables.

Instead of wasting your time trying to learn everything there is to know about relational data-bases, you'll focus your efforts on learning how to write select statements, join tables, and other common operations that make up that critical 20%.

This is why doing is so important.

It also can help to shadow an expert and watch them work, or even assist them in an apprentice-like situation.

By just seeing someone who uses the technical skill you are developing and what their 20% is, you can learn what you need to know quickly.

On the job training especially can be extremely effective.

READ WHAT EXPERTS ARE WRITING

I'll leave you with one final idea to help you develop technical skills.

Become an avid reader of what experts who already possess that technical skill are writing.

When I was learning my craft, I would spend about **30 minutes each day** reading various blogs related to subjects I was learning about.

When I really wanted to get an in-depth knowledge of C++, I devoured Scott Meyers' *Effective C++* books (http://simpleprogrammer.com/cg4-effective).

Oftentimes, just hearing an expert's opinion on a subject can grant you **deep insights you wouldn't be able to gather on your own.**

It's one thing to understand the syntax of a programming language or how to use a framework; it is another thing to understand the idiomatic usage of either.

Study how experts are applying the skills in the real world that you are trying to learn.

Read about the problems and arguments experts have regarding the intricacies of a technical skill, and your understanding will deepen.

PRACTICE, PRACTICE, PRACTICE

Hopefully, I've given you a few good tips to learn technical skills and to develop them further.

It should be pretty clear to you now that **learning by doing is critical**—especially when dealing with technical skills.

It should also be pretty clear to you that **you need to have an actual plan to learn** and **a clear goal** of what it is exactly that you want to learn.

I want to leave you with one final point.

Practice.

It's going to take time to develop any technical skill. In order to get good at something, you are going to have to practice a lot.

Try not to get frustrated by how long it may seem to take, especially when you feel like you aren't making progress.

If you put in the time, **the skills will come** as long as you are following a solid plan with a clear goal.

Just keep at it and trust the process (https://simpleprogrammer.com/cg4-trust).

CHAPTER 5

WHAT PROGRAMMING LANGUAGE SHOULD I LEARN?

One of the most common questions I get from new programmers starting out in the field of software development is which programming language they should learn.

For some aspiring developers, **this question ends up being a stumbling block they never get over.**

I've coached plenty of developers who were always second-guessing themselves or changing their minds and kept jumping from programming language to programming language, always worrying about making the wrong decision.

If you've stressed over which programming language you should be learning, this chapter is for you.

First, I'm going to dispel some of that doubt; then I'll give you some real practical considerations for choosing your first programming language to learn.

THE ACTUAL LANGUAGE DOESN'T MATTER ALL THAT MUCH

Yes, you read that right.

What language you learn doesn't actually matter nearly as much as you might think it does (https://simpleprogrammer.com/cg5-what-language).

There are several reasons I make this statement, but one of the main ones is because so many programming languages, at their core, are very similar.

Yes, the syntax is different. Yes, programming languages may look different. They may even have completely different sets of features.

However, at their core, all programming languages share more than you might first suspect.

Almost all programming languages will have basic constructs for branching, looping, and calling methods or procedures and a way to organize code at a high level.

There are even many programming languages that are so similar that if you know one language, you almost already know the other.

C# and Java are pretty good examples. JavaScript is very similar to either of those.

Learning your first programming language is always the most difficult. Once you learn a programming language, learning a second one is easier. After you know two or more programming languages, each additional programming language is exponentially easier to learn.

If you don't even know one programming language well—or at all—it might be difficult to believe these statements, but **I've learned at least 10 different programming languages over the course of my career**, and I can guarantee you that the first and second ones were by far the most difficult.

Not only are programming languages more similar than you might think, but you'll also easily be able to switch to a different programming language and learn it later on.

This means even if you learn one programming language and decide it's not the right one, or you get a job where you'll be using a different programming language, it's not a big deal. You'll already have done the hard work of learning your first programming language.

You'll also probably find that many developer jobs—especially at big companies like Microsoft or Google—don't require that you know a specific programming language.

I've even had plenty of interviews where I was asked to solve a programming problem in **whatever language I felt most comfortable** doing it in. There were no constraints, no one specific language that I absolutely needed to know.

CONSIDERATIONS FOR PICKING A PROGRAMMING LANGUAGE

Therefore, **I really don't think it matters all that much what programming language you decide to learn first**, but if you are still having some trouble making a decision, I'm going to give you a few things to consider.

JOB PROSPECTS AND FUTURE

I'd say, for most of you, **the most important thing to consider is what job a particular programming language is likely to help you get** and what the future of that language is.

Now, for most popular programming languages, at any given time there are going to be plenty of jobs available.

Different programming languages may rise or fall in popularity, but if you are concerned with job availability, you might want to consider one of the main, popular programming languages.

At the time of writing this book, I'd say those are:

- C#
- Java
- Python
- Ruby
- JavaScript
- C++
- PHP

There is no shortage of jobs for developers who program in one of these languages.

That said, depending on where you live in the world, you may need to be a bit more selective if you aren't willing to relocate.

For example, if you live in some small town in Arkansas and there is only one technology company and that technology company does everything in Java, I suggest you learn you some Java (https://simpleprogrammer.com/cg5-learn-java).

I would imagine for most people this won't be the case, but if it is you, then I guess your decision is pretty easy.

If you are willing to relocate or you are planning on doing freelance programming, you could probably specialize in a more eccentric and less widely used language and do pretty well by being an expert in an area where there are few experts.

But, if you are just starting out, I'd try to stick to something a bit more mainstream.

Another consideration to take into account, along with job prospects, is **what the future is likely to hold for the programming language you are considering.**

At the time of writing this book, Objective-C would probably not be a good choice of a language to get started in, simply because most iOS developers are switching to Swift and Apple is heavily investing in the Swift programming language (https://simpleprogrammer.com/cg5-swift).

If you've already been programming in Objective-C, I wouldn't worry; there will still be plenty of jobs and legacy Objective-C applications to maintain. It just might not be the best choice for the future.

Of course, none of us have a crystal ball, so **it's pretty difficult to predict which languages are going to be popular and which ones aren't.**

Awhile back I predicted the death of JavaScript (https://simpleprogrammer.com/cg5-java script-doomed). That didn't exactly happen.

I just went to a conference where one of the speakers was a co-inventor of Objective-C, which first came into being in the early 1980s.

The speaker, Tom Love, wrote a book in which he basically stated that the JavaScript language was dead. At the time of writing this book, it's now one of the top five most-used programming languages in the world. (I've heard it claimed to be number three.)

The point is, **you never know what is going to happen.**

Ruby took years before it became popular.

JavaScript is arguably one of the worst designed languages ever and was originally used for making little pop-up or alert boxes on web pages; now it's an extremely popular language.

So don't try and guess the future, unless you do have a crystal ball. In which case, forget programming. Wall Street is where you need to be.

HEY JOHN

Why do you hate JavaScript so much?
JavaScript doesn't suck, you do.

I know it might sound like I'm just making stuff up and that I have an axe to grind in regards to JavaScript.

Perhaps you might think that I had some childhood trauma with JavaScript which left me with deep emotional scars.

Well, let me tell you a little story about how JavaScript was born—it's pretty short, bear with me.

In May of 1995, Brendan Eich, who was working at Netscape at the time, created JavaScript in 10 days as a quick effort to create a simple "glue language" that was easy for web designers and part-time programmers to use. (And I got that right out of Wikipedia (https://simpleprogrammer.com/cg5-javascript).)

So, all I am saying is that JavaScript, originally, was not very well thought out and was kind of thrown together in 10 days.

That's a fact, that's what happened—don't shoot the messenger.

With that said, I don't **hate** JavaScript.

I just don't think it's the most elegantly designed language, and I don't prefer it. That's all.

Now. With that said, the newer version of JavaScript, (now known as ECMAScript), is much better and has been enhanced to make up for many of JavaScript's original shortcomings.

I actually—though I hate to admit it—kind of like it now... kind of.

Regardless, my opinion doesn't really matter.

I'm a realist. Obviously JavaScript is an extremely popular language and it is used everywhere.

So, like it or not, I have embraced it—while reserving my right to talk shit.

Oh, and in case you are still not convinced, why do you think one of the best selling JavaScript books of all time was called *JavaScript: The Good Parts*" (https://simpleprogrammer.com/cg5-javascript-good).

TECHNOLOGY THAT YOU ARE INTERESTED IN

One excellent consideration when picking a programming language is simply what technology you are interested in.

If you start with a technology, the programming language choice may be easier.

I know plenty of developers who are interested in developing Android apps because they love the technology.

For most of them, Java is going to make sense because that is the native language in which to develop Android applications. (Although, you could also develop Android applications in many other languages, like C#, Ruby, and even JavaScript.)

It definitely doesn't hurt to pick your first language based on what you are most interested most, because learning your first programming language can be difficult.

The more you are interested in and excited about what you are learning, the easier it will be to stick with it and get through the difficult parts of the learning curve.

I really wanted to develop an iOS application because I had just gotten an iPhone and I was excited about the technology.

That excitement made it much easier for me to learn Objective-C and build my first iOS app.

Had I not been excited about the technology, I probably wouldn't have made it very far.

Don't be afraid to pick a programming language based on what excites you or what you are interested in. Your enthusiasm can carry you through the rough patches in the learning process.

DIFFICULTY LEVEL

Another major consideration would be difficulty level.

Some programming languages are just much more difficult to learn than others.

I usually don't recommend starting out by learning C++ (https://simpleprogrammer.com /cg5-not-back) because, in comparison to many other programming languages, C++ is rather difficult to learn (https://simpleprogrammer.com/cg5-learn-c-plus-plus).

C++ has you dealing with managing memory and pointers and quite a few other nasty constructs that can throw a beginner for a loop.

It's a great language—still one of my favorites—but not the easiest one to learn.

A language like C#, Lua, Python, Ruby, or PHP is going to be much easier starting out.

There are even beginner languages specifically tailored to learning programming, like Scratch or Basic.

I don't want to discourage your from learning a more difficult language like C++ if that is what you really want to do, but you should at least know what you are getting into and decide if you'd rather your first language be something easier.

RESOURCES AVAILABLE TO YOU

You also might want to consider what resources are available to you for learning a programming language.

Some obscure programming language may not have as many books, online videos, or other resources available, which might make them more difficult to learn.

Other more popular programming languages may have plenty of tutorials online, bootcamps you can enroll in, and books and other resources you can utilize, so be sure to look into how many and what resources are available out there for you.

While this isn't as big of a concern today as it used to be since there are so many resources for beginners out there, it's still something to take into consideration.

You might also want to consider what resources are specifically available to you, like a computer or software.

A somewhat difficult-to-learn programming language may be an easier choice, simply because of how many interactive online tutorials there are.

You can learn JavaScript online through your web browser without installing anything on your computer.

A language like C++ will require downloading some tools and software, which might not be easy to do or as easily available.

For the final resource, I'd consider looking to the people you know.

Who can you turn to for help?

Is there someone that can answer your questions if you get stuck or help accelerate your learning?

I certainly wouldn't make resources the biggest consideration to take into account when choosing your first programming language, but it's still one you should contemplate.

ADAPTABILITY

Finally, let's talk about adaptability.

Different programming languages are going to be more adaptable to different situations and technologies.

For example, the C# programming language, at the time of writing this book, is one of the most adaptable thanks to companies like Microsoft and Xamarin (now part of Microsoft).

If you learn C#, you are not just constrained to Windows or web programming.

C# is available on just about every platform today, so it is highly adaptable.

You can use C# to write Linux and Mac applications, and you can even write Android and iOS applications, completely in C#.

Plenty of other programming languages are also highly adaptable.

For instance, Ruby has been ported to many different platforms and is used in quite a few areas of technology.

JavaScript is also highly adaptable. You can even use JavaScript to control Arduino boards and do robotics. (Check out my good friend Derick Bailey's article on how to do it (https://simpleprogrammer.com/cg5-johnny-five).)

Other programming languages are not as adaptable.

If you learn R or Go, for example, you are going to be a bit more restricted to the technologies and platforms those languages were designed for.

More and more programming languages—especially popular ones—are being ported to more platforms and used in a variety of different technologies, but there are still some that are not as versatile.

So, if you think you might want to be a web developer today but do Android development tomorrow, or you want to get involved in a bunch of different platforms or technologies, **you might want to consider how adaptable the language is you are trying to learn.**

SOME FINAL THOUGHTS ON PICKING A PROGRAMMING LANGUAGE

Even though I've given you some considerations to take into account when choosing your first programming language, **I want to stress the point that the actual language is not all that important.**

What is important is that you pick something and stick with it long enough to get through the learning curve required to gain proficiency.

Plenty of programmers who are starting out get frustrated, because they feel like they are **just not getting it.**

I'll talk about this more in the next chapter on "Learning Your First Programming Language."

Just hang on and stay the course, and you will gain proficiency. I promise.

It can be tempting to get bored, or think you are learning the wrong language, and so keep switching languages, but—trust me—that is not a good idea.

Finally, consider this. When I first started programming, knowing a language in-depth was one of the most important skills a programmer could have.

I would pour over C++ books and try to learn every intricacy of the language.

That is no longer as important a skill today.

Today's programming is done at a higher level. **Programming today involves utilizing libraries and frameworks much more than language features.**

Sure, it's important to know a programming language—and to be good at it—but absolute mastery just isn't as valuable a skill as it was.

That is why I say don't worry so much about what language you learn first. **Just make sure you do learn one and stick with it**—at least for now.

CHAPTER 6

LEARNING YOUR FIRST PROGRAMMING LANGUAGE

Ok, so you've decided what programming language you want to learn and now you are all set to learn it.

All you need to do is crack open a book and start reading, right?

Well, not exactly. I mean, you can do it that way—if you like frustration.

Remember how we talked about how **you learn best by doing?**

That's the plan for this chapter.

I'm going to give you the layout for the ideal way to learn your first programming language, and not just to learn it, but to become extremely comfortable and proficient in it, if not master it.

Learning your first programming language can be the most difficult thing about learning to program, but it doesn't have to be.

Most programmers—my past self included—learn by reading a book, trying a few things out, scratching our heads, and then rereading a book and continuing to try things out until it finally "clicks."

What I'm about to share with you comes from coaching and teaching many software developers through not only learning their first programming language but also improving their skills in that language. I also bring my own experience mastering languages like C++, C# and Java.

Basically, in this chapter, I'm showing you **what I would do—knowing what I know now—if I were in your shoes and were learning my first programming language today.**

START BY LOOKING AT A WORKING APPLICATION

Most beginner programmers, when they want to learn to program, pick up a book and start reading.

There are some excellent books out there which attempt to teach you programming in a very hands-on approach. However, I think **the best place to start is by looking at the source code of an actual working application** and trying to figure out as much of what is happening as possible.

This is difficult.

It's going to feel uncomfortable, but that's ok. Get used to feeling uncomfortable (https://simpleprogrammer.com/cg6-5-softskills).

What I want you to do is to pick an open source application—preferably a popular one that is likely to be well-designed—and start looking through the source code.

You can find plenty of projects on GitHub (https://simpleprogrammer.com/cg6-5-github), so I'd recommend checking there.

It's beyond the scope of this book, but it's even better if you can download the code and build and run the application yourself.

If you have a friend that can help you with this, that's great. If you don't, it's ok.

What is important is that you **explore the code to get a feel for what the programming language syntax looks like and read the code to see if you can understand or make sense of anything.**

Use the application itself, if possible, so you can get a feel for the relationship between the code and what the code does.

Like I said, this is going to feel very uncomfortable.

You might feel like you're not understanding anything.

I repeat, that is ok. Just do your best and see if you can figure out how one or two things work or what you might change in the code to change the functionality in some way.

Moreover, get a feel for how things are named and how they are organized.

Pretend like you are an archaeologist trying to understand the writing of some ancient civilization.

By starting out this way, **you are going to have a serious head start over most programmers who have no idea what the programming language they are trying to learn even looks like.**

It's always a good idea to get a lay of the land before embarking on any journey.

Programming is no different.

FIND A FEW GOOD RESOURCES OR BOOKS AND SCAN THROUGH THEM

Further continuing with the theme of getting the lay of the land before setting sail, the next step is not to read a programming book cover-to-cover. Instead **pick out a few books or other resources—such as videos, articles, or tutorials—and scan through them.**

Again, this is going to be at least somewhat uncomfortable because much of what you are looking at isn't going to make much sense.

But... **the idea here is to scope out the territory.** You just want to get an idea of how big this thing is that you are about to learn and what the general concepts are.

This extra work upfront will pay off later when you have an idea of what types of things you are going to learn and how the concepts are going to build on each other.

If you have taken my "10 Steps to Learn Anything Quickly" (https://simpleprogrammer.com /cg6-10-steps) course, you might recognize that what you are essentially doing here is getting the big picture and determining scope.

LEARN HOW TO CREATE HELLO WORLD

Ok, at this point you are still not "reading a book" or taking a training program.

You'll be doing that soon enough—if you want to. (You can actually learn a programming language without doing that, if you follow these steps. I learned Go and Dart in about two weeks utilizing only online documentation (http://simpleprogrammer.com/cg6-pluralsight) and a similar process to what we're discussing here.)

What you want to do at this point is to **create the most basic kind of program you possibly can in whatever programming language you are learning.**

Remember how we talked about learning just enough to get started in the chapter on "How to Develop Technical Skills?"

That is the goal here.

You want to get started as soon as possible so that you can develop the confidence and knowledge to apply what you will be learning and put it immediately into practice.

What you are going to start with is a very basic program called "Hello World."

Most programming books begin by having you create a "Hello World" program, which usually just prints "Hello World" to the screen.

The idea here isn't really to learn all that much about the language, but rather to **become familiar with and test out the basic tool chain required to build and run a program** in your programming language of choice.

If you are reading about your programming language, it should contain an example of a "Hello World" program you can create.

If not, just do a Google search for "Hello World + *your programming language.*" You should have no trouble finding an example.

By creating a "Hello World" program, you'll also learn the basic structure of a program in your programming language.

LEARN BASIC CONSTRUCTS AND TEST THEM OUT WITH REAL PROBLEMS

Now comes the point where, if you have a book on your programming language or tutorial of some sort, you can start reading or working through it.

At this point, what you are reading or consuming shouldn't be quite as mysterious as it would have been if you just dove in.

What you want to do now is familiarize yourself with each of the basic constructs of the programming language you are learning, and then write some code that uses these constructs.

You'll want to try and think of problems or applications associated with what you are learning that are as realistic as possible because, when you apply a skill to an actual problem, you understand and remember it better.

Here is a list of some of the basic constructs most programming languages should contain:

- Ability to write output to the screen
- Basic math capability
- Storage of information as a variable
- Organization of code into functions, methods, or modules
- Invoke a function or method
- Performance of boolean logic evaluations
- Branch conditional statements (if / else)
- Looping statements

Here is some good news.

Once you know these basic constructs and how to use them, you'll have the basics of programming in any language. Yes, the syntax might be different, but this is the core of programming.

You will probably spend a good amount of time in this phase.

Just work your way through, learning each of the constructs of your programming language one at a time, and apply each construct by actually writing some code.

If you are working on your own, you'll need to identify what all the constructs are and in what order it makes sense to learn them.

If you are going through a book or tutorial (or preferably multiple books and tutorials), the path should be laid out for you and should even have some examples and challenge assignments for you to do.

Try to make sure you always understand what you are learning and how it is applied.

Now is a great time to go back to that original source code you looked at in the first step and see how much more of it you understand.

KNOW THE DIFFERENCE BETWEEN LANGUAGE FEATURES AND LIBRARIES

One thing that often trips up beginning programmers—especially with the programming languages of today—is knowing what is part of the language and what is part of the standard libraries that come with the language.

Often the distinction is not very clear because, idiomatically, you are going to write code that uses the standard libraries very often.

That's ok. You are going to need to know the conventions for programming in the programming language you are learning, but **you should take special care to try and figure out what is part of the actual language and what is part of the libraries** that are often used with the language.

This might seem like nitpicking, but I think it's important because it will take that scrambled mess of syntax that you probably have floating in your head at this point and help you categorize and organize it to make more sense.

What you'll realize is that, **for most programming languages, the actual language part itself is not that large** and is relatively easy to learn, but the standard libraries are large and knowing your way around them is going to be the more difficult endeavor.

Programming today is more about knowing how to use libraries and frameworks than being an absolute expert in the language.

That is one of the reasons why this distinction is important.

By realizing what is not part of the language but is rather part of the library and learning how to look up libraries for common tasks you want to accomplish in the language, you'll become a much better programmer.

REVIEW EXISTING CODE AND WORK THROUGH UNDERSTANDING EACH LINE

At this point you should be familiar with all of the major concepts of the programming language you are learning, and you should have used most of the programming language features in real examples.

You also should have a decent understanding of the difference between the language itself and the libraries that are used in conjunction with the language.

You still might not exactly feel comfortable with the language or that you actually know it.

This is the stage where you may sort of feel like you can understand how everything works, but you have no idea how you would put it together to write a real application.

(Kind of like learning to speak another language.)

Many beginning programmers tend to get a bit stuck at this stage and feel frustrated, thinking they'll never be a real programmer.

One of the best ways to push forward from here and make sure you don't have gaps in your knowledge is to **start looking at existing code, line by line, making sure you understand exactly what each line and statement in the code is doing.** (Even if you don't always understand the why, being able to know the what is still progress.)

HEY JOHN

Don't I need to know the why? What good does it do me to just know what the code does if I don't understand why it does it?

Think of it this way: if you don't understand the what, you can't possibly understand the why.

If you don't know what the words in this book mean, you can't understand the individual sentences and if you can't understand the individual sentences, you won't understand the concepts.

That's why we start at the lowest level.

I want to make sure you know what every single line and statement in the code is doing, because without that you don't have any shot of understanding the why—or how it all fits together.

So, you start there and the why comes later.

Yes, it's important to understand the why and how the individual lines of code work to make up the program and make it function, but in order to do that you first have to understand the language itself.

So, right now just focus on learning the language.

The rest will come, I promise.

You can take the existing source code for a project you looked at in the first step and start randomly going through files in the project.

Open a file and go through each line of code in the file, making sure you understand exactly what it is doing.

If you don't understand—and there will be plenty of things you won't—take some time to think about it, and look up anything you don't understand.

This is tedious. It might even be boring, but it's totally worth it.

When you get to the point where you feel like you can read any line of code and understand what it is doing—again, the why is not as important at this stage—you are ready to move on.

BUILD SOMETHING... LOTS OF SOMETHINGS

Now it's time to really start using the programming language.

At this point, you should already have written a few small programs and utilized most of the features of the language, but you'll get a greater feel for the language once you start actually building real applications.

Pick a few small project ideas—nothing huge—and start building applications.

Don't pick anything too ambitious and don't try to do anything platform specific or UI intensive at this point. Preferably, your applications will just print text to the screen and take input from the keyboard for now.

The idea is **to build some simple applications that focus on utilizing the programming language you are learning and the standard libraries**, not additional frameworks for platform features—we'll get to that next.

By doing so, you will build confidence in the programming language and your ability to use it, and you'll learn what language constructs to use to reach the goal you are trying to accomplish.

Here are some simple project ideas to get you started:

* Create a program that **solves a mathematical problem** by getting inputs from the user.
* Create a **Choose Your Own Adventure type of program** where the input from the user determines what happens next.
* Create a very **simple text-based adventure game** where the user can issue commands to pick up objects, move through rooms, etc.
* Create a program that is able to **read input from a text file and write output** to a different text file.
* **Create a chatbot** that talks to the user and pretends to be human or gives humorous responses.

APPLY THE PROGRAMMING LANGUAGE TO A SPECIFIC TECHNOLOGY OR PLATFORM

Up until this point, you should have mainly been learning about and using the programming language you've chosen in isolation.

This is intentional because you need to understand and be comfortable with the programming language itself and its standard libraries before adding the extra complexity of the environment and other frameworks you might use to build a real-world application.

In order to create something useful with a programming language, you are going to need to apply it to a specific technology or platform.

At this point, you should decide on a few small projects you can complete which will require you to utilize the programming language on a specific platform.

For example, let's suppose you are learning Java.

Up until now, you would be writing Java code that would work on any platform that Java could run on, since you'd be mostly using the standard libraries and just working with input and output to the screen or a file.

At this point, you might decide to use Java to build an Android application.

You will have to learn how to build Android applications and about the Android framework. However, you'll already be familiar with Java, so you won't be trying to learn a huge amount of concepts at once without knowing what Java is or what Android is.

You can, of course, learn Android and Java together—in fact, I did a Pluralsight course teaching exactly how to do that (https://simpleprogrammer.com/cg6-java-course)—but to get a real mastery of the language and avoid confusion, isolating the language from the platform or technology and then combining them is probably going to be much easier.

Now you will be developing specific, specialized skills with the programming language you are learning that will be useful for getting a job.

Pick whatever platform or technology you think you are most likely to want to work with in the future and start creating a few small applications using it.

I'd also recommend that you specialize in just one technology or platform at this point (https://simpleprogrammer.com/cg6-specialize). You can always learn more later.

By specializing, you will not only limit what you have to learn at this point, but you will allow yourself to gain a deeper knowledge and competency in a particular technology, which will make you much more confident and greatly increase the marketability of your skills.

SOLVE DIFFICULT ALGORITHM PROBLEMS WITH THE LANGUAGE TO MASTER IT

By now you should be pretty comfortable with the programming language you are learning.

You should know it pretty well and have used it in a variety of different applications.

You should have a specific technology or platform you've applied your skills to and feel comfortable creating basic applications using that technology.

Nevertheless, **you still might not feel like you have a mastery of the programming language.**

Don't worry; this is also normal.

When I was first learning C++, I remember how even after I understood everything about the language, had actually used it to create several applications, and was even working as a developer writing C++ code, I still didn't feel like I had a real mastery of the language.

I felt like I was a good C++ programmer, but not a great one.

I really wanted to get my C++ skills up, but I didn't know how.

Then, I discovered this coding competition site called TopCoder (https://simpleprogrammer.com /cg6-topcoder).

Every week, there was a new set of programming challenges where you could compete against other programmers to solve some fairly difficult algorithm problems.

At first I was horrible. I couldn't even solve the easiest problem.

I would look at other people's solutions, and I would have no idea how they came up with that solution or even how their code worked.

They were using C++ in a way that I never imagined.

But then, over time, as I kept trying to solve problems and I looked at how other people had solved the problems, I started to get better… much better.

I started to see patterns in how certain types of problems were solved.

I started to really understand how to utilize features of C++ that I had previously ignored.

I learned how to effectively use the standard libraries and language features along with data structures to solve complex problems.

I became not just proficient at C++ but excellent at it. I finally felt as though I had mastered the language.

That's what I want you to do.

You don't have to go on TopCoder to compete, but **there are plenty of places where you can practice solving algorithm-type programming problems.**

I've already mentioned one good resource for these kinds of problems, but here are some more:

- *Cracking the Coding Interview* (https://simpleprogrammer.com /cg6-cracking) by Gayle Laakmann McDowell
- Programming Pearls (https://simpleprogrammer.com/cg6-pearls) by Jon Bentley
- Project Euler (https://simpleprogrammer.com/cg6-euler)
- Codility (https://simpleprogrammer.com/cg6-codility)
- Interview Cake (https://simpleprogrammer.com/cg6-interviewcake)
- TopCoder (https://simpleprogrammer.com/cg6-topcoder) (check out the practice rooms for the algorithm contests)

These problems will be extremely difficult at first, and that is ok. They are supposed to be.

What you'll find is that, over time, you'll start to recognize that there are only a handful of types of problems, and you'll start to be able to identify how to solve them immediately.

At first, you'll have no clue what to do, and like I said, that's ok—just keep trying.

Also, **don't forget to look at how other people have solved the problems you are struggling with.** Try to understand why they solved particular problems the way they did.

This was one of the best ways I was able to learn how to solve these kinds of problems.

I would look at the solutions of the top coders on TopCoder, and I would learn a great deal.

Once you can solve these types of programming problems with the programming language you are learning, you will not only be pretty close to mastery of the language, but also **coding interviews will be a piece of cake for you** while other candidates are sweating through their shirts.

CHAPTER 7

GOING TO COLLEGE

In the next three chapters, I'm going to talk about **three different strategies or paths you can take to get started as a software developer.**

First, we'll talk about **going to college**; then we'll talk about **enrolling in a coding boot camp**, and finally we'll talk about **self-education**.

Any of these paths are viable, but I want to lay out the pros and cons of each path and give you a solid strategy that will help you, if you choose to embark on that particular path.

Ok, let's get started by talking about going to college or a university, the traditional education route.

I'm not going to spend much time talking about what college is since I'm assuming you've heard of it.

Instead, I want to talk about what this specific choice involves.

If you choose to go down this path, it means you are going to enroll in an accredited school which will take anywhere from two to six years to get a degree in a program like Computer Science, Computer Programming, or something similar.

This is the route most software developers take, but is it the best one?

Let's find out.

ADVANTAGES

First, let's talk about the advantages of going to college.

Your parents probably think there are plenty of advantages—in fact, they probably think college is the only option—but I want to be as objective as possible.

Even though I'm not exactly a fan of traditional education myself, I have to admit there are still some real benefits to getting that piece of paper.

MANY COMPANIES STILL ONLY HIRE DEVELOPERS WITH DEGREES

Even though we are in the 2010s, many companies are still pretty short-sighted when it comes to their hiring practices—especially for developers.

Often, you'll find that larger corporations with HR departments will pretty much only hire software developers with degrees (https://simpleprogrammer.com/cg7-degrees) **from accredited colleges or universities.**

This doesn't mean you can't get a job at one of these companies without a degree, but it might be very difficult to do so.

This is true in my own experience: Before I finished my degree in computer science, I was hired as an employee at Hewlett-Packard. I had already been working as a programmer for the past few years. In fact, I was a contractor working onsite at HP.

Normally, HP doesn't hire anyone who doesn't have a degree, but they approved me as an exception since I had been recommended and had already proven myself as a contractor.

It took jumping through many hoops for me to get an offer, but **when the offer finally came, I was sorely disappointed.**

Instead of taking into account my experience and ability, I got classified into a non-degree category, meaning they put me at the very bottom of the pay scale and told me I was lucky to get an offer at all.

I only tell you this story to give you an idea of the prevailing mindset at certain companies who typically hold a degree in higher regard than they should.

By getting a real degree, you will potentially open yourself up to more opportunities you wouldn't have access to as someone who is self-taught or went to a coding boot camp.

There are plenty of companies that will hire someone without a degree—and not discriminate against them—but overall, choices without a degree will be more limited.

Just a fact of life.

Bottom line: **having a degree will give you more job options than you might have without one.**

GOOD BASE KNOWLEDGE OF COMPUTER SCIENCE CONCEPTS

Many self-taught programmers are very good programmers but lack knowledge of some of the computer science concepts which are taught in college.

Today, these skills are not as important as the more practical aspects of software development, but **I do believe every software developer should learn about operating systems, data structures, algorithms, predicate logic, computer architecture**, and many of the other topics found in most computer science degree programs.

These topics can be difficult to learn on your own—especially if you don't even know they exist.

As we'll discuss in the next chapter on "Getting a Job," you'll find that **many top companies give coding interviews** (https://simpleprogrammer.com/cg7-interviews) that specifically target this kind of traditional computer science knowledge.

I'm a very pragmatic person and I am, for the most part, against traditional education systems, but I do feel **that more programmers need to understand some of the underlying basics and theory behind the code** (https://simpleprogrammer.com/cg7-code) **they are writing.**

While college is less likely to give you the pragmatic knowledge you need to work as a software developer today, most degree programs will give you the depth of knowledge in computer science concepts that can be extremely useful when getting into more complex programming scenarios, like working with real-time systems, developing new algorithms, and making them efficient. Newer fields like machine learning also need people with a deeper understanding of these computer science concepts.

STRUCTURE

One thing traditional education does better than anything else is give you structure.

Some people simply cannot operate without a clear structure in place, telling them exactly what to do and when.

Many people have aspirations of becoming a software developer, but never end up doing it because they get overwhelmed by all the information they need to learn and don't know how to organize that information in a way that will progress them down the course of self-education.

Other wannabe software developers are simply **too unmotivated** and **lack the self-discipline** required to self-educate.

If you wouldn't identify yourself as being a self-starter or you have problems taking action when the path is not clearly laid out for you—be honest—you would probably benefit from the structure a college or university provides.

If you try to learn on your own, you have to decide what and when to learn, and how much time each day to dedicate to learning.

If you enroll in a computer science program or other program at a college or university, you'll pick some electives and have some say in your schedule, but you'll have everything else planned out for you. Then, you just have to stick to the plan.

INTERNSHIPS AND OTHER OPPORTUNITIES

Colleges and universities are often able to offer internship opportunities or other connections and resources that you might not have access to on your own.

Many companies recruit directly from colleges and have pre-established relationships with them, which can make getting a job easier.

Many colleges also have programs and opportunities available with different foundations, conferences, and other events that can greatly help you with networking and making the right connections.

This can definitely be a huge advantage, especially if you want to work for a big technology company like Google or Microsoft early on in your career.

A seasoned developer might be able to get a job at one of these larger technology companies based on merit and experience, but for a software developer just starting out, internships are a great way to get your foot in the door. Since most internship programs are run through colleges and universities, you must be a student or have recently graduated in order to have access to them.

DISADVANTAGES

Ok, now it's time to get into the disadvantages of going to college.

This is the part of the book your parents aren't going to like.

Unfortunately, there are some definite disadvantages to going to college. Some obvious, some not so obvious.

TIME

The first and most obvious drawback is time.

Going to college is going to take a minimum of four years out of your life. That's time where you can't really be working as a full-time software developer and gaining experience to put on your resume.

This is a pretty big commitment. A large amount can happen in four years' time.

Therefore, you really want to think about whether the benefits of having a degree are worth giving up four or more years of your life.

There is also the time commitment of college itself. **Not all of the activities and time you spend in school will directly benefit you.** You'll be expected to take core classes that have nothing to do with becoming a software developer, so you can conceivably see that as a waste of time.

Taking tests is also arguably a waste of time, as it doesn't benefit you directly.

The same can be said of listening to lectures, especially if you could have absorbed the same amount of information in a quicker way.

Traditional education is not designed to maximize the use of time, as often the programs must be taught to the lowest common denominator. (Not true for all schools, of course, but in general.)

This is one of the main reasons I am against traditional and compulsory education. I just feel it isn't very efficient, which is something you should consider before you dive in.

COST

Next up is money.

Everyone wants more of it, no one wants to part with it, but if you go to college, you are most likely going to have to part with a great deal of it.

I'm sure I'm not telling you something you don't already know when I say that **school is expensive, and it's getting more and more expensive every year.**

If you go to college, expect to pay a large sum unless you get a scholarship or start out in a community college—more on that in a bit.

If you want, or are required, to live on campus or you have to finance your education, you can expect the bills to be even larger.

I know plenty of software developers and non-software developers who are still paying for their higher education many years and even decades after getting their degrees.

That sucks.

It can be very difficult to justify the cost of an expensive education when you consider the lost years of pay you would have received from working during that time, as well as the interest on school loans in comparison to the increased salary—if any—you get from having a degree.

Yes, this viewpoint is a bit jaded, but I've coached and counseled too many software developers who racked up huge school bills getting their degrees. Many of them **ended up in financial messes** that will be extremely difficult to extract themselves from.

Don't worry, though. I have some ways to mitigate this problem if you do want to go to a traditional college, which I'll talk about in the strategy section.

One final word of advice.

Make sure you actually add up all the costs of going to college, including interest, room and board, and lost employment income, so you at least know what you are getting into.

Claiming ignorance and asking the government to wipe out your student loan debt is not only irresponsible; it's just plain stupid.

OUTDATED OR NON-REAL WORLD EDUCATION
It takes a long time to publish a textbook.

It takes a long time to create a degree program and get it approved or to add new classes to an existing program.

Often professors in colleges and universities are very disconnected from the kinds of software development which are being done in the real world.

As a result, educational programs at colleges poorly reflect the skills and technologies which are most critical to know for success in a real software development job.

Yes, a computer science background can be helpful, but it's just not as pragmatic as learning how to use source control, Agile methodology, or even the most popular and widely used JavaScript framework.

To be fair, many traditional schools are realizing this weakness and taking some steps to make their degree programs more relevant to what is happening in the software development world today—but many are not.

That is part of the reason I am writing this book.

I want to give you all the soft knowledge you need to know about a career in software development because I feel that most colleges and universities don't provide it.

You can, of course, overcome this limitation by learning the other aspects of software development on your own, but at that point you really have to question why you are paying for a degree in the first place.

DISTRACTIONS

There is a reason why there are rankings for the top party colleges in the country.

There is a reason why some people say college was the most fun time of their lives.

College is full of distractions.

Alcohol, parties, protests, sports, concerts, snoring roommates... distractions are everywhere.

I know plenty of software developers who took six or more years to get their degree because they couldn't just buckle down and study. They got too distracted by all the other things college has to offer.

While some people might see this as an advantage, **if you are serious about becoming a software developer, the college atmosphere can be a huge distraction.**

I don't think many young, high school graduates consider this aspect of going to college.

They just assume they'll be able to study and get the work done and party on weekends.

It doesn't work like that.

When I did go to college, there was a party every night. It was extremely easy to neglect studies, sleep in, skip class, and do everything but school work.

Yes, you can avoid all of that stuff and just focus on what is important, but make sure you at least know what you are getting into.

HEY JOHN

But my parents are making me go to college. They say I have to do it. They'll disown me if I don't.

I was at a Sushi restaurant here in Pacific Beach, San Diego the other night and I was talking about how this homeless person said that I should be running on the beach, on the sand, and not running on the pavement near the beach.

I was saying how he had a good point and perhaps I should listen to him, when my 6-year-old daughter piped up and said "Be your own man. You are Simple Programmer."

Obviously something I've been saying has been rubbing off on her.

I was pretty shocked, but she was right.

Yes, I know your parents raised you and I know that you may feel like you owe them something for doing what just about every warm blooded mammal is biologically wired to do, but the truth is you don't.

You have one life and it is yours to live.

You don't owe anyone anything and no one owes you anything.

Ultimately, at the end of the day, you are the one who has to live with the consequences of your choices, not your parents, not your guidance counselor, not your friends, just you.

So, while it may feel like you don't have a choice, you always do.

Don't get me wrong. I'm not saying "don't go to college," but what I am saying is that you need to decide for yourself whether it is right for you and not let someone else tell you what you are going to do.

This is difficult, I get it. Been there done that; had my own dad hang the phone up on me and practically disown me when I told him I was going to invest in rental properties.

But, sometimes you have to make difficult decisions in life and sometimes you have to be willing to accept whatever consequences may came and the fact that some relationships may be ruined.

Trust me though, you'll be a much happier person in the long run living your life instead of letting someone else live it for you (https://simpleprogrammer.com/cg7-living).

STRATEGY

If you are choosing the traditional route and going to college, it's important to have a plan.

You don't want to end up with loads of debt and few benefits, like too many college graduates today.

Let's talk about **a few strategies** you can utilize to get the most bang for your buck.

START WITH A COMMUNITY COLLEGE

First of all, I'd highly suggest going to a community college (https://simpleprogrammer.com /cg7-community) for the first two or even three years of your degree in order to save a ton of money.

If you get a scholarship, you can ignore this advice. However, if you are paying out of pocket or are taking on student loans for your degree, **going to a community college first can save you a bundle**, and you can still get a degree from a more prestigious college or university.

The key here is to make sure the credits and program you take at a community college will transfer over to the school where you'd eventually like to get your degree from.

So, make sure you check that out first.

AVOID DEBT

Next, I'd really recommend not going into debt, if you can manage it.

Debt is horrible. **Debt can ruin your life.**

Some people see educational debt as good debt, like a mortgage on your house or investment property, but I don't.

I find that the debt incurred from school rarely pays off and it forces you down a path you may not want to follow. It's like **shackling yourself to a huge weight** you are going to have to carry around for the next five, ten, or even more years.

Don't do it.

Instead, here are some ways to go to school and avoid debt:

1. **Take a year off, get a job, and save money.** You don't have to go to college right after high school. Saving up some cash can really help you avoid going into debt.

2. **Get scholarships.** Not for everyone, but if you can manage to get a few scholarships, this can greatly help to reduce expenses.

3. **Get a part-time job while going to school**, which enables you to pay for school. It's not fun, but it will pay off in the long run.

4. **Live at home.** Yes, it sucks, but you'll probably get more work done and you'll definitely pay a lot less money.

5. **Move to a state where education is free**, like Alaska. Or move to Germany temporarily.

You can even combine these tactics to reduce debt further.

Trust me, it might seem like going $40k into debt to get your education will be worth it, but it's going to take you a really long time to pay back that debt—especially with interest.

And what happens if you can't find a job after that huge investment?

MAKE LEARNING YOUR RESPONSIBILITY

Going to school and getting a degree is great, but it doesn't mean you learn anything.

If you are going to spend the time and money to go to a college or university, you better get something more than just a fancy piece of paper.

Unfortunately, no one can teach you anything. You have to learn it yourself, regardless of where you learn it or from whom.

Always remember that **education is your responsibility.**

Don't read textbooks or do assignments just to pass the test and make the grade.

Instead, **focus on actually learning and applying what you are learning as much as possible.**

That is how life works in the real world. No one is going to "teach" you anything. It's going to be up to you to learn, so it's better for you to get used to it now.

I can't tell you how many college graduates I come across who have spent tens of thousands of dollars and years of time on an education that is completely worthless. They thought that going through the motions and getting a degree would make them educated and guarantee them a job.

It won't, so if you are going to enroll, **do the work and take the responsibility of learning upon yourself**, rather than give the responsibility to the degree program you enrolled in or the professors who are teaching you.

DO SIDE PROJECTS

Going to school will take a huge bite out of your work experience time.

It's a serious deal to dedicate four to six years of your life to something.

One of the biggest problems new graduates have is that since they don't have experience, they can't get experience, and they have a difficult time finding a job.

One really good way to avoid that problem is to do side projects (https://simpleprogrammer.com/cg7-sideproject) while you are still in school.

College is the perfect time to build up your portfolio or to start building a side business which can give you some valuable experience and perhaps even some income while you are waiting to start your career.

Side projects can also help you to apply what you are learning so that you'll be less likely to forget it and more likely to gain the deep understanding needed to apply knowledge in the real world.

Plus, **how many stories can you recall of college students who started side projects and then became millionaires off of them?**

Microsoft, Facebook, Yahoo, Dell, and Google all started from side projects in dorm rooms, basements, or garages.

That doesn't mean you are going to get rich off of doing a side project from your dorm room, but you never know. At the very worst, you'll learn something and you could end up creating your own job for yourself when you graduate.

INTERN

I mentioned this earlier, but I would highly recommend taking advantage of the opportunity to participate in internships in college.

Internships can be one of the easiest ways for a new software developer without experience to get a job at a big company like Google or Microsoft, or even just to get a job period.

Internships can also make up for the lack of real world experience in many degree programs.

You really don't want to get your degree and then be hitting the pavement with all the other new grads with no experience.

Therefore, make sure you take advantage of an internship program if you can—even if it doesn't pay well.

You can make money later in your career. Right now you need experience.

GET YOUR DEGREE WHILE YOU ARE WORKING

Here is the strategy I used to not go into debt, not lose years of experience, and still get my degree.

I went to school for a year, then when I got my summer job that turned out to be a good full-time job, I dropped out and worked for a few years Then I re-enrolled in an online school that I could do while I was working my regular job.

As a result, **I never had to live like a poor person.** I had four more years experience than most college graduates and I still got my degree.

Also, since I was working a full-time job as a software developer already, **my degree was super cheap and easy to obtain.** Plus, I could apply what I was learning to my work.

Now, I realize not everyone can do this.

If, however, you are a self-taught developer or you already have a job, I think **this is an excellent option.**

You could even do this while working in another, somewhat related field.

The only drawback is that it's quite a bit of work to do a regular job and go to school—it certainly takes self-discipline—but if I were starting over today, this is the route I would take for sure.

Next up, we'll talk about a less traditional and much more debated way to get into the field of programming: enrolling in a coding boot camp.

CHAPTER 8

CODING BOOT CAMPS

In the not-too-distant past there were only two choices if you wanted to become a programmer: go to college or teach yourself.

In the past few years—at least at the time of writing this book—**a new option has emerged.**

For many, this is an exciting option that offers new opportunities and ushers in a new age of computer programmers who believe anyone can learn to code—in as little as three months.

From the programming elitists who say that you have to spend years in school or hacking out code at 12:00 am in order to really call yourself a coder, this is a scary threat.

Like it or not, coding boot camps have emerged, and it looks like they are here to stay.

WHAT IS A CODING BOOT CAMP?

Before we can get into the advantages and disadvantages of coding bootcamps, we need to first talk about what **exactly a coding boot camp is.**

A coding boot camp is much like it sounds.

While there is huge variety in what each coding boot camp teaches, how they teach it, and how long the boot camps are, they are all focused on one basic idea.

They teach you to become a programmer FAST.

Most boot camps aim to teach you enough to get a job as a software developer in a compressed amount of time by **just focusing on what is really important and by having you really focus on as much real world type programming as possible.**

Is a programming boot camp a good idea (https://simpleprogrammer.com/cg8-bootcamp)—and is it the right choice for you?

Let's find out.

ADVANTAGES

First, let's talk about the advantages of attending a coding boot camp instead of either following a traditional education route, i.e. college, or learning completely on your own.

Contrary to popular belief, there are certainly a large number of advantages to going down the coding boot camp route.

Enough that **if I were starting out today, I'd probably enroll in one myself.**

In fact, even as an experienced developer, **I'm tempted to enroll in one** to see what it is like to learn a new technology at one of these boot camps.

Maybe I'll go undercover and do that one of these days.

SHORT LEARNING TIME

One of the biggest advantages that you'll find a coding boot camp offers is the **compression of learning into a very short period of time.**

Going to college or even learning on your own could take years.

Some boot camps promise to get you a job as a software developer in as little as three months.

Now, while this claim may seem difficult to believe, I'm convinced, and here's why.

Some boot camps have you **working 10-12 hours a day, six days a week**, doing nothing but learning to code and practicing programming.

I believe many developers can get the equivalent of several years of experience in that time because, **in a typical workplace, you might only code about 20% of your time**—if that.

If you apply yourself and really buckle down, I could see you feasibly learning in an even shorter timeframe than three months.

We'll talk about the possible disadvantages of this approach in a little bit, but I ultimately see this as a huge advantage.

Time is money (and vice versa (https://simpleprogrammer.com/cg8-money)). Invest your time to make money, leverage that money to make more, then buy back your time for a net profit.

I'd rather immerse myself in something completely for three to six months than learn it slowly over a period of years.

I'd rather jump in, get going, and get a job in the real world as soon as possible, because that is where all the most valuable experience comes from.

As advantages go, it's pretty clear that this one can't be overlooked, as long as you are willing to accept that you can actually learn to program in this short time frame—which I definitely believe is possible.

Difficult, but possible.

HIGH PLACEMENT RATE

It's undeniable that **many boot camps have an extremely high placement rate for their students** with real jobs working at real companies—especially in Silicon Valley.

Now, not all boot camps are created equal, but **I have heard of good boot camps having placement rates as high or higher than 90%.**

This is an insanely valuable advantage.

To think that someone could go from making $30k a year to making $80-$100k a year as a software developer in as little as a few grueling months.

That is pretty awesome.

If you get a college degree, some degree programs will try and help you get a placement, but most leave you on your own—unless you enroll in an internship program.

I know plenty of college graduates who can't find jobs and frequently complain about it on my YouTube channel (https://simpleprogrammer.com/cg8-youtube).

I don't know anyone who has completed a boot camp and hasn't been able to find a job.

Granted, I'm sure that not all boot camp graduates are able to find a job easily, but since one of the biggest advantages that a boot camp offers is the ability to get you a job, many boot camps set up great relationships with employers to help them do just that.

Boot camps have a vested interest in you getting a job after completing their program.

In fact, some boot camps actually give you a full refund of your tuition and only make money when you find a job, at which point they take a cut of your first year's salary.

It is difficult to get a job without experience, so I consider this to be a significant advantage.

LOW PRICE

While some people complain about how expensive boot camps are, I find them to be extremely cheap for the value you get (https://simpleprogrammer.com/cg8-bootcampvideo)—especially compared to traditional college tuitions.

Boot camps range in price from free to around $20,000 at the top end.

When you consider that cheap college tuition might be around $10-$20k per year for 4+ years, **even the most expensive boot camp is really quite cheap.**

I also really like the idea that the amount of money a boot camp charges is an amount that most people could save up for and afford without having to get loans. (Yes, it might take a while to save that much, but saving $40-$80k for college is an impossible task for most.)

I will tell you, though, that **I would not price-shop boot camps.** I would base my decision on which boot camp to attend on many other factors, leaving price only as a final consideration.

No need to be penny wise and pound foolish when it comes to investing in your career and yourself.

All in all, the value you get out of a boot camp for the price you pay creates a ridiculous arbitrage situation for anyone willing to do the hard work and take advantage of the situation.

FOCUSED STUDY

Another major advantage of a boot camp is **the opportunity for a very focused and intense study of the craft of programming.**

While you may focus for periods of time when going to college—especially when finals are coming up—more of your energy is scattered as you are learning information over several years and it's mixed with other subjects.

Not so with a boot camp.

Some boot camps have students working six days a week at 10-12 hours a day, focused solely on learning to code.

While some people may see this as a drawback, **I've always found the best way to learn and improve at anything is through long periods of very intense focus.**

You've probably heard that the total immersion technique is the best way to learn a foreign language, and I'd say it's pretty much the same for programming as well.

This kind of focus is one of the reasons why boot camps can cover a large amount of information in such a small period of time.

REAL WORK-LIKE SETTING

As I mentioned in the last chapter, **most college and university degree programs don't do a great job of preparing a student for what programming in the real world is like.**

I was just talking to a beginner programmer today who had recently received his degree, and he was complaining how **he didn't feel like college prepared him for what the real world of software development was like** and how he was trying to learn these important skills on his own.

Since boot camps are usually focused on taking someone who has conceivably never written code before and getting them ready to immediately start working in a real job as a programmer in as short a time period as possible, **you can bet that most coding boot camps will be structured in such a way as to mimic real programming environments.**

The focus within most boot camps is pragmatic in nature, which I find to be highly advantageous if you want to get up to speed and working as soon as possible.

WORK WITH OTHER HIGHLY MOTIVATED PEOPLE

I actually left this advantage out on my first draft of this chapter because, honestly, it didn't occur to me.

I'm happy to give credit where credit is due, **and the credit in this case belongs to David Trom-holt** who left this comment on one of my YouTube videos about coding boot camps (https://simpleprogrammer.com/cg8-bootcampvideo):

> *"For those who are wondering why some people are willing to pay a lot of money to go to a bootcamp, it's not because they don't know that you can learn this stuff on your own, obviously there's an abun-dance of cheap or even free resources on the web.*
>
> *But you can potentially get more personal growth by going to a bootcamp, there's a social aspect to it, and some people learn better when they have a specific structure to follow.*
>
> ***It can be extremely motivating to be surrounded by other like-minded students**, and the type of inspiration you take in is more direct than if you get everything from a book or a video."*

This is an excellent point and a great advantage that I didn't even think of.

Many coding boot camps are set up like a hybrid classroom / work environment where you work and learn directly with other students.

Not only can this be motivating, but it is some good training for what it's like to work on a team.

DISADVANTAGES

So far I've listed quite a few advantages for coding boot camps, but almost every one of these advantages has a corresponding disadvantage, depending on how you look at it.

Coding boot camps are not for the timid or lazy. If you fall into one of those categories, many of the advantages I talked about above might have already appeared to you as one of the disad-vantages we'll cover below.

HUGE TIME COMMITMENT

Even though you'll be learning to program rather quickly in calendar time, there is a massive time commitment required to attend and graduate from a coding boot camp.

This isn't something you do in the evenings, or as a hobby. It's not like working out or going for a run. A coding boot camp is pretty much a full-time commitment.

If you enroll in a coding boot camp, **expect it to completely consume your life.**

You are pretty much going to have to quit your job and drop everything else you have going on to focus only on learning to code for three or even six months.

Some of the longer programs might go at a slower pace, but the time commitment is still going to be much more intense than going to college or learning slowly on your own.

Like I said before, some coding boot camps require students to be in the classroom or working on projects 10-12 hours a day, six days a week.

CAN BE EXTREMELY DIFFICULT

That brings me to the next major disadvantage: **coding boot camps—at least the good ones—are notoriously difficult.**

We've already talked about the time commitment, but doing well in a coding boot camp is going to require more than just showing up. **You are likely going to have to work your ass off.**

Most coding boot camps are extremely fast paced, taking you from knowing nothing about programming to writing real code in the first week.

There is a huge amount to learn in a very compressed amount of time, so **there is exactly zero room for slacking off**—especially if you have no programming background at all.

If you are the kind of person who thrives under challenging situations, you may actually find this to be a good thing, but I imagine most people will consider this at least somewhat of a disadvantage, one that should not be overlooked.

STILL SOMEWHAT EXPENSIVE

Even though coding boot camps are much cheaper than traditional colleges, **they are still expensive**, and they can seem even more expensive if there isn't an option of financial aid.

As far as I know, there are no government programs that help pay the cost of your coding boot camp or give you student loans that you can defer until you graduate. (Perhaps there are, but I'm sure they are not common.)

Anyway, I suppose this disadvantage is relative.

For a lawyer looking to switch careers and learn programming, $10k might seem like a bargain price and extremely cheap.

However, for an 18-year-old kid who just graduated high school and never had a job making more than $10 an hour, the tuition for a coding boot camp can seem extremely expensive.

If you wish to attend one, no matter your situation, you'll have to budget yourself wisely.

PLENTY OF SCAMMY CODE CAMPS

This is probably the worst disadvantage I can think of when it comes to coding boot camps: **there are so many bad ones out there.**

A coding boot camp is a great way to make a large amount of cash quickly—and anyone can start one.

As I've been writing this chapter, I've even been thinking to myself that I should open one.

Remember, **you have to be extremely careful** when picking a coding boot camp.

The last thing you want to do is to spend several thousands of dollars, quit your current job, and devote three months of your life to something, only to find out it was all a waste of time and money.

While there are plenty of legitimate coding boot camps out there with good track records and happy students, there are many more fly-by-night companies trying to make a quick buck off of the coding boot camps craze.

An experienced programmer might be able to spot these scams from a mile away, but for someone just starting out in the field, it can be very difficult to tell legitimate operations from money-grabbers. When we talk strategy, I'll show you some ways you can choose a good coding bootcamp for yourself.

NO DEGREE TO FALL BACK ON

Even though a coding boot camp may teach you to program and help you get a job as a software developer, **it doesn't mean you are set for life.**

If you decide to change professions or want to apply to a company which requires applicants to have a degree, you might be out of luck if you invested in a coding boot camp instead of a college or university.

It all depends on how risk averse you are and how much importance you place on having an actual degree.

Once you break into the field of software development, a degree isn't nearly as important, but others might disagree—and who knows if that will change in the future.

MAY BE LACKING IN SOME AREAS OF COMPUTER SCIENCE KNOWLEDGE

Remember how I said that boot camps are pragmatic?

That can be both good and bad.

It's good because you are going to learn exactly what you need to know to get a job as a software developer and write code, but it can be bad because **you might be missing some other knowledge which could genuinely help you in your career** long term.

In fact, the reason why so many experienced programmers seem to have a large amount of animosity towards coding boot camps probably stems from this concern.

Coding boot camps tend to focus on how to develop software, not the whys or science behind it.

This can sometimes result in an **overconfidence in your abilities** without really understanding what you are doing.

Imagine a doctor who didn't attend medical school and sort of learned on the job while working with a few other doctors.

It's not quite the same thing as learning programming by going to a coding boot camp, but many experienced programmers—who in my opinion think far too highly of their skills—tend to think it is.

Now, while I think they are just being a little **overprotective of their jobs**, they are partially right.

Of course, it's easy to remedy this problem by going back and learning some of the computer science concepts not covered in your boot camp later on in your career, but most developers never seem to find the time to go back and do it.

Therefore, realize that even if attending a coding boot camp can teach you to code and get you a job as a programmer, **it may leave you with some knowledge gaps that you may want to go back and fill in** if you don't want to be held back from reaching your full potential.

STRATEGY

Alright, let's get to my favorite part: strategy.

I've advised many starting programmers on how best to prepare for attending a coding boot camp, so I've thought about this quite a bit.

I'm going to share with you some of the tips I've given to those wannabe coders and some advice I'd follow myself if I were just starting out and planning on going down the boot camp route.

RESEARCH TO MAKE SURE YOU AREN'T BEING SCAMMED

First of all, **do the research to make sure you aren't enrolling into one of those less-than-reputable coding boot camps** I mentioned earlier.

This should go without saying, but enough people get sucked into opportunities that seem too good to be true that I think it is worth mentioning—just to be sure.

Make sure you don't bargain hunt when shopping for a coding boot camp.

It is much better to pay a few thousand more dollars and actually learn something valuable and get a real job as a software developer than to save a few bucks.

The easiest way to check out a coding boot camp is to **talk to its previous students.**

I would be very wary of enrolling in any boot camp that hadn't already had several classes of students you could interrogate.

Make sure you talk to multiple previous students about their experiences with the boot camp, what they learned, and how easy it was to find a job after graduating.

This is a basic step of due diligence that can save you from being scammed out of thousands of dollars and help you avoid many days of heartache and regret.

Take the time, do the research, and be willing to pay a higher price for a higher quality result.

SAVE UP TO PAY IN FULL

Going into debt to pay for college is a bad idea, and—in almost all situations—I'd say the same thing about a coding boot camp.

There is no guarantee you are going to get a job after graduating from a coding boot camp, so don't max out your credit cards, take a hammer to your piggy bank, mortgage your house, and borrow against your 401k to attend one.

Instead, **be smart about it.**

While you are researching boot camps, be saving money as well.

Sure, it might take you a bit longer before you can enroll and start your career as a newly minted programmer, but you'll also be hedging your bet and not be overcommitting yourself financially to something you can't afford, solely on the hope of future prospects.

In just about any arena, this kind of short-sighted thinking is a recipe for disaster.

CLEAR YOUR SCHEDULE COMPLETELY

As humans, we tend to overestimate what we can accomplish in a day.

To-do lists never end up getting done.

We always pack more into our schedule than humanly possible.

If you are going to spend the time, money, and effort to attend a coding boot camp, **I would suggest clearing everything off of your schedule** and giving all your time and focus to that endeavor.

Yes, it might be possible to hold down a job and attend a coding boot camp at night or to continue to work on a side project (https://simpleprogrammer.com/cg8-sideproject) or go to school, but because coding boot camps tend to be so fast paced, I wouldn't take the risk.

If I were attending a coding boot camp today, **I'd completely eliminate everything else off of my schedule**, except perhaps workouts, and make sure I gave it all I had—and that's what I suggest you do as well.

STAY AFTER AND NETWORK AS MUCH AS POSSIBLE

I'd also highly advise spending as much time at the boot camp as possible.

Stay after and work more on your projects.

Talk to people in the boot camp.

Get in good with the instructors and offer to help them with anything they might need help on so that you can have a chance to learn even more.

Show that you are committed and willing to help others, and I promise it will go a long way. People will see you working hard, they'll see your earnestness, and they'll remember that, which will come in handy when you do go looking for that job.

MAKE SURE YOU ARE THE TOP OF THE CLASS

If a coding boot camp has a 90% placement rate of students into real jobs, after the boot camp is over, **you want to be damn sure that you are not in the bottom 10% of the class.**

If I were you, I'd aim to be in the top 10% of the class.

In fact, **I'd be vying as hard as I could for the top spot** because that spot is almost guaranteed a great job.

So give it your all. Breaking into the software development industry without any experience or a degree is extremely difficult. I wouldn't want to take any chances, especially if I was paying a big chunk of cash and committing a large amount of time to the endeavor.

LEARN THE BASICS AHEAD OF TIME

Last but not least, **come into a coding boot camp with as much programming knowledge as possible** in the language you are going to be learning.

If you want to be one of the top students in the coding boot camp and you want to make sure you get the most out of it, you want to make sure you don't get left behind.

Every advantage you can have, you should try to take, and one of the biggest advantages you can start with is to already be at least somewhat familiar with the programming language and technology you will be learning in the coding boot camp.

Set yourself up for success. **Don't assume you are going to learn everything you need to know in a coding boot camp.**

Instead, come in with the attitude that you are going to the boot camp to **accelerate your learning** and leave with the knowledge of how to apply what you have learned to a real world setting.

But maybe coding boot camps aren't for you. Perhaps you are more of a "lone wolf."

No matter, I've got you covered.

In the next chapter we'll talk all about self-teaching and what it's like to learn completely on your own.

CHAPTER 9

TEACHING YOURSELF

Many programmers are self-taught.

It's not rare in the world of software development to come across a programmer who learned how to program on his own.

Some of **the best programmers learned programming out of necessity** when doing another job, and found they needed to automate some set of common tasks.

That doesn't mean teaching yourself programming is easy.

There are plenty of eager software developers in training who struggle with teaching themselves and get frustrated along the way.

A self-taught programmer is a unique animal in the world of software development.

I can tell, almost immediately, when I am working with a self-taught programmer versus someone who went to school or coding boot camp.

Self-taught programmers tend to think they can take on just about any challenge.

But... sometimes they get in over their heads or they move too fast, often being labeled as cowboy coders (https://simpleprogrammer.com/cg9-success).

That doesn't mean all self-taught programmers are the same, but there are some distinct advantages and disadvantages when learning to code on your own.

If you are considering learning on your own, you should be aware of the advantages and disadvantages before you embark on this exciting and sometimes frustrating journey.

ADVANTAGES TO SELF-TAUGHT PROGRAMMING

First, let's talk about advantages — and there are plenty.

Most of the advantages here are based around flexibility.

When you learn on your own, you have ultimate flexibility. Some people see this as a good thing, others as a bad thing.

I tend to think of it as a mixed blessing.

Flexibility is great when you can **utilize it to allow you to do more** and go down the path you want to go down.

It's not so good when the lack of structure leaves you **feeling like you don't know what to do and lacking the motivation to find out.**

But, that's not the only advantage.

Cost, and the acquisition of the skill of self-education are also really good reasons to choose the self-taught road.

Let's delve a little deeper... shall we?

COST IS LOW OR NOTHING
Teaching yourself to program can save you a huge amount of money.

Today, **anyone can conceivably learn to program just using the free resources available on the internet.**

We really do live in an amazing time as far as access to information, especially about programming.

The web abounds with free tutorials, blog posts, reference manuals, and even complete copies of books which one could use to learn how to become a software developer.

In fact, if you are reading this chapter as a blog post on my blog at https://simpleprogrammer.com, **it's completely free.**

Even many of the programming tools and development environments are free for programmers learning their craft.

Now, **that doesn't mean free is always the best way to go.**

Often it's worth paying some amount of money (https://simpleprogrammer.com/cg9-personal) to get access to a more curated set of learning materials.

But, again, that route is still much cheaper than college or a coding boot camp.

A few thousand dollars can buy you far more books (https://simpleprogrammer.com/cg9-books) than you can ever read and gain you access to literally thousands of online courses through sites like Pluralsight (https://simpleprogrammer.com/cg9-pluralsight), Lynda or Udemy.

If you are cash-strapped, this reason alone might be enough to convince you to go down the self-taught programmer route.

SELF-EDUCATION IS ONE OF THE MOST VALUABLE SKILLS YOU CAN LEARN

Whenever I give a talk on the top five soft skills every software developer should know, self-education (https://simpleprogrammer.com/cg9-softskills), or learning to learn, always makes the top of the list.

I can't stress enough how valuable of a skill this is, not just in the field of computer programming and software development, but in life in general.

People who master the skill of self-education have a whole world of possibility and opportunity open up to them that those who rely on others for education and learning do not.

There is almost nothing you can't do in life if you have the ability to teach yourself (https://simpleprogrammer.com/cg9-learning), so **I place an extremely high value on learning this skill.**

That doesn't mean you have to learn this skill by learning to program on your own, but it is a great way to develop it since it's such a difficult and demanding endeavor.

There are few things that are more difficult to learn in life than learning to program on your own.

I know some people will disagree with me on that statement, but I have taught myself many skills and I have been a teacher of all kinds of life skills for a long time, and I've only encountered one challenge greater than that of learning to code: learning to be an entrepreneur.

YOU CAN LEARN AT YOUR OWN PACE

One of the major struggles people have with traditional education or boot camps is that they either move too quickly or too slowly.

Different people, with varied backgrounds, intelligence levels, and concentration abilities are going to learn and grasp things at a different pace.

It can be frustrating to be in a setting where the teacher is teaching at a slower pace than what would be optimal for you, because it feels like you are wasting your time and you may become bored and not pay attention.

On the other hand, **it can also be equally frustrating when you are sitting in a class that seems to be moving too quickly** and you are having trouble understanding what is going on.

By teaching yourself how to program, you can avoid this problem completely and move at the pace that is most comfortable to you.

In the end, you'll probably have a better understanding of what you are learning, because you'll be able to completely explore a concept before moving on to the next one.

If you consider yourself a slow learner or a very rapid learner, this could be a big advantage that you may want to consider.

I almost always try to learn things on my own for this very reason.

YOU CAN WORK AROUND YOUR SCHEDULE

When you decide to go to college or a coding boot camp, you are committing a huge amount of time in both your daily schedule and your life to one specific endeavor.

This can be great if you don't have other commitments and you have the luxury of focusing on just learning to program or getting your degree, but **if you already have a hectic schedule and you don't want to quit your full-time job, learning on your own can be a much better choice.**

In fact, it may be your only choice.

I learned programming on my own and then completed my degree on my own through a correspondence school.

I needed that flexibility since I already had a really good job that I had no interest in leaving.

So, if you don't want to drop everything else in your life to focus on learning to program, this could be a pretty big reason to learn on your own.

YOU CAN GO DEEP ON SUBJECTS YOU ARE INTERESTED IN

One of the things I found best about learning on my own is that I could go really deep into the subjects I was most interested in.

When I did go to a traditional college, I was constantly frustrated by having to move on before I felt like I had completely explored a topic.

I often felt like we were just rushing through the material so we could complete the textbook—not really trying to learn.

If you find yourself to be a very curious person who really wants to dig deep and understand what they are learning, you will probably be frustrated in college—and perhaps in coding boot camps—where there is often an emphasis on rushing to cover the required material, rather than going deep to gain true understanding.

DISADVANTAGES TO SELF-TAUGHT PROGRAMMING

Learning on your own definitely has some great advantages, but it has some definite disadvantages as well.

That same flexibility that is great for working around your schedule and letting you set your own course can be a detriment when you feel like you don't know what to do and no one is guiding you.

Here are a few disadvantages you might want to consider before becoming the facilitator of your own educational journey.

YOU HAVE TO FIGURE OUT WHAT TO DO AND WHAT TO LEARN

Remember how I said flexibility was both a blessing and a curse?

Here is why.

When you have absolute flexibility, it can be extremely difficult to decide what to do.

What do you learn first?

How do you know if you are doing it right?

How do you know if you are done?

These are just some of the questions that come up when you are trying to teach yourself programming.

That is part of the reason why I laid out a step-by-step process for learning your first programming language in the chapter "Learning Your First Programming Language."

I always say that **everyone wants freedom, but not many people can handle it.**

If you are not a self-starter and you have problems with motivating yourself and walking down paths that aren't completely paved, you might want to consider learning programming via a more guided pathway.

NO HELP WITH FINDING A JOB

While colleges don't often offer a huge amount of direct support for finding a job after you graduate, there are usually internship programs or networking opportunities which you can take advantage of to greatly increase your chances of getting a job after getting your degree.

Coding boot camps are even more focused on helping graduates get placed into companies after completing their programs.

But, when you are on your own… you are on… your own.

It can be pretty tough to find your first job as a self-taught programmer.

Getting your foot in the door and proving that you know what you are doing without any experience, certificate, or degree, can prove challenging.

But it can be done. In the next section of the book, "Finding a Job," I'll talk more about how, but this is definitely something you should consider, before you fully commit to the self-taught route.

IT'S EASY TO LOSE MOTIVATION

Not many people can push on and accomplish a goal without motivation (https://simpleprogrammer.com/cg9-unmotivated).

It's an extremely valuable skill in life, but it's a rare one and is difficult to develop.

Most people only do things when they feel motivated to do them—which is usually when they first start.

That is where committing to a structured program like a formal degree at a college or even a three to six month program at a coding boot camp can help.

When you feel obligated to complete something because you **threw down a large wad of cash**, or committed a large amount of time already, it can be easier to push on, even when motivation wanes.

It can also help to be around other people whose motivation and enthusiasm may rub off on you, for those times when you are lacking it.

Learning on your own can be difficult if you can't either work without motivation or you aren't very good at self-motivating (https://simpleprogrammer.com/cg9-manifesto).

Remember, everything eventually gets boring. The newness wears off.

At some point, studying programming at 7:30 PM, after a hard day of work is not going to seem so fun. Will you be able to push through and do it anyway?

Or will you be better off with a formal structure that guides you a little more firmly?

SOCIAL ISOLATION

Let's not forget social isolation.

This is a very tough one for many people to deal with and it's one of those problems most people never suspect they will have.

Colleges and coding boot camps provide plenty of opportunities for you to socialize and work with other people seeking a similar goal.

At first, studying on your own might not seem so bad, but **after a few weeks of being locked up in your room or office by yourself in front of your computer, you can start to go a bit stir-crazy.**

I spend quite a bit of time in my office by myself, so I know this from personal experience.

I find other ways to get out and socialize when I can, but even I have short fantasies of going into a regular office and being around people, rather than being alone for most of the day.

This is definitely something you might want to test out and see how you do, before you make a final decision.

LIKELY TO HAVE GAPS IN KNOWLEDGE

I know I've given you quite a few disadvantages so far to learning on your own.

I don't mean to paint an overly bleak picture, because I am a big advocate of self-education. **I just want to make sure you know what you are getting into**, because this route has the highest chance of failure for most people.

So bear with me while I tell you one more disadvantage. Last one, I promise.

Just like I mentioned with coding boot camps, learning on your own is likely to leave you with some definite gaps in knowledge, but probably in different areas than what you would experience going to college or a boot camp.

Many self-taught programmers lack some of the best practices and orthodoxy that college or boot camp graduates may have.

That is because when you work in isolation and solve problems on your own, you start to develop your own ways of doing things.

This isn't necessarily bad, but it can be if the way you figure out how to do things greatly differs than what is commonly accepted and you aren't willing to learn and change once you get a real job.

You can, of course, combat this by purposely trying to add computer science material to your self-study program and working on shared projects, like open-source for example, but **just be aware that you are likely to have some gaps in your education** that you won't be aware of.

STRATEGY

I've already covered quite a bit of strategy on self-education on the chapters on "Learning Your First Programming Language" and "How to Develop Technical Skills," but I'm going to dive into a few more tips that I think will help you on your path to learning on your own.

As I've mentioned before, you'll probably find my "10 Steps to Learn Anything Quickly" (https://simpleprogrammer.com/cg9-10steps) course to be of some value as well, since it gives you a good system to use for teaching yourself just about anything.

COME UP WITH A PLAN

When we fail to plan, we plan to fail.

Isn't that how the old saying goes?

It may be cliché, but it is so true.

I can almost guarantee you that if you don't come up with an actual plan for how you are going to learn to become a software developer, you will inevitably fail.

Planning is extremely important in any endeavor where you are working on your own and setting your own course. Trust me, as an entrepreneur, I know (https://simpleprogrammer.com/cg9-plan).

So, **make sure you actually plan out what you are going to learn**, how long you are going to spend learning, and the actual steps you need to take to get from where you are now to where you want to be.

The plan isn't going to be perfect, and you are going to revise it along the way, but that's ok.

The important thing is to always have some kind of realistic plan that you've actually spent time thinking about.

Don't just crack open a book and naively think you are going to learn how to code.

You can start right now by downloading the free Software Developer Skills Assessment (https://simpleprogrammer.com/career-guide-toolkit). This tool will show you the scope of knowledge and skills you'll need, so you can pick areas where you're weakest and get to work on them.

SET A SCHEDULE

If you follow only one piece of advice from this section, follow this one: **set a schedule.**

I can almost guarantee you failure and frustration if you do not set an actual schedule for when you are going to be focusing on your self-studies.

You can decide how long or short or how often, but **plan it ahead of time and stick to the schedule**, like your life depends on it.

I coach software developers for a living. I teach people how to be more productive, get in shape, reach their goals and basically kick ass. And I can tell you that **people who do not commit to a schedule pretty much always fail.**

I fail when I don't create a schedule.

I would have never even made it this far in writing this book if I didn't commit to a schedule of writing so many minutes per day.

Right now there is literally a timer ticking that is telling me I have 21 minutes of writing left for today.

The cumulative effect (https://simpleprogrammer.com/cg9-progress) is one of the most powerful effects for making progress in any area of development. Use it to your advantage by creating a schedule and making a little bit of steady progress each and every day or week.

NETWORK WHILE YOU ARE LEARNING

Remember how I said that one of the major disadvantages with learning on your own is that you don't get the benefit of someone helping you find a job after you are done?

That means your network is going to be extremely important.

What you don't want to do is decide that you are done learning to program and are ready to go look for a job and suddenly find that you don't even know where to start and you have no network to help you.

Start building your network right away.

Start attending meetups and user groups in your area.

Go to code camps and other activities.

Start a blog. Get involved in the community.

Then, when you are ready to find a job, it will be much easier.

Don't wait to do this kind of stuff until the end. Start now.

FIND A MENTOR

It doesn't have to be Yoda, and you don't need someone to walk with you through every step of your learning process, but **you should find at least one software developer you can turn to to ask some questions or get some help when you really need it.**

Don't expect someone to officially accept you as their mentee. That rarely happens and it's a bit weird in today's society.

But, do know at least one or two people you can turn to when you get stuck.

Having a resource you can depend on (https://simpleprogrammer.com/cg9-mentor) in moments where you just don't get it or don't know what to do can save you hours of frustration.

Before you start down your learning path, know who you are going to ask if you desperately need help, even if you have to pay for their advice.

Oh, and while you are at it, see if you can become a mentor to someone else as well.

There is no better way to really deepen your understanding of a subject than to try and teach it to someone else—plus it feels good to give back and help a fellow human being.

BUILD AT LEAST ONE SIDE-PROJECT

Nothing will help you learn better than applying what you are learning to a real problem and using it to create a real solution.

But aside from that reason, which we pretty much already covered in previous chapters, side-projects can be extremely beneficial (https://simpleprogrammer.com/cg9-sideprofit).

I always like to double-dip in the benefit I get out of my time.

The chapter I'm writing now is going to first appear as a blog post on my blog.

I'm standing at my desk while typing this chapter, which is burning some extra calories.

I'm churning out at least 1,000 words a day to keep my writing skills sharp and improve them.

For the hour I spent today, writing this chapter, I'm going to be getting at least three benefits.

That is what a side project can do for you.

A good side project can provide these benefits simultaneously:

- Give you a **real problem** to practice on and apply what you are learning
- Create a **portfolio of real work** you can use to show at an interview
- Create some possible **side income** or a new business
- Create some **useful tools for yourself** while you are learning to code
- Build **confidence** in your abilities
- Provide an outlet for fun (if you like that kind of thing)

If you are going to be writing code anyway, **you might as well make that code be doing something useful that might benefit you in multiple ways.**

Don't worry if you don't know exactly what you are doing. You will learn along the way.

Even if you build something you deem as "crap," at least you'll have built something and at the end of your education, you'll have something to show for it — or multiple somethings.

SUBSCRIBE TO A SITE LIKE PLURALSIGHT
Full disclaimer here, I authored 55 courses for Pluralsight (https://simpleprogrammer.com/cg9-pluralsight).

But... even if I didn't, honestly, I'd still be telling you to sign up.

Why? **It's an insane amount of value for such a low price.**

I wish something like this existed when I was learning to program.

There is a ridiculously large amount of content available on just about every programming topic you can think of—taught by experts—for a pretty cheap price.

Even if you don't go with Pluralsight, there are plenty of other alternatives like Lynda.com, Treehouse, Udemy and more.

I would definitely be taking advantage of this cheap training, because it's an excellent way to learn on your own and have some structure to it.

I can't stress enough how much of a value video training sites like these are for someone who is trying to learn on their own.

Alright, so now you know enough—or should be well on your way to knowing enough—to get started as a software developer. (Although you probably have some important decisions to make on how to best go about your new venture.)

From here on, we are going to take a different turn with the book. In the next sections, we will delve into actually getting a job as a software developer.

We'll begin our journey with a nice long discussion about internships.

SECTION 2

GETTING A JOB

Choose a job you love, and you will never have to work a day in your life.
—Confucius

That's not exactly true, but it's a pleasant thought.

And certainly, picking a job you love can bring you much greater happiness than one you dislike.

Although, again, I'd say that any job you think you love, you'll eventually dislike—even hate at times—it just goes with the territory.

Regardless, before you can actually love or hate a job, you have to get one first, right?

That's what this section is all about; finding that job.

You may be a beginner just getting started in your software development career, either fresh out of college, boot camp or your own self-created educational program, or you might be a battle scarred software veteran looking for your next assignment; either way there are certain things you need to know.

You've got to be able to craft at least a semi-decent resume.

You've got to be able to get an interview and hopefully pass it.

And if you get an offer, you've got to learn how not to be an overly eager, nervous chump and actually negotiate that offer.

And what about those recruiters?

Friends or foes?

Can you really trust them?

Contractor? Salaried employee?

Which is better?

Job hunting is a skill that you spend perhaps the least amount of your career doing. Nevertheless, it's an extremely important part of being a software developer, because the kind of job you take, where it's located, who you work with, what you work on and how much you get paid all have a very significant impact on your life.

With that in mind, in this chapter I've tried to package up everything you need to know about finding your next job.

And to make it as simple as possible for you to jump in and actually land your programming job, I've also created a supplemental "developer job hunt action plan" that you can get for free here (https://simpleprogrammer.com/career-guide-toolkit).

This action plan will walk you step by step through the process I'll outline in the next several chapters. You'll also get several additional tools and resources, including a job application progress tracker, and my best tips for crafting the perfect resume.

Ready to get going?

We'll start off with some beginner advice about internships and getting a job without experience and then we'll jump right into the job seeking process and some of the other questions and situations you may encounter with looking for a J-O-B.

Let's dive right in since as much as you might L-O-V-E programming it's also nice to get P-A-I-D.

CHAPTER 10

INTERNSHIPS

If you are just starting out, one of the best and easiest ways to get a job is through an internship.

This is especially true if you are trying to get a job with one of the "Big Four" big technology companies (https://simpleprogrammer.com/cg10-degree) like Microsoft, Google, Facebook, or Apple.

Many large technology companies only hire interns or experienced software developers.

Internships provide a unique opportunity for a company to evaluate a potential employee before they hire them.

They also provide a unique opportunity for you, as a software developer just starting out, to experience what it is like to work for a real company—even though your job duties might not be all that realistic.

Internships aren't for everyone, but if you have the opportunity to get one, especially if you are just starting out, I'd highly recommend taking that opportunity even if the pay is not very good or pretty close to nothing.

The sacrifice of working for peanuts for a short period of time at the beginning of your career can have a huge payoff in the long run.

In this chapter, we'll cover **what an internship is** and tackle some of the **difficult issues around pay** and getting an internship. I'll also give you some **tips on being a good intern** and **securing a job** afterwards.

WHAT IS AN INTERNSHIP?

Even though you may be familiar with the term, I think it's best if we start out by talking a little bit more about what exactly an internship is, especially as it relates to the software development world.

An internship is usually a temporary position in an organization—paid or unpaid—that is available to students or professionals who are just starting out.

Unlike most jobs, an internship position usually doesn't require you to have any working experience. This is one of the reasons why it can be a really good opportunity for you if you are just starting out.

It's difficult to get a job without experience, and it's difficult to get experience without a job. Remember that old catch-22?

Companies hire interns for a wide variety of reasons.

Some companies want to appear to be "doing good" and "giving back," so internships are really just token positions for positive PR. (I'd try to avoid those types of internships.)

Other companies **want to snatch up new talent right out of college** because they want to inject new blood into the company, and have the opportunity to groom a young mind, preparing them for a long-term career with their corporation.

Still, other companies are just looking for **a cheaper way to get work done.** They see internships as a win-win situation where they can give someone an opportunity and get some work done they couldn't afford to get done otherwise.

And I'm sure there are many more reasons for hiring interns.

But what about an internship itself? What does it entail?

It's difficult to say, because **what an intern does can be just as varied as why companies hire interns** in the first place—although the two are often related.

Some internships are like real jobs, where you are expected to become part of a software development team and work just like any other member of the team.

In these kinds of internships, you are often assigned a more experienced developer as a mentor. This person will train you and help you to get the hang of things.

Other internships are literal competitions where there are several interns hired, and they all compete to secure a couple of positions.

Often in those types of internships, all the interns are put on the same team, working on an intern project together, which sort of acts as a double test to see how each intern gets along in that kind of environment.

Similarly, there are often **internships where a company picks out a specific project** they don't have the resources to accomplish, and they utilize interns to do it.

These kinds of internships may be a good chance to prove yourself, but you might not get much help. You are likely to be told what the end result should be and cut loose to do it.

Finally, **you have internships where you are basically the "errand boy (or girl)."**

These types of internships can be a bit frustrating because you might not actually be working on projects that are going to utilize your skills as a budding software developer, but might instead be fetching coffee or doing some other menial task.

It's probably a good idea to get an idea of what you'll be doing as an intern before signing on as one.

Ask directly, and try to contact previous interns to get an idea of what the job will actually be like.

Before we move on, I do want to say one more thing about the "errand boy" type of internship.

It's not necessarily a bad thing. **Often proving that no task is below you and that you are willing to do whatever it takes is an extremely admirable character trait.**

Companies who have these kinds of internships are testing for just that—not always, but often.

SHOULD I GET PAID?

Hah.

Sorry, couldn't help myself.

This is a great question though—and so complicated.

It really depends on the opportunity.

I'll go on the record saying that if a billionaire offers to allow me to intern for him, I'll gladly accept no pay and camp out on his lawn, just to learn.

I'd suggest you do the same.

With that said, that doesn't mean you shouldn't be paid for your efforts if you can.

Most internships are paid. There are even some laws regarding internships and paying wages. I'm not a lawyer, so I'm not going to advise you specifically concerning those things, but you should certainly look into them if you're serious about pursuing a paid internship.

What I will say is that **pay is irrelevant when you are considering an internship** because an internship really shouldn't be about pay at all—that is far too short-sighted.

Believe me. I'm the same guy that will tell you to negotiate the hell out of your pay to get the best deal you can (https://simpleprogrammer.com/cg10-salary), but when it comes to internships, it's a different story. Here's why.

First of all, you have to consider **what it is you are after when you are trying to get an internship.**

Mostly, it should be to **get experience** and **get an opportunity** you wouldn't be able to get otherwise, so that you can **get a good-paying job later.**

An internship is not about making money.

It's sort of like an apprenticeship.

If you are going into an internship position with the goal of making money, you've got the wrong idea.

Instead, you should be thinking about **how this experience is going to help your career or open up opportunities for you.**

When you think about it that way, does it really matter if you are paid $10 an hour, $30 an hour, or even nothing?

It's supposed to be a short duration gig, so the total amount of monetary difference isn't going to matter very much.

This is one of those places where you don't want to be penny wise and pound foolish.

So, yes, if you can get paid, get paid, but **don't let pay be the determining factor in deciding what internship to take** or whether to take one at all.

I'd rather work for a billionaire for free than get paid a large amount of money to waste my time working for an idiot.

HOW TO GET AN INTERNSHIP

Now, we are getting to the good part: how to actually get an internship.

It's not always easy.

Plenty of competition. Few positions. Everyone eager, dressed up in their nice suits and dresses.

How do you stand out? How do you even find an internship to apply for?

Well, if you are going to college, that is the obvious first place to look.

Most colleges and universities have internship programs you can sign up for, and they can help you out. To me, this is a no-brainer.

However, this actually might not be the best way to get a good internship—more on that in a minute.

If you aren't going to college and you are self-taught, or you came through a boot camp and didn't get a job, **you are going to have to be a little more creative**, which isn't a bad thing.

If you just do a Google search on "Software Development Internship," you'll find thousands of internships to apply for. You'll even find websites entirely devoted to internships.

Again, not a horrible idea. Go ahead and do that and apply for some of the ones that seem interesting to you.

This method still isn't the best, though.

Think about how many people are going to be applying to those internship positions.

Think about how many **cheap, abusive companies**, who are just trying to **get free or extremely cheap labor**, are going to be posting internships like those.

Want a better idea?

How about this one: **Make your own internship opportunity.**

Instead of applying for internships that already exist, here is what I would do.

First, I'd figure out the **internship and hiring laws** where I live.

I'd find out exactly what needs to be done from a legal and paperwork standpoint to hire an intern.

I'd do all the research, so that if I approached a company that didn't have an internship program, I could actually show them how valuable it could be to them and how easy it would be to set one up. (I'd even offer to do it for them as my first internship job.)

Next, **I'd start making a list of companies** where I felt like I could gain the most valuable experience and contribute the most to.

I'd try to figure out what local companies I would either want to work for or could provide me with some great experience or learning opportunities.

Then, I'd take that list and **try to figure out who I know at those companies** or who I know that knows someone working for one of those companies.

After that, I'd **pick my best prospects and research them.**

I'd learn about the company history, what they produce, who they hire, what kind of jobs they have, and what work they do.

I'd look up social media profiles of people who work at that company and I'd try to reach out to a few of them explaining, "Hey, I'm new to the profession, and I am really interesting in learning. Could I buy you coffee?"

Finally, I'd start **reaching out to the companies directly**, preferably through someone I knew or someone I had bought coffee for, and I'd start making my pitch.

I'd pitch them on how I could add immediate value to their project by giving them some real details from what I learned about their company and talking with people who worked there.

I'd talk about how I was **eager and hungry** and willing to work my butt off to do whatever it takes.

I'd get very specific on what I could do for them and the value they would get for hiring an intern.

I'd even be giving specific examples of **projects I could immediately start working on** for them.

If they objected, or said they didn't have an internship program, I'd say, "No problem. I can show you exactly how to set one up," and I'd reiterate the long-term value of having an internship program for their company.

I don't like to compete with a bunch of people trying to get the same opportunities. I like to create my own opportunities.

And I can tell you, as a business owner and entrepreneur, if someone approached me in this way, trying to get an internship with Simple Programmer (https://simpleprogrammer.com /cg10-homepage), they'd have a very high chance of success.

Oh, and if you do go into an interview for an internship, here's what I'd stress more than anything else:

* **I'm eager and hungry** to learn and contribute as much as I can.
* I'm the **hardest worker** you'll ever find in your life.
* **I don't have to be managed**. Set me on a project, and you can consider it done.

Don't try and flaunt your skills or experience or try to impress them with what you know.

Focus on demonstrating a basic level of competency in the job and the traits above, and you'll have a much better shot than trying to convince them you have the experience of 10 years of programming when you have 0.

WHAT MAKES A GOOD INTERN?

Ok, so you got the internship. All systems go.

What now?

I know you want to knock their socks off so that you'll get offered a full-time position, but how exactly do you create enough of a force to send their argyles flying?

Well, let's start with the biggest frustration companies have with interns and internship programs, and why so many companies don't think it's worth the investment—even if it means getting free work.

I'll speak from direct experience here, since I don't have any interns currently.

Interns are a pain in the ass because you constantly have to supervise them, answer questions, and tell them what to do.

It actually costs me more money to hire an intern who works for free than not.

Why?

Because if I have to spend my valuable time telling someone what to do or correcting their mistakes, **I am actually losing time and money.**

How do you as an intern correct this problem?

Simple. Turn the equation around.

As an intern, your job is simple: save your boss as much time as possible.

This means you have to be **self-directed**, to be able to **figure out what needs to be done** and to do a quality job with **minimal supervision** and feedback.

Yes, that might not be the ideal learning environment for you, but it is the way you are going to create the most value and not be annoying as hell.

That doesn't mean you don't get any feedback, don't get to learn anything, or even that you have to come up with all of your own projects.

However, **you should realize that you are there to make everyone else's jobs easier**, not the other way around.

This service-first type of attitude will not only carry you far in your internship, but **it will also groom you to become a leader**—because that's exactly what real leaders do (https://simpleprogrammer.com/cg10-leadership). They serve to make other people's jobs easier.

Now, obviously you have to get some benefit out of the arrangement, and trust me, if you act in this manner, you will.

You'll learn far more by observing, anticipating needs, and helping others with their jobs and tasks than you will by doing your own job and having others help you.

Plus, the point of an internship is not really to gain experience or learn—don't get me wrong, you'll accomplish both of those things. Isn't the real point to get a job?

Let's talk about that next.

HOW TO TRANSITION AN INTERNSHIP INTO EMPLOYMENT

Ok, you've managed to get the internship. You've knocked their socks off. You've demonstrated that you are a person who can make everyone else's jobs easier and work without constant direction and supervision. Now it's time to get the job, but how?

The good news is, if you've done what I've told you above, this part should honestly be easy.

In fact, it should be so easy that you'll **have to do practically nothing.**

If you come onto a team and immediately start adding value, making other people's jobs easier, and producing quality work without having to be told, when your internship is up, the company you are working for is going to be **clamoring to hire you.**

I'm not even kidding on this one.

Seriously. Again, as a business owner myself, **I absolutely guarantee you I'll hire you if you can demonstrate your ability to make me more money than I pay you.** There is no reason not to.

If you are doing your job as an intern and creating as much value as possible for your employer, you literally will not have to do anything after your internship is up.

They will come after you because they will not want to lose—yes, that's right, *lose*—such a valuable asset.

If, for some reason, they aren't pounding down your door, though, a polite email would be a good idea.

Say that you really enjoyed working there and the opportunity they provided you, then politely ask for next steps to continue the relationship.

But, honestly, **if you have to send that email, you probably didn't do a great job as an intern.**

But don't worry if you blew it, or if you couldn't even get an internship to start with, there's still hope.

Up next, we'll talk about the "hard way" to get a software development job, when you have no experience, you have no internship, but you do have determination.

CHAPTER 11

GETTING A JOB WITHOUT EXPERIENCE

When you don't have any experience, it can be extremely difficult to get a job.

In the last chapter, we talked about one way to get around this through the internship process, but that isn't always an option.

No need to lose hope, though. **If you can't get an internship and you don't have experience, you can still get a job**—and I'm about to show you how.

This chapter isn't going to be about getting the job so much as **preparing yourself to be able to get a job** as an aspiring software developer without any, or with very little, experience.

In the next chapter, we'll go into the details of how to best apply for and find jobs—whether you are experienced or not.

Before you start applying, **you need to make yourself as marketable as possible** (https://simpleprogrammer.com/cg11-marketyourself) and that is what this chapter is all about.

THE BIGGEST RISK FOR COMPANIES HIRING A DEVELOPER

Let's start off by talking about the biggest risk factor for most companies when it comes to hiring a software developer.

Do you know what it is?

Well, having been on both sides of the table multiple times and being a business owner myself, I can say that **in most cases it's hiring someone who doesn't actually know how to code.**

A software developer who doesn't know how to code—or is really bad at it—actually adds negative value and can cost the company even more money than merely paying their salary would entail.

In such a case, it's better to never hire this person at all.

When I worked for Hewlett Packard, part of my job was to interview "top-notch" C++ programmers to add to our team. These programmers would join my team of proven top-notch C++ developers whose job it was to debug the most complex problems and triage them to be fixed by the product development team.

Oftentimes, I'd sit at the interview table and look at a resume of a supposedly "expert C++ programmer" who had over 15 years of experience, and **I'd ask them one simple question about C++, but they couldn't answer it.**

One simple question.

I'd ask them to write some code, and *they'd have 100 excuses* (https://simpleprogrammer.com /cg11-excuses) for why they couldn't write code right now or why their code to a simple problem didn't work.

These were supposed to be expert developers.

Remember, these people had excellent resumes, made it past HR, made it past a technical phone-screening interview, and were now **sitting in front of me, desperately trying to bull shit me** into believing they actually knew how to code.

Why do I bring this up?

Because I want to emphasize that **any good technical interviewer has seen it all before** and has hired enough bad programmers to know that their primary job is to prove that you don't actually know how to code.

HEY JOHN

Are interviewers really out to get you? Do they really want to see you fail?

So… I do a bit of dating coaching for guys mostly.

One of the things I coach guys on is how to approach a woman that he might be interested in and how to start a conversation.

I always tell these guys that when you approach a woman, say at a bar, most of the time it seems like she doesn't want to have anything to do with you and finds you annoying. She gives the impression that you need to get lost.

But, secretly, most single women are really hoping you'll be "that guy."

That awesome guy who is the man of her dreams—confident and self-assured and does what he thinks is right, disregarding the disapproval of her or anyone else—a manly man, to be politically incorrect.

I tell these guys that the reason a woman may act as if you are annoying or that she wants nothing to do with you is because she's testing you.

She wants to see if you really are the confident man that approached her or if you are just pretending to be that guy and somehow mustered up the courage to say "hi," while at the first sign of disapproval you'll crawl back into your hole and cry yourself to sleep.

It's the same with an interview.

A good interviewer really, really wants you to succeed.

They want you to be "that guy" or "that girl."

Believe me, they don't want to keep having to interview and turn people down, but just like that pretty girl at the bar, they have to test you—make sure you aren't full of shit.

So, if they are smart, they are actually going to try to prove that you don't know how to code.

> It's going to seem like they want you to fail—even though they secretly want you to succeed.
>
> Be prepared for that, don't let them rattle your cage.
>
> Keep your cool, be cool… see if you can get her to buy you a drink.

Any company that you would want to work for is going to guard as much as possible against hiring developers who don't know how to write code.

This is one of the reasons why—even though so many software developers complain about it—so many companies do whiteboard coding interviews (https://simpleprogrammer.com /cg11-whiteboard). (It's really difficult to bullshit one of those.)

OVERCOMING THAT RISK

Where am I going with all this?

Simple. **If you have no experience, your primary strategy to getting a job as a software developer is to prove that you can code and that it's not BS.**

Everything else I'm talking about in this chapter is going to be based on the idea that you want to alleviate that risk as much as possible.

When it comes to interviews, not everyone is as hard on potential developers as I am (https:// simpleprogrammer.com/cg11-hard), but I can tell you that even the dumbest interviewer will be at least somewhat suspicious of the abilities of someone who doesn't have any programming experience at all on their resume.

In fact, you probably won't get an interview at all unless you can figure out how to instill enough confidence in your coding ability or competence to be able to overcome that severe handicap in the first place.

So, what we really want to do here is **make it pretty clear to any company considering you for a position that, even though you don't have direct work experience, you are an experienced programmer**, and you have some external proof that you know how to code.

That is what is going to help you get your foot in the door.

HAVE AN ONLINE PRESENCE

First of all, you should have an online presence of some sort.

One of the first things a potential interviewer is going to do when you are being considered for a job is to Google your name.

In fact, the HR person who got your resume is probably going to do this even before you get close to an interview.

It's going to be really bad if the first thing that comes up is your mugshot for that indiscretion you had with public urination one spring break in Pacific Beach, followed by a Facebook photo of you doing a keg stand and flipping the bird.

It's going to be really good if what comes up is your professional blog where you have a bunch of articles about the specific software development technologies you are specializing in, and it looks like you keep it up-to-date.

Every software developer should have a blog.

It doesn't matter if you are an experienced developer or if you are just starting out. You should share what you are learning and write about your chosen specialty in the software development field.

If you don't already have a blog, sign up for my free course on how to create a blog (https://simpleprogrammer.com/cg11-blog).

I'm not going to go into the details of creating a blog and specializing here, but I've heard every excuse you can possibly think of as to why people don't have a blog. So let me say, regardless of experience, regardless of whether you think you have nothing worthwhile to say, just do it.

At the very least, a blog will show that you have some passion and dedication to your interest in software development and that you are the kind of person who likes to learn and help others.

Aside from a blog, **it also helps to have other good things come up when your name is Googled.**

A Twitter account, perhaps a Facebook page, or something else that shows you are active and involved in the software development community is going to go a long way in helping you establish credibility, despite lacking experience.

I'd highly encourage you to **Google your own name and see what comes up.**

In today's world, this is your real resume, regardless of what kind of resume you create.

HAVE A PORTFOLIO

Having an online presence is great, but without experience, you are probably going to want to have a bit more substance as well.

It's a really good idea to have a portfolio of some of the work (https://simpleprogrammer.com /cg11-portfolio) **you've done** that shows you know how to code and provides an example of your code.

This is going to go a long way to alleviate that risk a potential employer would have in hiring someone who lacks experience.

If a potential employer can see code that you've written and projects you've created, they can be more sure that you at least have some idea of what you are doing and can probably write code for them.

Now, there isn't any way to prove that you wrote the code yourself or that it is even your code, but if you have a decent portfolio of projects you created, it's more and more believable.

I'd highly recommend creating some small projects while you are learning to code, or after you've learned to code, and demonstrate your ability by writing an entire application from start to finish.

You can put these projects online using a service like GitHub (https://simpleprogrammer.com /cg11-github).

In fact, it's worth taking a moment to talk about GitHub, which can act as an online portfolio and is already used to judge, to some degree, the ability of even experienced programmers.

GitHub is an online and open repository for many code projects, especially open source ones, based on the source control system, Git.

But today, it's much more than that.

Many software developers are judged by their GitHub profile, which shows what projects they committed code to (https://simpleprogrammer.com/cg11-open), what projects they've created, how often they commit code, and how popular their code is.

Using GitHub is one of those ways to prove you have ability when you lack actual employment experience.

If I were starting out without experience, I would make my GitHub profile as impressive as possible.

Your GitHub profile can essentially act as an online portfolio for your work.

Even if you don't use GitHub, though, you should still have a portfolio of your work.

Another great way to create a portfolio is to **create actual mobile applications** that you can deploy into one of the mobile app stores.

It's really easy for anyone to do this today, and there are multiple benefits beyond just creating a portfolio for yourself.

You could also make some money, and you might even be able to build your own side business—more on that below.

I'd aim for having a portfolio of at least 3-4 applications or projects you've built.

They don't have to be big, but they shouldn't be completely trivial either.

Try to demonstrate your skill in the technology you are striving to get a job in. It also helps to show some coding ability to do something like call a web service or utilize a database.

You might also want to include unit tests or automated tests of some sort to show that you have the ability to write test code.

You will want to show off the best of your abilities with these sample projects in your portfolio.

It can also be a good idea to bring your laptop into an interview with one of these projects already loaded up so that you can show the interviewer the code you wrote and go through why you designed things the way you did and how you created one of the applications in your portfolio.

Honestly, **I would not try to be a software developer today without some kind of portfolio**. I think it is the single best way to demonstrate your proficiency because, for the most part, it's incontrovertible proof that you know what you are doing.

CREATE YOUR OWN COMPANY

Many people laugh when I tell them this idea of gaining experience when you don't have any, but it's perfectly legitimate.

Way more companies than you probably realize are actually run by a single person or a skeleton staff of part-time workers or contractors.

There is absolutely no reason why you cannot create your own software development company, develop an application, sell or distribute that app, and call yourself a software developer working for that company.

You can do this at the same time you are building your portfolio and learning to code.

If I were starting out today, **I'd form a small company by filing for an LLC**, or even just a DBA (Doing Business As) form (you don't even need a legal entity), and I'd build an app or two that would be part of my portfolio. Then, **I'd publish that app or apps in an app store** or sell it online in some way.

I'd set up a small website for my software development company to make it look even more legit.

Then, **on my resume, I'd list the company and I'd put my role as software developer.**

I want to stress to you that **this is in no way lying and it is perfectly legitimate**. Too many people think too narrowly and don't realize how viable and perfectly reasonable of an option this is.

I would not advocate lying in any way.

If you build an application and create your own software development company, **there is no reason why you can't call yourself a software developer** for that company and put that experience on your resume—I don't care what anyone says.

Now, if you are asked about the company in an interview, you do need to be honest and say it is your own company and that you formed it yourself.

However, you do not need to volunteer this information.

I don't think being the sole developer of your own software company is a detriment either.

I'd much rather hire a self-starter who formed their own software company, built an app, and put it up for sale than someone who just worked for someone else in their career.

I realize not all employers will think this way, but many will. You'd probably be surprised how many.

In fact, Simple Programmer literally started this way.

PREPARE FOR INTERVIEWS

Anyone looking for a job should prepare for interviews, but someone without experience should especially do so because you are going to be judged much more harshly, and you are going to have to answer many more tricky questions.

So, do your homework. **Spend plenty of time preparing for interviews** by both studying questions you are likely to be asked and doing mock interviews with friends, relatives, or whomever is willing to help you.

Get a camera and record yourself doing an interview.

Play it back and watch to see what you look and sound like.

Go get a book like *Cracking the Coding Interview* (https://simpleprogrammer.com/cg11-cracking) and make sure you can pass any kind of coding interview you get.

You are going to have to really prove yourself, so you need to be extra prepared.

When you have no experience, you are starting off with a distinct disadvantage, so you will have to work extra hard to overcome it in an interview.

BUILD YOUR NETWORK

This is another one of those things that anyone looking for a job should be doing, but you especially need to do this if you don't have experience.

The best way you are going to get an opportunity without experience is if someone is willing to take a shot on you and give you a chance because either they know and like you or they know someone who will vouch for you.

Make sure that you are attending community events (https://simpleprogrammer.com/cg11 -community) like meetups or developer organizations.

Work hard to build up a network with people who work for various companies you might want to get a job at.

Again, this is just another way to overcome the disadvantage of not having experience.

If I were starting out without experience, I'd be spending extra effort building my networks.

OFFER TO WORK FOR FREE

I'm slightly getting into tactics here, since this will apply mostly for someone without experience and I'm not going to cover this in the next chapter on finding a job, but I don't want to leave this one out.

One really good way to eliminate risk for a company that is considering hiring you when you don't have any experience is to basically offer to work for free or—even better—offer a money-back guarantee on your work.

I know this sounds crazy—and I admit, it's a bit difficult to pull off.

You are probably not going to take this approach when you go through the normal resume / interview process, but if you are working through your network or reaching out directly through an informal interview process, you might really want to consider this tactic.

You do have to have a lot of confidence (https://simpleprogrammer.com/cg11-confidence) **to pull this off, though.**

You have to project the idea that you are so sure that you can succeed that it is well worth taking a chance on you and that you are even willing to work for free or with a money-back guarantee to prove it.

You'll have to be fairly persistent and you'll have to really think outside of the box—like I said, this isn't going to likely work in the typical resume / interview process. However, **if you are an out-of-the-box thinker and you have an affinity for salesmanship or very high charisma** (https://simpleprogrammer.com/cg11-charisma)**, you can make this work.**

In fact, if you pull this off confidently enough, you may even get hired without having to work for free or offer a guarantee. Just making this kind of offer can give a prospective employer enough confidence in your abilities that they are willing to take a chance on you and hire you straight up.

Like I said, this is a long shot, but I have heard multiple stories of software developers successfully pulling off this tactic.

Besides, if nothing else is working and you are desperate, **what have you got to lose?**

OFFER TO WORK ON A SMALL PROJECT

If offering to work for free or with a money-back guarantee seems too bold, cocky, or risky—or perhaps all three—there is a smaller version of the same idea which can help reduce risk for an employer by giving you a chance to prove yourself before being hired.

You can always offer to work as a contractor or consultant on a very small project first in order to demonstrate your abilities.

Again, this is going to require at least some out-of-the-box thinking, but if you pitch this right—especially to a company that "is not hiring right now"—you might be able to pull it off.

In fact, **many companies hire employees as temporary contractors first to "test drive" them.**

Another variation of this same tactic is to gain some experience by **doing some really cheap freelance work.**

You can sign up on a site like Upwork.com (https://simpleprogrammer.com/cg11-upwork) to work as a freelancer and bid on jobs.

If you are willing to work for a really low rate, you might be able to get a job even without experience.

Perhaps you would expect to make $25 an hour doing a programming job. You could always offer to do work at $5 an hour just so you could gain some experience.

Project some confidence. Say that you would normally charge $25 an hour and that you can do as good of a job as someone who charges that rate or higher, but you are trying to gain some experience, so you are willing to work at a much more discounted rate.

I've even hired freelancers on Upwork who have clearly lacked the experience, but their rate was so low and they were so eager to get experience that I decided to give them a shot.

At a very low rate, I figured I didn't have much to lose and if they turned out to be good workers, I'd be getting a hell of a deal.

It doesn't have to be Upwork, either. I did an interview with Marcus Blankenship (https://simpleprogrammer.com/cg11-marcus) and he talked about how, when he first started out doing freelance web development work, he worked for a ridiculously low rate just to gain experience.

As long as you present your offer effectively and you are willing to take a big pay cut, **you can trade a lower paycheck for experience**—which will be much more valuable in the long run.

WORK IN THE MAILROOM

I don't always advise the mailroom tactic because it can get you stuck in a role that you don't want to be in, and it can be difficult to transition into a software developer position in certain organizations. Sometimes, though, this is the best choice when you lack experience and you need to get your foot in the door.

Earlier in my career, I had very little experience and the hiring craze of the dot-com boom had just ended.

It was sort of difficult to get a software development job.

I tried applying to many different jobs and I even had several interviews, but **after three months, I didn't have any real prospects.**

Finally, I decided to call a buddy of mine who worked at HP and see if there was any way he could get me back in there.

He said that there were no software development jobs he could help me with but they needed a QA person, and he was pretty sure he could get me the job if I wanted it.

I knew that I didn't want to be in QA, but I felt like once I was working at HP, I'd be more likely to get a software development job there eventually, so I took the job.

It didn't take me very long before I started helping out one of the programmers that was sitting near me, and after some time I was moved into a software development role and eventually promoted.

Even though it might not be ideal, you could start in another position in a company and work your way up to a software development role.

There are, of course, challenges in doing this, and it is difficult to get someone to change their perspective of you if you come in as a certain role and now want to transition to a software developer. Nonetheless, if you are lacking experience, this technique can work.

It will at least help you get your foot in the door.

GET CERTIFICATIONS

I'm not too big on certifications (https://simpleprogrammer.com/cg11-certification), but I do think they become much more valuable when you lack real job experience.

Getting certifications won't prove you know anything and it won't guarantee you a job, but it is another way to alleviate some of the uncertainty a prospective employer may have with hiring someone who lacks experience.

At one point in my career, I lacked .NET experience, but I really wanted to get a role doing .NET development because I liked C# and thought it was the future.

The problem was, even though I had some C++ experience, no one wanted to hire me for a .NET job—especially since I didn't have a college degree at the time, either.

So, what did I do?

I got every single .NET certification I could.

I got my MSCD, then my MCAD, and even my MCDBA for good measure.

I had just about every developer certification you could get from Microsoft.

Within a year, I was moved into a .NET position, despite any real-world experience using the technology.

Now, like I said, this might not work for you, but I don't think it can hurt—especially when you lack experience.

BE PERSISTENT

Finally, remember that **the squeaky wheel always gets the grease.**

I used to put at the bottom of my email signature, "I am the squeaky wheel," to remind everyone that I'm going to keep coming at you until you give me what I want.

I owe my success in life more to being persistent than anything else (https://simpleprogrammer.com/cg11-persistence).

When you don't have experience, you should make up for it with gumption.

Be the kind of go-getter who doesn't take "no" for an answer and people will be likely to eventually give you a shot—experience or not.

Many people are afraid of following up for fear that they'll blow their chances or be annoying.

Be annoying. It's better than being forgotten.

Besides, if you are persistent enough and you do it in a way that is as least annoying as possible, you'll come across as someone who is eager and hungry.

I've been on both ends of this.

I've followed up with 10 emails before getting a favorable response from someone I was trying to get in contact with.

I've also received emails asking for my time which I've blatantly ignored until the sixth or seventh one made me take notice and realize that someone this persistent might be someone worth spending some time with.

If you don't have experience, you are going to have to get it somehow.

Don't give up. Keep following up. Keep doing what you are doing, and eventually you'll find your break.

CHAPTER 12

HOW TO FIND A JOB

Every week, I get emails or comments on my YouTube videos from software developers—some of them quite experienced—who can't seem to find a job.

I have heard every kind of excuse (https://simpleprogrammer.com/cg12-noexcuse) or reason why they can't get one.

Some developers complain that the **older developers have made it too difficult for younger developers to have a chance**—that we've taken up all the good jobs.

Meanwhile, some developers complain that no one wants to hire older developers and everyone is ageist.

Others complain that **it has to do with their race, religion, or political affiliation.**

Still others complain that **their skill set is useless**, and no one wants to hire a developer who doesn't have experience with the latest and greatest technology.

While some of these arguments may be true—and, yes, discrimination occurs—**the underlying cause is that these software developers don't know how to get a job.**

At the time of writing this book, **there is a huge demand for software developers.** So many positions go unfilled.

Yet, many software developers complain about not being able to land a job.

How can this be?

How can it be that there are so many vacancies in our industry, yet frequently developers will tell me they have applied for hundreds of jobs and have been rejected by all of them?

The problem lies in **not knowing the right way to find a programming job** (https://simpleprogrammer.com/cg12-nojob) and I think it's an easy one to solve.

In this chapter, I'm going to give you **the best tips and tricks** I've learned on how to help software developers get jobs.

THE COOKIE-CUTTER APPROACH (TRADITIONAL APPROACH)

I'll be upfront with you on this one: I don't like the cookie-cutter approach.

I really don't like the normal way of finding a job because it requires so much wasted effort, and it rarely leads to the best results.

However, rather than just skipping to my preferred way of finding a job, I'm going to go over the standard approach of creating a resume, filling out an online application, and submitting your resume; something that most software developers—and most professionals in general—do.

The reason I'm going to start here is that **so many software developers are doing this in such a wrong way.**

I've heard countless stories of developers blasting out hundreds of resumes in a single day to every single job posting they could find on Monster.com and wondering why they aren't getting any results.

If you are going to take the standard cookie-cutter approach, you should at least be doing it correctly.

I'm going to show you how.

IT'S A NUMBERS GAME

First of all, you have to understand that the whole process of blindly applying for jobs, the way most people do, is **purely a numbers game.**

It's just like sales.

In fact, **you should really treat the whole thing like a sales process.**

Create a sales pipeline and perhaps even use a CRM system like many sales organizations do to track your prospects through the pipeline.

(For an easy way to start measuring how efficient your "sales pipeline" is, you can download this software job application tracker (https://simpleprogrammer.com/career-guide-toolkit).)

You'll have something that looks like this:

Jobs applied for > Responses received > Telephone screens > Interviews > Offers

At each stage of the pipe, you should expect only a small number of prospects to make it to the next stage.

For example, suppose you apply for 100 jobs.

Perhaps you'll get 30 responses following up with you in some way.

Out of those 30, perhaps 7 will ask you to do a telephone screen.

Out of those 7, perhaps 2 or 3 will ask you to come in to do an actual interview.

And perhaps you'll get one job offer out of all that work.

If you want more job offers, you can essentially do two things:

1. **Put more prospects into the pipe** (apply for more jobs).

2. **Increase the percentage of prospects** that make it from one stage of the pipeline to the other.

In other words, you could apply for 1,000 jobs and then get 10 offers, or you could apply for 100 jobs with better performance along each step of the way and also get 10 offers out of it.

To recap, it's either more prospects in the pipe or better flow through the pipe. That's it.

If you want the best results, you do both.

How is it, then, that so many developers tell me they've applied for hundreds or thousands of jobs and still received zero offers?

Well, there is some luck involved, but most likely it's one of two things:

- **They are lying**, or rather, grossly overestimating the actual number of jobs they applied for.
- **They really suck** at applying for jobs. Their percentages of prospects moving from each segment of the pipe is really, really low.

Most likely, it's both.

But have no fear. I'm going to show you how to increase both effectively.

HAVE A GOOD RESUME

First of all, if you are going to be playing the numbers game, you want to have the highest number of prospects making it to the next level of the pipe as possible.

One of the best ways to do this is to have a really good resume (https://simpleprogrammer.com /cg12-resume).

If your resume is crap and you get filtered out at the first step, you are going to be wasting a large amount of time, and your overall pipeline is going to be extremely inefficient.

Yes, **a really crappy resume might eventually get you a job**, but the worse your resume is, the more jobs you are going to have to apply for in order for the numbers game to work out.

I don't know about you, but I'd rather apply for 50 jobs than 5,000 jobs.

One of the first things you should do is to get your resume as polished and effective as possible.

I know some people still disagree with me on this topic, but I**'m 100 percent convinced the best way to do this is by hiring a professional resume writer** (https://simpleprogrammer.com /cg12-expert) **who specializes in technology industry resumes.**

Yes, **a professional resume writing service might cost you $500** or more, but in the end, that is going to be a small investment for the benefit you are going to get.

I'm not going to go into the details here since the next chapter is all about resumes, but one of the best ways you can increase the effectiveness of your resume is to have it professionally written and formatted by an experienced resume writer who knows how to write resumes for software developers.

CREATE A QUOTA OF JOBS TO APPLY FOR

Next, let's tackle numbers.

I like to use quotas (https://simpleprogrammer.com/cg12-quotas) **to make sure progress is continually made.**

I am going to finish this book on time because I have a specific quota of writing at least 1,000 words a day and working on the book 50 minutes each day.

You should have **a quota for the number of jobs you are going to apply for each day** when you are actively looking for employment.

What that number is will depend on what the job market is and how many jobs are available to you, but if you are currently out of work and you need to find a job, it should be at least five jobs a day.

It would not be ridiculous to try and apply for 10 jobs a day.

Figure that each job you apply for will take you around an hour.

What? An hour to click "apply?"

No, an hour because you are not just going to click apply. **You are going to specifically apply for each job by writing a custom cover letter and altering your resume to better match each job.**

Is this a large amount of work?

You bet it is!

Is it effective?

Hell yes!

Remember, not only do we want to increase the number of prospects in the pipe, but we also want to **increase the chances of each prospect moving from one stage to the next.**

So, if you only click "apply" on Monster or some other job site, you'll be able to apply for a large number of jobs really quickly, but you'll be sacrificing a large amount of effectiveness.

Also, consider how large the job market is, which is going to be predominantly based on your geographical region.

If there are 50 new jobs per month, you could do a sloppy job of applying for all 50 in one day, but then what would you do for the next week or two?

Sit on your hands and hope you get an interview?

Wouldn't it be better to apply for five jobs a day but spend an hour or so on each application, greatly increasing the likelihood of success?

HOW TO APPLY FOR JOBS

When you apply for a job, your goal should be to make your resume and cover letter match the job description and any other information you can gather about the company as much as possible.

The idea is that, when the hiring manager or person reviewing the job applications looks at what you submitted, **they are stunned by how perfect of a match you are.**

This doesn't mean you lie or make things up to put on your resume or in your cover letter.

Instead, you should **try to take your existing experience and highlight the most relevant parts that match the job description**, remove the irrelevant parts (or minimize them), and use some of the words or phrasings that are used in the job description.

Be careful here; you don't want to just parrot back everything in the job description, because then it will be obvious that you just made everything you submitted match exactly what they wanted.

That being said, **you should match as closely as you can** without seeming too obvious.

Take a careful look at the job description, and get a feel for what the most important skills and characteristics are being looked for in the job.

Modify the ordering and emphasis on your resume to reflect back these points and to show yourself in the best light possible.

Rephrase job descriptions and accomplishments in a way that best shows their transferability to the new job.

Do a little bit of research on the company as well and write up a cover letter that sells the hiring manager on why you are specifically the best applicant for the job. Mention something that only someone who actually did some research on the company would know.

In the cover letter, you should be making a clear connection between the skills being requested for the job and how your experience is relevant and makes you the perfect match.

Yes, this is a large amount of extra work.

It's going to take extra effort.

You are going to have to have several versions of your resume, and each job you apply for will be a further variation of those variations.

But... if you are really serious about getting a job, and you want to stand out, this is what you have to do.

It's easy to click a button and apply for 500 jobs with the same resume and cover letter—that is the lazy thing to do.

MEASURE RESULTS

One thing you'll want to do as you are applying for jobs in this manner is to measure your results.

You should keep track of **how many jobs you applied for; what days on which you applied; what response you got**, if any; **what version of your resume** you used; and anything else that might be relevant to your job search.

What you want to do is to have some solid data, so you can see what is and what is not working.

Think of a job search like an advertising campaign.

You have to test various advertisements to see which ones get the best responses.

I'll often have developers whom I am coaching track the results from the original version of their resume and then track the results they get once they have it professionally written.

Oftentimes, they'll see a 300 percent or more improvement in the response rate they get from job applications using the new resume.

You need to have this kind of data so that you can alter your plan.

ALTER YOUR PLAN

Measuring things is pointless if it doesn't result in you taking action.

As you are getting back data about how effective your current version of your resume is, the way you are writing your cover letter, or anything else that's relevant, **you should be using that data to alter your plan and try new approaches.**

Test out a new version of your resume.

Perhaps test a different layout or formatting.

Maybe test using a chronological resume instead of a functional one or vice-versa.

Many unemployed software developers who complain to me that they've applied for hundreds of jobs knew they weren't getting any results after applying for 50 jobs, yet **they still used the exact same resume and cover letter for the next 100 jobs they applied for.**

To me, this is straight up lunacy.

How can you do the same thing over and over and expect to get different results?

It makes no sense.

So, **get feedback from what you are doing and alter your plan until you start seeing results.**

Perhaps stick to the same plan for a week and then at the end of the week, go back and look at all the data you have and then decide what you are going to try differently the next week.

If you take this approach, you can almost be sure that you'll eventually find a job.

The problem is most software developers don't want to go through all this effort. They just want to complain and say that no one will hire them.

Don't let that be you.

WORK DIRECTLY WITH A RECRUITER

Another more traditional tactic you can take to find a job is to work directly with one or more recruiters.

I'll talk more about how the recruiting industry works in an upcoming chapter, but as far as applying for jobs goes, **a recruiter can be a big help**—especially if you have marketable skills.

If you can find a good recruiter who has contacts at several different companies, they can help you to fix up your resume to match jobs they are recruiting for, and they can often help you to get an interview with one of their clients.

Here is the thing to remember about most recruiters, though:

Recruiters never want to look bad in front of a client.

When working with a recruiter, you need to convince them you are not going to embarrass them by completely blowing an interview or showing yourself to not be technically competent or a liar.

Do your best to project as much confidence as possible, and a recruiter is much more likely to get you placed with one of their good clients.

Try to think about it from their position. Your performance, good or bad, is a reflection on them and can affect their own professional interests. If you don't conduct yourself competently, a recruiter is unlikely to take a risk on you.

THINKING OUTSIDE THE BOX

Ok, so everything we talked about so far is the traditional, cookie-cutter way to get a job, and it can work if you do it correctly, but it's not the best way to either get a job or to get a good job with a high salary.

A majority of jobs—especially the good ones—are not advertised.

Don't believe me? Check out this *Wall Street Journal* article (https://simpleprogrammer.com /cg12-offline) that says as many as 80 percent of jobs are not publicly advertised.

How do you get one of those jobs?

You have to think outside the box.

You have to stop thinking that the only way to get a job is to look for a job posting and apply for it.

Yes, like I said, that method can get you a job, but there are perhaps a thousand other ways to get a job.

Don't be afraid to be creative.

Too many people believe that the standard approach and "best practices" are the only ways to do things, but they aren't.

There are no rules. There are only guidelines.

It's up to you to decide how to best accomplish any task you set out to do, including finding a job.

Below, I'm going to give you a few ideas on how to "think outside the box" in terms of job searching, but it is in no way an exhaustive list.

The whole idea behind thinking outside the box is that you do things that aren't orthodox and aren't exactly what someone tells you to do.

So, if you are brave and willing to do what it takes, read on.

BUILD A NETWORK

I've mentioned this already, and before this book is done, I'm sure I'll mention it at least a dozen more times.

Build a network.

One of the most effective ways to get access to jobs that aren't advertised is to know someone who knows someone who's looking to fill a position. Have a reputation within your network that is so good that as soon as someone hears you are looking, they are jumping all over to try and pull you onto their team.

The only way this is going to happen is if you are willing to invest the time and resources in building a strong network.

There are two main ways that I know of to build a strong network (https://simpleprogrammer.com/cg12-alone).

1. **Meet lots of people** (https://simpleprogrammer.com/cg12-conference).
2. **Give them lots of value.**

Most people try and build a network the wrong way.

They wait until they need a job or something else and then they start "meeting people."

As soon as they meet someone, they start spewing all about themselves and how they are looking for a job.

No one cares what you want.

I'll say it again.

No one cares what you want.

People only care about what they want.

When you try and network by telling people about what you want, you are doing the opposite of making people like you; you are teaching them to avoid you.

Instead, what you need to do is to meet plenty of people before you ever need anything from them, and when you do meet them, find out the best way you can serve them.

What can you do for them?

How can you help or contribute to them and give them value?

If you do this, you will build a strong network, and you'll never have to "look" for a job again— I promise.

It takes time, though.

So where do you start?

Well, as a software developer, **I'd be trying to attend as many meetups and software development groups as possible.**

In any geographical area, there are plenty of weekly or monthly groups you can attend.

You will meet developers, recruiters, and managers, and make plenty of other great connections in places like these.

For an added bonus, **offer to present to the group.**

You'll be able to build up a huge amount of credibility quickly if you offer presentations to the whole group that gives them value.

Remember, this is a slow process focused on giving value to others first.

You build a network by investing in it.

You have to sow before you can reap.

If you are patient and attend plenty of events in your community, you will eventually build a powerful network.

SPECIFICALLY TARGET COMPANIES

Another major strategy you can employ for finding a job is to specifically target companies you want to work for instead of applying for jobs that companies are posting.

The difference is that you do some research and **you find a company you would like to work for**, or perhaps a few companies, and you put all your resources and energy into finding a way into that company.

When I was really looking for a remote job as a developer—and there weren't that many—I successfully applied this strategy.

I found one particular company that I knew had a team of completely remote developers.

I learned about the company.

I learned who worked for the company.

I started following the blogs of developers who worked for the company.

I started commenting on their blogs and building relationships with these developers.

The next time they were looking to hire a developer, **guess who multiple developers from that company recommended for the job?**

And guess who got the job?

There are many ways to apply this tactic. This a very general strategy.

In fact, I'll give you some specific applications of it below.

The basic idea is that you pick out the company instead of the job, and you find ways to get into that company.

It might be by **finding people you know who work for the company** or **making new connections** to people working in the company.

It might be by **offering that company something of value.**

It might be by **simply being so persistent** that the hiring managers of that company learn your name and that you won't give up.

A coworker of my wife's fervently wanted to work for a particular company in Boise, Idaho called Healthwise.

For two years, she applied for just about every single job they ever opened up.

She made friends with employees already working for the company.

She persistently followed up until they relented and eventually hired her.

She's still working there.

BUILD SOMETHING USEFUL

One great way to specifically target a company is to build something useful to them and use that to get their attention.

I know several engineers who have been hired directly by companies because they built some kind of tool that used the software the company had built, or they specifically built a tool that they knew the company could use.

I've heard of designers getting hired because they redesigned a company's website and sent them the new design for free.

Imagine if you took some popular software you were using, built a new feature or revamped it in some way to make it better, and then presented what you did to the company who built the software.

Now, you'd have to add some real value and you'd have to not just be showing off, but if you created real value for them, for free, don't you think they'd want to hire you?

Plenty of people find something wrong with a popular website and then tell the company how they would improve it, but f**ew people actually build a mock-up where they have actually implemented a solution to improve it.**

START AT THE TOP

Here is a bit of a trick from sales: start at the top.

When most developers reach out to a company to offer their services and try to get a job, they usually end up starting at the bottom.

They might contact HR or a development manager or even an individual software developer, all of whom might have little say over making a hiring decision—especially if there isn't already a requisite for a job.

Instead of starting at the bottom, **try starting at the top.**

See if you can find a way to get in contact with the CEO of the company or even the CTO or Director of Engineering.

One way to do this is to call a published number for the company and simply ask to speak to that person.

Don't say you are a job seeker looking for a job. Instead, say you have a unique opportunity you want to present to him or her, or say you have a business deal.

If you do get to speak to one of these "top dogs," **be confident and have a good pitch.** Don't just ask them for a job. Come up with something of value that you can give them and their company.

Ask them if they could put you in touch with someone who you could follow up with to further discuss what you can do for their company.

Does this sound ludicrous? Insane, perhaps?

You might think this would never work, right?

Well, **that is the whole point of out-of-the-box thinking.** So many people believe they have to start at the bottom or go in the front door.

There is no reason you can't get an audience with a CEO or CTO of a company and have them refer you down to a hiring manager, saying, "I want this guy. Do you have a spot where we could get him in?"

Successful enterprise salespeople use this technique all the time. There is no reason why you can't as well.

UTILIZE INBOUND MARKETING

This is the drum I'm perhaps most famous for beating.

I've put out a whole course on "How to Market Yourself as a Software Developer" (https://simpleprogrammer.com/cg12-marketyourself) that basically teaches you how to utilize inbound marketing to get jobs to come to you instead of you going out to look for them.

I've successfully used this technique myself. In fact, **the whole reason you are reading this book is because of the success I've had with this technique in my career.**

Countless opportunities have come my way. I've received hundreds of job offers, spoken at events all over the world, and **drastically altered the course of my life** because of inbound marketing.

So, what exactly is inbound marketing?

Simple. It's just **creating content or some other kind of value that gets people to come to you instead of you going to them.**

As a software developer, you can build a blog (https://simpleprogrammer.com/cg12-blog), make video tutorials, write books, write articles, appear on podcasts, and many other things to build a reputation, get your name out there, and get people—and opportunities—coming to you.

Some people might call this the "get famous" approach, but you don't have to be famous to make this work for you.

All you need is to be known for one particular thing (https://simpleprogrammer.com/cg12-bigmistake) **in the field of software development.**

The key is to pick some very specialized area of software development and become the expert in that area.

The smaller the area is, the easier it is for you to become number one, which should be your goal.

Once you've established this area of specialty, jobs will come to you. I guarantee it.

INTERVIEW THE INTERVIEWER

This is another approach that gets you in via the backdoor and gets you right through the gatekeepers.

One great way to get yourself an opportunity where there might not be an open job at the time is to interview the interviewer.

With this technique, you are going to speak to a contact at a company that you want to get a job at, perhaps a development manager, a CTO, Director of Technology, or some other person who would have some kind of hiring decision ability.

You are going to tell this person you are researching information for either an article you are writing or you'd like to interview them for a podcast you are creating.

You could even say that you are recently getting into the field and you'd like to ask an experienced person about the profession.

The idea is to figure out some way you can get into the office and get a conversation with this person.

Most people will gladly jump at the opportunity for free press or the chance to help an aspiring software developer learn more about the field.

Whether you actually end up publishing the interview or not isn't all that important—although I see no reason why you wouldn't since someone else is giving you free, valuable content you can publish.

At this point, you are just planting a seed.

Now you have someone in a company that you'd like to work for who knows who you are and probably likes you since people tend to like people who are interested in their favorite topic: themselves.

In a few weeks, months, or when a job happens to open up at that company, you can follow up.

You can also follow up if you publish their interview on your blog or podcast.

In fact, if you are going to apply this technique, why not interview the CTOs of all the top tech companies in your area?

Then, you can make a roundup post of all the interviews, publish it on your blog, and benefit from some inbound marketing as well.

BE PERSISTENT

Finally, I'm going to leave you with the same advice I left you with from the previous chapter: **be persistent** (https://simpleprogrammer.com/cg12-grit).

Too many people give up way too quickly because they don't understand or believe in the power of persistence (https://simpleprogrammer.com/cg12-persistence).

Yes, it's possible to burn bridges by being too persistent and annoying.

However, you have to go way further than you think to get to that point, and even then, you don't really have that much to lose if you weren't going to get the job anyway.

Don't get me wrong. I'm not saying to be overly pushy and that you can bully your way into a job.

What you should be doing is constantly following up, changing your tactics, and pushing forward as hard as you can if you really want to get the best opportunities in life.

Doors won't always open for you. Sometimes you have to take a crowbar and pry the doors open.

Don't give up until you've tried all of these techniques—more than once.

CHAPTER 13

CREATING A RESUME

Ah, resumes.

I have a love-hate relationship with resumes.

Resumes are so important to getting that perfect job, but they seem like such a waste of time.

It seems like no one actually reads a resume, but rather gives it a quick look and forms a strong opinion about you almost instantaneously.

That is why **resumes are both so important and so useless.**

Still, every software developer should have a good-looking, well-written resume (https://simpleprogrammer.com/cg13-resume) that helps them get the interview they so badly want.

Yet... I find that most software developer resumes, well, suck.

If you are reading this, your resume probably sucks.

I don't mean that as an insult. It's just reality.

You are probably good at writing code, not at writing resumes.

When it comes down to it, **resumes are more about advertising than anything else.**

You can think of a resume as a one-page advertisement for you.

In fact, if you want to have a good—nay, a great—resume, you have to think of it that way.

The simple truth is, **for most jobs you apply for, the only thing anyone will ever see is a quick 15-second glance at your resume.**

It's in those 15 seconds that the course of your life literally can be determined.

Interview or reject.

Top of the stack or circular file system.

Like it or not, a good resume is important.

In this chapter, I'm going to help you to create a great one.

FIRST STEP: DON'T CREATE A RESUME

I'm not joking.

Really, don't.

I get quite a bit of flak for this statement, but **unless you are actually a professional resume writer—or perhaps a copywriter—you shouldn't be writing your own resume** (https://simpleprogrammer.com/cg13-advice).

Yes, I know that sounds inauthentic.

You are worried about being a fraud.

Someone who can't write their own resume is obviously not qualified for a job.

I'd never hire someone who farmed out their resume to a resume-writing service. I can spot it a mile away.

Trust me, I've been doing this long enough that I've heard every excuse.

In my book *Soft Skills: The Software Developer's Life Manual* (https://simpleprogrammer.com/cg13-lifemanual), I have a short chapter on resumes. I give the same advice that I'm giving you here, and plenty of people have told me, "I like the book except for that resume-writing part; I don't agree with it."

So, believe me, I understand that opposition.

Nevertheless, the simple fact remains: s**oftware developers who get their resumes professionally written by a good professional resume writer get more job offers and higher salaries.**

I've seen it firsthand. I've had countless programmers who followed my advice and told me about how much of a difference it made, and to me it just makes sense. Here's why:

There is an art to writing a resume.

Writing, especially persuasive writing, is a skill.

Like I said before, a resume is basically a one-page advertisement for you.

It's not much different than a magazine ad that is trying to sell you the latest gizmo, gadget, or beauty product.

There is no reason to think that you, being a programmer, would have any real proficiency in writing a resume.

When I have work done on my house, I hire someone to do it.

Not because I can't put a floor in or figure out how to tile a bathroom, but because, even though I might be able to get the job done, **I know that someone who has done that job 1,000 times before is going to be a significant margin better than I am** going to be trying to do it my first time. (I also acknowledge that I suck at these kinds of things.)

Not only is it not worth the 20 hours of my time it would take to tile my own bathroom versus paying someone to do it in four hours, but also it's just not in my wheelhouse of skills—and I'm OK with that.

Think about your job.

The CEO of your company could probably figure out how to put up a webpage, write JavaScript, and program your product.

But he doesn't. Why not?

Because he's got you. You are the professional.

He knows that his time is better spent doing other important things like pretending to work and playing golf instead of programming.

Writing your own resume is just as silly as having a CEO of a company write code.

Yes, it's possible and, with a large amount of effort, a decent job could be done, but why not hire the professional to do it?

So, my advice to you—even if you won't listen to it—is to hire a professional resume writer, but be particular with who you choose.

Any old resume writer will not get you great results.

PICKING A RESUME WRITER

Picking a great resume writer is really important.

Everything I said above is worthless if you hire a bad resume writer who does a worse job than you could do on your own.

I suspect some of the people who are so against the idea of hiring a professional to write their resumes have either **had a bad experience with a not-so-professional resume writer themselves or have been subjected to resumes written by some liberal arts major who couldn't find any other job** and decided resume writing looked like fun.

Therefore, it's pretty important you get this figured out, don't you think?

When looking for a professional resume writer, **you want to first try to get referrals.**

See if there is anyone you know who used a professional resume writer and got good results.

You should be looking for a resume writer who specializes in either software developer resumes or technology resumes.

The worst thing you can do is get a resume writer who doesn't know anything about technology and writes something like, "I spearheaded the C++ing of the project single-handedly by applying SQL to the polymorphic programming code."

Bam. Wastebasket, and you look like an idiot.

Ask a prospective resume writer for samples of their work.

They should be able to provide you with real resumes they wrote for clients with fictitious names put in—or even real ones if they got permission.

Make sure you get samples of actual software development resumes, so you can see if they can actually write a good resume for a programmer.

By reviewing their writing, you will have a pretty good understanding of the kind of resume you are going to get.

If you can't get samples, do not hire this person.

I also wouldn't price shop very much here. Quality should be your number one concern.

Expect to pay anywhere from $300 to $500, but an even higher investment would not be ridiculous.

Think about this as an investment.

Having a great resume can easily land you a job paying 10 percent or more of a higher salary.

It can also mean the difference between 6 months of job hunting and a few weeks of job hunting.

If you make $80,000 per year and now you can get a job making $88,000, a $500 investment doesn't seem so pricey anymore, does it?

I am usually hesitant to recommend a resume-writing service, but you can find the one I've currently been sending people to here (https://simpleprogrammer.com/cg13-service).

WORKING WITH A RESUME WRITER

Just hiring a good resume writer is not enough.

A resume writer can only create good output if they have good input—that part is up to you.

Make sure to have the following information prepared for a resume writer:

- The **exact dates** of all of your previous relevant work
- **Titles and job descriptions** of each job
- As many **major accomplishments** you can think of for each job
- All your **education history**
- Any **certifications** you have or other honors
- A list of what you consider your **most important or relevant skills**
- A few **sample job descriptions** of the job or jobs you'd like to get hired for
- Anything else you think would be relevant

Getting all this information can be a large amount of work.

You might think, "Well, what is the point of hiring someone to write my resume if I am going to have to do all this work anyway?"

The point of hiring someone to write your resume is not to do the grunt work of compiling data; it's to present that data in a short, succinct, and compelling format that makes you look as appealing as possible.

That is what you are paying a resume writer for.

The better and more detailed information you give a resume writer to work with, the better end result they'll produce.

You'll probably also want to ask the resume writer you hire to **produce a few different versions of your resume** geared towards different positions or presented in a different way.

You'll also probably want **a sample cover letter** that you will *greatly* **alter** when you apply for specific jobs.

The idea here is just to get something that will be well-written which you can base your *highly customized* **cover letters** on when you apply for individual jobs.

One last tip: if you are not happy with the resume or the work the resume writer is doing, don't just be polite and not say anything—speak up!

This is your future and your career; if you want a good result, you have to be willing to demand it.

If you know it's not going to work out, don't be afraid to fire that resume writer and move on to another one.

WHAT MAKES A GOOD RESUME

Whether you use a resume writer or write your resume on your own—ahem, *cough* don't do it—**you should probably have a good idea of what exactly makes a good resume.**

This is going to sound strange, but after coaching thousands of developers on aspects of life, I've gotten to be pretty good with human psychology, so listen up.

One of the most important things that makes a good resume is...

It looks good. Yes. It looks good.

What? The vanity, the betrayal!

Do people really judge an entire person's career, their worth as a human being and programmer—nay, their very soul—based on looks alone?

Yes, they do, so have a good-looking resume and wear a suit and tie to your interview.

I'm not even kidding here; people really do judge a book by its cover.

One of the reasons I highly recommend getting a professional to write your resume is because, not only will they make it sound good, but also they'll make it look good.

Honestly, this is the most important thing because if your resume looks like crap, it might get tossed without even getting looked at at all.

OK, now onto less superficial things.

Besides looks, **a resume needs to communicate, quickly and effectively, what you are all about and what value you can bring to a prospective employer.**

I still see resumes that start with an objective section—that's just plain nonsense.

No one cares what you want.

No one cares that you'd like to find a job where you can utilize your skills, C# and ASP.NET MVC architecture, while working on an effective team in the medical technology field.

What they do care about is what value you can provide and how much of a hot commodity you are.

The point of a resume is to act as a one-page ad for you—more specifically for the super sought-after, legendary, software developer that you are.

Your resume, then, should be **short and to the point, as specialized as possible, and highlight the most important Herculean achievements** you've amassed over the course of your career.

There are plenty of ways to accomplish this.

You can do it with a traditional resume format: chronological, functional, etc.

You can do it with something a little more avant garde.

You can even do this with a video presentation where you are on camera introducing yourself and talking about your "greatness."

(By the way, I always advise recording a video resume in addition to your paper resume today. It's a great way to show your personality and bring something a little extra that is likely to go a long way in getting you to the interview stage.)

An excellent resume is not at all about how much you can cram into a single page, but rather the opposite.

The more you can say with less, the bigger impact you'll have, and the more likely someone will actually read the contents of your resume.

Ultimately, you want to portray very clearly what your skills and expertise are, how you've used them in the past to achieve great results, and how those skills might be transferred to the future position you are applying for.

That's it.

WRITING YOUR OWN RESUME

I really don't recommend writing your own resume, but if you are going to do it anyway, I might as well give you some tips.

What follows are some of the most important things to consider when writing a resume in today's working environment as a software developer.

START WITH LINKEDIN

Like it or not, LinkedIn—at least at the time of writing this book—has become the de facto standard professional networking site and web resume.

You are going to need a LinkedIn profile, and you can bet any prospective employer is going to check it, so you might as well start here.

Do the standard fill-in-the-blanks resume to complete your LinkedIn profile, but take the same care you would to create your regular "paper" resume.

Don't just rush through this one and think it doesn't matter.

Also, don't fudge dates or information here, because I can just about guarantee you, i**f you have major discrepancies between your resume and what your LinkedIn profile says, you are going to get called out on it.**

Having to explain how you didn't actually lie on your LinkedIn profile, and that it's just a misunderstanding or clerical error is not a great way to start an interview.

So make your LinkedIn profile complete, make it reflect the truth, and don't forget to solicit everyone you've ever worked with for recommendations—those really do make a difference.

MAKE IT ABOUT THE VALUE YOU PROVIDE

Everything you write in your resume should be thought about from the perspective of the value you provide (https://simpleprogrammer.com/cg13-valuable), **not what you want.**

A resume is not a Christmas list of what you want in a job.

It's also not a trophy case where you admire how good you are and brag unrelentlessly.

Instead, it's all about showing how you can provide value to a prospective employer based on your current skills and what you've done in the past.

For each job you apply for, customize the resume to show the unique value you can bring to the specific job you are applying for.

WHAT YOU DID, HOW YOU DID IT, AND THE RESULTS YOU GOT

I'm not going to get into the nitty-gritty because I'm not an expert resume writer, and there are plenty of other resources you can find online that show you the format of a resume or how to lay one out.

I do, though, want to talk about one detail in your job history and descriptions that I feel is extremely important.

Instead of writing generic stuff like:

"Used Java and the Spring framework to help develop an application for creating cat-shaped logos."

Use this format:

- What you did
- How you did it
- The results you got

And be specific.

Something more along the lines of:

"Designed and programmed a unique and innovative cat-morphing algorithm using Java and the Spring framework, which improved the performance and adoption of an application for creating cat-shaped logos by over 500%."

Then, like a good copywriter, tighten it up, and make it even more specific:

"Derived a new cat-morphing algorithm based on the Traveling Salesman problem. Refactored the cat-morphing module to implement the new algorithm, using the Java Spring framework to improve maintainability. Performance improved 508%, and time spent on bug fixes dropped 34%."

In fact, it took a professional copywriter, my friend Josh Earl, to arrive at that final rendition.

As he put it:

"What metrics does the hiring manager have on HIS performance review, and how can you show that you'll make him look good?"

Which is exactly why I suggest you hire a professional resume writer in the first place.

HEY JOHN

How should I put this... should I bullshit on my resume?

Not unless you want to get called out on it in an interview.

One of the most uncomfortable things in an interview is when the interviewer says "so, I see it says here on your resume that you are an expert in C++. Can you write a simple 'hello world' program in C++?" and you nervously walk up to the whiteboard, pick up a marker, make a few scribbles and have to set it back down and say, "no, I can't."

That sucks. That really sucks!

Now, don't get me wrong. That doesn't mean you can't put down a programming language you are learning or skill you are mildly proficient in. Just make sure you state it as such.

> Don't get caught in a lie.
>
> Make sure you can support and defend everything you put on your resume.

KEEP IT SHORT

One of the first resumes I ever created in my software development career was a six-page monstrosity.

I listed, in detail, every job I ever held, every single technology I used at that job, every certification I had, and what I ate for breakfast for the last two years.

Well, maybe not the breakfast part, but I think you get the point.

A resume that is six pages long does not get read.

Even when you send that resume to your mom, she only pretends to read it.

A resume, just like a good advertisement, should be as short as possible to get the sale—or, in this case, the interview.

Most of the time, that means you are going to want to **have your resume fit on a single page.**

This also means you'll have to make your resume very focused and to the point.

It may seem counterintuitive, but trust me, this is a good thing.

You want someone who picks up your resume and quickly scans it to get a very focused idea of what kind of software developer you are and what kind of relevant experience and skills you have.

It's very tempting to list every technology and skill that you have on your resume—especially if you have a large number of them—but you must resist the urge.

For example, suppose you are applying for a C# job as a web developer using the ASP.NET MVC framework.

You might have a skill section where you list programming languages, like so:

Programming languages: C, C++, Java, C#, Lua, Python, Perl, JavaScript, Visual Basic, Go, Dart, Objective-C, Cobol, Swift

Seems like a good idea? Right?

Wrong.

Even if you know all those programming languages, you are probably not an expert in all of those, and most of them are irrelevant to the job you are applying for.

The signal is likely to get lost in the noise.

Either you'll be creating the impression that you are a liar and just keyword-stuffed your resume, or that you are a jack-of-all-trades and not an expert in C# and ASP.NET MVC.

It would be much better to have a section like this:

Relevant Skills: C#, JavaScript, ASP.NET MVC

That doesn't seem nearly as impressive, but it is much more focused.

At the interview, you can talk about how you know 50 other programming languages. You could also have some other jobs on your resume that highlight a few other languages or technologies you used in the past, but you always want to be as specific as possible.

Think of it this way: suppose you had a nasty tax problem and the government sent a court summons for tax evasion, and you needed to hire a lawyer to represent you in court.

Would you rather hire a lawyer whose expertise was:

Divorce law, tax law, marine mammal law, criminal law, real estate law, cow-tipping legalities

Or one who listed this as their expertise:

Tax law, corporate law

The first one might be more impressive overall, but who are you going to trust to represent you in court?

I know which one I'd pick.

Short, to the point, relevant.

You don't have to list every single job and every single skill.

You can even put on your resume "relevant skills" or "relevant experience."

PROOFREAD

This one should go without saying, but I've seen enough resumes with huge spelling mistakes and typos that I'm going to specifically call it out here.

You should proofread your resume at least five times. Forwards and backwards.

Then, you should have two other people proofread your resume.

Nothing says, "I'm an idiot and I'm careless and don't pay attention to detail," like a resume with typos, grammatical errors, or spelling mistakes—especially spelling mistakes.

"Porgrammer" does not equal "programmer."

Some employers will throw your resume directly into the trash bin if there is a spelling mistake or typo without even looking at anything else.

It may seem harsh, but would you ever want to hire someone for any important job if they lacked attention to detail or were careless?

Would you hire the tax attorney to represent you in court for tax evasion if he misspelled lawyer?

HAVE MULTIPLE VERSIONS

We've already talked about this a little bit when I told you how to apply for a job and that you should have a resume writer create multiple versions of your resume, but let's rehash it here for good measure.

You are going to want to have more than one base version of your resume that you can use for different kinds of jobs you might apply for.

Most software developers, especially those starting out, are willing to take different kinds of jobs using different technologies.

If this is you, you should specifically create base versions of your resume targeted at these kinds of jobs which would highlight the specific skills and technologies needed for those jobs.

You should still customize your resume for each and every job you apply for, but having a few different base resumes to start from may help save you time and keep you somewhat consistent in how you apply for jobs.

MAKE IT UNIQUE

Finally, we'll wrap up this chapter by talking about an often-overlooked resume factor: uniqueness.

The idea of a resume is to stand out.

When you are applying for a job that 100 other software developers are also applying for, you are going to want to find some way that you can stand out and be as unique as possible.

This doesn't mean you have to do anything crazy, but it is a good idea to do something slightly unconventional or to do something that will make your resume stand out in some way.

You want someone who looks at your resume to remember you because you appeared unique or special.

One great way to do this is to get creative with the format of your resume.

Once upon a time in my career, I created a skills section on my resume, and I used stars to indicate from one to five how high my skill was in a particular technology or language.

Since then, I've seen this tactic used by many developers, but at the time that I did it, it was fairly unique, and I received a great deal of comments from recruiters and interviewers who remembered that I was the guy with star ratings on my skills.

Some employers or interviewers will appreciate uniqueness, and others won't, so it's hit and miss, but I'd rather stand out in a few places—and get outright rejected—than to be forgettable and dull everywhere.

This concept is called polarization, and it's good when used appropriately.

I've often coached software developers to include a short video version of their resume—or just a short video introduction—as a unique way to stand out.

Don't be afraid to be creative. Like I said, some people won't like it, but plenty of people will. And you'll stand out in their minds.

One word of caution, though: **don't let your creativity interfere with the readability and communication of your resume.**

Remember when everyone started putting Flash intro pages on their websites?

If you don't, that's ok, but there was this era in the technological world where everyone thought it was cool to make Flash websites that had horrible navigation (see Web Pages That Suck (https://simpleprogrammer.com/cg13-suck).)

Anyway, it was creative but a bad idea because that kind of design greatly detracted from the content of the web pages and made them difficult to use.

So, be creative and be unique, but use that creativity to enhance your message, not detract from it.

CHAPTER 14

THE INTERVIEW PROCESS

Nothing can be more terrifying for a software developer than an interview—**especially if it is a coding interview on a whiteboard** (https://simpleprogrammer.com/cg14-whiteboard)**.**

Although, with the right preparation and mindset, an interview can actually be **something you look forward to** as a chance to show your stuff and exhibit your best skills.

I know the above statement may seem difficult to believe, especially if you've had not-so-great interview experiences in the past, but **I've also had some pretty horrible interviews in my career** as a software developer, and I've learned from those experiences.

I can tell you, without a doubt, the right preparation makes all the difference.

I remember my first interview with Microsoft, as a young developer who thought he knew everything.

Microsoft flew me out to their Redmond campus for a full day of interviewing.

Things got off to a very bad start.

As soon as I arrived at my hotel and began to unpack, **I realized I forgot my pants.**

I found a department store where I could buy some pants for the next day, but little did I know my trouble was just starting.

I had no idea what a Microsoft interview was like, and **I was absolutely not prepared.**

The next morning, a driver picked me up and took me to the Microsoft campus where my liaison explained to me how the interview process would work.

I'd be spending all day going to six or seven interviews.

The day would either be a half-day or a full day.

After the first four interviews of the day, including a lunch interview, if it didn't look like I was going to be a good hire, they'd send me back to my hotel early to pack; otherwise, I'd have three or four more interviews.

Stressful enough for you?

My very first interviewer asked me to code a Win32 function on the whiteboard.

I was not prepared.

I stuttered. I sweated. I scrawled something illegible on the board.

It was pretty clear I didn't know what I was doing.

The interviewer tried to help me out to no avail.

I made excuses. I stalled for time. I produced nothing close to the desired output.

I lied to cover up my inadequacies.

The next interview was no better. More whiteboard coding, more complete, embarrassing failure.

If you are going to be cocky, you better at least know what you are doing.

My ego was quickly deflated.

The lunch interview was a mercy killing.

We just chatted about Microsoft and life. I felt like I was a lame horse being taken out to the pasture and given a few sugar cubes before...

BANG!

Before I knew it, I was back on the little bus, heading back to my hotel.

I did not get a job offer.

I did, however, learn quite a few lessons, and I became much better at interviewing later in my career.

This chapter is all about not making the same mistakes I did.

Let's carry on, shall we?

KINDS OF INTERVIEWS

I hope that, by starting up this chapter with an embarrassing story about myself, I've loosened you up a bit, because now I'll be sharing one of the most important things about interviewing you should know: all the different kinds of interviews you can expect to have as a software developer.

I've tried to catalogue here what I think are **the most common variants and types of interviews you are likely to see** with the hopes that you'll avoid the kind of embarrassing episode I had to endure at Bill Gates' torture chamber.

In this next section, I'm going to talk about the **different kinds of interviews**, but we aren't going to go much into the preparation for them since you probably won't know what kind of interview you are up against until you are either at the interview or scheduled for it.

Have no fear, for, after we talk about the kinds of interviews, we'll cover how to prepare for them—I promise.

PHONE SCREEN

It's pretty common to have a phone screen before you'll be seriously considered for a job.

Most major companies that hire developers will make sure to screen any potential candidate they want to bring in for an interview before incurring the cost of doing so.

A phone screen is usually technical in nature, but it can also have some non-technical questions.

You may end up with both a technical and non-technical phone screen.

Back when I interviewed for Microsoft, they gave me both types of phone interviews.

Like I said, **the purpose of the phone screen is not to decide whether to offer you a job, but rather to weed you out.**

You want to pass a phone screen by showing that you are technically competent and that you aren't some kind of psychopathic freak.

Usually a phone screen interview will be composed of some basic technical, qualifier questions and a few personality questions.

As long as you are properly qualified for the job, **these interviews should not be very difficult.**

In fact, often a non-technical person asks you a standard set of questions and records your answers.

So just answer the questions, don't read too much into the responses, and try to give as much detail as possible, so it is more difficult to screen you out.

ONLINE TECHNICAL INTERVIEW

This is a new kind of interview that has only really started to appear in earnest in the last few years, but I **believe we'll see more and more interviews conducted in this fashion.**

This kind of interview is much like a phone pre-screen, but instead of taking place over the phone, **it will take place over a Skype call, or another video chat equivalent, where you will be asked to solve some programming problems or even do pair programming with an interviewer so they can quickly assess your talent remotely.**

Many remote teams are employing this kind of interview because it closely resembles the conditions of working as a remote developer.

This is also a very difficult interview to bullshit.

If you are screensharing with an interviewer while you are working on a programming problem, it's going to be pretty clear whether or not you really know how to code.

Another variation of this interview entails being **given a coding assignment or a link to a programming assessment test** where you will have a controlled environment and time limit to complete some number of programming problems.

Preparing for either of these types of interviews is going to be very **similar to preparing for an in-person coding interview**, which we'll discuss in-depth a little bit later.

You will want to make sure you have a good mastery of solving algorithm-type problems in your programing language of choice and that you have a good understanding of data structures.

STANDARD TECHNICAL INTERVIEW

By far, this is the most common type of interview.

In my programming career, most of my interviews were one-hour, in-person, technical interviews where the interviewer asked me a series of technical questions about the technology I would be primarily using at the job. It didn't really go much deeper.

I would suspect the reason why these kinds of shallow interviews are so prevalent is because most software developers who are asked to conduct interviews don't really know how to interview someone. They just Google a list of common interview questions related to the primary technology or programming language they are interviewing the candidate on and then simply ask them.

Obviously, you can be pretty prepared for this kind of interview by doing much the same.

Google common programming questions for your technology and know the answers to them.

CULTURE FIT INTERVIEW

This kind of interview is usually conducted by a manager or, in a small company, the CEO or startup founder.

The goal of this kind of interview is to **see if you will fit in with the team personality-wise** (https://simpleprogrammer.com/cg14-nontech).

For this kind of interview, you might be taken out to lunch and asked some basic questions about yourself and your past experience.

The interviewer is usually looking for some indication that you have some kind of personality flaw that would be detrimental to the team.

For example, if you seem to always get in conflicts in your past jobs because you assert that you are so much more knowledgeable in the right way to do things and everyone at your previous jobs were so ignorant, that's a pretty good indicator that you are going to be trouble.

Also, at a lunch interview, if you are very nervous and can't have a good time and relate to the interviewer(s) by having a decent conversation, it also might be an indicator that you are not going to be a good fit.

It's pretty difficult to know what an interviewer is looking for here, so you want to **be yourself as much as possible and avoid any antisocial behavior.**

PANEL INTERVIEW

Honestly, this is probably one of the worst kinds of interviews for most people—especially if it is combined with a coding interview.

With a panel interview, **you are interviewed by several people, lined up in a panel, at the same time.**

The panel might take turns asking you questions or asking you to clarify on someone else's previous question.

You should **expect a mix of both technical and personality-type questions** with everyone scribbling copious notes about each of your answers.

Most often, a panel interview is conducted at the end of a half-day or after a full-day interview as the final test, so be prepared.

CODING INTERVIEW

This is also another kind of the worst, dreaded interviews—perhaps the most dreaded of all.

In a coding interview (https://simpleprogrammer.com/cg14-12things), **you'll be asked to solve some algorithm problem by writing some code.**

Often, you'll be asked to write that code on a whiteboard without the use of an IDE.

Most software developers who haven't specifically prepared for this type of interview do not do well at this request.

Writing code on a whiteboard while someone is watching can be extremely unnerving, especially if you are not confident about how to solve the problem you are being asked to solve.

Big companies like Microsoft, Google, and Apple often employ these kinds of interviews, so if you want to get a job at one of these companies, you had better be prepared.

The best way to get good at these kinds of interviews is to study specifically for them. These challenges require a different mindset and approach to problem solving than you may be used to.

For an in-depth walkthrough of exactly how I approach these problems, download the Interview Prep Crash Course (https://simpleprogrammer.com/career-guide-toolkit) that's included with this book. You'll get to watch as I break a problem down into whiteboard "pseudo code," then move to my IDE to implement the final solution.

Then don't forget to practice, practice, practice.

ALL-DAY OR HALF-DAY INTERVIEW

This kind of interview usually consists of several technical interviews, a culture fit interview, and possibly even a panel interview at the end.

Usually bigger companies are going to conduct all-day or half-day interviews, but I've also been interviewed in this manner by smaller startups that had heavy funding.

The reason why is because it's expensive to coordinate and have multiple staff members each spend an hour interviewing every candidate for a job.

These interviews are pretty grueling.

I already told you about my experience at Microsoft, but I've also had two all-day interviews ending in a panel interview at HP, both of which went much better than the Microsoft one.

I really dislike these interviews. All it takes is for one interviewer to dislike you, and the entire day could be ruined since one bad vote can usually vote you off the island.

With these kinds of interviews, **expect to go from interviewer to interviewer during the day, to have a lunch interview, and then some kind of interview with management or a panel at the end.**

It's tempting to think that if a company is going to fly you across the country, put you up in a hotel, and spend all day interviewing you, that it's just a formality and you already got the job.

But I assure you that is not the case—trust me, I know.

WHAT YOU NEED TO KNOW

OK, so now that we've talked about the different kinds of interviews, let's talk about what exactly it is that you need to know for an interview—technical or not.

I am going to speak in general terms here because, obviously, **the specific job and technology will dictate what amount of the knowledge you need to have** and the types of questions you'll be asked.

However, I think you'll find it useful to **get a general idea of what you need to know** and then once you know that, **work on the specifics yourself.**

HOW TO SOLVE CODING PROBLEMS

Even though not all interviews will require you to solve algorithm-type coding problems, the most difficult—and probably the most important—ones will.

You should take the time to master the skills required to solve coding-style interviews by becoming good at solving coding problems and by gaining **a good, working knowledge of data structures.**

Yes, it's a bit difficult to master this skill, but it will pay off immensely.

Most programmers can't handle coding interviews and don't know how to solve common coding problems.

For that, again, I'll recommend Gayle Laakmann McDowell's book, *Cracking the Coding Interview* (https://simpleprogrammer.com/cg14-cracking). Additional information can also be found in the chapter on "The Technical Skills You Need to Know."

(At this point, you might think I'm best buds with Gayle. I've actually never met her. She has yet to return one of my emails. Her book just happens to be one of the few books dedicated to teaching you all the types of coding problems that you are likely to face in a coding interview.)

I also wrote a blog post about how to crack the coding interview (https://simpleprogrammer.com/cg14-12things), which you may find useful.

If you prefer to learn by video, I did a course on Pluralsight about Preparing for a Job Interview (https://simpleprogrammer.com/cg14-prep), which shows you step-by-step how to solve algorithm-type problems and break them down. I actually find them fun.

Once I got good at these types of interviews, I became extremely confident in any interview I would go into because I knew I could tackle the most difficult challenge they could throw at me.

(Oh, also do a search for FizzBuzz. Don't get blindsided by this one—you'll thank me later.)

COMMON TECHNICAL QUESTIONS ABOUT YOUR TECHNOLOGY / EXPERTISE

This one should go without saying, but I've sat on the other end of the interview table from a supposed .NET developer who couldn't answer what the CLR was, as well as, a C++ developer who thought polymorphism was a kind of religion, enough times to know that I have to make it pretty clear.

You need to know your shit.

Seriously. Know the stuff about your programming language or technology that any idiot Googling "Java interview questions" can find.

You should know the answer to every single question in the top three results from Google on your technology choice + interview questions.

If you don't, it's completely your fault because this one is so easy.

Yes, an interviewer may still stump you from time to time, but **you should at least know the most commonly asked questions.**

If you are interviewing for any object-oriented programming language, you better know what encapsulation, inheritance, polymorphism, data abstraction, interfaces, and abstract base classes are at the very least.

I'm pretty sure I asked about each one of those topics in every single technical interview I ever conducted, and I was also asked about them at least 50 percent of the time I was interviewed.

You can usually find plenty of books (https://simpleprogrammer.com/cg14-exposed), blog posts, and other resources that contain lists of interview questions for whatever programming language or technology you are going to be interviewing for, so I won't try to list them here.

I did do a "Preparing for a Job Interview" (https://simpleprogrammer.com/cg14-prep) course on Pluralsight which goes over some of the most common questions for common technologies.

PERSONALITY AND PSYCHOLOGICAL QUESTIONS

Be ready to answer all of the common personality and psychological questions most interviewers default to asking.

You should be prepared to answer questions like:

- What is your greatest strength?
- What is your worst weakness?
- Where do you see yourself in five years?
- What was a challenge or conflict you got into at work and how did you handle it?
- Why do you want to work here / want this job?
- Can you tell me a little about yourself?
- Why are you leaving your current job?

I'm not going to go over how to answer these questions here.

You can find plenty of advice on how to answer these types of questions online.

The short of it is that **you want to be as genuine as possible without revealing too many negative details, and you want to keep everything as positive as possible.**

Accept responsibility, show growth. **Never blame anyone else** for anything.

Make sure you have at least practiced and thought about answers for all of these questions and any other similar ones you are likely to be asked, especially for questions like "Why are you leaving your current job?"

HEY JOHN

Umm, yeah that question about your worst weakness. How do I answer that?

Well, ah, yeah. That's a tricky one isn't it?

Here's the thing.

Just about any attribute can both be viewed in a positive or negative light—a strength or a weakness.

Perfectionist?

Positive: extreme attention to detail.

Negative: can get so obsessed with making things perfect, that you sometimes lose sight of the bigger picture.

Just use this to your advantage.

You could answer this question by saying something similar to this:

"Well, I tend to be a perfectionist, which is great, because my extreme attention to detail means that I don't make many careless mistakes and I produce high quality work, but I can also sometimes become a little too obsessed with making things perfect."

See the formula?

Lead with the strength side of the weakness, heavy on the strength, light on the weakness.

Flip the good quality to slightly bad, so that it doesn't look like you are saying you have no weakness, but at the same time you aren't revealing a major character flaw.

Some people think the best way to answer this question is to just be brutally honest and reveal something really bad.

Don't do this. I'm not saying to lie—never lie— but there is no need to tell your interviewer that you stalked your girlfriend in high school or that you have a tendency to be lazy.

Always put your best foot forward.

Demonstrate how you turn weaknesses into strengths.

INTERVIEW TIPS

Alright, now let's get into some actual tips to help you do the best you can in an actual interview (https://simpleprogrammer.com/cg14-10tips).

Before we get into these tips, I want to talk about one of the most important tips, which you can find a whole chapter on in my book, *Soft Skills: The Software Developer's Life Manual* (https://simpleprogrammer.com/cg14-lifemanual).

This tip is that **you shouldn't be relying on the interview as the time to impress the interviewer.**

The best possible thing you can do to help you "pass" an interview is to have the interviewer already like you before you get into the interview.

Even though technical skills are important, **most interviewers end up hiring people they like.**

How could you possibly get the interviewer to like you before the interview?

What sorcery is this, you ask?

Simple. Think outside of the box.

In the chapter, "Finding a Job," I talked both about the traditional way to get a job by blasting out resumes as well as some techniques that are more out-of-the-box.

If you've used one of the out-of-the-box techniques, there is a good chance you came in via a referral instead of a cold job application and resume.

In that case, the interviewer may already know who you are or have a good impression of you.

If you have a blog or YouTube channel, the interviewer may also know who you are ahead of time.

And, finally, I've talked to many software developers who—when they knew who was going to interview them—actually **reached out ahead of time for a pre-interview** and to introduce themselves. (This works surprisingly well.)

The point is, if you can build rapport ahead of the interview and think of ways to make it so that the interviewer already likes you before you even step foot in the door, you are going to have a much better chance of landing that job.

I've had situations in my career where I was able to do this so well that the interview was just a formality, and I literally just chatted with the interviewer for an hour. (The best interviews feel like that, anyway.)

Regardless, if you can't gain that advantage, here are some tips that will apply in just about any interview situation.

DRESS RIGHT

I've got a bit of an against-the-grain opinion on this one, but **I believe you should always dress up as best you can for an interview.**

I know that many software development shops allow everyone to wear flip-flops and shorts, and they may even say you can at an interview, but don't do it.

For an interview, **you should dress two levels above the standard office dress code.**

If you are a guy, I'd almost always recommend coming into any interview with a nice suit, and if you are a lady, I'd recommend the equivalent dress or power suit.

If you are a power ranger, you definitely want to wear your power suit (couldn't resist).

Although, I wouldn't wear a tuxedo. That might be overkill (unless of course you are interviewing for a secret agent position).

Yes, it's true the interviewer might say that you didn't need to wear a suit and that you are "over-dressed," but don't trust what people say.

Even if the interviewer feels that you are overdressed, looking sharp and professional causes a first impression that is difficult to shake.

I can't see any disadvantage to having an interviewer think you are extremely professional.

Let the other job candidates dress in t-shirts and jeans, but you dress up as best you can and create a strong, unconscious bias that you are the more professional, better candidate.

You don't have to take my advice here, but whatever you do, at least dress one level higher than what the standard office wear is.

Please do not wear shorts to an interview, no matter how badass you think you are.

For specific how-to advice on dressing for a job interview, you may want to check out the "what software developers should wear" guide and suggested wardrobe list available for download here (https://simpleprogrammer.com/career-guide-toolkit).

BE ON TIME

On time is 10 minutes early.

Not 15, not 20.

Not 10 minutes late.

Not right at the time you are supposed to be there.

If you are driving to the interview, plan to be there 30 minutes early, but wait in your car for 20 minutes if you get there as early as expected.

This is called a buffer.

If you have trouble being on time for events, always plan to arrive 30 minutes early and spend 20 minutes answering email, reading a book, or something else. (Outside of the building where no one can see you. I shouldn't have to say this, but I do, so here it is.)

Then, if something comes up—and it always does—you are still on time.

DON'T LIE

It's tempting to lie or fudge the truth, but don't do it.

You don't have to volunteer every negative piece of information about yourself, but if something comes up, address it. Don't sweep it under the rug.

This especially goes for answering technical questions.

If you don't know the answer, just state that you don't know but are interested in learning the answer or that you will find out the answer when you get back home.

Don't try and bullshit answers to questions you don't know. It's obvious and if the interviewer knows his or her subject well, you'll just sound unconfident, arrogant, and dumb.

I've interviewed enough software developers to know that bullshitting an answer never leaves a good impression.

It's OK not to know the answer to every single question the interviewer asks.

You will create a much better impression by honestly and humbly admitting your lack of knowledge in an area and your eagerness to correct that fault than any kind of deception or bullshit you can come up with.

It may even work in your favor to have at least one question that you admit you don't know the answer to.

DON'T DEFEND YOURSELF

Interviews can be high-stress situations where you can easily feel like you are being judged— you are.

In these kinds of situations, it can feel like you are being personally attacked—you aren't.

It's easy to slip into a defensive response when asked certain questions about your work experience or skills.

It's easy to slip into a defensive response when you don't know the answer to a question the interviewer asks, and you might feel embarrassed or like they are trying to make you look like an idiot.

Resist this temptation at all costs.

Nothing shows more of a lack of confidence than a backpedaling, defensive person who can't handle anything negative about themselves or being perceived as not knowing the answer to something.

If you feel like you are being "attacked" during an interview, go with it.

Have a stoic resolve which shows that your confidence in your abilities is so high that you can admit your weaknesses and you aren't afraid to look dumb or incompetent.

ELABORATE

An interview is like an audition.

You want to get as much stage time as possible.

So don't blow it by giving one-word answers to questions the interviewer asks—or even one-sentence answers.

Always elaborate.

What do I mean?

Instead of just answering the question—especially a technical one—add more details.

Talk about how you used a particular technology or concept.

Give your thoughts about it, especially your controversial ones.

You'll be seen as having understanding and a depth of knowledge rather than as someone who memorized a bunch of definitions that you don't really understand.

You also have a chance to show your personality and show how you explain and share your ideas.

Don't go overboard and tell your entire life story to the interviewer, but always elaborate on any non-trivial questions.

One huge advantage of this approach is that even if you are technically wrong, you will get credit for analytically thinking about the problem or question, especially if you think out loud.

BE CONFIDENT (NOT ACT)

You can fake everything but confidence, so don't even try it.

Instead, **actually be confident going into an interview.**

Faked confidence comes off as either insecurity or arrogance.

Real confidence comes off as being comfortable with who you are, where you are, and just having a good 'ol time.

How can you actually be confident?

Well, by preparing, of course.

The more prepared you are for an interview, the more confident you'll be going into one, so do the difficult work up front.

As the Greek lyrical poet Archilochus once said, "We don't rise to the level of our expectations, we fall to the level of our training."

DEMONSTRATE THIS ONE, ALL-IMPORTANT MESSAGE

I am self-motivated. I figure out what needs to be done and I do it.

Everything you say to the interviewer should indicate this.

As an employer myself at Simple Programmer, I can tell you that this trait is what I am looking for more than anything else.

I want to hire people who I can count on to get things done and require minimal guidance from me.

I want people who figure out what needs to be done and do it.

Those are the most effective people.

Those are the kinds of people you don't have to manage because **they manage themselves.**

Demonstrate—in as many ways you can—this all-important trait.

Specifically say it if you have to.

PRACTICE, PRACTICE, PRACTICE

Unless you've got a hardline into the Matrix, if you want to get good at anything you'll need to practice

So do it.

Practice mock interviews.

In the mirror.

With your pets.

Have your friends and family interview you.

Go out and get real interviews—just for practice.

Record yourself on video and play it back, so you can watch and cringe.

Do whatever it takes to get the practice you need.

Practice coding problems on whiteboards.

Practice, practice, practice.

I can't say it enough.

Practice.

CHAPTER 15

SALARIES AND NEGOTIATION

This may be one of the most important chapters you read in this book—no, really.

Using the advice in this chapter, you may be able to earn yourself hundreds of thousands or even a million dollars or more over the course of your career.

The reason why is two-fold.

First, if you negotiate correctly, **you can increase your starting salary** at a job you take by a fairly large amount—much more than you can ever expect to get from raises.

And second, **raises are almost always based off a percentage of your current salary.**

That is why **it is absolutely critical to get a good salary when starting a new job and to negotiate as best as possible.**

Unfortunately, most developers severely undercut themselves and either don't even negotiate at all, or immediately roll over and accept the first offer they are given (https://simpleprogrammer.com/cg15-tooquick).

I fully understand this mentality, especially if you just want to get a job, but it's important to think about the long term.

In this chapter, I'm going to take you from first getting an offer and the things you need to consider, all the way to the negotiation phase, where I'll give you some of the best advice I have about making a counter offer.

One last thing before we get started:

This information is so critical to your financial future that I've put together a condensed Software Developer's Negotiation Checklist that you can download for free (https://simpleprogrammer.com/career-guide-toolkit).

Print this out and keep handy when you're negotiating your salary or raise—you'll be glad you did.

KNOW YOUR SALARY RANGE

The first thing you should do is know your salary range, the area of technology, the job title, and the geographic location of the job you are applying for.

Let's break some of these down.

You should know what the salary range is for the specific job you want at the company. Sites like Glassdoor.com (https://simpleprogrammer.com/cg15-glassdoor) can help you with that.

You can also ask around.

If you know someone who is working at the company, don't ask, "How much do you get paid?"

Instead ask, "Is x to y dollars a reasonable salary expectation based on what you know? And if not, what would you say is reasonable?"

Whatever number they say, increase it by at least 10%, since no one wants to help someone else get paid more than themselves.

You are not going to have perfect data on this, but **before you go into any kind of salary negotiation or evaluate a job offer, you should at least have a pretty good idea of the range the company usually pays someone in an equivalent title or position.**

In fact, large companies might even have an actual official pay scale that you can get your hands on.

For example, when I worked at HP, my manager had an official pay scale with different pay grades that he could show me.

Sometimes, all you have to do is ask.

However, you shouldn't use this as your only data point.

You should **do additional research to find out what software developers of different levels of experience and working with specific technologies are being paid, on average** (https://simpleprogrammer.com/cg15-range).

Ask around and search for this data. It won't be that difficult to find.

Yes, I know this is extra work, but it's also plain old common sense.

Any time you are about to enter serious negotiations on a money matter, you should have your facts straight.

If I'm going to buy a new or used car, you can bet I'm coming prepared with the car's Kelley Blue Book value, what other dealers or sellers are pricing the same or comparable vehicle at, and the dealer's invoice, if I can find it.

So many software developers ask me what number they should name when asked about their salary requirement (hint: don't name any), or whether an offer is good or not, but if they would have taken the time to do a little research in advance, they'd already know.

Trust me, this research can pay off well, so do it.

GETTING THE OFFER

So, let's skip ahead a little bit—since negotiations can happen before or after the offer—and talk about when to expect an offer and what to do when you get one.

Most companies will tell you ahead of time if they are going to send you an offer, although I've received a surprise email or courier with one from time-to-time.

It's debatable whether it's more beneficial to negotiate before the offer is made or after.

If you negotiate before getting the offer, you risk not getting one in the first place.

But, if you negotiate after, you risk not setting the stage properly and getting an extremely low offer that will be difficult to negotiate out of.

All-in-all, I prefer to do the bulk of the negotiation after getting the offer because at that point the hiring manager has made a firm decision to hire you, which will be an advantage in negotiating.

When you get an offer, it's important to remember that an offer is just that: an offer.

It does not mean you absolutely have the job—although chances are likely—and it does not mean you are guaranteed anything in any way.

Offers can easily be rescinded, although it rarely happens.

You should carefully read the offer and pay attention to any deadlines for responding. (Those can be negotiated.)

Look for the details like the start date, yearly or monthly salary, job title, benefits like vacation or health insurance, and any other details that are important to you.

All of these points are negotiable, so it's important to consider everything.

You may be tempted to just immediately accept an offer, especially if you've been looking for a job for a while. Don't.

It's always worth trying to negotiate, at least to some degree.

Before we move on, let's talk about one more important point when it comes to getting an offer: the time frame.

I've had plenty of job interviews where I've waited for weeks before getting an offer or a rejection letter.

Chances are, if you got the job, you will get the offer fairly quickly within a few days of the interview—although this isn't always the case.

It is always a good idea to follow up (https://simpleprogrammer.com/cg15-persistence), especially if you can indicate subtly that you have another option you are considering.

Many programmers are afraid to follow up, but I can't understand why.

Do you think that someone who wants to hire you for a job is going to decide to not hire you because you sent them an email asking about when to expect a decision or you followed up in some way?

It's more likely that being aggressive and a go-getter will move a hiring manager from a "maybe" to a "yes," so definitely follow up.

Salary Isn't Everything

We've already hit on this slightly, but let's dive a little deeper into what makes up the entire package of a job offer.

Far too many software developers just look at one number—salary—when considering a job and an offer.

Not only does this approach take many negotiating factors off the table and make your position weaker, but it also may cause you to short-change yourself by taking a job offer that appears to be worth more money, but actually isn't.

Let's consider a few scenarios, shall we?

Imagine having two offers. One is for $90,000 and the other is for $80,000.

The $90,000 offer, we'll call it "Offer A," is from a small company. They are going to give you a .05% equity in their company which vests after three years.

The CEO indicates that, since they are a small startup, typical working hours are around 60 hours a week.

Vacation time is "generous" and is combined with sick days to form a "take vacation when you need it" policy.

Health insurance is provided, but only covered at 80%, and you have to pay $200 pre-tax into it via your paycheck.

There is a 401k retirement plan, but no company matching.

Your job title will be Senior Software Developer.

The $80,000 offer, we'll call it "Offer B," is from a pretty large Fortune 500 company. You won't get any equity in the company, but you may get stock options as a bonus, if the company has a good quarter.

The company seems to have a good culture. Many developers work from home. They usually have social events where they take half-days on Fridays. You don't get the impression that many people even work 40 hours a week. Work-life balance is an HR policy.

Vacation is being offered at "two weeks," which increases after several years of service. You also get five paid sick days.

Health insurance is fully provided with no extra cost at 100% coverage.

There is a 401k retirement plan with 2% matching.

There are a few other small benefits like an on-site, heavily discounted cafeteria, discounted child care, gym membership, etc.

Your job title will be Software Engineer II.

We could spend all day talking about the differences between these offers, but I want to start with the most important and best way to compare two offers from a financial perspective.

Let's talk about hourly rate.

You see, salary tends to hide this.

In order to get the real hourly rate you will be paid, we need to take into account the following important factors:

- Expected hours you will work in a week
- Expected compensation, including bonuses
- Vacation time
- Value of benefits you will use (especially health insurance)

This can get fairly complicated, but let's try to keep it simple, since we are only looking for big differences. It's not worth considering that one job ends up being $35 / hour and the other is $36.

Let's take both offers and try to come up with an hourly rate.

Offer A:

Hours worked in a typical week: 55 (give them the benefit of the doubt)
Straight compensation: $90,000
Bonuses: $0 (equity is usually worthless)

Vacation time: 5 days (when a company has an unlimited vacation policy and has 50-60 hour workweeks, you typically take very little, if any, vacation.)
Health insurance: $700 a month

$90,000 + 0 + ($700 * 12) = $98,400
$98,400 / (55 hour per week * (52 - 1 week vacation))
$98,400 / 2805 (total hours worked per year) = $35 an hour

Offer B:

Hours worked in a typical week: 40
Straight compensation: $80,000
Bonuses: $2,400 (assume 3% average)
Vacation time: 10 days
Health insurance: $1,500 a month
401k match: $400 a month
Other benefits: $200 a month

$80,000 + $2,400 + ($1,500 + $400 + $200 * 12) = $107,600
$107,600 / (40 hour per week * (52 - 2 week vacation))
$107,600 / 2000 (total hours worked per year) = $54 an hour

Now, before you get all upset, I'm not saying a big company is necessarily better than a startup. It could be the other way around, but look at the difference here.

When you look at how much you are actually being paid an hour on one job where the salary is lower, **the actual hourly value is about $54 an hour while the other job, which pays $10,000 more, is actually only about $35 an hour.**

This is huge!

Even if I am off on some of my estimates, you can easily see how looking at salary alone is deceptive and can lead you down the entirely wrong path.

Always, always do this kind of calculation when you get a job offer.

Now, of course, it doesn't just come down to money.

You might be much happier at one job versus another, so definitely take that into consideration as well.

But as far as negotiating is concerned, make sure you are making a fair comparison from a financial perspective.

We'll talk about negotiating next, but think about how much of a difference this kind of information makes when considering what to ask for.

Knowing this information, you might ask the startup company for $120,000 in order to make it comparable or a better deal than the large company offer.

Without this information, you might have assumed the startup company's offer was actually better.

NEGOTIATING

Ok, now that we've properly set the stage, we can actually talk about negotiating.

Without having the background knowledge we covered above, I'm sure you can see how your negotiations would be much less effective.

First of all, **let's talk about why negotiating is so important.**

I hear plenty of times from software developers that they didn't want to hassle with negotiating and risk losing the job, so they just took the offer.

Often, these well-meaning developers try to convince me it wouldn't have made much of a difference anyway.

Respectfully, I disagree. Here's why.

One big reason is that **it is much easier to impact your salary when you first begin a job than through getting raises at a job.**

If you can raise your overall compensation by 10%—which is usually easily obtainable—you can possibly put yourself ahead by 2-3 years in terms of raises, which usually are around 2-3%, but might actually be 0%.

This alone might not seem like a huge deal, but the power of compounding—what Einstein called the 8th wonder of the world—can make it so. Let's see how.

We'll just use salary negotiations for this example, but ultimately you want to negotiate on every factor we talked about in the previous example to influence the overall compensation.

Suppose you took a job for $80,000 instead of negotiating and getting $90,000.

The chart below assumes a 3% raise every year.

Let's see what the difference would be after 10 years.

Year 1	$80,000	$90,000
Year 2	$82,400.00	$92,700.00
Year 3	$84,872.00	$95,481.00
Year 4	$87,418.16	$98,345.43
Year 5	$90,040.70	$101,295.79
Year 6	$92,741.93	$104,334.67
Year 7	$95,524.18	$107,464.71
Year 8	$98,389.91	$110,688.65
Year 9	$101,341.61	$114,009.31
Year 10	$104,381.85	$117,429.59
Total	**$917,110**	**$1,031,749**

That represents a difference of $114,639. That might not make you rich, but it is a pretty decent amount of money.

That assumes you stay at the same job for 10 years and get 3% raises, but what happens if you switch jobs and negotiate again or you negotiate your raises?

And what happens if you take that extra money you are making and invest it?

Oh, and, if you are curious what the difference might be over the course of your entire career, say 30 years, it's $475,754.16!

POSITIONING

One of the first things to consider when entering any negotiation is the relative positioning of both parties.

This is one of the main reasons why I spend so much time teaching software developers how to build a personal brand and market themselves (https://simpleprogrammer.com /cg15-marketyourself).

The better your position is coming into a negotiation, the better the outcome you can get from the negotiation.

The person who can most afford to walk away from a deal always has the best position— remember that.

Probably **your best possible position** is to have a company seek you out specifically and try to recruit you based on your unique talents, abilities, or reputation—and for you to already have a very nice, high-paying job along with several other offers.

Oh, and you also have plenty of money in the bank to live off of for the next three months or more.

Does this seem like fantasy?

It's not. When I was still writing code full-time, before I went out on my own, I was able to put myself in this exact position, and it was great.

Let's look at the contrast.

The worst position you could be in is to have applied for a job without a referral. You are barely qualified for the job since they asked for someone with a college degree, and you don't have one.

The interview didn't go well, and you were the third choice for the position. The other two candidates declined the offer.

You don't have another job lined up. You are about to get kicked out of your apartment, and you have a bunch of unpaid bills.

Can you see how you'd be in a much better negotiating position in the first case as compared to the second?

Before you even get into negotiations, you want to do as much as possible to try to get yourself as close to the first case as you can.

You never want to be caught in what I call "the squeeze.".

This is a situation where your choices are extremely limited, and you are forced to make some suboptimal choices because of some constraint like finances, a deadline, or some other calamity.

So, what can you do to improve your position?

First of all, you can make sure you are not desperate.

Don't quit a job before you have another job lined up—even if your boss is a jerk.

Try to have a few months of living expenses saved up at all times. Anyone can do this and it will keep you out of quite a few squeeze situations in your life. (Trust me on this one.)

Try to **apply for a job from a referral** if at all possible. (See the chapter on finding a job for more info on that.)

Be extremely well-prepared for an interview so that you can have the strongest performance possible. If you "ace" an interview, you are going to be in a much stronger position than if you barely squeak by.

See if you can **get multiple offers lined up** at the same time.

Make sure you k**now the job market, the company you are negotiating with, and the salary information** we talked about above. Knowledge is power. In any negotiation, the party with more knowledge is in a much better position than the party who lacks it.

Establish a good reputation. **The better your reputation is, the better your position will be.** This is one of the main reasons I advocate for every software developer to have a regularly updated blog and learn some basic marketing and branding skills.

Before you begin any negotiation process, evaluate your position and the position of the company you are negotiating with.

WHOEVER NAMES A NUMBER FIRST, LOSES

Remember how I said knowledge is really important in positioning?

One of the biggest pieces of knowledge you or a company can have about you is salary information.

In just about any negotiation, whoever names a number first loses, or is at least at a distinct disadvantage.

Under no circumstances should you reveal your current salary and you should never name the salary you are looking for until you've been given an offer first.

Yes, I know this is easier said than done.

Yes, I know companies will directly ask you both your current salary and what salary you want for the job you are applying for, but there are several ways around this.

First of all, if you are asked what your current salary is, you can say that **it is confidential information from your current employer** and you wouldn't feel right giving out that information.

You could simply state you prefer not to say.

If pressed why, you could say that **you consider the entire compensation package** which includes benefits and other non-tangible items, so you wouldn't want to talk in terms of salary alone.

You could also take a more blunt approach and simply state that **you feel like talking about your current salary would put you at a distinct disadvantage** in negotiating your salary at this job, because if your salary was significantly lower you would get less than you are worth, and if it were significantly higher, you might not get an offer which you might have considered.

This exact same advice can be applied when you are asked to name a number for your current salary expectations.

In addition, you could say that **you will entertain any reasonable offer** or that you would like to know about the entire compensation package rather than to just name an arbitrary number.

(This is actually a very smart thing to say when you consider how much of a difference the overall compensation package made to the hourly value of the two offer examples we looked at above.)

Here's an example from a blog post I wrote on this topic (https://simpleprogrammer.com /cg15-negotiate).

"Suppose you applied for a job and you expected that the salary for that job was $70,000. You get offered the job and the first question you are asked is what your salary requirements are. You state that you are looking for something around $70,000. Perhaps you are even clever and say somewhere in the range of $70,000 to $80,000. The HR manager immediately offers you a salary of $75,000. You shake hands, accept the deal and are pretty happy—only there is one big problem: the HR manager had budgeted from $80,000 to $100,000 for the job. Since you named a number first, you ended up costing yourself potentially as much as $25,000 a year—whoops."

DON'T BE AFRAID TO COUNTER OFFER

In just about all situations, when you do get a job offer, you should counter offer.

This is what is known as **an arbitrage situation** because there is very little downside but a very large upside.

What I mean by this is that you have **very little to risk and a large amount to gain.**

It would be rare for an offer of employment to be revoked simply because you made a counter offer.

In most cases, the worst they will do is say "no."

So, **you should almost always make some kind of counter offer.**

What kind of counter offer you make will greatly depend on the situation and context.

You should, however, have a clear goal in mind for what you would like to get out of any negotiation and the minimum you are willing to accept, before going into negotiations.

This will make it much easier for you to know what your counter offer should be.

I've also learned that, when it comes to negotiation, **usually whoever makes the biggest move or concession ends up losing** in the long run.

In one of the only legal battles I've ever had to seriously endure in my career, I was in negotiations over a settlement that was in arbitration.

The original damage to me was around $10,000, but my lawyer came in asking for an initial settlement of $50,000.

The first round of negotiation ended with the other party countering our $50,000 request with his own offer of exactly zero dollars.

My inclination was to immediately drop the asking amount to $25,000 or so, so that he'd at least start coming up.

To my shock, both the judge and my lawyer agreed that the best number in this case would be around $45,000.

What happened next was magic.

Suddenly we were looking at a counteroffer of $9,000.

Again, I was inclined to counter back at around $15,000 or so to "meet in the middle." (https://simpleprogrammer.com/cg15-split).

My lawyer and the judge both agreed that coming back with $39,000 would be the best number.

This continued back and forth with the other side coming up and us barely moving down, until we ended up somewhere close to $16,000. (Remember, my original goal was just $10,000.)

What I learned from this negotiation is that **you should be extremely careful moving down from what you want and instead try to force the other party to come up.**

I also learned that by having someone represent you, through the power of agency, you have much more leverage than representing yourself.

So don't be afraid to counter offer and when you do, know what you want, aim much higher than that number, and come down slowly.

And don't be afraid to make more than one counter offer.

There is a limit. I probably wouldn't make more than two or three because, at that point, your prospective employer will probably be questioning how badly you actually want the job, but you should at least make one and, in most cases, two.

EVERYTHING IS NEGOTIABLE

When you negotiate, do not just negotiate on salary alone.

Remember how we broke out all the components of an offer and actually figured out the hourly rate difference between Offer A and Offer B? Even though Offer B was for $10,000 less salary, it turned out to be a much better deal than Offer A.

If you only negotiate on salary, you'll be leaving a large amount of your negotiating power off the table.

It's always important to remember that different aspects of a deal have different values to different people involved.

While salary might be really important for your prospective employer because they have a set range and HR policies that prevent them from going above it, they might be able to be much more flexible with vacation days, medical benefits, or some other perks that could impact the overall deal just as much or even more than salary alone.

It's crucial that you not only look at every component of a compensation package or offer, but also negotiate on as many points as possible if you want to maximize your opportunity.

Even working hours can be negotiated ahead of time.

It is very possible to negotiate that you will only work 40 hours max per week at a job with a startup company where most employees work 50 and 60 hour weeks.

It's also not unreasonable.

Negotiating something like this ahead of time can be extremely valuable, especially if you can put those other hours to good use.

The point is to negotiate on all points. You will have more to work with and can increase your overall compensation much more than you will by just negotiating on salary.

DON'T SUCCUMB TO TIME PRESSURE

One of the best negotiating tactics possible is to put the other party under time pressure—artificial or real.

When you are under time pressure, you feel rushed, so you are more likely to make a bad decision.

You'll notice used car salesmen and timeshare vacation salespeople heavily employ this tactic, along with a large amount of pressure.

Make sure you always have time to think about and consider your options.

One of the best ways to do this is **to ask or to simply state that you need more time.**

Just because you received an offer that has a deadline three days from now doesn't mean that you have to make a decision in that time frame.

If you need more time—or if you are waiting for other offers, see below—just say you need a few more days to consider the offer.

If the company you are working with won't "play ball," you can try making a fairly high counter offer right at the deadline.

This can often buy you more time as they will have to come back with another offer and give you more time to think about it.

Just make sure you are not making a rushed decision based on the time limit. In many cases, it's better to pass in life than make rushed decisions.

MULTIPLE OFFERS

If you are fortunate to be in a multiple-offer situation, you might find it stressful because you don't know what to do.

It's great to have options, but is it ok to play your options against each other?

And how do you do it?

First of all, you should have multiple offers if you are doing things right.

Try and make it so that you have more than one offer on the table at the same time.

Schedule your interviews and apply for jobs in such a way that maximizes this potential.

In the real estate business, some savvy agents will "pre-market" a house by advertising what date it will go on the market.

When that date rolls around, they get multiple offers at the same time and often can trigger a bidding war.

So, there is value in having multiple offers, but **you have to play it carefully.**

I think the best way to play it is to **let the parties involved know that you do have multiple offers you are considering, but don't directly use or reveal that information to each party.**

What I mean by this is that you should be honest that you are considering other offers because you want to find the best opportunity for your future and where you can make the best contribution.

This is perfectly reasonable, and it puts a certain amount of pressure on a prospective employer to give you the best offer possible and raises your value in their eyes since you are a "hot commodity."

Nevertheless, **you should not go to one prospective employer and say, "Well, so-and-so company offered me X amount of dollars and Y amounts of vacation, so you'd need to at least offer me Z. Plus, they have a cafeteria. What do you have?"**

That is a really good way to have the pending offer withdrawn and to have them say, "No, thank you."

No one likes to feel like someone is putting the squeeze on them.

It's one thing to be honest that you have more than one offer, but it's another thing to use that information to try to bully someone by forcing their hand.

If a prospective employer asks about how big another offer is and what you are considering, it might be ok to reveal a little bit of information, but you'll have to be really careful to do it in a modest way that doesn't sound like you think you are all that.

Use discretion and consider the situation and context.

Ultimately, **the real value in having multiple offers does not come from directly playing offers against each other, but in having options.**

Having options gives you the most valuable negotiating position: the ability to walk away.

When you have two or three offers, you can confidently negotiate each one hard and not worry if you lose one or two.

Just tread carefully and don't be a jerk.

CHAPTER 16

HOW TO LEAVE A JOB

The best way to leave a job seems pretty obvious, but enough software developers completely screw this up to make me think it is worth a short chapter.

Leaving a job in the wrong way can have disastrous results on your career and can possibly permanently damage your reputation, especially if you live in a small town.

There is often quite a bit of emotion involved in leaving a job.

Anger, frustration, and even guilt are usually the key motivators that can cause an otherwise rational person to make extremely unwise and irrational decisions when leaving a job.

I've left plenty of jobs (https://simpleprogrammer.com/cg16-safety) in my software development career in order to pursue new opportunities, and I've had my share of mistakes.

In this chapter, I'm going to talk about how and when you should leave a job and also give you some general advice on the dos and don'ts of vacating your current position of employment.

WHEN YOU LEAVE A JOB

Let's start by talking about when you should leave your job.

Far too many software developers stay at a dead-end job where they aren't happy and are not growing for far too long.

There are many reasons for this.

Some programmers are afraid that they won't be able to find another job.

Others are used to a certain level of comfort and don't want to risk that by entering a new work environment.

Yet others are in a job they know they should leave, but are **clinging desperately to the false hope that the toxic environment they are currently in** (https://simpleprogrammer.com /cg16-coworkers) **will eventually change.**

Perhaps the most common reason developers stay in a job too long is because they don't realize the other opportunities that are out there.

How do you know if you are sticking around too long and that it's time to move on?

One of the best indicators is **a lack of growth.**

If the job you are in is not providing new challenges for you and you don't see any opportunity to grow as a software developer—and as a person—it is probably a good indicator that it is time to move on.

It is really easy to get stuck in a rut because you are comfortable or are afraid of change and the unknown.

But all growth in life is only achieved by making yourself feel uncomfortable (https:// simpleprogrammer.com/cg16-softskills)**.**

There are plenty of job opportunities that offer a huge amount of growth, but there are other jobs where you know that the work no longer challenges you and you don't see any path for growth.

As soon as you know you are in a dead-end job, you should be preparing to move on.

I've seen far too many software developers stay in the same job, with the exact same job title, for 10 or even 15 years.

If you aren't growing, you're dying. Grow.

Another really good reason to leave a job—perhaps the best one—is that you've identified the work environment to be "toxic." (https://simpleprogrammer.com/cg16-toxic).

I receive horror story emails from programmers every day where they tell me about how their boss verbally abuses them on a daily basis or their coworkers passive-aggressively belittle them constantly through abusive code reviews (https://simpleprogrammer.com/cg16-codereview).

Life is too short to deal with shitty people.

Eject jerks from your life.

If you are in a toxic work environment, don't keep hoping it will change. **Get out.**

Don't play the victim when you have power to change your situation.

No one should tolerate a professional work environment where they are constantly being psychologically abused.

However, not all reasons for leaving your current job are negative or emotional.

Sometimes, you'll have a better opportunity come along that you should take simply because it is a better opportunity.

I've left plenty of great jobs in my career just because a much better opportunity presented itself.

Business is business. We all have to do what is best for ourselves career-wise.

If you have reservations or feel compelled to be loyal to your current workplace, always remember: no one else is going to look out for you.

That doesn't mean that you should job hop at every opportunity that comes along which might be better than your current job, but **if you see a really good opportunity, don't be afraid to take it.**

HOW TO LEAVE A JOB

Now that we've covered when, let's talk about how.

Seems obvious, right?

You just quit! There, done.

Well, it's not quite that simple. There are a great deal of complex emotions to deal with when leaving a job, especially if you've had the same job for several years and have many friends at work.

In general, **you want to make the break as clean and non-personal as possible.**

You want to make sure not to justify yourself, but to simply make your decision stand.

Benjamin Disraeli, a former British Prime Minister, is famous for saying, "Never complain and never explain," and I think this advice is especially apt when it comes to leaving a job.

DON'T WORRY ABOUT "THE TEAM"

Honestly, this is perhaps the toughest part of leaving a job.

There is a huge amount of guilt associated with abandoning "the team."

If you are a conscientious person and you've been working in a team towards a goal, **it can feel like you are letting people down** if you suddenly leave the job and move on.

You have to fight this feeling and realize that life will go on without you, and you must also concede that **you are not as important and critical to the team as you think you are.**

One of the most common excuses I hear from software developers who are considering leaving their current job is that **the project will fall apart without them** or that they'll be abandoning the team.

I've been there myself—on both accounts.

You have to realize **this is partially hubris at work here.**

We want to feel like we are so important and critical to the team, but the truth is **anyone is replaceable.**

You are not abandoning the team; you are making a career and business decision.

I actually stayed at my last job well beyond when I should have left, mostly because of the feeling I had that leaving would be abandoning my coworkers.

I felt bad about moving to my next opportunity because I didn't want to disappoint my current boss, and I didn't want to leave "my team" high and dry.

But you have to do what is best for you.

They'll get over you and they'll understand.

GIVE TWO WEEKS NOTICE

One mistake that is often associated with the guilt of abandoning the team is giving far too much notice when leaving a job.

My advice is to give two weeks notice and that is it.

When I left my last job, I gave two weeks notice and then I was asked to stick around for an extra two weeks.

Quite honestly, I should have said no, but because I already felt guilty about leaving the team, I caved in and said yes.

I ended up wasting two weeks of time that I could have productively spent on my new venture, and I really didn't get any benefit from it.

I ended up drawing out an already difficult situation and making it more awkward, and I also risked something happening which could have messed up my future plans.

When you stay longer than two weeks, you can quickly wear out your welcome, and you can jeopardize the opportunity you are moving to by delaying the transition.

Nothing is worse than staying at your current job an extra two weeks and in that time having something happen at the company you are supposed to be moving to, which causes them to rescind the offer.

You could suddenly go from two good jobs to no job—all because you tried to do the right thing.

So, do give notice. It's not professional to just quit on the spot, but make sure it's just the standard two weeks.

If your current employer needs you for longer than two weeks, work out a consulting arrangement for some amount of hours per week so that you can start on your new job and not put it at risk.

If your current employer isn't willing to pay you as a consultant after the two weeks are up, then they don't need you as much as they thought they did.

Don't be guilted into staying longer.

Again, you have to do what is best for you.

HEY JOHN

I don't live in the US. Where I live we are required by law to give X weeks or months notice!

I'm not a big fan of indentured servitude or slavery, but I suppose it is what it is.

I vehemently oppose the idea that someone can legally compel you to work for them.

Plus, it just seems plain stupid.

I mean suppose you are required to give three months notice.

Do you just sit on your ass for three months collecting a paycheck?

Can they actually make you work during that time?

Seems stupid to me.

But, since I am not yet emperor of the world, I don't get to decide these things.

Regardless, if the law or even custom where you live is that you have to give longer than two weeks notice, then just do it.

The point really is not about two weeks, it's about not giving more notice than either required "cringe" or generally deemed acceptable / appropriate / customary, etc.

DON'T THREATEN TO LEAVE A JOB

If you are going to leave a job, just leave it.

Do not, do not, threaten to leave (https://simpleprogrammer.com/cg16-nothreats).

Plenty of bad things can happen to you if you threaten to leave a job. It's a really bad idea.

You may think that presenting an ultimatum—saying if something doesn't change or you don't get your way or get a raise, then you'll quit—is the best way to get what you want, but it isn't. Trust me.

What is likely to happen is that as soon as you make a threat to leave a job, your boss will start looking for your replacement.

No one likes to feel as though they are being bullied.

Once you establish yourself as someone who is willing to resort to threats to get what you want, you'll be considered a loose cannon and a potential liability.

If you have a problem with your work environment, it is ok to make it known and to ask for a change, but if that change doesn't come, you have two choices: live with it or quit.

Plenty of software developers have walked into the boss's office thinking they were too valuable to be let go, tried to throw their weight around by threatening to quit, and **immediately found themselves packing up their shit.**

I can recall one incident when I was working at HP. I really wanted to be put on the .NET development team since that was my specialty and I was already consulting on that team's architecture meetings, but for political reasons, I wasn't allowed to move to the position.

I was not happy.

I made it known that I really wanted to be moved to the team and that I could make a much bigger contribution on the .NET team.

Nothing happened.

So, when I'd had enough, instead of threatening to quit, I simply made up my mind and found a new job.

I gave my two weeks notice and fully planned to leave.

At the last minute, literally as I had my hand on the door to exit the building, one of the high-up section managers at the company called me into his office.

He said that since I hadn't made a threat and had instead simply left, he was going to give me an offer to stay at HP with a much higher salary and a position on the .NET team.

He made it clear that plenty of developers had tried to get what they wanted in the past by making threats, and they had a strict policy to never negotiate under those conditions.

DON'T GIVE ADVANCE NOTICE

This is just plain stupidity, but I see it all the time.

Again, this is usually motivated by guilt or by a person trying to be forthright and do the right thing.

One of my good friends was planning to quit his job and move to freelance work in two months' time.

He thought he'd be upfront about it and let his boss know his plans, so they could prepare as much as possible and it wouldn't come as a shock.

I told him not to do it and instead to give the professional standard of two weeks notice.

He said he had a great relationship with his boss at work and that he wanted to give him the heads up.

He thought nothing bad would happen.

Can you guess what happened?

As soon as he gave his "two months' notice," his boss said, "Nah, that's ok, you can just leave now."

He was shocked.

He didn't even get two weeks.

But it makes sense.

It's a big liability to have an employee hanging around when you know they are going to leave in two months.

You can't give them any major projects, you don't know if they'll actually quit sooner, and you don't know if they'll do any work or just collect a paycheck.

So, **as tempting as it is, do not give advance notice.**

Do not tell your boss you are planning to stay for two more months or a year or whatever it is.

Just keep it to yourself and when you are two weeks out, then break the news.

Besides, what if your own plans change?

Quite a bit can happen in two months.

THE WORLD IS INCREDIBLY SMALL

Incredibly.

I've run into people I knew in high school in a hotel corridor thousands of miles away.

I've met people in foreign countries who I've randomly talked to and they happened to be friends with my friends back home.

The reason why I'm telling you this is because the next two things I'm going to talk about are all about recognizing how small the world is, and because of that, how fast you can ruin your reputation.

I've seen, firsthand, software developers who have blackballed themselves from employment in a geographic area because of how they left a job.

You always want to leave on the best terms possible, whether your departure is voluntary, involuntary, or you just have to get the hell out of there.

TRAIN YOUR REPLACEMENT

One of the best things you can do in order to leave a job on good terms is to do an excellent job of training your replacement.

It's tempting to not do this, especially if you've been fire—I mean, laid off.

You have to fight your ego, which says that no one can do as good of a job as you and tells you that if you train your replacement then no one will miss you. Instead, realize the greater importance of long-term legacy and reputation.

Contrary to popular belief, **it's actually in your best interest if things do not fall apart after you leave.**

Many software developers get this foolish notion that if the company they leave is hurting after they leave, it means they were valuable.

The opposite is true.

A good leader starts training their replacement the moment they take a new job.

A good leader knows that they become immensely more valuable by building teams, companies, processes, and infrastructure that allow things to run smoothly without them.

A self-conceited jerk with self-confidence issues, scared of showing any form of insecurity, believes themselves to be a critical part of an organization which will ultimately fail without them.

Therefore, when you are on your way out—voluntarily or not—**make sure to do the best job you can during those two weeks training your replacement.**

Document everything you can. Take all the knowledge from your head and transfer it to the company, so they can function as well as possible without you.

Not only is this the right thing to do, but it may also pay off someday when someone runs into someone else in an airport and strangely your name comes up. Know what I mean?

DON'T SAY ANYTHING BAD IN THE EXIT INTERVIEW

I just don't get this one.

You are on your way out the door.

If your boss was a tyrant and your coworkers smelled like homeless people, it doesn't matter anymore because you are on your way to freedom.

So why, **why, would you say anything bad or critical or anything that could in any way possibly hurt you during an exit interview?**

Just don't do it!

Nothing good can come from it, but plenty of bad can.

You have to understand that this is not the time to fix all the problems with the work environment you are now leaving, just because you have a sympathetic ear.

Not only is it too late, but it also doesn't matter anymore—YOU ARE LEAVING.

So, when you get asked about what could be improved, what problems there are, why you are leaving, or what you liked least about the job, etc, just say something pleasant.

Do not say what you really think!

Resist the urge.

I implore you.

Nothing good can come of it.

Do you really think they are going to give you a medal and a check for $10,000 for improving the organization?

No. Not going to happen.

Yes, many times, exit interviews are well-intentioned attempts to improve the company and working environment, but fixing company culture issues doesn't happen by listening to grievances of ex-employees on their way out the door.

Do not participate in a game that will not help you in any way, but which has a very high chance of burning bridges, trashing your reputation and causing a witch hunt.

I'm going to end this chapter now because I don't want to continue beating a dead horse, but I think you get my point.

CHAPTER 17

SWITCHING MID-CAREER (LATE ENTRY)

Some of the best software developers I know didn't start out their careers with any interest in software development.

It may be difficult to believe, but **sometimes having a different background—in a completely unrelated field—is a huge benefit when going into the field of software development.**

I'm not entirely sure why this is the case (although I have some ideas of course), but time and time again, I've seen software developers with only a few years' experience, but broad experience in another field, end up surpassing software developers with much more experience.

If you are thinking about becoming a software developer, but you've been in another, unrelated field for some time, hopefully this chapter will provide you with encouragement and some ideas of how to best make that transition.

THE BENEFITS OF SWITCHING MID-CAREER

Most of what I am going to be talking about here is my own speculation, since I started out my career in software development and later transitioned into the role I am in now, rather than starting out in some unrelated field.

But, like I said, **I've met enough really successful software developers who started out in completely different fields** to have at least a rough idea of what makes them so successful.

One huge benefit I've observed for people who have switched into software development from another field is that t**hey often bring with them a large swath of people skills and soft skills** (https://simpleprogrammer.com/cg17-lifemanual) which are more rare in the software development field.

It's no secret that software developers sometimes lack these people skills and other soft skills. Nor is it any secret that I find them to be extremely valuable (obviously, since I wrote a book teaching them and have pretty much built an entire business around the idea (https://simpleprogrammer.com/cg17-homepage)).

I find that soft skills developed in other professions translate really well into the software development field and have the tendency to move people who possess them ahead of the normal learning curve.

Having them may give you a distinct advantage, especially if you worked in a field where soft skills or people skills were highly valued.

I've also found that the **mindset of success** (https://simpleprogrammer.com/cg17-mindset) tends to be widely applicable, and that if a person is successful in one professional vocation, the chances are they'll be successful in any vocation they pursue.

You'll likely find this to be the case if you are currently in another field—even a very distantly related one—when beginning to make the transition.

Finally, I would say that the **ability to think outside of the normal constraints** that many software developers and highly technical people think within can be a huge advantage as well.

There is a high tendency for what is called "cargo-cult" programming where programmers are likely to do things not because they work, but because other developers are doing them and they are seen as "best practices."

Having an outside perspective can give you the advantage of thinking in a way that is unclouded by preconceived notions and ideas that are a bit pervasive in the programming community.

While brand new software developers without any experience in any vocation may also have this same perspective, they are often more susceptible to falling into the same traps because they lack the depth of experience and confidence in their own thinking that someone with more experience likely possesses.

Again, I don't know the exact magic formula that seems to make software developers who started in a different background so successful, but these are a few of my ideas.

THE DISADVANTAGES

I don't want to paint an overly rosy picture of switching into software development from another field.

It's certainly not easy and there are definite disadvantages.

It's also true that you are not guaranteed to be a stellar programmer just because you used to be a nurse.

One huge disadvantage that blindsides many transitioning developers is the complexity and amount of knowledge required to be a computer programmer.

There are plenty of fields where you could learn something in college or even have some on-the-job training, and in a few months you'd be able to do the job.

I'm not saying that software development is the only difficult field there is or that anyone can do another vocation without training, but **software development is several magnitudes more difficult than the average profession.**

Yes, that statement may piss some people off, but it's completely true.

In fact, if you are having a difficult time accepting that statement, you might have a difficult time making the transition, because you will likely not be prepared for all you need to learn.

So, **it can definitely be a disadvantage to come into this field thinking it's just like any other field or job you can learn.**

You will have to do a good deal of studying and intentional practice to become even mildly proficient in this field—which is part of the reason for writing this long volume.

Another major disadvantage is obviously time.

This can be overcome somewhat by the advantages I listed above, which can accelerate your learning curve, but you are still going to have to play some catch-up if you want to fill the holes in your knowledge caused by a lack of direct experience.

Even if you have only spent three years in the field, and are as good as a software developer who has spent 10 years, you are still not going to have seen as many situations and problems as that person—in most cases—so that lack of experience may make some things a bit more difficult.

HOW TO DO IT

Ok, now that you've got some idea of what you may be up against, let's talk about how to overcome some of these disadvantages and how to be as successful as possible when transitioning mid-career into software development.

Plenty of people have done it.

I've even received emails from software developers who've made the transition late into their fifties, so it's certainly possible.

Here's how.

TRANSITION AT YOUR CURRENT JOB

It's difficult to break into the field of software development.

I've already spent a good deal of time in previous chapters talking about how to get your first job, because it definitely isn't easy.

No one really wants to hire a software developer without prior programming experience.

How, then, do you get that job if your resume says you've been an accountant for the last 20 years?

Well, one way is to start transitioning into software development from your current job.

Many software developers I know started out in a completely different field and found that they could **learn a little programming here and there to help them with their work or to build some kind of tool that would help everyone at their work.**

If you are interested in becoming a software developer, you might want to look around in your current work environment and see if you can find places where you could start using your newfound skills.

This is a great way to transition into software development because if you start programming at your job—even if it's just small projects—you can then put that on your resume.

You may even find that you can create a software development role for yourself within the company you are working for, just by **automating things or building tools** which end up being valuable enough that your current employer will pay you to keep doing what you're doing.

Start by taking on some of these side projects at work during your own time and then perhaps ask for permission to start transitioning some of these activities into your full-time position.

If you can pull this one off, you may not even need to go out and apply for a programming job.

Once you are officially programming at work, you can always find another programming job somewhere else.

LOOK FOR A WAY TO USE YOUR EXISTING BACKGROUND

Another tactic I've seen successfully employed is to **use your existing background in an unrelated field to give you valuable domain expertise** at a software development company who develops software for that unrelated field.

For example, suppose you have 20 years of experience as a nurse and you want to get into software development.

Yes, you could learn programming and then try to apply for any software development job that came along.

However, it might be a much better idea to look for software development companies which mainly operate in the healthcare industry, or even healthcare companies who might employ software developers.

By specifically applying for these kinds of jobs, you'll be giving yourself a distinct advantage over other applicants who lack the domain expertise you have.

In software development, domain expertise can be enormously valuable, because understanding the why and purpose of the software in a particular industry can prevent many errors from being made.

It may be much easier for a software development company to hire a developer with 10 years of software development experience, but someone who knows software development and has 10 or more years of domain expertise is going to be a much rarer find.

I was just talking to a developer who had a genetics background and ended up getting a job with Oracle, because his previous career was in genetic and biological chemistry, and Oracle was looking for developers to work on a product they were creating that involved genetic research to help cancer treatment centers.

Try and use your existing, seemingly unrelated experience by finding a way to make it related.

Just about anyone can do this, because software exists in just about every major industry.

BE WILLING TO START FROM THE BOTTOM

Finally, I'd say that if you are switching into software development mid-career, you need to be willing to start at the bottom with the knowledge that your previous work experience will ensure you don't stay there long.

It can be difficult to make a transition from a high-paying job where you have seniority and perhaps a reputation, to being a lowly grunt being paid peanuts, but if you want to switch careers, you are going to have to be willing to do that—at least in the short term.

The software development world is more of a meritocracy than other industries, so it doesn't really matter how much experience you have or who you know so much as what you can do— although reputation obviously plays an important part.

I'd advise you to plan on starting from the bottom, realizing that most of your skills are not going to carry over, and to be ok with that.

This will help you to avoid the frustrations you might otherwise face if you expect to make a lateral transition into this field.

Like I said, though, if you already have experience in another industry and have achieved success there, many of the soft skills you have developed will be likely to accelerate you through the ranks of software development.

You just have to be patient to begin with.

CHAPTER 18

GOING FROM QA OR ANOTHER TECHNICAL ROLE TO DEVELOPMENT

I decided to dedicate a whole chapter to this topic because it's one of the most common questions I get asked. **Making the transition from QA or some other technical role to being a software developer** (https://simpleprogrammer.com/cg18-moving) **can be extremely difficult.**

I made the transition myself—in fact, I had to do it twice.

The first time I made the transition was when I had just started out in my career.

I had been a self-taught programmer and had taken a year of college in a computer science program, but **I couldn't find a job as a programmer**, so I started a job doing QA as a contractor for HP.

Initially, my job was brainlessly simple.

I'd go through stacks of printed tests, which I compared to a "master" printout, and I'd look at the differences to see if they were known issues or new bugs that had been introduced in the latest printing firmware.

The job was pretty boring.

We were just supposed to look at flagged differences and decide if they were a big deal or not.

I wasn't happy with that. I wanted to know what caused the differences, so I started digging a little deeper.

I asked to have access to the actual print instructions which were sent to the printer for each test.

The print instructions were either in PCL or PostScript, two popular printing languages.

I spent my own time and any downtime to learn both PCL and PostScript.

I became an expert in both.

Then when I looked at errors, I would go through the printer test and modify them, using my understanding of the printer languages to test my theories about why specific printer language commands were causing the problems.

Pretty soon I was filing detailed bug reports with snippets of printer code, indicating exactly what printer language commands were likely to be behaving incorrectly and causing the errors.

It didn't take long before the software development team became interested in pulling me in as a resource to show them how and what I was doing.

I was eventually asked to write printer tests, and thus I officially became a programmer and got an actual programmer title.

Later in my career, I went through a similar experience when I couldn't find a software development job and again found myself at HP, this time in the role of a QA test lead.

This time, I was sitting next to a fairly new software developer who didn't have a good grasp of C++.

When we'd chat about some of the problems he was facing, I'd come over to his cubicle and give him some tips and help get his tasks done.

I didn't take any credit and **only tried to make him look as good as possible.**

After a few weeks of this, he started telling his boss how much I knew about C++ and how it seemed like a ridiculous waste to have someone who knew this much about software development writing test cases.

When a big deadline came up, the software development team asked to borrow me as a resource to help meet the deadline.

Once I was working with the development team, they didn't want to give me back (https://simpleprogrammer.com/cg18-righttime). Thus my role was switched to software developer once again.

THE BIGGEST HURDLE YOU'LL FACE

Perhaps the biggest hurdle you will face in switching from QA or some other technical role into software development is the perception people have of you.

Once you have a role within a company, people tend to always see you as that particular role, regardless of your skillset or how you grow.

In the software development world in particular, there is usually a sharp distinction between software developers and testers (or QA).

Because of this bias, coming into a new company as a software developer is often easier than transitioning to a software development role from being a tester or other position.

This can be extremely frustrating—especially if you've outgrown your previous role.

You will have to be patient, and realize that although it will take time for perceptions to change, they eventually will.

The more you can involve yourself in the software development side of the organization and take on more programming tasks, the more that other people in the organization will start to see you in the new role.

Sometimes, though, you may have to move to a completely different company to escape the box you've been put into.

Let's talk now about some strategies other software developers and I have used in the past to make the transition from a non-developer technical role to software developer.

MAKE YOUR GOAL KNOWN

My first piece of advice for you would be to go ahead and make your goal known as widely as possible (https://simpleprogrammer.com/cg18-tell).

Let your coworkers know that you are aspiring to move into development.

Ask for a meeting with your boss or manager, and frankly tell them that you'd like to move into a software development role and that you are willing to do whatever it takes to get there.

When you talk about this goal with your boss, make sure you discuss how your testing background will benefit the company when you eventually move into a programmer role.

Talk about the benefits your company will gain from you making the transition.

The more it is known that you want to move into a software development role, the more you'll start to chip away at the bias people might have about keeping you in your current role, so don't be afraid to openly talk about it.

But talk is cheap.

If you keep saying that someday you want to become a software developer and you aren't doing anything to learn programming, you are going to sound like a hopeless dreamer.

Make sure you back-up your talk with action (https://simpleprogrammer.com/cg18-action).

When you do have this conversation with your boss, see if you can **get a list of requirements or a course you can take that will move you from your current role to one working as a software developer.**

If you can nail down a list of things you need to learn or milestones you need to achieve, you can create a much more solid case for making the transition, when you are ready.

I've used this exact technique to not only switch into new roles but also to get promotions.

I've simply asked what I would need to accomplish or what skills I would need to improve to get a promotion, then I've gone and done all of those things and asked for the promotion.

It's not foolproof—you could still be denied your request—but if you've got a list of what you need to do and you've done it all, then it's pretty difficult to form a case against your advancement.

ASK FOR OPPORTUNITIES

If you really want to move into software development, don't wait for someone to hand you the title and assign you work. Instead, ask for opportunities to do some programming even while you are in your current role.

Ask your boss for one or two simple assignments.

Ask if there are any bugs you can fix.

And keep asking.

You may be refused the first few times or it may seem like too much of a hassle to assign you a task that someone is going to have to explain to you, but **if you are the squeaky wheel and you keep asking, there is a good chance you'll eventually get something thrown your way**—even if it's only to shut you up.

MAKE YOUR OWN OPPORTUNITIES

Sometimes, though—quite often, actually—you are not going to get opportunities to do software development, even if you ask.

Like I said, it might be because explaining a task to you would take more time than it's worth, and most projects are always behind.

It might be because, frankly, your boss or coworkers don't believe you have the technical chops to take on software development work because they see you as "just a tester" or "Linux admin" or "technical support person," or whatever it might be.

You might have to make your own opportunities.

You might have to take it upon yourself to look for areas where you can help out and contribute without getting in anyone's way or taking up their time asking questions.

Often these opportunities lie in what I call the "dirty work." (https://simpleprogrammer.com /cg18-obstacle).

That is the stuff that no one wants to do.

It's the coding equivalent of cleaning the toilet.

Perhaps it's debugging this really nasty bug that no one has been able to figure out.

Perhaps it's writing up documentation for an API or building a tool to make things easier for everyone else.

It's probably going to be the boring work that is difficult, but if you want to find a project that no one will fight you for, it's likely to be "dirty work."

Be ready to roll up your sleeves and dig in.

USE YOUR OWN TIME

Some bosses might assign you some small programming tasks you can do as part of your regular workload.

Some bosses might be ok with you spending some of your time picking up the "dirty work" kind of projects I mentioned above.

However, that will not always be the case.

In fact, in many work environments, **you are likely to get a slap on the wrist if you start doing software development work when you are supposed to be doing your regular job.**

In those cases, if you really want to get your shot at software development, **you are going to have to be willing to give a little—or a lot—of your own unpaid time to further your mission.**

Even if you are given some work time to work on software development tasks in your current role, it's still a good idea to devote some extra, unpaid hours to those tasks, so that you can move the needle much further, much faster.

Be willing to get in early or to stay after work to get extra projects done.

If you are having a difficult time finding anyone who will let you work on tasks involving software development, you will probably have much more success if you are willing to do the work on your own time.

It's an offer that most companies would find difficult to refuse.

LOOK FOR BRIDGES

One really good way to make the transition from a job like QA to software development is to **find a bridge job that will put you between the two roles.**

For many testers, **automation is a great bridge** (https://simpleprogrammer.com/cg18-bat).

If you can start taking on test automation tasks, you'll get a chance to write code to automate manual tests.

Convincing your boss to let you do test automation (https://simpleprogrammer.com /cg18-manual) **is usually going to be an easier sell than convincing him to let you become a junior developer without any real experience.**

It's a win-win situation because you gain valuable, real programming experience, and your company gains the benefit of automated tests, which make the entire organization more efficient.

Plus, this is a difficult niche role to fill for many organizations. It's not always easy to find test automation experts.

Once you have the title of test automation engineer or software developer in test, it's going to be extremely easy to move into a regular software development role at any company because **now you have real experience being paid to write code.**

In fact, you might find that test automation is more fun and rewarding than doing testing alone or regular software development. You might even find it pays better than an entry level programming job.

(I love designing automated testing frameworks (https://simpleprogrammer.com /cg18-selenium). *It's one of my favorite technology areas, which I find extremely rewarding and challenging.)*

There are bridge opportunities to software development from many other technical jobs as well.

For instance, **Linux administrators can become tool developers** or easily **move into devops positions** where they can use their Linux administration skills, scripting, and programming to automate tasks and build tools that benefit everyone.

Technical support people can move into roles where they do technical support for developers or even become higher-tier support technicians who **dive into the code to try and solve customer problems or gather information to send to developers.**

Look for ways you can leverage your existing skills and responsibilities in some kind of development capacity, and you can create your own bridge job.

MOVING TO A NEW COMPANY

Most of what I've talked about in this chapter has assumed that you'd be making the transition from QA or some other technical role to software developer within the same company, but that is not always possible or desirable.

How, then, do you go from a tester at one company to a developer at another company?

Actually, most of the same advice I've given you in this chapter still applies; it's just that your job title doesn't change until you switch companies.

What I mean by this is that you should be trying to get some kind of development experience at your current job—even if you can't move into a software development role—simply so that you can put that experience on your resume when you apply for a software development role in another company.

Even if you built some tools on your own time that helped you do your job, you have the opportunity to put that on your resume as real development work, which is going to greatly help you get your first development job.

Bridge jobs are also going to be extremely useful here, especially if you can get your title to have developer or engineer in it.

MY LAST PIECE OF ADVICE

Don't get discouraged.

It's often more difficult to transition from another technical role into software development, simply because of the bias I talked about before, where people tend to see you as "just a tester" or "just a server admin," etc.

However, if you are willing to do the extra work and be "so good they can't ignore you," as Cal Newport says in his book of the same title (https://simpleprogrammer.com/cg18-ignore), **you are eventually going to hit success.**

Keep learning, keep improving your skills, keep looking for opportunities and making your own, and you'll get what you are after.

Patience and perseverance are key.

CHAPTER 19

CONTRACTING VS. SALARY

There are two basic types of employment in the software development industry.

You can either be a contractor of some sort, or you can be a salaried employee.

In my career, I've been both, and each has a distinct set of advantages and disadvantages.

In fact, **in some companies there is an entire culture built around the differences between contractors and employees.**

When I worked at HP, first as a contractor, then as an employee, there was this notion of "blue badgers" and "orange badgers."

Orange badgers were the contractors, and they were typically paid less, had no benefits, were treated like second-class citizens, and were even at times told they couldn't use the HP walk-ways or participate in any onsite activities.

Blue badgers were HP employees who had a blue badge that signified their elite social status. They were employees and entitled to all the benefits contractors didn't get.

It was difficult to become a blue badger. Every contractor hoped to become one, but few did.

But that is just one company culture.

I've also been places where the entire hierarchy was flipped around.

I worked on a government project where contractors were paid two to three times more than the government employees and were considered to be the "elites."

In that government environment, no one wanted to be an employee; instead everyone wanted to be a contractor.

I remember when they offered government jobs to many of the contractors and most of us refused because why would we take a huge pay cut for just a little more stability?

As you can see, the **decision between being a salary worker and a contractor isn't just about money**, and it is very situational.

In this chapter, I'll help guide you through that decision as we talk about the types of contractors—there are more than one—and the considerations of each type of employment.

TYPES OF CONTRACTING

Let's begin by talking about contracting.

I'm going to define contracting as any job that is not a salary job, although there are a few salaried consulting or contracting types of jobs where you are paid a salary while you are billed out to a client on an hourly basis. (Do not take these jobs; they are for suckers.)

HEY JOHN

Why are these jobs for "suckers?"

To put it simply, it's because you get all of the downside with none of the upside and you have the illusion of job security.

Many consulting companies hire out enterprise architect positions or solution architect positions which look like and sound like regular salaried employment positions, but really they are just consulting positions where the consulting company is paying you a salary out of the hourly rate they are billing the client for your time.

These jobs usually have 50% to 100% travel requirements and appear to have really high salaries.

Sounds good, right? What's the catch?

The catch is that you aren't really in a regular salaried position.

There is no job security.

You are just staff augmentation for a consulting firm that is only keeping you on staff while they can successfully bill you out on a project.

As soon as they don't have a project to bill out on, you get laid off or "benched" without pay.

You are taking all of the risk and receiving all the negative attributes of being a consultant, but you aren't getting the high hourly rate that you should be receiving.

Plus, you'll be traveling all the time and will be required to submit timesheets showing at least 40 billable hours per week—or more.

When I say contractor, I mean hourly worker of some sort.

Before we can dig into the details of being a contractor, we need to know the types of contracting.

AGENCY CONTRACTOR

The first type of contractor is what I call an agency contractor, known in the US as a W2 contractor.

This is the type of contractor who is working for an agency which bills them out to a client. They do not work for the client directly.

With this kind of contracting, you'll usually fill out some time sheet for how many hours you bill, and you'll get paid an hourly rate as a contracted employee of the agency you are working for.

Some of these relationships can be extremely predatory.

What I mean by this is that **it is not uncommon for an agency to hire software developers to work for one of their clients and bill that client 200% to 400% more than what they actually pay the software developer.**

I've worked on contracts before where I know that some of the software developers were being paid $25 an hour while the agency was billing the client over $100 an hour for their work.

Now before you get all crazy and start a protest, understand that due to the nature of this type of employment some markup is necessary and reasonable.

With this type of contracting you are technically an employee of the agency, and that agency has some overhead associated with keeping you employed.

In the US, agencies are responsible for paying employment tax, handling payroll, possibly providing some benefits like vacation or sick days and a few other expenses.

You should always expect some kind of markup.

I always advise contractors to know their markup (https://simpleprogrammer.com/cg19-markup) and to negotiate it.

INDEPENDENT CONTRACTOR

My definition of an independent contractor is a contractor who still primarily works for one client. They may even work for that client through an agency, but they operate as their own business.

In the US, we sometimes call this corp-to-corp billing. (Or 1099 employment.)

Essentially as an independent contractor, you own a business or legal entity that you do business under and you have a contract with a client or agency for a particular job.

The biggest difference here between this type of contracting and being an agency contractor is that **you are not on the agency's payroll.**

Instead, you are responsible for all your own overhead. **You are essentially self-employed.**

As a result, **you should expect to be paid a higher hourly rate** for an equivalent job, since you are responsible for paying your own self-employment tax, payroll, and any benefits.

FREELANCER

Finally, we have the freelancer.

I define a freelancer as someone who is an independent contractor who works for multiple clients or takes on multiple small jobs instead of working primarily for a single client.

This kind of contracting really involves running your own business because you have to deal with the overhead of finding clients, setting up your own contracts, invoicing and everything else associated with running a business.

I think of a freelancer as a contractor hired to work on a specific project or do a specific job while I consider an independent contractor or agency contractor to be some sort of staff augmentation.

If you are looking to get the highest rate possible (https://simpleprogrammer.com/cg19-million), freelancing is probably the most difficult option, but if you know how to market yourself, you can do pretty well (https://simpleprogrammer.com/cg19-really).

Remember, though, these are just my definitions and ways of explaining the differences between the types of contracting arrangements.

There are, of course, other ways to classify contractors and all kinds of variations and hybrids of these types of employment, so don't take this as gospel.

SALARY JOBS

If you aren't a contractor, you are probably in a salary position or you are unemployed.

A salary job, in my definition, is any job in which you are not a contractor and instead you work directly for the company that is paying you, and they pay you on a non-hourly basis.

Of course, there are some direct employment jobs in the software development world where you are technically an employee and paid hourly—but those are fairly rare.

Usually if you are an employee, you are paid a salary.

A salaried job usually means that the hours you work do not determine the pay you receive.

This can be both a good or a bad thing, depending on how many hours you end up working. (See the chapter on salaries and negotiation for more details on the economics of this.)

MONEY

Let's jump right into the discussion about contracting versus salary by first talking about that all too important resource: money.

In most cases, you will be directly paid more money as a contractor for an equivalent job.

Don't believe me? Okay, suppose you had a company that offered to pay you as either a salaried employee or a contractor.

Perhaps the salary for the job was $80,000 a year.

It's quite possible that as a contractor you might be offered a rate of $60 per hour.

Now, if you do the math on that, $60 x 40 hours a week x 52 weeks in a year equals $124,800.

This seems like much more money than an $80,000-a-year salary job, but—if you remember the chapter on salaries and negotiations—you know that there are other factors that make up the total compensation which can drastically alter the deal.

BREAKING DOWN A CONTRACTING RATE

Let's take this simple case and work out some scenarios to see why you would be paid more as a contractor than as a salaried employee.

We'll start by backing two weeks out of the 52 for vacation and another week for holidays. (Contractors, especially independent contractors, usually are not paid vacation.)

So, $124,800 - (3 * 40 * 60) = $117,600.

Now, we'll subtract out health insurance. Let's just value it at $1,000 a month, which is probably pretty typical of what a company pays for an employee's health insurance.

So, $117,600 - $12,000 = $105,600.

Then, we'll add up a few other benefits the company would usually pay, like 401k matching, perhaps bonuses, gym membership, etc. We'll be conservative and say this costs the company $300 a month.

So, $105,600 - $3,600 = $102,000.

Now, if you are an independent contractor, you have to pay your own self-employment tax. If you are an employee, the company has to pay half of it, which is about 7.5%.

We can do this one of two ways. We can either take the $80,000 salary and figure out the company's share of 7.5%—which they can pay to you directly as a contractor—or we can take your pay as a contractor and take out the 7.5% to see what you'll net.

I'm going to take the second approach because I want to show you how to compare a salary job to a contract job rather than how a company can afford to pay you more as a contractor. Make sense?

So, we have 7.5% of $117,600 = $8,820.

I used the $117,600 number because I am assuming you will probably take your own vacation and holidays, but if you were going to work 40 hours a week all 52 weeks, this would be different.

We now have $102,000 - $8,820 = $93,180.

Not as big of a difference now is there?

What looks like a $45,000 difference can easily be just $15,000.

From the employer's perspective, **hiring someone at $80,000 might cost the company $100,000 - $120,000 a year in total costs.**

WHY CONTRACTORS GET PAID MORE

I know many software developers who directly compare a salaried rate to a contract rate by simply multiplying the contract hourly rate by 40 hours a week and 52 weeks a year and then proclaim that they'd never be an employee because they get paid so much more as a contractor.

While it is generally true that contractors are paid more, **you can see that a large part of that extra pay is an illusion.**

Furthermore, often companies will pay more for a contracted employee because of flexibility.

An employee is more of a fixed cost whereas a contractor can be easily removed when their services are no longer needed.

It's also worth mentioning here that **freelancers typically will need an even higher hourly rate** (https://simpleprogrammer.com/cg19-really) to get close to an equivalent salary because of a few additional factors.

Freelancers are going to have more overhead since they will be running a business with more clients and there are costs associated with that.

They'll also have to spend unbillable time working to manage books and find new jobs to bid and work on.

Also, they may also not be able to easily fill up 40 hours of work each week.

Overall, **I generally say that a freelancer's bill rate needs to be 2x the equivalent hourly rate of a salaried position in order for it to be equivalent.**

For instance, an $80,000 salary job might be equivalent to a freelancer billing out at:

$80,000 / 52 / 40 = $38 an hour
$38 x 2 = $76 an hour

Before you decide to become a freelancer, think about this.

(You can find a more detailed discussion in the careers section in my Soft Skills: The Software Developer's Life Manual *(https://simpleprogrammer.com/cg19-lifemanual) book.)*

UTILITY VALUE OF BENEFITS

Now, I know what you might be thinking: "I don't need all those benefits, John; I just want cash!"

It is important to consider not just the face value of the benefits but the utility value.

For some people, being a contractor can be an extremely profitable position versus regular salaried work because they simply don't care about or won't use the benefits provided to a salaried employee.

If you take our example above, and you decide that you don't care about vacation or holidays and want to be able to maximize income by working 40 hours a week, 52 weeks a year, you could add back in the $7,200 we took out for vacation time and holidays.

(But be careful here. Of course you might not PLAN to take any vacation or time off, but shit happens. You get sick, relatives die or become terminally ill, your dog needs a kidney transplant and you need to take off work.)

If you were willing—and allowed—to work overtime, you might estimate your average week to be 45 or 50 hours a week as a contractor, and that would again bring your overall compensation up.

One of the contracts I worked on had a max time of 50 hours per week that was automatically allowed. Since I maxed that out every single week, contracting became much more profitable for me.

Also, **perhaps your spouse works and has health coverage for you already**—or you just don't want to have health insurance.

In that case, the health insurance benefits may be worthless to you.

If you are like me and you don't ever invest in a 401k (https://simpleprogrammer.com /cg19-retire) but instead put your money in real estate (https://simpleprogrammer.com /cg19-realestate), you might not care about that benefit, either.

Plus, at least in the US, if you structure your company correctly, and you are earning enough money for it to be worth doing, **you may be able to reduce self-employment tax on a large amount of your income by being an employee of your own company** and paying yourself a smaller salary than the total contracting fees you get.

Ultimately, what does this boil down to?

At least in monetary terms, **choosing between being a contractor or employee is very situational.**

It is going to depend on what benefits you use, how many hours you will and can work and even if your spouse is employed or not.

At least now you should have a framework you can use to realistically evaluate the choice between being a salaried employee or contractor.

Not quite as simple as dividing by 52 and then 40, is it?

WORK ENVIRONMENT

I've already alluded to some of the differences in work environment with my story at the beginning of this chapter, but let's dig a little deeper, shall we?

In most work environments, just like in all social and cultural systems, divisions and classes develop.

Some companies have huge distinctions between contractors and employees, but in other companies the differences are not as noticeable.

Don't be fooled, though; they always exist.

Some of the differences in the way people are treated have to do with labor laws which define contractor and employee positions.

Some companies, in order to avoid lawsuits around contractor benefits, will be very deliberate in making the distinction between the two positions, and this doesn't always create the best working environment—especially if you are a contractor.

At some companies, the hiring process for an employee is more rigorous and selective than the hiring process for a contractor. If the number of employees is fewer than the number of contractors, it can create even more of an elitist mentality.

Generally, I've found the larger the company, the more this is true—except in US government, where strangely it is a bit reversed.

The reason why I am telling you this is that **I don't want you to be surprised if you feel like a bit of an outsider if you take a contracting job at a large company.**

While there's nothing wrong with being a contractor, it's also important to be aware that you may not be included in the company culture.

Again, not all companies are like this. I've found in smaller companies there isn't much of a difference between contractor or employee at all.

A good consolation, though, is that you are likely to be paid more, and when everyone else is working overtime and not getting paid, you'll feel pretty good putting those 50 hours on your timecard and getting paid for it.

OTHER CONSIDERATIONS

Here are a few other considerations besides money and work environment which may help you decide if you want to pursue some sort of contracting arrangement or salaried employment.

Do you like to be part of a group or organization—a tribe, if you will?

If so, you should think about how being a contractor might make you feel "left out."

If your long-term aspirations are to grow with a team and be part of a company that is achieving a mission in the world, being a contractor might make you feel a bit more like a hired mercenary.

I've had this experience myself.

In fact, at one point in my career, I moved from a very lucrative contract position in a government program that was paying me $100 an hour to a salaried position, which was comparatively less, simply because I wanted to feel like I belonged to a team, and I was tired of just working for money.

Also, **contracting positions usually don't carry as much klout on your resume.**

In general, it is easier to get hired as a contractor, but there is a big difference between being a Microsoft employee and working as a contractor at Microsoft—at least in the eyes of hiring managers, where they'll see being an employee much more favorably.

Doesn't mean contracting jobs will necessarily hurt you, though.

For instance, you can structure the wording on your resume to put emphasis on where you worked and what you did, not your method of employment.

Finally, **upwards mobility may be difficult** unless you are willing to switch contracts every one or two years.

I know several contractors that have been working for HP for over 15 years who are still being paid close to what they were when they started.

Yes, they have been enjoying a somewhat cushy job, but if you are going to stay somewhere for 15 years, you should probably be an employee and climb the corporate ladder.

Most software developers have no idea about the difference between being a contractor or salaried employee, so congratulations, you are ahead of the game.

Up next, we'll be talking about another mysterious world to most software developers: recruiting.

You might be surprised how it actually works.

CHAPTER 20

HOW THE RECRUITING INDUSTRY WORKS

I can remember the first time I started working with a recruiter.

I had no idea how the recruiting industry worked.

I took my freshly created resume, sent it to a recruiter, and said, "Find me a job."

It didn't go so well.

I kept calling day after day, asking the recruiter if they had made any progress on finding me a job.

I was under the false impression that "my recruiter" worked for me.

It was only after some time and quite a few negotiations and placements that I realized recruiters—at least for the most part—don't work for you. They work for the company who has the job opening and has hired the recruiter to fill it.

(There is one exception, which I'll talk about a little later on.)

I know this may seem obvious to you, but I was oblivious to it. I just wanted a job.

In the years I've worked as a software developer and coached many other software developers to find and get the best jobs, I've learned quite a bit about how the recruiting industry works.

It's actually pretty crazy.

But while it's crazy, it's also important that you know how the industry works so you can better navigate the choppy waters of getting a software development job.

It's very easy to be taken advantage of, led on, and manipulated if you don't understand this complex industry.

In this chapter, I'm going to share with you everything I know about the recruiting industry and give you some advice on how you can effectively apply this knowledge to get a good job and not end up with the short end of the stick.

Let me mention a couple of caveats before we get into it:

First, **I'm not a professional recruiter**, so most of my information is from what I have learned and observed.

Second, **the recruiting industry is complex.** I'm sure more than an entire book could be written on the topic. Here I'm simplifying, generalizing, and giving you a summary.

This is in no way meant to be a comprehensive description of the entire recruiting industry.

Still, I think you will find the information in this chapter useful and surprising.

TYPES OF RECRUITERS AND AGENCIES (AND HOW THEY GET PAID)

Recruiters go by many different names: headhunters, employment agencies, staff augmentation, those annoying guys who send you unsolicited LinkedIn requests for jobs you aren't even remotely qualified for.

However, **not all recruiters and recruiting agencies are the same**—and not all of them get paid the same way, either.

Understanding each type of recruiter and how they get paid can help you to understand how to work with them—and even which ones to avoid.

Let's break down each of the major types of recruiters, how they make their money generally, and what this means to you.

INDEPENDENT AND SMALL RECRUITERS

These are typically the most annoying recruiters.

Some of these recruiters work on their own. Some of them work on some kind of heavily weighted commission structure and are actually contracted out en masse by larger firms with a sort of scattershot approach.

Since these recruiters or small agencies don't have a large presence and reputation, **they have to aggressively solicit potential candidates** to try and fill a position.

Why are they so aggressive, you may ask?

Ah, it's all in how they are paid.

You see, **most recruiters get paid a commission based on a percentage of a candidate's salary.**

Before I tell you how much, go ahead and take a guess to see if you can figure it out—the answer may surprise you.

Did you guess?

In general, recruiters are paid between 20 to 35 percent of the annual salary of a candidate they place.

As you can imagine, in the software development industry—especially with recruiting for top jobs—this can be a large amount of money.

Is it all beginning to make sense now?

Can you see why recruiters would be so aggressive and fill up your LinkedIn inbox with messages?

Independent recruiters are often the most aggressive because they don't have to share their commission with an agency they work for, or they get a much larger chunk of it.

Let's use some actual numbers, so you can understand how powerful of a motive it is for a recruiter to place someone.

Suppose a recruiter is hiring for a Senior Software Engineer position and the salary is about $100,000 a year.

An independent recruiter is likely to get a 25 percent commission on placing someone in that job.

So $100,000 * 25% = $25,000.

That is a pretty large score.

Now, like I said, recruiters usually aren't completely independent, so they won't get the full $25,000, but some are and do get that full amount. The ones who work for smaller agencies, where they are more like contractors themselves, will take a large chunk of that commission.

However, that is not the only way they operate.

Recruiters can also recruit for contract positions. (See the previous chapter on contracting versus salary for more information on contracting.)

For these positions, recruiters place a candidate and then get a markup on what that candidate is being paid.

Let's suppose a company is looking for a contractor and is willing to pay $75 an hour.

A recruiter might offer that job at $50 an hour, even though the company is paying $75 for every hour that contractor works.

In this case, their markup or margin would be $25 an hour.

I'm sure you can see how this would be quite lucrative as well.

LARGE AGENCIES

Large agencies are going to operate in a structure similar to small agencies and independent recruiters with only a few differences.

The biggest difference is going to be reach and how commissions are handled.

Large recruiting agencies will likely have good relationships established with major employers, so they will be much more effective in getting someone placed than a smaller recruiting agency with fewer connections—at least from the perspective of the job searcher.

Often, large agencies can have enough of a relationship with a large employer that they almost take over the hiring process from the employer, and if they deem you a good fit for a job, you are very close to getting the job already. (This mainly applies for contract positions.)

In those cases, the only way to get in might be through that agency.

With a larger agency, as might be expected, the recruiter takes less of the commission.

It's likely the actual recruiter may get 50 to 60 percent of the recruiting free with the rest going to the agency.

There may also be a split with an account manager who handles the big corporate accounts for the recruiting agency.

EMBEDDED AGENCIES

Many corporations make use of what I called embedded agencies or on-site staffing.

In this case, **a large agency gets a contract with a major employer to bring staff on-site to fill positions or even to manage entire projects on their own.**

Here, the line blurs between recruiting agency and consulting firm quite a bit, especially if they have their own managers or on-site manager contractors.

When I worked at HP, there were a few of these embedded agencies on site who had hundreds of contractors working for them that they recruited and managed on site at HP.

When I was first recruited into one of these contract jobs, the recruiting agency did almost all the interviewing and just briefly put me in an interview with an actual HP manager before hiring me to work on site.

These agencies and companies that embed external agencies on site often run afoul of hiring and co-employment laws—at least in the US.

There have been many suits filed regarding co-employment at major corporations because the line is so blurred in this case.

HEY JOHN

What is co-employment? How do I know if I'm being taken advantage of? Do I need to sue?

I'm not going to get into the nitty-gritty since I'm not a lawyer and it's a fairly complex topic, but the gist of it is that when a company has a staffing agency bring in some contractors who are technically employed by the staffing agency, there is a big risk that the client could be seen by the courts as a primary employer and responsible for providing benefits to the contractor.

There is a "20-factor" or "common law" test that is applied to identify whether or not a contractor should be counted as a "common law employee."

Back in the year 2000, Microsoft got slapped with a lawsuit in which they had to settle to the tune of $97 million dollars worth of benefits because the court ruled that some of their long-term contractors should be counted as "common law employees."

Like, I said it's a fairly complex issue, but it can be very bad news for employers who utilize staffing agencies who then bring their own contractors on-site.

As far as being taken advantage of by co-employment, personally, I wouldn't worry about it—and I wouldn't sue.

What I mean, is that even though legally the contractors working at Microsoft were awarded "benefits" from Microsoft because of co-employment issues, it was pretty much a dick move to sue them.

Suing your employer—or excuse me, co-employer—is not exactly something you want to have on your resume.

And, in my opinion, if you take the job and accept the terms, that's on you.

I'm all for not being taken advantage of and for negotiating the best rate you can, but when you agree to work for a certain rate and work on a client's site, like I said, that's on you.

You can only be taken advantage of when someone does something you didn't agree upon or alters the deal without your consent.

Could this be the case in some co-employment situations? Sure, I suppose, but I wouldn't worry about it.

INTERNAL RECRUITERS

Many medium-to-large-sized companies have their own internal recruiters who go out and find candidates for a job and get them into the interview process.

I've been contacted several times by internal recruiters working for Microsoft or Google (https://simpleprogrammer.com/cg20-smart) whose entire job is to find talent to bring into the company.

Often, these internal recruiters are not recruiting for a specific job but are instead recruiting for a specific person they think would do well at the company and bring in added value, so they might have multiple positions to match you up with.

Unlike agency recruiters, **internal recruiters are usually paid a fixed salary** with perhaps some portion of it based on commission or some kind of bonus.

This is important to know because they have much less incentive in placing you than an agency recruiter does, and if you don't work out, they have to stick around to deal with the aftermath.

AGENT RECRUITERS

This is probably the rarest type of recruiter, and you aren't all that likely to get contacted by one.

That being said, I have seen more and more of these types of recruiting arrangements showing up in various forms.

This kind of recruiter actually does work for you—or more accurately represents you—since they are your actual agent, just like a book agent or talent agent.

You pay them either a placement fee or a certain percentage of your salary, in most cases.

You would have to be a rockstar kind of developer to gain the advantage of using this kind of an agent—or for one to even be interested in representing you.

Again, they're pretty rare, but it's not a bad way to go if you think you have a highly valuable skill and you'd like someone else to greatly assist in your negotiations.

WHAT THIS MEANS FOR YOU

Ok, at this point you might be thinking that this is interesting information to know, but you might be wondering how this applies to you as a job searcher.

This information should help you **know how to deal with recruiters more effectively by understanding their motives and what type of recruiter they are.**

Being aware of just how much a recruiter stands to gain—especially an independent one—from getting a job filled should influence how you deal with them.

First of all, **you should realize that many recruiters are going to be contacting as many potential candidates as possible to get the best chance of finding someone to fill the position they are recruiting for.**

Always remember that although a LinkedIn email from a recruiter might make you feel like a special little snowflake, in most cases you are not. They are just copying and pasting your name into a template message.

This is, of course, not true when it comes to internal recruiters. **Internal recruiters have much less incentive, so they are much more likely to be scouting you directly based on your skills and talents.**

If you contact a recruiting agency, you should remember they are not interested in finding you a job but are more interested in filling as many jobs as possible.

Therefore, you want to **present yourself as strongly as possible** since they will ultimately decide what jobs to put you in for.

You want to **appear as someone who will get hired easily** and who **will interview extremely well.**

You should also realize that a recruiter is likely to do everything they can to push you through the pipeline as quickly as possible.

This means that you might not necessarily be a good fit for a job and they might tell you really good things about a job or company to get you there. **They might even lie to you or to an employer about you.**

There is a large amount of money on the line.

This isn't to say that all recruiters are bad or unscrupulous, just that you need to watch out for yourself and realize how cutthroat the recruiting industry really is.

FIRST SUBMISSION

If you are job hunting, **you should also be aware of what positions a recruiter may submit you for and how that may affect you.**

In many cases, **the first agency to submit a candidate's resume for a job is considered to be the source of the lead and is owed the commission.**

For instance, imagine a scenario where you have a company that has a job opening, which they advertise on their site. They have also employed two recruiting agencies to fill the position.

You talk to one recruiting agency, Agency X, and give them your resume, and they submit you for the job.

Later, you are searching around and discover the job on the employer's site directly—not even knowing it's the same job—and you submit your resume there.

Finally, a recruiter from another agency, Agency Y, calls you up and says you'd be perfect for the job and that they happen to know the hiring manager directly and can easily get you in.

A few days later, the hiring manager for the job and Agency Y both tell you they wish they could help you, but Agency X already submitted you for the job, so you have to go through them.

If Agency X doesn't follow up very well or offers you a really bad deal because they have a high margin, you could be stuck.

Therefore, **make sure you know when a recruiter submits you for a job and what client it is with before authorizing them to do so.**

NEGOTIATING YOUR SALARY

You should also consider how recruiters are paid when negotiating your salary, both as a full time salaried employee and as a contractor.

Suppose you are applying for a position at a company who is also utilizing a recruiter.

You know that they are willing to pay a recruiter perhaps $10,000 to $20,000 to fill the job.

If you apply directly and get an offer, you can potentially ask for a $10,000 to $20,000 bonus and have a good chance of them saying yes since they were prepared to pay that much anyway.

You should also, of course, know what your markup is going to be (https://simpleprogrammer.com /cg20-markup) **if you are being recruited for a contract position.**

Not only should you know that markup but also you should negotiate it so that you can keep more of what you are being billed out as.

HEY JOHN

This sounds a bit ridiculous. I mean, how would I even go about asking for the $10,000 to $20,000 the company was going to pay a recruiter? And is someone really going to tell me how much they are marking up my contracting rate?

I know you are skeptical, but you would be amazed how much information people give you, or what you can get if you just ask.

Sometimes you ask for the moon and you get it.

Here's a story from my own personal experience which demonstrates both.

Once upon a time, I was being recruited for a contract position working for a state government agency.

A friend of mine, who was already on the contract, had recommended me, and another contractor, who was also on the project, had mentioned he had worked with me in the past and read my blog. So the project manager for the job wanted to bring me in to chat.

Now, he wasn't able to directly hire me, because that government agency had to hire contractors via one of three staffing companies which were contracted to fill positions for this particular project.

But, after having an informal interview, I was basically told to pick one of the staffing companies they were working with and tell them that if they submitted me for the job, I'd basically get it.

It was a pretty good position to be in, I'll admit, but I thought, wow I should probably know what the government agency is going to bill the staffing company, so that I can negotiate a little better and make sure I'm not taken advantage of.

So, guess what I did?

Well, duh, I simply asked the job's project manager what rate they were going to pay the staffing company.

And guess what he did?

Well, he pulled out a spreadsheet that showed what pre-negotiated rates they had with each of the staffing companies for the position they were looking to fill.

It turned out that the position I was going to be filling would be billed out at $95 an hour.

With that information I went to each of the staffing agencies, told them about the position and that I'd be instantly hired for it, and asked them what the best rate they could offer me was.

One company said, "$30 an hour."

Another came back at "$50 an hour."

And a third came back at "$55 an hour."

I decided that since I was bringing the business directly to them—essentially putting it in their lap—that I was willing to accept, at most, a 20% markup on my services.

So, I told each staffing company that if they wanted to fill the position, they'd have to pay me $75 an hour out of the $95 they were billing the client.

Two of the staffing companies scoffed at me and thought my demand was absurd.

I was told they "don't work that way" and that "they don't negotiate markups" and that I was "ridiculous for even trying to know my markup."

But, I held my ground and said that I had other alternatives and I would not allow someone to make more than a 20% markup off of me when I was bringing them the business and I had the connection with the client.

The third staffing company wanted to play ball. They negotiated to $65 an hour, which I declined and said "thanks anyway."

A few hours later, I got a call from the owner of the staffing company while he was on the golf course.

Not only was he impressed that I had the "balls" to negotiate with them and actually find out my markup, but he was willing to meet my demands since as he put it, "he had nothing to lose in the deal."

Now, I'm not saying it will work out for you every time, like it did for me in that story, but the point is, I asked hard questions, made huge demands and got what I was asking for.

If I didn't try, I would have probably been paid $50 an hour instead of $75, which is a pretty big difference.

You have to understand that in many of these situations, the person you are talking to or negotiating with doesn't have any real skin in the game.

What does that project manager care if he tells me what they are billing the staffing agency?

It doesn't affect his bottom line.

He's still going to have to spend that amount of his project's budget on a contractor, whether the contractor gets more of the cut or not. (In fact, he was secretly rooting for me, encouraged me to negotiate and wanted to know how well I did after the negotiations were over.)

And even for some staffing companies, the recruiter might just be doing their job, or they might not care, or they may just be so cocky that they let information slip that they shouldn't have.

Anyway, the point is you never know unless you ask.

Fight for what you want and you just might get it. In most cases the worst that can happen is someone can say "no."

USING A RECRUITER OR GOING SOLO

Let's wrap up this chapter by talking about one last important topic to discuss when it comes to recruiters: should you use one or not?

Oftentimes, you'll be in a position where you could apply for a job directly or you could go through a recruiter.

Or you could reach out to recruiters to help you find a job instead of searching completely on your own.

Which is better?

It depends on a few things.

There are some distinct advantages and disadvantages to look at here.

First of all, consider that **some jobs with exclusive recruiting arrangements may only be accessible via a recruiter or a specific agency.**

When it comes to those jobs, you may not even have a choice.

It's also likely that **some big recruiting agencies will have a virtual lock on recruiting for a specific company** since they have such good relationships established.

In many of those cases, if the recruiting agency thinks you are valuable, they can move you right into a job very quickly by utilizing the trust they've already established.

This can be especially useful to get into large corporations where the traditional hiring process might be hugely discriminating.

Recruiters may also help you negotiate better than you can do yourself, and they usually have a vested interest in you getting the highest pay possible.

Indeed, the power of an agency in negotiation is very useful (https://simpleprogrammer.com /cg20-yes).

Often, if you can have someone negotiating on your behalf, you can get a much better deal.

The downside is that **you may get less than what you could get if you were directly hired by a company since they have to pay the recruiter as well.**

This is especially true with a contract job where you could probably get a much higher hourly rate if you negotiated directly and represented yourself.

If you consider yourself a good negotiator (see the chapter on salary negotiations), you might be better off applying directly to a job than going through a recruiter.

In contrast, if you are not a good negotiator, you may find that even with the overhead of a recruiter being paid to place you, you still come out ahead.

Finally, consider that **a good recruiter may be able to help you represent yourself in the best possible light.**

Likely, they can help you make some changes to your resume, which may help you present as a stronger candidate for a job, and they may have some inside knowledge that could help you during an interview.

All in all, I would say that it depends on the job and how highly you value the recruiting agency.

A good recruiting agency with a strong reputation and good rapport with the client could be a huge asset in a job search, but a recruiter who does nothing but pass on a bunch of resumes, trying to get a commission with as little work as possible, is not going to be much help at all.

SECTION 3

WHAT YOU NEED TO KNOW ABOUT SOFTWARE DEVELOPMENT

"There are known knowns. These are things we know that we know. There are known unknowns. That is to say, there are things that we know we don't know. But there are also unknown unknowns. There are things we don't know we don't know."
—Donald Rumsfeld

The sheer number of things you have to know in order to be an effective software developer is astounding—crushing at times, especially for new programmers.

Programming languages, source control, testing, continuous integration, web development, HTML, CSS, design patterns, databases, debugging, methodologies, SCRUM, Agile… the list goes on and on.

There is so much to learn that if I were to try to teach you all of it, this book would be a ten-volume set. (And outdated as soon as it was published.)

So, what can we do instead?

How can you learn all that you are supposed to learn about software development?

Well, by focusing on eliminating as many unknown unknowns as possible.

That's what this section is about.

The goal of this section is to tell you a little bit about everything you need to know to be an effective software developer.

If you are just starting out, most of this will be new to you.

If you've already been programming for awhile, this section should help you fill in any gaps.

If you are a seasoned veteran, this section will probably help you identify weak points.

The idea here is to give you a basic overview of everything you need to know to be a software developer, so that you aren't surprised when someone says continuous integration or SCRUM, and then later on you can fill in the gaps and turn some of these known unknowns into known knowns—as Rumsfeld would say.

To that end, I'd also suggest that you download the Software Developer's Skills Assessment (https://simpleprogrammer.com/career-guide-toolkit) that's included with your copy of this book. This tool is a visual "heads up display" that can help you identify weak spots you didn't even know you had.

We are going to cover a large amount of information here, but we are only going to wade into about our knees—so try not to get too overwhelmed.

Remember, the goal is not to necessarily learn everything right now, but just get the basics and really eliminate as many unknown unknowns as possible by shining the light on them.

So, get your flashlight and let's go a spelunkin'.

CHAPTER 21

OVERVIEW OF PROGRAMMING LANGUAGES

Often, new developers think it's important to know a large number of programming languages—but it's not.

While I don't think it's important to be an expert in every language that exists (https://simpleprogrammer.com/cg21-more), **I do think it's very useful to be aware of the major programming languages and their differences**, so you can have a good idea of what tool to use for the job.

In this chapter, I'm going to give you **a fairly biased look** at what I consider to be the major programming languages you are likely to encounter and should be familiar with.

I know plenty of people will disagree with me, but my opinion on programming languages comes from my experience using them.

I do believe that even if you don't completely agree with my choices of programming languages and descriptions of them, you'll also find that most experienced developers would at least agree with 75 percent of what I am going to say here.

In the software development world—as you may know already—75 percent confidence in something is pretty dang high.

Also, you'll notice there aren't programming languages like COBOL, Ada, Fortran, etc. on this list because even though some people might argue that they are major programming languages, you don't see them around very often, so I don't think they are worth talking about here.

If you want a full list of programming languages, check out this one on Wikipedia (https://simpleprogrammer.com/cg21-list).

C

C, originally created at Bell Labs by Dennis Ritchie between 1969 and 1973, is one of the older programming languages in use today. It is still quite popular, despite its age, and **is arguably the most used programming language worldwide.**

Many of the other major programming languages of today have their roots in C.

In fact, if you learn to program in C, you'll probably find it easier to pick up other languages like C++, C#, Java, JavaScript, and many others.

C is a bit of a tricky language because it is so powerful. It is very low-level, allowing developers to access the memory on a computer directly and to manipulate many low-level parts of the computer.

You'll find C used in many operating systems, low-level hardware, embedded systems, and even a good number of older games.

C is often considered a system's programming language.

C++

C++ is the programming language that often gets mixed in with C. This is mainly because many C++ programmers don't grasp the object-oriented concepts in C++ and write what would be called C code with some C++ features.

If you work on legacy systems written in C++, you are likely to see a large amount of this type of code.

C++ is technically a superset of C, which means that a C program should compile with a C++ compiler (although there are a few exceptions).

C++ was created by Bjarne Stroustrup at Bell Labs to extend the C language in order to provide some useful features from Simula, adding object orientation, classes, virtual functions, and many other features.

Today, C++ is still widely used—especially in game development—and it continues to be updated, now called "modern C++."

However, C++ is a very complex language. It's not one that I recommend beginners start with because of the level of complexity.

It's extremely powerful, but it's also, as they say, easy to blow your foot off with.

C#

C# is one of my favorite programming languages of all time because of how expressive yet easy it is to use.

I feel like C# is an elegantly designed language, and it seems to grow and evolve fairly rapidly even today.

C# was originally created by Microsoft as the flagship language of the .NET Runtime.

It was created by Anders Hejlsberg, who was highly involved with the creation of Delphi and Turbo Pascal.

C# started out as very, very similar to Java. In fact, it has been called a copy of Java, which I can't really argue against.

In fact, I first picked up C# so quickly because I knew Java, and in my mind it was basically the same thing with just a few minor differences.

Recently, however, C# and Java have diverged quite a bit—although, again, I'd say that if you know one of these languages, you are 90 percent on the way to knowing the other.

C# is an object-oriented language that could be described as similar to C++, but is much simpler and now has many functional features.

JAVA

Java is extremely similar to C#, but it's older, so technically C# is extremely similar to Java.

It was created in 1995 by James Gosling at Sun Microsystems as a write-once, run anywhere language. The idea was that Java could run on a virtual machine which could run on any computing platform, thus enabling Java programs to be easily cross-platform.

Java is object-oriented and largely based off of C and C++, but again, just like C#, is very simplified, not allowing direct memory manipulation and other low-level constructs that can get you into trouble.

Today, Java is owned by Oracle and still continues to grow and thrive—although it's now managed by a committee, whose members tend to slow down advancement.

PYTHON

Python is one of those languages that I'd like to dive into deeper some day.

It's an extremely elegant and simple language with one of the core objectives being readability.

Python was created in 1989 by Van Rossum who is called by the Python community "benevolent dictator for life."

Python can be written in an object-oriented, procedural, or even functional way, and it is an interpreted language, meaning that it is not compiled.

In comparison to C++, Java, and C#, Python code is often much more terse since more can be expressed in fewer lines of code.

Python is extremely popular today and is growing in popularity—as far as I can tell.

It's **one of the main programming languages used at Google** and is a great beginner language.

RUBY

Now, here is an extremely interesting language.

Ruby was actually created in Japan by Yukihiro "Matz" Matsumoto around 1993. (I had the honor of Matz being a commentator on the Japanese translation of my *Soft Skills* book (https://simpleprogrammer.com/cg21-lifemanualjapan).)

The idea was to create an objected-oriented scripting language.

Ruby didn't really start to take off and become a popular programming language until years later, though.

One of the big catalysts of Ruby's success was the creation of Ruby on Rails (RoR) by David Heinemeier Hansson (also known as DHH) in 2003.

Since then, Ruby has risen and slightly fallen in popularity, but it is **still an extremely popular programming language today because of how easy and fun it is to use to program.** In fact, that is one of Matz's major design goals for the language.

You'll find that many coding boot camps teach Ruby as the primary programming language since it is a very good beginner language.

JAVASCRIPT

Here is another interesting programming language that doesn't seem to want to die.

JavaScript was originally created by Brendan Eich in 1995 and was **developed in just 10 days!**

As you can imagine, this resulted in a language with many problems. JavaScript looks a lot like C#, Java, or C++, but it behaves much differently.

JavaScript was initially used as a simple scripting language for the web, but, as I'm sure you have discovered, it has become the primary language of the web—and beyond.

Newer versions of JavaScript, or more precisely ECMAScript, have fixed many of the deficiencies of the language and made it more suitable for large-scale development.

Pretty much every web developer today has to have at least some understanding of the language since it is so widely used.

HEY JOHN

Why has JavaScript become such a popular web development language—especially if it's, well, not the best?

That's actually a really good question.

I would say the primary reason has nothing to do with how good of a language it is or how suited it is for web development, but rather convenience and opportunity.

Early in the days of the web, JavaScript was included in just about every browser, mostly to do simple things like show a popup or dialog—not at all like it is used today.

Also, JavaScript didn't have to be compiled, since it's an interpreted language.

This simply means that the language could run inside the browser and be executed one command at a time instead of having to be compiled first—which is also pretty convenient for the web, since the JavaScript could be delivered with web pages and executed inside the browser.

Other technologies like Flash, and even other scripting languages came along—and some would argue they were superior, but I think JavaScript ultimately won out because you could count on it being everywhere and so many developers had to know at least the basics of it anyway.

PERL

While not as popular as it used to be, Perl is still a widely used language, especially in the Unix scripting space.

In fact, Perl was originally created as a scripting language for Unix by Larry Wall in 1987.

It became widely popular in the early days of the web because of its flexibility and ability to parse strings, which made it great for CGI scripting. (If you don't know what that is, don't worry, but consider yourself lucky.)

I've always sort of hated Perl because I've found it to be an ugly language which is extremely difficult to read.

But, despite my misgivings about the language, I have to admit that its designation as "the Swiss Army chainsaw of scripting languages" is accurate.

Perl is extremely flexible and extremely powerful—I just can't understand anything I or someone else wrote in it two days later.

PHP

Here is a language which people love to hate—myself included.

PHP is not a very elegant language. In fact, it feels a bit "dirty" in my opinion, but it pretty much, along with JavaScript, powers a majority of the web today.

Facebook was first written in PHP. The ever-popular blogging software WordPress is still written in PHP.

There is a huge list of extremely popular websites that at least started out as PHP, and many of them still use it.

It was originally created by Rasmus Lerdorf in 1994 and actually evolved without any kind of written specification until 2014. (Yes, you read that correctly.)

PHP was never even intended to become a programming language. It was just a set of dynamic tools to help build simple web pages, but once the cat was out of the bag, it was impossible to put back in.

For all of PHP's shortcomings, it is easy to learn and use although it has many dark alleys to get lost in.

It's not my favorite language, but many beginners start out modifying existing PHP code to "cut their teeth."

OBJECTIVE-C

Here is another language which rose from obscurity to dominance in a matter of a few years.

Objective-C was originally created by Brad Cox and Tom Love in the early 1980s. The idea was to add object-oriented capabilities from SmallTalk to C.

Objective-C was widely forgotten—and almost dead—except for Apple picking it up and deciding to use it in its Mac OS X operating system.

Even still, it didn't become widely popular since only Mac developers were really using the language until Apple introduced the iPhone and iOS, which beckoned in millions of new programmers to struggle with the strange syntax of the language.

I was one of them, as I had to learn Objective-C to port my first Android application over to iOS.

I have to say, I'm not a big fan of the language.

It has a very high learning curve, and it's quite verbose to even do the most simple thing.

Luckily, iOS developers today don't have to learn Objective-C and can use a slightly more friendly language, Swift.

SWIFT

This programming language is Apple's new flagship language for iOS.

I'll admit, at the time of writing this chapter, I haven't played around with Swift myself—although if I pick up iOS development again, I'll certainly check this language out.

Swift has been purposely designed to work with Apple's Cocoa and Cocoa Touch frameworks (the ones used for iOS and OS X development).

It's also designed to easily integrate with the large amount of existing Objective-C code out there.

Swift supports many of the popular features of Objective-C that make Objective-C so dynamic and flexible, but also is much simpler and concise.

If you are going to do iOS development today, it's probably a decent idea to skip Objective-C and go straight to Swift.

GO

Go is a relatively new programming language which was created by Google.

I really like Go because it's concise, yet also powerful.

(I created a course on Go which you can find on Pluralsight (https://simpleprogrammer.com /cg21-gocourse).)

Go was created in 2007 by Robert Griesemer, Rob Pike, and Ken Thompson and is very similar to C, but with some great additions and simplifications.

Unlike C, Go has garbage collection, so you don't have to manage memory. It also has some concurrent programming features built right into the language, making it extremely performant and making concurrency a first-class feature of the language.

When you start to program with it, you can tell overall that it's a really well designed language by how concise much of the syntax is.

Like C, Go is primarily a system's programming language, but it is spreading out to more areas including the web.

ERLANG

Erlang is a functional, deeply interesting programming language, designed to be distributed and concurrent. **It also supports hot swapping of code** where you can change the code in an application without stopping it.

It was originally created in 1986 by Joe Armstrong, Robert Virding, and Mike Williams at Ericsson, but was open-sourced in 1998.

The language was originally created to help improve the development of telephony applications—hence the hot-swapping since you don't exactly want to have most telephony applications go down.

Erlang could easily be considered the most robust programming language (and programming environment) around today.

HASKELL

This programming language is very academic in nature.

Haskell is a purely functional programming language which was first designed as an open standard for a handful of functional languages that existed in 1987. The idea was to consolidate the existing functional languages into a single comment, one that could be used for functional language design research.

Haskell 1.0 was designed in 1990, by a committee believe it or not.

In recent years, Haskell has become more popular and not just for academics.

Since **Haskell is a purely functional language** and strong static type system, it can be a difficult programming language to use and learn, but it is also quite powerful and produces highly predictable code without side effects.

GLOSSING OVER THE DETAILS

Again, I want to stress a few things about this list of major programming languages.

Obviously, it's time-sensitive and highly biased, so if your favorite programming language or the new hotness isn't listed here, it could be for either of those reasons.

I also glossed over the details of the programming languages because **I don't want us to get sucked into trying to define static versus dynamic languages and object-oriented or procedural languages versus functional languages.**

(But, if you do want to deep dive into the topic, I'd recommend reading "Types and Programming Languages" (https://simpleprogrammer.com/cg21-types).)

In fact, in programming environments today, many languages don't clearly fall into the old categories of static or dynamic or object-oriented and functional since many languages incorporate features in multiple categories.

Rather, all you need is an idea of the major programming languages there are and a quick synopsis of each one so that, if you are interested, you can explore whatever languages interest you most on your own.

HEY JOHN

But, but, you missed my favorite programming language. What about Rust? What about Cobol? What about Scala, Lisp, Haskell for goodness sake! And hey, hey I need to know about interpreted languages and scripting and compilers and all that don't I, don't I?

Woah there, boy.

Woah there... Let's take a deep breath.

Count to 10, now exhale.

There you go.

Ok, so I hear you. I did explain above that my choices were biased and that I may have not included your favorite language.

It's all good though. The point of this chapter is not to tell about every major programming language you might find out there in the wild, but rather just to give you an overview of some—yes, some—of the major ones.

The truth is, you don't need to know every single option.

I know Baskin Robbins has 31 flavors, but it doesn't mean you need to take one of those little pink sample spoons and try every single flavor before you make a decision.

So, don't sweat it.

If you see a language is missing from this list, it's all good.

If you are really interested in that language you can look it up.

I just wanted to give you a small taste of what you are likely to see and some general knowledge of the heavy hitters.

And as far as interpreted languages, compilers, static versus dynamic typing and all that, well yes, it is important to understand those things, but it's going to take more than a chapter to do it.

The focus of this section of the book is to let you know what you need to know, so you can have a basic overview and then can study those things in much more depth on your own.

So don't mistake my not talking about how programming languages work as me saying that stuff isn't important.

It's definitely important, but there are entire books on programming language theory and design that cover all of that much more in-depth.

Alright, that concludes our very short overview of programming languages. Next up let's get into the different kinds of development and software developers.

CHAPTER 22

WHAT IS WEB DEVELOPMENT?

I'm going to be completely honest with you: I'm not a huge fan of web development (https://simpleprogrammer.com/cg22-hate).

Don't get me wrong. I've done plenty of web development, but in comparison to developing desktop apps or mobile apps, web development is… well… trickier.

In general, you know what your runtime environment looks like with desktop or mobile development. If you're building a Windows app, you might use .NET. If you're building for macOS, you might use Objective-C. But in either case, you know which version of which operating system you support, and which language and features are available.

With Web development, however, this changes. You don't have as much control over the runtime environment because there are at least 5 major players in the Web Browser world: Microsoft Internet Explorer, Microsoft Edge, Google Chrome, Apple Safari, Firefox. There are plenty of other "lesser" players like Opera, as well as, mobile device browsers, "web" TVs, video game consoles, and more.

That's a lot of mouths to please, or hands to err… your shit is going to break, ok?

Then, there are the myriad of different versions of all of these browsers that people use.

Web development is tricky because each of these different browsers and browser versions can support different features and behaviors.

But, like it or not, **as a software developer, you have to know about web development—at least the basics.**

In fact, most software developers today are web developers.

It's true; web development has taken over the world. It's the King Kong of development platforms.

Desktop development used to be the norm, but more and more applications have moved to the web—or at least to web-based technologies—and continue to do so.

Even with the rapid growth of mobile development, web development is still critical because as cell phones and tablets get more powerful, it will be easier to create cross-platform apps by making them web apps which run in the browser.

That means, **whether or not you are planning to become a web developer, you need to at least be familiar with web development, how the web works, and the major technologies involved.**

In this chapter, we are going to cover some of these basics.

A QUICK OVERVIEW

Web development itself and how it is done has changed greatly over the years, but one thing has remained the same: **web development is about creating applications which run in a web browser.**

Some of these applications have their logic living on a web server which renders HTML, CSS, and JavaScript to create an application.

Other applications only utilize the server to create their initial state, download the logic to run the application, and then use the server only to retrieve and store data.

Regardless of how web development is done, **the basic technologies are the same: HTML, JavaScript, CSS**—and a large amount of patience... to test all the web browsers, which... you'll invariably be required to support.

Web developers today utilize about every major programming language to create web applications.

This is possible because the user interface of a web application is really just plain text in the form of HTML and CSS, which can be generated by any programming language capable of generating text and responding to HTTP requests. (Which would be just about any programming language by the way.)

JavaScript—another plain text file format—is also used today to manipulate HTML in a web browser, through what is known as the DOM (Document Object Model). The DOM is a representation of a webpage in the browser, which can be used to directly change the user interface displayed in the browser without directly creating new HTML or CSS code.

HOW THE WEB WORKS

It's difficult to understand what web development is if you don't have at least a general idea of how the web works.

Some things have changed over the years, but **the basic functionality of the web and its underlying technologies have mostly remained the same.**

Consider this brief primer a very condensed and basic explanation of how the web works.

First of all, we have the web browser.

The web browser is able to parse and render HTML and CSS into a visible format which we call a web page.

A web browser is also capable of executing JavaScript to do various things, including modifying the underlying structure of a web page.

The web browser has to send a request to a web server in order to get a web page to render.

This is done through a protocol known as HTTP, or Hypertext Transfer Protocol.

When a request for a particular resource or URI (Uniform Resource Identifier) is sent to a web server, that web server finds the requested content—if it exists—and sends back a response to the browser.

The browser then parses and renders that response, which is what the end user sees in the web browser.

Now, obviously there is much more going on under the covers, but **the basic idea is that the web browser makes a request and the web server responds by returning back HTML, CSS, and JavaScript.**

Why is this important to understand if you want to do web development?

Because, as you can imagine, **a web application has to be thought about a bit differently than a normal desktop application.**

In a desktop application, you might be able to hold various bits of state in memory and be able to access that state data when you switch to a different page or section of the application.

For web applications, **you have to work around the fact that the underlying HTTP protocol is stateless.** Because of this, web applications have to continually make requests from the server for every action that happens in the application. (I'm generalizing here, but this is mostly true.)

This also means you must have some way to manage the application state between requests and keep track of the individual users that are using the web application simultaneously.

There are frameworks and patterns that make this easier to do, but it's critical to understand that web development is much different than other kinds of development due to the statelessness of HTTP and the constant client-server interactions.

With what sounds like a complicated programming process, and difficult-to-manage application runtime, it's easy to wonder how we got here. Where did the modern web come from, and why are we using the technologies that we are using now?

A BRIEF HISTORY OF THE WEB

Web development started in a very different place than where it is now.

Early web developers spent most of their time creating static HTML pages and all navigation was done using hyperlinks.

An early web developer didn't really create an "app." They created a set of static web pages that had information and perhaps a few pictures, all linked together with hyperlinks.

It was all really quite boring and not very posh at all.

So much so, that there weren't really any web developers at that time, just webmasters—and I was one of them, for the United States Air Force, when I was 16, during my summer job. Ah, those were the days...but they were short-lived.

There needed to be a way to make web pages more interactive.

Early developer conversations probably went something like this: "Wouldn't it be cool if someone could put their name into a box, click a button and get back, "Hi John, you are such a stud."?

(Note: this is NOT, I repeat NOT the first interactive web page I ever made. I'm just using this as an example.)

It also would be cool to be able to conditionally render some content and not other content, and to begin tracking state.

Now, not only could the web page say, "Hi John, you are such a stud," but it could remember that I'm John when I load the next page (along with how studly I am), as well as, show me a completely differently rendered web page, for studly stallion webmasters like myself.

A technology called CGI ("Common Gateway Interface") was used to create the earliest web applications. These apps could conditionally generate HTML using data, like query strings, that the browser sent to the server.

But, this wasn't exactly easy because, as a web developer, you'd have to parse the request you got from the browser and generate your own response, making sure to implement the HTTP protocol correctly and generate some valid HTML.

This did become easier when web development frameworks began popping up. You may have heard of technologies like ColdFusion or ASP. These were some of the early web frameworks which made CGI and the dynamic generation of HTML easier.

Now a web developer could generate conditional HTML by using special tags, markup and logic.

Translation: things got easier... much easier.

This kind of technology worked like a templating language and allowed a huge number of developers to create real web applications for the first time... sorry, webmasters.

But, alas there needed to be a way to make web pages even MORE interactive.

Eventually with browser technology evolving and computers getting faster—as well as a growing demand for more complex applications—web developers started using **JavaScript to expand the capabilities of many web applications.**

Around the same time, web developers started using CSS (Cascading Style Sheets) to make it easier to style and change the style of web applications. HTML became responsible for defining content and CSS became responsible for the layout and style of that content.

But, it appears that web developers—and users—are never happy and just can't be satisfied with dynamically generated, stylish web pages, so they had to take it a further.

There needed to be a way to make web pages even MORE interactive—and even more cool.

Think of it as the nuclear arms race of web technology.

Rendering everything on the server is slow and doesn't feel responsive, so **technologies like AJAX (Asynchronous JavaScript and XML) were invented to allow web pages to update dynamically without refreshing the page.**

Eventually entire web applications were built dynamically without any page refreshes at all. These types of web applications are known as SPAs, or Single Page Applications.

We'll see what happens as the web continues to move forward and evolves, but it looks like the web is going to **continue to become more like the desktop applications of the past, and the web browser is going to become more and more like an actual operating system.**

In fact, this has become so true that Google created a web-based OS called Chrome OS in which the OS is basically the Chrome web browser.

And that's a brief history of the web—as I see it… in a nutshell. (A really small nutshell.)

PRIMARY WEB DEVELOPMENT TECHNOLOGIES

All right, now that you have the basics of how the web works and understand a little bit about how the web evolved over time, let's talk about a few of the most common web development technologies you are likely to encounter.

HTML

This is the keystone of web development. HTML is the basic building block of the web and all web development is eventually based on it.

You can build an entire web application using just HTML—although it won't really do that much (and I'd probably call it a web page).

HTML (Hypertext Markup Language) (https://simpleprogrammer.com/cg22-design)**, is used to create the content and structure of a web page.**

HTML consists of a series of tags that define the parts and components of a web page.

For example, you might use the <img> tag to embed an image on a page. You can use an <h1> tag to create a title. Or you can define an <article> to tell the browser where the main content for the page is located.

There are dozens of commonly used tags, and many more less commonly used tags for organizing the content and structuring the document.

A web browser will parse the HTML and use it along with CSS and JavaScript to render a page.

CSS

Before CSS existed, HTML was used to both specify the content and structure of a web page, as well as, to dictate how it should be displayed and styled.

This was a problem because it meant that in order to change the styling of a web application—for example, to make all the buttons a different color or to change a font size—the HTML would have to be changed in many places in the application.

CSS was invented to solve this problem by cleanly separating the content of a web page from the styling of it (although the two do overlap from time to time).

CSS (Cascading Style Sheets) (https://simpleprogrammer.com/cg22-design) **can be linked to in a web page in order to define the styling for that web page.**

An entire web application can link to a set of CSS pages which set the style for the entire web application.

Then, if you want to change the color of a button, you can just modify one CSS file, and all the buttons for the entire web application will change.

Quite a useful technology.

evil looking hand gesture as I slowly stroke my chin

long pause

If you are good with CSS, there is quite a bit you can do to change the presentation of a web page, from making elements appear or disappear, to changing the locations of elements, resizing, changing fonts, and just about anything else you can imagine.

But CSS isn't without it's own set of limitations and problems. It can be challenging to write CSS in a manner that is easy to maintain or that is well organized, allowing other developers to easily see what is happening.

Unlike programming languages, CSS has not supported variables, functions or other forms of encapsulation. This means repeating your color specification everywhere you need it, instead of using a variable. It also means repeating elements like border size and spacing, instead of applying those elements with a function.

CSS is adopting many of these ideas in new and future versions, but it is taking a long time for this happen.

HEY JOHN

What about CSS preprocessors? My buddy keeps talking about them, but I don't quite understand what they are.

It's not something you absolutely have to know about, but...

It's worth noting that many web developers today use what are known as CSS preprocessors.

What are CSS preprocessors, you ask?

Well, they are kind of like magic for CSS in that they make it easier for you to write CSS in a programmatic way that isn't as repetitive.

When you have a large web application it can be burdensome to maintain all the CSS for that application and much of that CSS is duplicated, because you have to define the same thing in many places.

CSS can get really complicated.

But a CSS preprocessor allows you to write your CSS more like the way you would write regular code and do all kinds of neat things like assign variables, perform loops, and even reuse big parts of CSS you've already defined.

Overall a CSS preprocessor makes your CSS code easier to maintain, less repetitive and can save you quite a bit of time.

JAVASCRIPT

When JavaScript first came out, it was a bit of a novelty that was used to do some very basic things on web pages, but JavaScript has evolved to take a much more central role in web development.

At its heart, JavaScript is a fully-functional dynamic language which can be executed directly in the web browser.

It makes web pages more interactive and allows for programmatic manipulation of web pages and their content.

It can directly interact with the DOM of a web page, to add, remove and change content.

It can add, remove and change CSS, to alter the display and formatting of the content on the page.

It can also run a full application's logic and processing—directly inside of a browser—to create business applications, games, visual effects and animations, and more.

(In fact, the once-popular and once-heavily-taxing-of-system-resources-game, Doom, has been ported to the web browser and implemented in JavaScript... sigh. Yes, this is really true (https:// simpleprogrammer.com/cg22-doom)*.)*

By using JavaScript to manipulate the DOM and CSS, the entire structure and style of a web page can be changed programmatically.

And this all happens inside the browser (unless you are using a technology like Node.js (https:// simpleprogrammer.com/cg22-node), which runs JavaScript on the server to actually parse requests and send back responses).

There are limitations to running a complete application in a browser, though—the largest of which is often the browsers that you must support.

If the browser doesn't support the features you need for JavaScript to do its work, you may need to keep the HTML creation and manipulation on the web server. (And cry a little.)

This is commonly referred to a server-side rendering vs client-side rendering in the browser.

The differences between server-side rendering and client-side rendering can be quite confusing, though.

SERVER-SIDE RENDERING

In the most simple model of web development, all web pages are rendered on the server and the HTML, CSS, and JavaScript of that page is sent to the web browser, where it is parsed and displayed to the user.

Server-side rendering simply means that the pages are fully constructed by the logic on the server.

So, with server-side rendering, the logic for the application lives almost entirely on the server.

As we talked about in the history of the web, this was the original way most web applications worked.

Today, technologies like ASP.NET or PHP still mainly utilize this model, although with the use of various JavaScript frameworks, even a server-side rendering technology can be used for client-side rendering.

CLIENT-SIDE RENDERING

With the increasing capabilities of browsers and JavaScript engines in browsers, there has been a strong movement towards what is known as client-side rendering.

Client-side rendering simply means that the content of the web page is constructed in the browser—via JavaScript—instead of on the server.

HEY JOHN

This may be a really stupid question, but you keep talking about Javascript. Do I have any options OTHER than Javascript for doing this and for web development?

First of all, there is no such thing as a stupid question, only inquisitive idiots.

But, in this case, your question is 100%, completely, totally, valid.

In fact, I've asked myself the same question many times—or variations of it, mostly while lamenting why some obscure idiosyncrasy of the JavaScript language is causing bugs in my application.

The honest answer is, there are plenty of alternatives—but, unfortunately, none of them are really viable.

You can actually program in another language besides JavaScript, but most of the other "JavaScript alternatives" actually end up getting compiled back down to JavaScript before they are run in the browser.

There are actually quite a few of these languages, like CoffeeScript, TypeScript, Babel, Elm, Dart even functional languages like ClojureScript.

Some of these languages are actually designed to run directly in the browser—well, certain browsers—like Dart, but most of them are happy with being compiled and becoming JavaScript before they are run in the web browser.

> We aren't going to get into the details here, but if you are interested in JavaScript alternatives, there are definitely plenty.
>
> Just know at the end of the day, whatever programming language you choose to write the client-side logic of your web application in, most likely it will be compiled to JavaScript anyway.

With client-side rendering, you can almost think of the web server delivering an "app" to the browser, and the browser executes that app internally to render the pages, create the navigations, and request any additional data from the server.

Behind the scenes, JavaScript is being used to create and manipulate DOM elements and even produce HTML or CSS that is part of the web page, or in this case, the web app.

As you can imagine, client-side rendering appears more seamless to the end-user because there isn't a need to make requests back to the server to have new pages rendered. The only requests are for additional data, which is then "plugged into" the web page dynamically.

This is why some client-side rendered apps are called SPAs or Single Page Applications.

There is usually only one page and the contents of that page are dynamically updated.

Both techniques can even be combined in a single web application (https://simpleprogrammer.com/cg22-meteor), where some parts of the user interface are rendered client-side and other parts and pages are rendered server-side.

When you have content being created in the browser, though, there will still be a part of the logic and process that lives on the server in the form of an HTTP API.

APIS

Part of being a web developer today involves understanding APIs or Application Programming Interfaces.

An API, as it's used in web development, is just a specification of some commands that one program can send to get the other program to do something or return some data.

Commonly SPAs, or Single Page Applications utilize APIs for sending data back and forth.

This is especially useful in client-side rendering applications because they need to be able to have some way to send and receive data and to communicate with the brains of the application, which is usually going to live on the server.

With server-side rendering the rendering is taking place on the server before the HTML gets sent to the browser, so the application can just get whatever data it needs while it's executing on the server.

With client-side rendering, the application is executing inside the browser, so it needs an explicit way to communicate with the server.

That's where the API comes in.

Not something we can dive into deeply in this chapter, but **just be aware that a large portion of web development today involves interacting with and programming against APIs**, particularly what are known as web APIs.

THE VERY BASICS

So, there you have it.

Those are the very basics of web development and when I say very basics, I mean very basics.

We haven't even talked about why HTTP is stateless, caching, databases and scalability, parsing and page rendering, and the many… many JavaScript frameworks that exist out there.

If you decide to become a web developer, yes, you will need to know all that stuff, but hopefully this chapter gives you a good place to start.

Next up, we'll head into one of my personal favorite kinds of development, mobile development.

(Side note: I want to give a special thanks to my good friend, Derick Bailey who helped me with revising this chapter and filling in some gaps in current and past web development technology where I was lacking.

Derick is an expert in web development, and teaches the intricacies of JavaScript at WatchMeCode.com (https://simpleprogrammer.com/cg22-watch) so I asked him to enhance the chapter a bit… although all the humor is still mine.)

CHAPTER 23

MOBILE DEVELOPMENT

One of the most intriguing areas of software development has always been mobile development.

Why?

Because mobile development presents a pretty unique opportunity for a one-person development team to build an actual, usable, meaningful app end-to-end in a relatively short period of time.

Mobile development also represents an entrepreneurial opportunity which is well within most programmers' reach.

Not to say that an ambitious software developer couldn't build a web application or desktop application by themselves, but mobile development is so much more accessible because mobile apps are expected to be small and singular in purpose.

Even in the gaming world, mobile applications can be a throwback to earlier, simpler times before 3D graphics and humongous code bases.

Retro-style games from the 8-bit and 16-bit era are somehow acceptable and even endeared on a mobile phone or tablet, where on other platforms they aren't nearly as widely accepted.

However, mobile development represents more than just an opportunity for the solo-developer to build their own project—**it's arguably the future of development**, as mobile devices are becoming a larger and larger part of our lives.

It's quite possible, at least at the time of writing this book, to become exclusively a mobile application developer, both independently and working for someone else.

In this chapter, we'll take a look at what mobile development is, go over some of the major mobile platforms, and talk a bit about the technologies that exist for doing mobile development, so that you have a good idea of whether or not mobile development is the right match for you.

WHAT IS MOBILE DEVELOPMENT?

Let's start out by defining exactly what mobile development is—it's not as obvious as it seems.

Mobile development isn't just about building phone apps, although that is certainly a large part of it.

Mobile development is doing any kind of development for any kind of mobile device.

Somewhat of a rhetorical definition, but stay with me here.

What I mean by this statement is that mobile development encompasses developing apps for phones, tablets, smart watches, and all kinds of wearable devices which run some kind of mobile operating system.

It doesn't necessarily mean developing purely mobile applications, since even web developers today have to think about how their applications are going to be used and accessed on a mobile device.

As we'll discuss a little later in this chapter, mobile applications can even be developed exclusively for mobile devices but entirely as web applications. This may even be the trend of the future as mobile devices become more and more powerful, and the browser takes an even more dominant role as the operating system of the future.

MAJOR MOBILE DEVELOPMENT PLATFORMS

Throughout computing history, there have actually been quite a few different mobile application development platforms, **but until recently, mobile development had not taken the limelight and no dominant platforms existed.**

That all changed with the introduction of the iPhone in 2007.

I remember back when I first started doing any kind of mobile development, when the Palm Pilot first came out.

One of my first entrepreneurial ventures—and probably the first application I completely built on my own—was a Magic: The Gathering life counter application written in C for Palm OS.

Since then, many mobile experiments have flourished for some time and then died on the vine.

Windows CE seemed so promising, but they just couldn't get it right.

Blackberry looked like it was going to dominate the world, and perhaps it did for a time.

But today—at least at the time of writing this book—**there are two main contenders**, and then there's the rest.

IOS

iOS is quite arguably the "big dog" when it comes to major mobile development platforms, partially because it was the platform that finally brought mobile development into the modern day and age by completely transforming the idea of a mobile device and mobile software.

iOS is, of course, developed by Apple, and it runs exclusively on Apple products.

At the time of this writing, **iOS runs on iPhones, iPods, iPads, Apple Watches, and Apple TV**, but I expect there will be more devices which will run iOS in the future.

iOS at its core is very Unix-like; it is based on Darwin (BSD) and M.

It shares some important frameworks with macOS, and its user interface is based on Apple's Cocoa UI, which is used in macOS applications, but has been modified and redesigned for touch devices and is called Cocoa Touch.

Apple provides iOS developers with several native tools and libraries to develop iOS applications, and, although you don't need to use Apple's development tools to build your apps, you do have to have a Mac running macOS to build your application.

iOS applications are typically built utilizing either Objective-C or the now more popular development language for the platform, Swift.

ANDROID

If you're not developing a mobile app on iOS, it's probably Android or both.

Android is the other dominant player in this space.

Android was a little later to the game, first being released in September 2008, almost a year later than iOS, but it has still managed to gain a pretty large share of the mobile market.

Technically, **Android is the mobile OS with the largest, most dominant share of the market**, weighing in at around an 80 percent share compared to iOS's 18 percent share.

Those numbers are a bit deceiving since Android is a fragmented market, consisting of many different devices made by different manufacturers, running different versions of the Android operating system.

Android, backed by Google, is open.

iOS, backed by Apple, is not.

Anyone can build an Android device, and it is designed to run on a variety of different hardware platforms and devices with very different form factors and capabilities.

iOS is designed to run, and only runs on, a specific set of Apple devices.

Android is based on the Linux kernel, and the source code for Android is released as open source by Google.

Like Apple, Google provides some native tools for Android development, but again, you aren't required to use them.

The native development platform for Android OS application is Java.

OTHERS

Everyone else left in the mobile OS market shares a measly, less than 2 percent share of the overall market.

Of the remainders, Windows and Blackberry are probably the largest, but still mostly inconsequential.

It's probably a matter of time before both of those mobile platforms completely disappear.

Because of their small market-share, I won't even talk about the others since I wouldn't encourage you to waste your time investing in any platform that has an extremely high chance of dying, but I'll say that there are some options for developing cross-platform mobile applications—which we'll talk about a little later on—that will allow you to develop for these marginal competitors at virtually no extra cost.

I would never consider developing exclusively for one of these platforms.

If you are going to develop a mobile application and become a mobile app developer, choose iOS or Android.

HOW MOBILE DEVELOPMENT IS DONE

When iOS and Android first came out, if you wanted to learn how to develop mobile applications for both platforms, you learned how to use the native tools each vendor provided.

For iOS, that was XCode and Objective-C.

For Android, that was an Android SDK plugin to Eclipse, or Netbeans and Java.

Oh my, how things have changed.

Today, there are many more options.

There are countless frameworks, tools, and entire platforms and ecosystems for developing mobile applications.

Just about every programming language is supported in one form or another, and mobile applications can even be built to run exclusively in a mobile browser.

Even though there are many options available, we can group them into a few large categories.

NATIVE DEVELOPMENT

Obviously, we can natively develop mobile applications using the tools the mobile OS vendor provides for us.

As I mentioned before, for iOS, this was initially XCode and Objective-C, but Apple created a new language called Swift (https://simpleprogrammer.com/cg23-swift), which is now the language of choice for developing iOS apps.

In the Android world (https://simpleprogrammer.com/cg23-android), not much has changed except that Google has put out its own Android Development Studio IDE. Java is still the preferred language (although, if you are really brave, C/C++ is officially supported).

When I created my first Android and iOS applications, I built them natively, but I wouldn't do that again today.

The biggest issue with native mobile development is that you have to completely rewrite the code for your application for both iOS and Android. (If you want to support Windows Phone or another small platform, you must do the same for that platform as well.)

It's not a huge deal, but applications typically need to be supported, so trying to support different versions of an application on two or more totally different platforms can be a bit of a maintenance nightmare.

Also, Android and iOS development are almost completely different.

The tools are different, the languages are different, the frameworks are different, and even the development paradigms are different.

If you want to create an iOS and Android version of an application, you have to be prepared to learn two very different, evolving platforms.

On the other hand, native development does have a few advantages.

The biggest one is raw speed—although some cross-platform frameworks like Xamarin can match it since they compile down to native code. We'll get to that in a minute.

Aside from using a framework that compiles down to native code, native code is pretty much going to be faster than any other solution.

If you develop natively, **you are also going to have better debugging tools** since you won't be operating with several layers of high abstraction.

You are also more likely to be able to **take advantage of some of the native features of the platform** and get closer to the hardware level. (Although, again, this may not be the case with some of the better cross-platform offerings out there.)

Overall, I think it's useful to know how to do native mobile development, but I don't think it's the best solution for delivering an app to multiple platforms.

CROSS-PLATFORM FRAMEWORKS AND TOOLS

The next option is to choose to use a framework or tool (https://simpleprogrammer.com /cg23-cross) that is designed to allow you to build cross-platform mobile applications.

There are many of these solutions to choose from depending on what you are looking for.

Some of these solutions actually produce native code and wrap the real native libraries, so they are just an abstraction over the native language and tools, but still require you to know and use the native libraries and frameworks.

Other solutions will build a hybrid application that has some native components and some web-based or HTML components and relies on the built-in mobile browser for creating most of the user interface and functionality of the application.

There is an ever-growing list of options to choose from, so choosing can be difficult.

The main considerations to think about when choosing a cross-platform framework solution are:

* What programming language you should use.
* Whether you want to take a native or hybrid approach.
* How many platforms you want your code to support.
* Whether you can reuse code or not.

PROGRAMMING LANGUAGE

What programming language do you want to use to code the application you are building?

Most cross-platform solutions support a single programming language.

You might not want to incur the learning curve of a new framework, mobile development and new programming language all at the same time, so you might want to pick a cross-platform solution which supports a language you already know.

NATIVE OR HYBRID

There are several cross-platform solutions which compile the final code down to the native format for the mobile operating system and hook directly into the native libraries and APIs.

My favorite one is Xamarin (https://simpleprogrammer.com/cg23-xamarin), which allows you to write your app in C# but still get all the benefits and features of a full, natively-built application.

There are many other options to choose from.

Other cross-platform solutions, like Cordova for example (https://simpleprogrammer.com /cg23-cordova), take a hybrid approach where the application is not a native application, but it looks like one.

Typically, native is going to be faster and look more like the mobile platform the app is running on, but some of the cross-platform hybrid solutions are getting so close to native that it can be difficult to tell the difference.

PLATFORM SUPPORT

Another major consideration is platform support.

Just about all cross-platform solutions support iOS and Android, but some cross-platform solutions also support desktop operating systems like Mac macOS or Windows, and others support the smaller phone OSes or even Raspberry Pi.

If you need to support Blackberry because that is what your customers are using, you will be constrained to cross-platform solutions which support it.

However, if you don't have specific needs for platforms other than iOS and Android, I wouldn't worry about cross-platform support beyond the two big dogs.

Games are a different consideration.

If you are doing game development, you might want to pick a tool which supports the widest number of platforms possible.

Tools like Unity 3D allow you to create games that can be run on just about every platform you can think of—even the web.

CODE REUSE

Finally, you should consider code reuse.

Just because a framework is cross-platform doesn't mean you'll be able to write all your code for the application once and have it run on all the supported platforms.

Typically cross-platform solutions which offer native support will have less code reuse because they will be tied more closely in with the native frameworks, libraries, and user interface elements and paradigms.

Therefore, you might have to choose between being more native and having the look, feel and design of the mobile OS platform you are running on, or sharing more code.

Recently, though, cross-platform solutions like Xamarin have come out with solutions which allow you to get some of the benefits of both.

For example, Xamarin uses a common UI library called Xamarin Forms (https://simpleprogrammer.com/cg23-xamarin) which allows you to have a much larger percentage of code reuse between platforms by creating another abstraction layer on top of the native UI and frameworks of the underlying operating systems.

Ultimately, code reuse depends on what kind of application you are building and how much you want the application to blend in with completely natively-built applications on the platform you are targeting.

MOBILE WEB APPS

The final option is to build a mobile application that is completely web-based.

Over the years, this option has become more and more feasible as the power and capabilities of mobile browsers have increased and adaptive web technologies have improved.

With this option, you build a web application, just like any other web application you would build on the web, but specifically design it to work on mobile devices.

Many mobile OS browsers even have hooks to support invoking native functionality from inside the web browser, so you can do things like get location data and access things like the camera on the device.

There are even quite a few frameworks out there to help you create mobile web applications which look like native applications when run on a particular mobile OS.

Honestly, **the future is mobile web apps**—we just aren't there quite yet.

MOBILE DEVELOPMENT CONSIDERATIONS

I personally think mobile development is an excellent choice for getting started in software development because it has a **low barrier to entry** and is an area of software development that will **continue to grow over the years.**

Just about anyone can become a mobile developer and even publish their own mobile applications—and perhaps also make some cash.

Plus, mobile applications are by nature limited in scope, **so a team of just one developer can produce a significant application in a relatively short period of time** which can act as a great portfolio of work to help land future jobs or contracts.

I often encourage beginner developers who are having a difficult time breaking into the industry to consider building a few mobile applications and getting them deployed on one of the mobile app stores.

Doing so can help you have the kind of prerequisite proof that you can actually write code and produce a complete working application.

Also, as I mentioned before, mobile development is likely to only continue to grow over the years, so the future prospects for mobile developers seem really good.

CHAPTER 24

BACK-END DEVELOPMENT

Software applications are like icebergs.

There is a portion of the application the user sees and then—in most cases—the largest part of the application remains unseen. This is the elusive and mystical "back-end."

In the chapter on web development, we mostly talked about web development as it relates to direct interaction with the end user—what we might call "front-end web development."

In most significant applications, the majority of the code is non-user interface code.

Complex systems have all kinds of logic that happen in the background that make them work.

Data needs to be stored and retrieved, business logic and rules need to be followed, and results need to be calculated.

All of this happens behind the scenes.

The back-end developer is the kind of developer who makes all this happen.

WHAT EXACTLY IS "BACK-END DEVELOPMENT?"

For the purpose of this chapter, I'm going to consider back-end development to be **any kind of development that doesn't involve writing code that produces a user interface.**

This could encompass back-end web development, but it might also involve writing APIs (https://simpleprogrammer.com/cg24-api), creating libraries, working with components of systems that don't have user interfaces or even some scientific programming endeavors.

In reality, even though front-end development gets most of the glory, **most of the code that exists in the world—arguably the most useful of it—is back-end code** that is never seen by the end user.

Simply put, back-end development is writing code that is not directly seen.

WHAT DO BACK-END DEVELOPERS DO?

What back-end developers do can vary greatly, depending on the size and scope of the application they are working on.

I've held many jobs where I was a back-end developer, working on the business logic in an application, and feeding data to and retrieving data from the front-end.

In the web development world, most back-end developers concern themselves with building the actual logic behind the application they are working on.

Often, front-end developers will build out a user interface, and back-end developers will write code that makes it all work.

For example, a front-end developer might create a screen in an application with a clickable button to get the customer's data.

A back-end developer might write the code that makes that button work by figuring out what data to fetch from the database for the appropriate customer and delivering it back to the front-end, where it is eventually displayed.

A back-end developer might also be heavily involved in the architecture of a system, deciding how to organize the logic of the system so that it can run properly and be easily maintained.

He might be involved in building frameworks or with the architecture of a system to make it easier to program against.

Back-end developers tend to spend much more time implementing algorithms and solving problems (https://simpleprogrammer.com/cg24-problems) **than front-end developers do.**

I've always liked back-end development work because it feels like more of a challenge.

That's not to say that front-end developers don't ever solve difficult problems, but often front-end development work is more about creating user interfaces and hooking them up rather than implementing the actual business logic that makes the app work.

PRIMARY TECHNOLOGIES AND SKILLS IN BACK-END DEVELOPMENT

While front-end developers need to know a set of tools used to create user interfaces, back-end developers usually have a completely different set of tools and skills that are required to do their jobs effectively.

One important skill back-end developers need is related to SQL and databases.

Most back-end systems are connected to some kind of database which stores the data for the application.

It is usually the job of the back-end developer to write, read, and process data from a database or other data source, so having skills like SQL can be extremely important.

Back-end developers—at least for web development—also need to be good with server-side languages for the technology stack they are using.

For example, while a front-end web developer might be focused on HTML, CSS, and JavaScript, a back-end developer might need to know more about PHP web frameworks, Ruby on Rails, ASP.NET MVC, or whatever server-side web development framework is being used to build the application.

Finally, I'd say that a **back-end developer needs to know much more about application architecture** since, for the most part, it is the back-end developer who is going to be building out the architecture and internal design of the application.

A good back-end developer will know how to utilize various frameworks and libraries, how to integrate them into an application, and how to structure the code and business logic in a way that makes the system easier to maintain.

If you like designing the infrastructure of an application, implementing algorithms and logic, and working with data, you'll probably enjoy working as a back-end developer.

WHAT ABOUT FULL-STACK DEVELOPERS?

I thought about dedicating an entire chapter to full-stack developers, but since we've already covered web development and back-end development, it's easy enough to talk about full-stack development here. Full-stack development just involves a developer who does both front-end and back-end development.

Really, full-stack development includes working on all of the components and layers of a system, or software development stack. It may even involve knowing about server hardware and architecture, or what would be considered "dev ops."

Today, more and more software development positions are looking for developers capable of doing full-stack development since it's valuable for a software developer to be able to work with the entire technology stack involved, rather than have one developer who works on the front-end while another developer works exclusively on the back-end.

Some of the reason for this is because more and more applications are blurring the lines between front-end and back-end development.

Many popular JavaScript frameworks, like Angular (https://simpleprogrammer.com /cg24-angular), allow you to create a large portion of what could be considered the business logic right in the user interface portion of the system.

Also, with more and more teams adopting Agile methodologies, **individual programmers are being asked to work on more than just their area of specialty, as tasks are being assigned to a team more so than an individual.**

While I think it's useful to be capable of being a full-stack developer—and you should definitely have enough knowledge to understand what is happening at every level of the software—I don't think it's the best idea to "specialize" in being a full-stack developer, because it isn't a specialization at all.

Basically, you should aim to get a broad knowledge of the most common technology stack you will be working with, but you should pick a primary specialty or two where you'll really get an in-depth knowledge.

All software developers should know how to create a user interface, the basics of the framework they are using, how to store and retrieve data from a database from within the application, and even how the infrastructure works to support the software, but they shouldn't try to be experts in all of those areas, because all of those areas are rather large and growing.

It's far better to have a general, working knowledge of everything in the technology stack and a specialized knowledge in a few areas.

Then, you can still call yourself "full-stack," but practically, you'll be much more useful to a team.

SUMMING IT UP

So, as you can see, there's not all that much to say about back-end development.

Not because back-end development is simplistic and doesn't require much development expertise and knowledge, but rather because the concept is so simple.

Back-end developers write code on the back-end—the code that works behind the scenes.

If you think about it, a majority of all code written is really back-end code.

I can guarantee you that there is more code working in the background, making everything happen than there is code that creates user interfaces.

So, even though front-end development seems to get all the credit and fame, the back-end developers are the real workhorses of the industry.

CHAPTER 25

CAREER IN VIDEO GAME DEVELOPMENT

Ever since I first touched a computer, I was absolutely in love with the idea of someday becoming a video game developer.

As a kid—and partially as an adult—I spent a large amount of time playing video games.

It's funny to say, but some of my fondest childhood memories and nostalgia involve video games, especially the NES and Super NES. And I can't forget all those awesome Sierra games like Space Quest and King's Quest.

Ah, those were the days.

I can pretty much say that the aspiration of being a video game developer was the main motivating force—at least early on—in my becoming a programmer at all.

There is a decent chance that either you, too, wanted to become a programmer because you wanted to make your own video games or that as a programmer now, you have at least some interest in the field of video game development.

If not, feel free to skip this chapter, but if you are interested in the wide world of video game development and are curious if it might be right for you, read on.

I've gotten so many requests for information about this topic (https://simpleprogrammer.com/cg25-viable) that, even though video game development isn't necessarily something you need to know about as a software developer, I decided to include it anyway.

A WARNING

I think that no discussion which seriously entertains the idea of someone becoming a professional game developer is responsible if it doesn't first start out with **a warning about why you should not become a video game developer.** So let me try to dissuade you from the crazy notion altogether.

Video game development is not for the faint of heart. It's an extremely difficult and demanding line of work, and the rewards are not nearly as great as you might think.

I have to admit that my experience on the topic is somewhat limited since **I've never been a professional video game developer** myself, but I have created my own games, taught courses on video game development, and know plenty of professional game developers, so I at least have some idea of what I am talking about.

First of all, you should realize that video game development is extremely competitive.

Think about it. Who doesn't want to become a video game developer?

If you are going to program something, why not video games?

I would guess that at least 70 percent of professional programmers have fantasized about becoming video game developers at some point in their lives—hell, I'm fantasizing about it right now.

So, **you should be prepared to face a huge amount of competition** for every single job that you apply for if you decide to embark on this road.

Not only is the competition stiff, but the hours are extremely long, especially for Triple-A studios.

Creating and releasing video games takes a huge amount of work, and a ridiculous amount of money could be invested in a single title.

As a result, **video game developers are often expected to work extremely long hours.**

I would be prepared to work no less than 60 hours a week, if you seriously want to entertain this career choice.

Finally, the pay is fairly low for the most part—definitely not what most people expect.

True, independent video game developers with a very successful title can make a fortune, and even experienced video game developers working for a studio can do fairly well if they have some successful titles under their belt, but those are the outliers.

When you further consider the insane amount of hours typically worked, the pay doesn't seem quite that high compared to a regular job.

If you really want to make money as a software developer, go work on Wall Street.

If you absolutely love video games and can't see yourself doing anything else— and you don't care about the cost or the money—perhaps… perhaps, video game development might be for you.

DEGREE OPTIONS

Even though I said that you can become a software developer without a degree—and I definitely believe you can—for video game development, **I would recommend getting a degree or at least going through some kind of vocational training program.**

Why?

Because video game development is difficult. Really difficult. There is a large amount to learn and so much of it is art.

You can easily get in way over your head, where you don't even know what you don't know or what is important.

You can certainly teach yourself video game development (https://simpleprogrammer.com /cg25-essentials) (I did), but are you going to teach yourself how to make video game graphics, how to design a story and level, 3D modeling, how to use the latest graphics engine, and all the other countless areas of specialty that are required to build one of the complex video games of today?

It's not that you can't learn all that stuff. It's more that to be a video game developer, you need to know the basics of all those things and more, and it can be quite useful to have a prescribed path to follow and to have some guidance along the way.

If you are creating small, one-developer games which you are going to release independently, you might be able to skip all that, but **if you want to get a job with a major game development studio, you are going to want to have a more complete education.**

Even now, I'm tempted to go to school to learn video game development. I think it would be a lot of fun.

Fortunately, there are actually quite a number of schools which actually specialize in video game development.

For the longest time, I wanted to go to Digipen University and Full Sail University because those were the two major schools that actually taught video game development.

Today, however, there is quite a large list of schools which either offer video game development programs or specialize in video game development completely.

Rather than list all of them here, you can check out an updated list on gamecareerguide.com (https://simpleprogrammer.com/cg25-schools).

SKILLS REQUIRED

Now that I've talked you out of video game development by telling you how hard it is, how crappy the pay is, and that you'll need to go to school for four years at an expensive game development university, it's time to really give you a kick in the nuts by telling you that you'll need to master C++ (https://simpleprogrammer.com/cg25-technologies).

Ha, I'm just kidding—sort of.

The truth is there are quite a few skills that you will need to become a video game programmer, skills that other types of programmers can get away without.

Let's start with C/C++.

I was only partially kidding when I said you needed to become a master of C++ (https://simpleprogrammer.com/cg25-master).

It is certainly possible to develop games without knowing C++. Plenty of games are written in all kinds of programming languages.

However, **many of the larger game studios, the ones who release massively processing-intensive games, still rely on C++** as one of the main languages of game development.

This could change in the future, or even by the time you are reading this book, but I doubt it.

Why do I doubt it?

Because video games are always cutting edge, pushing whatever the current hardware is to the extremes.

That means that even if C++ stops being used, some other, close-to-the-metal language is going to take its place in order to get the maximum performance on the hardware the game is running on. (Perhaps quantum computers will solve this problem.)

Another really important skill for video game developers is **experience with a video game engine.**

Right now, at the time of writing this book, Unity 3D is one of the most popular video game engines out there, so it's not a bad idea to develop some skills with this game engine.

There is also the slightly more complex Unreal Engine, and a few others that you might want to be familiar with.

Most complex games today use some kind of game engine rather than writing their own, so having a skill set and experience in at least one game engine is pretty critical.

Finally, I'll say that **math is also an extremely important skill** (https://simpleprogrammer.com /cg25-math) **as a game developer.**

Most programmers can get away with a rudimentary amount of math, honestly.

But video game developers have to understand how to do matrix transformations and all kinds of other complex calculations—especially if you are working with 3D games.

Yes, the game engines can handle some of this for you, but you still need to know what is going on.

There are, of course, a whole list of other skills you'll need as a game developer, but I wanted to point out what I think are the three most important ones that other types of programmers would be much less likely to concern themselves with.

WORKING FOR A BIG GAME STUDIO

There are two major career paths for video game developers: you can work for a big studio or you can be independent.

Working for a big studio is what I've really focused on in this chapter since most video game developers who actually want to make a living will be going down this road at least at some point in their careers.

This option is going to make sense for most video game developers because it is going to guarantee them a paycheck, and they are going to be able to be a video game programmer and focus on the programming aspect of video game development rather than having to know how to do all the other things related to releasing a video game.

That doesn't mean this is the best choice.

Certainly, there are going to be major drawbacks.

You might not be able to work on the cool parts of the game you'd like to work on.

You might instead have to work on one simple aspect of the game that seems pretty boring to you.

For example, you might be assigned the task of coding the collision detection algorithm to determine when a sword makes contact with an enemy, which might just involve a bunch of complicated vector math.

You might work really long hours and find that video game development doesn't feel like playing and creating video games, but just like work.

You do, though, have the opportunity to be part of something very large.

By working for a studio, you can work on a massive game that you could never develop completely on your own.

You also might get a chance to work with some really cool and experienced video game programmers who you can learn from.

BEING AN INDEPENDENT

If you don't work for a large video game studio, your other choice is to either be independent or work for a small independent game company.

This choice sounds like a large amount of fun—and I bet it is—but it also carries a huge amount of risk.

Video game development is difficult and extremely competitive.

It's very difficult to create a best-selling video game or even to create a profitable video game at all.

A huge amount of time and money can go into creating a game which may not even be released, or if it is, flops completely.

I've looked at income reports from independent game developers who I thought were pretty successful, and to say they were disappointing is a huge understatement.

Yes, there are exceptions. Maybe you'll create the next Minecraft, but don't count on it.

Instead, I would suggest pursuing independent game development only if you have to call all the shots to make your game, and you are willing to make whatever sacrifices you have to have that freedom.

Honestly, if I were to actually pursue game development professionally, this is the route I'd choose.

I like the idea of having complete creative control over a game.

I like the idea of learning how to create the graphics for my game or directly working with an artist to do so.

I like the idea of designing the levels and gameplay myself, not just programming it.

And you might, too, but you will have to weigh the costs and see if it's worth it to you.

HEY JOHN

What about virtual reality?

I'm actually all-in on virtual reality.

I got an Oculus Rift pretty recently and I was amazed to find how far virtual reality has come along since I had first encountered it with the Virtual Boy, way back when.

Surprisingly, it's also one of those emerging areas of game development where a single game developer or small team still has a chance to make a big splash since there still seems to be a bit of a gold rush and much of the work needed to make a 3D game a VR game is actually pretty easy.

I've had the chance to talk to a few VR game developers and they basically use the same tools that you would use for a normal 3D game, like Unity 3D, but it is rendered as VR.

The key is creating a good VR gameplay experience and utilizing the unique control options for VR games.

I would say that VR is definitely an area that is worth looking into, especially because the skills needed to create VR games are going to carry over to many non-game, commercial applications as well.

I can see all kinds of learning platforms and training simulations taking place in the world of VR.

RESOURCES AND SUGGESTIONS

I thought I'd end this chapter by giving you a few suggestions and resources you can utilize if you are interested in learning more about game development.

Now, I haven't been a professional game developer myself, so **take my suggestions here with a grain of salt**, but I have learned how to program games and have taught some courses on it. All of my game development experience is self-taught.

With that said, **I'd highly suggest that if you are pursuing game development that you start by creating a large number of games.**

Start with some really simple games and then try to create more complex games.

Instead of inventing your own original games, try to make copies of existing games that are progressively more and more difficult.

For example, the first game I made when I was teaching myself game development was Pong.

Then, I tried creating a simple space shooter game.

Not only is this a great way to develop your game programming skills and learn about making games without having to come up with brilliant ideas and get stuck in the design of games, but it will also **help you create a portfolio of games you can show if you apply for a game development job.**

So many programmers I talk to really want to be game developers but don't know where to get started. My answer is always, "Start making games."

As for resources, one of the best ones I know of is a site called Gamasutra (https://simpleprogrammer.com/cg25-gamasutra).

This site is probably the best on the internet for finding information about game development, game development news, and for hearing real stories from game developers.

Gamasutra also has some sister sites in their network with more focused topics and an excellent collection of resources.

If you are interested in checking out my courses on game development, you can check out these Pluralsight courses I created:

- Beginning HTML 5 Game Development With Quintus (https://simpleprogrammer.com/cg25-quintus)
- Building Your First Game For Android And The PC Using Java (https://simpleprogrammer.com/cg25-androidpc)
- Introduction to 2D Game Programming with XNA (https://simpleprogrammer.com/cg25-xna)
- Cross Platform Game Development with MonoGame (https://simpleprogrammer.com/cg25-mono)

Good luck and have fun. Perhaps I'll join you someday.

CHAPTER 26

DBAS AND DEVOPS

Producing working software involves much more than just writing code.

Most substantial software applications require some kind of data storage, and they have to be built, tested, and deployed somewhere.

And you know what?

We need people who know how to handle that kind of stuff and to do it.

This is where the roles of DBAs (database administrators) and DevOps come in.

You might be wondering why you need to know about all that—can't you just write the code?

Well, yes, sometimes you can just write the code, but more and more teams are becoming cross-disciplinary, and software developers are being required to take on—or at least contribute to and work with—a variety of different roles.

Software development, especially in Agile environments (https://simpleprogrammer.com /cg26-agile), is more of a team effort (https://simpleprogrammer.com/cg26-team), and we've added a whole bunch of best processes and "ways things should be done" as we've learned over the years how to deliver better and better software. (Or at least we think we have.)

Anyway, as a software developer, you may be asked to wear several different hats, especially if you work for a startup or small company where there isn't a dedicated DBA or operations team.

It's not unlikely that someday you'll be asked to install a database or set one up to work with an application.

Likewise, you may be asked to help determine the process of taking the working application code, getting it built and tested, and deploying it to a production server.

Or, you may also be asked to work with one of these strange creatures who call themselves DBAs or DevOps... dudes?

Anyway, regardless of the reason, you should probably learn something about your technological brethren.

Oh—and we'll get to Quality Assurance later; that deserves a whole chapter by itself.

DBAS

First, let's start with DBAs.

What exactly is a DBA, or database administrator?

Well, the role can vary from organization to organization, but **generally it involves hurting developers' feelings by telling them their code sucks** and is utilizing too many database connections and telling them "no" a lot when they ask if they can do various things involving the database.

For the most part, though, the DBA is responsible for setting up, maintaining, securing, optimizing, and monitoring the databases, and perhaps even setting up database schemas or writing stored procedures.

Some DBAs tend to be very operational in nature and don't do much in terms of actually creating database tables and writing any kind of database code.

Other DBAs are more like database programmers in addition to the operational work they do on the databases.

DATABASES NEED CARE AND FEEDING

Not every development team is going to have a DBA.

In fact, **many organizations are going to have developers—that's you—doing many of the DBA duties**, so it is useful to know your way around a database and some of the basics of installing and maintaining one.

For many software applications, the database is an important piece of the business, so whether the role of maintenance and administration falls directly into the hands of a DBA or is distributed amongst developers, it's quite important that someone does the work.

Databases grow over time and can be pretty big resource hogs, so it's critical to pick the right hardware to run a database on and to determine when it's time to upgrade.

Databases also contain some pretty important data, so care has to be taken to back them up regularly, and someone needs to put together a disaster plan to restore a database or keep things running if one happens to fail.

And let's not forget performance. Over time, databases which are not well designed or tuned can get slow and inefficient, so special care has to be taken to profile the database and determine how the data should be arranged or indexed to make things faster.

I could go on and on, but I think you get the point. **Databases don't just raise themselves.**

DO I NEED TO BE A DBA?

No, but I'd highly recommend you invest some time in learning how to:

- Install and set up a database.
- Create and restore backups.
- Create tables and schemas.
- Create stored procedures.
- Index tables and how indexes work.
- Write some basic SQL code to perform basic operations like queries, inserts, updates, etc.
- Join tables.

Like I said, you don't have to be an expert in all this stuff, but knowing the basics will be extremely helpful in your job as a software developer, whether you have to do some of this stuff yourself or you have to work with a DBA.

HEY JOHN

Wait, what? I don't know what a schema is. Stored procedure? Join tables?

It's ok. Calm down.

That's all database stuff.

It's not important that you know all this stuff right now, like I said. But I can see that you are curious, so even though this section of the book is about what you need to know—not about teaching it to you—I'll go into a bit more detail.

Schema – think of it as a blueprint for the database. The schema defines what tables the database is divided into and what the format of that stored data is.

It also defines just about everything else about a database.

Think of it this way; with a schema for a database, you should be able to construct a complete empty copy of a database.

Stored procedures – think of stored procedures like functions or methods for databases or even… wait for it… procedures, because that's essentially all they are.

Just a bunch of SQL code that usually lives directly on the database that can be called to do something.

A logical way of organizing some common operations you might want to do on your database.

Just like how you organize code in your applications.

And joining tables. Well, that's just like it sounds. It's just combining tables in the database in some way to get either a cross-section, union or some other combination of data from one or more tables.

It's a pretty common database operation.

Here's an example: suppose you had a table called "customers" which stored all the customer data in your database, and you had another table called "orders" which stored all the order data.

Suppose you wanted to get all the orders for a particular customer.

You could join the customer and order table together and pull the customer's data along with all of that customer's orders by doing a query that joined the customer and orders tables together.

Obviously there's much more to databases, and it's definitely worth learning about them, but perhaps that gives you a little bit of a better idea of what I'm talking about.

DEVOPS: A NEW ROLE

It's not too often that completely new roles are invented in the IT field, so the role of DevOps is both unique and a little, shall we say, loosely defined.

What exactly is DevOps?

Well, **it's a conglomeration or a mashup, if you will, of development and operations.**

In my mind, I think MacGyver (https://simpleprogrammer.com/cg26-macgyver).

If you ask different people, you'll get many answers, but for the most part they'll agree that DevOps is all about doing whatever needs to be done to get the code built, tested, deployed, and running in production.

But to really understand and appreciate DevOps (https://simpleprogrammer.com /cg26-Phoenix), you have to understand...

OPERATIONS: HOW WE USED TO DO IT

You see, before there was DevOps, there used to be just developers and operations (sometimes called IT).

Developers wrote the code, then they threw it over the wall to QA.

QA would say it sucked and throw it back.

The code would go back and forth a few times before one party or both finally gave up, and then they'd collectively throw the code over another wall to the operations team.

The operations team would complain about how inefficient the code was, how it was going to break the server, and how developers don't have any clue about security, then throw it back.

The developers would curse at the operations guys who are just trying to give them a hard time, make a few minor changes, and throw it back.

Finally, the operations team would take the code, deploy it to the server, everything would break, and everyone would blame everyone else.

Ok, perhaps I'm being a little dramatic here, but the point is that **we used to have very disconnected teams in the world of software development.**

In the past—and for some organizations still today—it used to be that developers would write the code, and operations would take that code and deploy it without either team knowing much about what the other team did.

This did create a large number of problems, but the problems were bearable until Agile software development came around.

Now teams are shipping new code once, twice, sometimes three times a week instead of every six months or so.

Development teams are building the code multiple times a day and running automated tests and quality checks against the code.

Things are no longer as simple as writing the code, building the code and deploying the code.

Instead, a whole set of operations and procedures emerged as a way to be as agile as possible and to be able to move code quickly from development to production.

WHAT IS DEVOPS?

Ok, so now that you know the backstory, what exactly is DevOps?

It's the multidisciplinary process of getting code from development to production and taking care of the code when it's there.

Instead of having two or three separate roles that don't know much about each other and are arguably hostile and antagonistic at times, **DevOps is about taking full ownership at every step along the way.**

In some organizations, there are specific DevOps roles where you might have a programmer who understands how to build and deploy the code involved in creating a build and deployment system to automate the process as much as possible.

In other organizations, the developer, tester, and operations roles are still separate, but they all work together to fill the role of DevOps through mutual understanding, cooperation, and collective ownership.

The important thing about DevOps is that it is a fundamental shift in thinking about how software should be delivered to production.

WHAT THIS MEANS TO YOU

Well, technically, **as a software developer, you are part of DevOps.**

Welcome. Congratulations. Here are your official DevOps wings.

Today, software developers are expected to know about more than just writing code.

You can't get away with throwing your code over the wall and letting it become someone else's problem, especially if you are working in a small company or startup.

You need to understand the process and tools that are used to move code from development to production—and ideally how to setup and use some of those tools.

Obviously, you should know how to use an IDE and build your own code locally; no one is going to do that for you.

However, you should also **know how to use source control** to check in and integrate your code with the other code in the system.

You should know the basics of continuous integration and how a build server works. (Don't worry, we'll cover most of this stuff in the upcoming chapters.)

You should know the **fundamentals and types of testing and how automated testing of various sorts fits into the bigger picture** of building and deploying the code.

You should know **how an application gets packed up** and ready for distribution or deployment.

You should **understand the deployment process and how to automate moving code from a build server to a staging server or production server** and **how configuration is managed** on various servers.

Finally, **you should know something about monitoring** an existing application to check for performance problems and other issues.

Yes, I realize this is a large amount of stuff to know, but you don't need to have in-depth knowledge about all these things—and you don't have to learn them all at once.

It's more important that you know what these tools and processes are and how they are used, so that if you needed to implement parts of this tool chain yourself, or assist in implementing them, you could.

Think of it this way.

Suppose you are a pitcher on a baseball team.

You don't need to know everything about every position on the team, but it's going to be difficult to talk about any kind of meaningful strategy if you aren't at least aware of the other positions and what they do.

You don't want to join a software development team and be completely oblivious to what happens after you check in your code.

And many software development teams don't want to hire developers who are.

Like I said, though, don't worry. I'm going to give you a basic overview of some of these topics in the upcoming chapters.

CHAPTER 27

SOFTWARE DEVELOPMENT METHODOLOGIES

Are you ready to put on your boxing gloves and enter the ring?

Are you ready to be confused?

Are you ready to endlessly debate semantics? To hire expensive consultants to tell you what you are doing wrong and coach your team to higher levels by getting everyone "certified?"

Well, **welcome to the world of software development methodologies.**

We don't have cake, but you are welcome to have a donut at our daily stand-up meetings.

Perhaps nothing causes more arguments in the software development community than the selection of software development methodologies and their intended implementation.

Software development methodologies define the processes we use to build software.

Some methodologies are fairly lightweight and don't tell you much besides a set of principles to stand by.

Other methodologies—like Extreme Programming—are extremely prescriptive and tell you exactly how you should build your software and run your entire team.

In this chapter, we are going to start from the past and look at the old model of development: the waterfall process, which is actually still in use in many organizations today.

Then, we'll jump right into the biggest fad in software development today: the quasi-defined, everyone-is-doing-it-but-no-one-is-doing-it-right methodology known as Agile development.

Finally, I'll introduce you to the basics of what I consider **the 3 main implementations of Agile** development which are being used today.

I have to warn you, I'm not going to attempt to cover every existing software development methodology that has ever existed.

Instead, I'm going to use my author's privilege again and tell you what I think you need to know.

TRADITIONAL WATERFALL

When I was first learning about software development, the traditional waterfall process was a given.

That's just how software was built.

We didn't call it waterfall.

We didn't make fun of it.

We just accepted it as the way to develop software and we did it—well, as best as we could.

(Note: this doesn't mean there weren't other software development methodologies out there. There were plenty of them; it's just that they weren't widely known or used, and many of them were only more formal ways of doing the waterfall methodology.)

Waterfall development is much like it sounds. It's building software one step at a time, with each step falling down into the next lower step until everything is downstream.

Built into the waterfall development methodology is the Software Development Life Cycle (SDLC).

This same SDLC shows up in just about every methodology.

In waterfall development, the SDLC is sequential.

In fact, you could say that **waterfall development is just following the SDLC step-by-step**, nothing more.

ARE YOU DOWN WITH SDLC?

Yeah, you know me.

I'm down with SDLC.

What is it?

It's a sequence of developing software that goes from requirements analysis, to software design, to implementation, testing, deployment, and then finally maintenance.

You progress through each phase and you only move forward, never back.

There is some overlap between phases.

Let's briefly talk about each phase so that you can be down with SDLC.

REQUIREMENTS ANALYSIS

In this phase, you gather all the requirements for the software.

What should it do? What features should it have?

What should it look like?

How should it behave?

You might gather this information by talking to customers or stakeholders, or by just making it up yourself, but you need to know what you are going to build before you build it. (Although as you enter the world of software development, if you haven't already, you'll quickly discover this is not the case in reality.)

SOFTWARE DESIGN

Now that you know the requirements of the software you are trying to build, it's time to figure out how you are going to build it.

At this phase, you take those requirements and turn them into architectural design for the system, low-level algorithms, and UML diagrams (if you like), and generally decide how the system is going to be built and work together.

The level of detail for software design is up for debate, but some level of design is always necessary.

In traditional waterfall approaches, you typically have what is known as big upfront design, which means that most of the details are planned out at a very low level during this phase.

If you are going to always go forward and never backwards and you have a fixed schedule, designing everything upfront seems to make sense, but in practical reality, requirements change, and there are so many unforeseen circumstances that this rarely works out.

IMPLEMENTATION

Ok, now it's actually time to code.

This phase of software development is supposed to be all about writing that code.

Here you turn the design from the last phase into actual working code.

I really don't think much more needs to be said about that here, so… moving on…

TESTING

Ah, so you have a beautiful piece of code that is elegantly designed, perfectly implemented, and shines like a thousand suns.

Then, some greasy-haired tester comes along and ruins it all by showing you how you deviated from the requirements and that none of your code actually works.

This is the testing phase.

The testers have been creating their test plans, writing their test cases, and preparing for this moment from the second they first saw you laughing gleefully in your cubicle as you enjoyed yourself, writing your code—no one should be that happy.

Now the testers run their tests, find the bugs, and after some debate and much shenanigans, you fix as many of them as possible until everyone agrees it's time to move on.

DEPLOYMENT

Now it's time to see if this baby actually works.

If you have multiple components that were developed separately, you strap them together and you could call that phase "integration," but either way you've got to deploy that code. Put it out there in the wild.

This might mean deploying the code to a server and then nervously flipping the switch, saying, "We're live."

This might mean making the gold standard CD that you'll ship out to all your customers.

Today, it might mean uploading your app to the app store.

Either way, you are now putting the software—and all your hopes and dreams—into the customer's hands.

Good luck.

I hope you really did fix those bugs...

MAINTENANCE

Oh, you thought you were done when you put that software out into production and shipped it to your customers?

Moved on to the next big thing already?

Not so fast. Most projects end up in the maintenance phase longer than any other phase.

Once software is out there in the wild, you still have to support it.

Now you'll be fixing bugs that customers find, adding new features, and keeping everything running smoothly.

This phase lasts as long as the software is still being used and supported.

And that's all there really is to the SDLC: get the requirements, design the software, build it, test it, deploy it and maintain it until the company goes out of business or some young whippersnapper gets the idea of beginning all over again and rewriting it.

AGILE

Agile really is the big game changer when it comes to software development.

Before Agile came along, most development projects were using some kind of waterfall development process, whether they acknowledged it or not.

What I mean by this is that they were sequentially building their software, going from one phase of the SDLC to another.

While some development projects were using some iterative approaches before the Agile movement took effect, and were breaking the SDLC into smaller cycles, that idea wasn't formalized until Agile.

So what exactly is Agile?

Well, even years after its introduction, we still don't really know.

Agile is a bit amorphous. You have to understand the history to understand why.

THE AGILE MANIFESTO

It all started at The Lodge at Snowbird Ski Resort in Utah.

Basically a bunch of authors from different development methodologies met together with industry leaders to try and find some common ground for how software development should be done in the industry.

The original group had 17 members, who discussed some of the problems affecting software development at the time, and together they formed what is known as **the Agile Manifesto**, which you can read below:

> *We are uncovering better ways of developing*
> *software by doing it and helping others do it.*
> *Through this work we have come to value:*
>
> *Individuals and interactions over processes and tools*
> *Working software over comprehensive documentation*

Customer collaboration over contract negotiation
Responding to change over following a plan

That is, while there is value in the items on
the right, we value the items on the left more.

It is based on **12 principles**, defined below:

Our highest priority is to satisfy the customer
through early and continuous delivery
of valuable software.

Welcome changing requirements, even late in
development. Agile processes harness change for
the customer's competitive advantage.

Deliver working software frequently, from a
couple of weeks to a couple of months, with a
preference to the shorter timescale.

Business people and developers must work
together daily throughout the project.

Build projects around motivated individuals.
Give them the environment and support they need,
and trust them to get the job done.

The most efficient and effective method of
conveying information to and within a development
team is face-to-face conversation.

Working software is the primary measure of progress.

Agile processes promote sustainable development.
The sponsors, developers, and users should be able
to maintain a constant pace indefinitely.

Continuous attention to technical excellence
and good design enhances agility.

*Simplicity—the art of maximizing the amount
of work not done—is essential.*

*The best architectures, requirements, and designs
emerge from self-organizing teams.*

*At regular intervals, the team reflects on how
to become more effective, then tunes and adjusts
its behavior accordingly.*

I think the principles better indicate what Agile is really about, rather than the manifesto itself.

AGILE ISN'T REALLY A METHODOLOGY

So as you can see, **Agile isn't really a methodology itself**, but rather it defines at a very high level how software development should be done, and is a sort of parent to other methodologies that are considered Agile in nature.

Agile ignited the idea that software should be developed and delivered incrementally and embraced the idea that requirements can and should change during the development of the software.

It also redefined some of the relationships between various members of software development teams by valuing face-to-face communication and self-organizing teams over heavy documentation and strict protocols.

Like I said, some development organizations were already doing some of these things and following methodologies which embraced one or more aspects of the Agile principles, but for the most part, the world at large was still mostly developing software with the traditional waterfall approach.

PROBLEMS WITH THE WATERFALL APPROACH

Before we dive into a few of the current popular Agile methodologies, let's take a brief moment to talk about why the waterfall approach sounds good on paper, but doesn't seem to work very well in reality (https://simpleprogrammer.com/cg27-waterfall).

One of the biggest issues with waterfall development is that requirements change—or rather, they are not known until later in the project.

If you try and take a step-by-step approach to developing software and attempt to get all the requirements upfront, it's not going to bode well for you if suddenly those requirements change or new ones are discovered.

If you've already fully designed the architecture of the system and you have to change some-thing, but you are in the process of implementing it, you either have to scrap a bunch of what you already did and go backwards, or you have to put your foot down and say no.

So, either the project slips or you build the wrong thing and piss off the customer.

As a software developer, it would be nice if nothing changed.

It would be nice if we could go and gather all the requirements, designs, or solutions and then implement them.

But life doesn't work out that way.

Really, Agile is about acknowledging that fact, accepting it, and building software develop-ment processes that work with that constraint, not against it.

That's Agile.

SCRUM

Now let's talk about some of the popular Agile development methodologies out there.

I'm not going to cover all of them—and to be honest with you, most teams that claim to be following one of these methodologies aren't really following them (https://simpleprogrammer.com/cg27-scrum).

They are following them in name, but not really in practice.

Most teams do what I would classify as some Agile-like development methodology.

So where does Scrum come in?

Scrum itself was created by Ken Schwaber and Jeff Sutherland somewhat simultaneously in the early 1990s.

In 1995 they wrote a joint paper which defined the Scrum methodology, merging their two approaches.

Scrum is a formalized and prescriptive methodology that defines specific roles on a software development team, the workflow for developing the software, and what specific meeting should take place in each iteration of development, also known as a sprint.

THE ROLES OF SCRUM

There are three main roles in Scrum.

First, the **product owner** (https://simpleprogrammer.com/cg27-fail) acts as the voice of the customer and ultimately determines what the priority of the work should be, as well as communicating with the rest of the business, other stakeholders and customers.

The development team not only writes the code but also performs the analysis, design, testing, and all the other tasks associated with delivering the software.

And finally, **the Scrum master** (https://simpleprogrammer.com/cg27-master) acts like a coach for the team by helping remove any impediments that would slow down the team, communicating with the product owner, and facilitating the Scrum process.

HOW SCRUM WORKS

The basic idea behind Scrum (https://simpleprogrammer.com/cg27-essential) is that software development is broken up into smaller iterations called sprints, which have a set amount of work that is locked down and done in that timeframe. The results are then incrementally delivered to the customer at the end of each sprint.

All of the features that need to be developed for the software are put together into what is known as a product backlog (https://simpleprogrammer.com/cg27-backlog). (These are basically like the requirements of the system.)

The product backlog is prioritized, and during every sprint, a sprint backlog is created where a certain set of product backlog items are pulled to be worked on during that sprint (https://simpleprogrammer.com/cg27-add)—which usually lasts one or two weeks.

At the beginning of each sprint, **a planning meeting is held** where backlogs are pulled into the current sprint, and the current team estimates the effort level of completing the backlogs.

Technically, the team is supposed to commit to getting all of those backlogs done during the sprint, but I've found that rarely happens in practice. (Commitment is difficult.)

Every day there is a quick stand-up meeting called a Scrum where everyone gives a really quick report.

The idea of the Scrum meeting is to keep everyone informed and remove any impediments that might be slowing down progress.

A Scrum meeting happens at the same time in the same location each day, and each team member answers three questions:

1. What did you do yesterday which helped the team reach the sprint goal?

2. What will you do today that will help the team reach the sprint goal?

3. Are there any impediments that prevent you or the team from reaching the sprint goal?

I've found it quite useful to require personal commitments for question 2.

So, I would change it to "what will I commit to doing today that will help the team reach the sprint goal?"

This subtle change makes quite a bit of a difference—in my experience.

During the sprint, the team works together to complete all the backlog items in that sprint, and **a burndown chart** is usually used to track the progress and velocity of the team in completing the backlog items.

The burndown chart tracks the remaining hours, story points, difficulty points, or whatever characterization method is being used to track the work left in the sprint.

When the sprint is over, **a review is conducted** where the functionality completed during the sprint is demonstrated to the stakeholders.

Finally, **a retrospective meeting is held** (https://simpleprogrammer.com/cg27-retro) where the team reflects on the past sprint and develops ideas for improvement in the next sprint.

ISSUES WITH SCRUM

When Scrum is executed correctly, I find it to be an extremely effective and valuable methodology for developing software.

Unfortunately, I've found that **in reality it is often not followed** very closely, and many allowances are made to compensate for failure or to try and game the system.

I've written up an extensive article on what I feel are the failings of Scrum in general (https://simpleprogrammer.com/cg27-die), so I won't go into details here, but I think it's worth talking about something I've already mentioned, which I think is the biggest reason Scrum teams fail to have the success they should.

Commitment.

Having been a Scrum master for several teams, where I coached many organizations on implementing Scrum, **I have found that the biggest thing which tends to kill an otherwise successful Scrum implementation is the lack of commitment**—both by the team and at a personal level.

It is really easy to pull backlog items into a sprint and agree to get them done if all goes well and according to plan.

It's a much more difficult thing to actually commit to getting them done.

Without the concept of commitment, the standards of accountability decline and the sprint loses meaning because the work pulled into the sprint is only a pipedream and is not reliable.

It is very much like creating a to-do list of things you are going to do in a day, trying your best to get them done every day and most days failing to complete the list.

The list itself starts to become meaningless over time and you start to wonder why you have it at all.

It's much more effective to make commitments that you fulfill 99% of the time, because then you can trust yourself and you, in turn, can be trusted (https://simpleprogrammer.com /cg27-commit).

I could talk quite a bit more on this subject, but I think you get the point.

KANBAN

While Scrum is a fairly formalized and prescriptive methodology—at least in workflow and organization—Kanban is not.

Kanban is similar, but it's a much more loosely defined methodology (https://simpleprogrammer.com /cg27-kanban), based more on principles than on instruction.

Kanban has its origins in the Toyota Production System and lean manufacturing.

Originally Kanban was created as a way to limit the work in production for manufacturing, which results in increased efficiency and less inventory.

When applied to software development, **Kanban is primarily focused on what is known as a Kanban board.**

A Kanban board is just a simple board with several columns in it, which represent the various stages of work as it flows through the development process.

The idea here is to make all the work being done on a project visible and to limit the total amount of work being done at one time (known as WIP, or work in progress) in order to identify and decrease bottlenecks.

Like Scrum, Kanban is based on the idea of self-organizing teams which are multi-disciplinary.

Kanban is easily applied to existing systems and processes and acts as a way to formalize and visualize the flow of work through those systems via the publicly visible Kanban board.

Kanban is very much focused on the idea of continuous improvement via feedback loops.

There is no defined way that software development teams use Kanban, so the process is going to vary from team to team.

Typically, you might expect that the team would have some kind of a backlog or list of work that needs to be done, and that work would be prioritized.

Then, someone on the team would pick up new work to be done and add it to the Kanban board.

The work would move across the board as it progresses from stage to stage.

Perhaps the work starts in analysis and design and then progresses to development and then moves to testing and finally deployment, but there may be various steps in-between or other ways or organizing the work.

I've always been a big fan of Kanban.

In fact, I use a variation of Kanban myself for most of the work I do (https://simpleprogrammer.com /cg27-plan)—including writing this book.

But I've always felt like there should be a bit more structure around the process.

Awhile back, I wrote up my own formalized version of Kanban which I called Kanbanand (https:// simpleprogrammer.com/cg27-kanbanand).

The goal was to create a little more structure and prescription in both the workflow and development processes.

EXTREME PROGRAMMING (XP)

The last Agile methodology we are going to discuss in this chapter is one of my favorites because it is so prescriptive and it promotes an extremely high-level of professionalism and rigor around software development.

Extreme Programming, or XP, was first created by Kent Beck around 1996; he released his first book detailing the process in 1999, *Extreme Programming Explained* (https://simpleprogrammer.com/cg27-extreme).

XP took many of the best practices at the time, like unit testing, test driven development, object-oriented programming, and a high-quality customer focus, and elevated them to a level that some people would call extreme—hence the name.

Due to its extreme and rigorous nature, it never caught on all that much, although some teams still practice it today. (Scrum is by far more common—or at least variations of Scrum that I like to call Scrumbut.)

HEY JOHN

You just said Scrumbut, what is that? It sounds interesting; is that some kind of a delicious, flakey pastry?

Ah, Scrumbut.

Yes that.

It's what I call it when a team says they are doing Scrum, followed by a long pause and then they say "but" and give a long list of exceptions to the Scrum process that they aren't doing.

Then they make all manners of excuses as to why they are doing things their way instead of just following the damn process like it was written!

As a consultant or a software developer trying to coach teams on Scrum or follow the Scrum process, it's as frustrating as hell and makes you want to pull your hair out.

> The biggest problem I have with Scrumbut though, is that it is a way to get around the pain in the Scrum process—the very pain that makes it effective.
>
> It's sort of like if you were trying to cook something on a stove. You turned on the stove, it was hot and you burned your hand because you weren't using hot pads to grab the handle of the pan. So you said, "you know what, I like everything about cooking with the stove except for the heat. The heat is just no good. Let's cook on the stove, but let's not use any heat."
>
> If instead you said, "hmm… the handle of that pan was hot, maybe we should put on some gloves or use a hot pad next time," you'd make much more progress.
>
> But, alas, most software development teams trying to implement Scrum just turn off the gas and wonder why their food isn't cooking.
>
> That's Scrumbut.
>
> I'm not bitter about it at all.

XP, like other Agile methodologies, embraces change and utilizes short development cycles or iterations to allow for change and the evolution of software over time.

The development process for an XP project is centered around an extremely focused set of disciplines.

XP practitioners will plan out what they are going to work on—much like Scrum—and then assign various points to the work to be done.

When the work is actually done, it begins with testing.

Acceptance tests define the done criteria which the work item must pass in order to be considered complete.

Before any actual real code is written, unit tests are created which define exactly what the code should do given various circumstances, subsequently driving the actual development of the code.

XP relies heavily on the idea of pair programming where two developers sit together and jointly work on all code that is being created.

The goal is always to d**esign and implement features as simply as possible, with the current needs in mind**, not the needs of the future.

The idea is that the code can evolve to handle more complex situations as they arise, rather than trying to optimize prematurely or provide extra flexibility, which often comes at the cost of added complexity.

The concept of collecting code ownership and coding standards is very important to the practice of XP.

XP is even so prescriptive as to require that no developers participate on overtime on the project.

As you can imagine, XP draws a large amount of criticism, and it is extremely difficult to follow without having a team in which all members are dedicated to the principles and practices.

To an outsider, XP can seem very much like a programming cult.

But I have to say I personally like XP and find it extremely effective when implemented correctly.

I've just always had an extremely difficult time convincing managers and development teams to fully adopt the process.

OTHER METHODOLOGIES AND NON-METHODOLOGIES

Let's be honest here: **most software development teams you work on will either be professing to follow some methodology and not really following it**, or will pretend to not be following any formal methodology at all.

I used to get pretty upset by this.

I used to get up on my soapbox and preach the values of following Scrum to the letter, or the benefits of actually implementing XP rather than just pretending to.

Or I would ask, "What methodology are you using to develop your software?" and when I get a an answer of "We don't have one," I'd lose my shit.

What I've come to realize is that **a specific methodology is not as important as having some kind of repeatable and measurable process** that can evolve and adapt.

It's great if your team is doing Scrum and improving upon how they do Scrum.

But it's also great if your team is taking some stuff from Scrum and taking some stuff from Kanban and XP and doing their own process that works—so long as there is some kind of process.

That is the key. A repeatable and defined process.

So, as you are learning about methodologies, I'd urge you to consider a few final points.

First, **a repeatable process is more important than a specific methodology.**

And second, **just because a methodology isn't listed here doesn't mean it's not a valid methodology** for software teams to use.

This is a long book, but a short chapter, so rather than trying to cover every software development methodology in existence—and there are many—I've tried to give you a basic understanding of the methodologies that I feel most software development processes today either utilize or heavily borrow from.

CHAPTER 28

TESTING AND QA BASICS

One of my first official jobs in the software development industry was that of a tester.

My job entailed looking at stacks of papers that were printed out by a new printer we were testing at HP and comparing them to the "master" printouts produced by older printers.

I didn't actually do the comparison of the pages myself; instead I would execute the tests, someone else would compare the printouts, and I'd look at the differences they flagged.

With each difference, I would review and decide, based on the test, whether the result was a true failure or defect. If it was the latter, I'd write up a defect report for a developer to look at—and possibly fix.

Later in my career, I took on a different role as a testing lead for a multi-function printer.

I'd decide what should be tested, how it should be tested, and then I'd come up with a testing plan and run the tests to verify the printer worked how it was supposed to.

It was through those experiences that I learned that **most developers have no clue about how testing is actually done**, and how valuable this understanding can be for developers who really want to excel in their careers.

I owe a large amount of the success I have had in my career as a software developer to my background in testing.

That background caused me to look at the code I was writing a little differently and to realize that my job as a software developer wasn't just to implement features and fix bugs, but to make the software I was writing work correctly and as intended.

Seems like a simple and obvious idea, but **if you don't at least know the basics of testing, you probably aren't going to have the best idea of what "working correctly and as intended" actually means.**

THE BASIC IDEA BEHIND TESTING

Usually, new programmers don't understand testing. They don't think it's necessary.

At a surface level it can seem a bit extraneous.

Do we really need to test that code? I ran it on my machine and it worked perfectly, so let's just ship it.

Testing, at its core, is really about reducing risk.

The goal of testing software is not to find bugs or to make software better. It's to reduce risk by proactively finding and eliminating problems which would most greatly impact the customer using the software.

Customers can be impacted by the frequency of an error or undesired functionality, or by the severity of the problem.

If you had a bug in your accounting software which caused it to freeze up for a second or two whenever a value higher than $1,000 was entered, it would not really have a huge impact; but that would be a high enough frequency to be very annoying to the customer.

On the other hand, if you had a bug in the accounting software that caused all of the data to become corrupted every 1,000th time the data was saved, that would be huge impact, but very low frequency.

The reason I define software testing in this way is because—as any tester will tell you—**you can never find all the bugs or defects in a piece of software and you can never test every possible input** into the software. (For any non-trivial application.)

So, the idea is not to find every single possible thing that is or can go wrong, or even to verify the software against a spec—as some people like to define software testing—because both are impossible.

(Oh, also if you ever find a complete spec for any application in your experience as a software developer, let me know.)

Instead, **the focus and main idea behind software testing is to reduce the risk that the customer is greatly impacted in a negative manner** when using the software.

Typically this is achieved by first prioritizing what areas of the software are likely to have the biggest impact (i.e. risk), and then deciding on a set of tests to run which verify the desired functionality in that area.

When the actual functionality deviates from the desired functionality, a defect is usually logged and those defects are prioritized based on severity.

Some defects get fixed, other defects are low enough impact that they are just noted and left in the system.

COMMON TYPES OF TESTING

The world of testing and quality assurance is huge (https://simpleprogrammer.com /cg28-testing).

Just like the development world has many concepts and methodologies for creating software, **there are many ways to think about how to test and the field is changing all the time.**

Even in name.

Early in my career it could be perceived as a slight or insult to call someone who worked in testing a tester; they preferred to be called QA (or quality assurance) professionals.

Just a year or two ago, I attended a testing conference and I made the mistake of calling someone a QA person. They corrected me and said that tester was the preferred term.

You can't win them all.

Anyway, let's talk about the different kinds of testing, so you can get a general idea of what someone is talking about when they throw around these terms—which you will hear often in the software development world.

This is not an exhaustive list by any means.

BLACK-BOX TESTING

One of the most common forms of testing—and really a way to describe a whole category of testing—is black-box testing.

Black-box testing is simply **testing as if the software itself was a black box.**

When you do black-box testing, you are only concerned with inputs and outputs. You don't care how the actual outputs are derived.

You don't know anything about the code or how it works, just that for a given set of inputs into the software, a given set of outputs should be produced.

Most testing is done in this fashion because it is largely unbiased. It either works or it doesn't.

WHITE-BOX TESTING

White-box testing is pretty much the opposite of black-box testing.

With white-box testing, you have at least some idea of what is going on inside the software.

Oftentimes, unit testing is called white-box testing, but I disagree. Unit testing is not testing at all—we'll talk about that more in an upcoming chapter.

Instead, **real white-box testing is when you understand some of the internals of the system and perhaps have access to the actual source code**, which you use to inform your testing and what you target.

For example, if you looked at code that did complex calculations for some accounting software, and you saw that there was a section of the code that did one set of calculations for values above a certain amount and another set of calculations for any other values, you'd be able to create tests that target both of those scenarios.

With black-box testing, you'd have no way to know these two conditions existed, so you'd be very unlikely to test for both of them, unless you just got lucky.

ACCEPTANCE TESTING

Acceptance testing goes by many different names.

Sometimes it's called user acceptance testing.

Sometimes it's called system testing.

The basic idea of acceptance testing is that **you have some tests which test the actual requirements or expectations of the customer, and other tests that run against the system as a whole.**

What I mean by this is that you don't just test one part of the software in isolation.

This kind of testing could be testing the functionality of the system or it could be testing the usability, or both.

The idea is that acceptance testing tests what is expected versus what actually happens.

AUTOMATED TESTING

This is another broad kind of testing which can take many forms and has many definitions, but I define automated testing as **any testing in which the execution of the test and the verification of the results is automated** (https://simpleprogrammer.com/cg28-bat).

So, you might automate the testing of a web application by running scripts which open up a web page, input some data, push some buttons and then check for some results on a page.

You could also automate the testing of an API by writing scripts which call out to the API with various data and then check the results that are returned.

More and more of testing is moving towards automated testing because manually running through test cases over and over again can be tedious, error-prone and costly—especially in an Agile environment where the same set of tests may need to be run every two weeks or so to verify nothing has broken.

REGRESSION TESTING

This brings us to regression testing, which is basically **testing done to verify that the system still works the way it did before.**

The purpose of regression testing is to make sure the software doesn't regress in functionality.

This is extremely important with Agile development methodologies—more on that in a future chapter—where software is developed incrementally and there is a constant potential that adding new features could break existing ones.

Most automated tests are regression tests.

In fact, **you could really make the argument that all automated tests are regression tests,** since the whole purpose of automating a test is so that it can be run multiple times.

FUNCTIONAL TESTING

Functional testing is another broad term used in the testing world to refer to **testing activities where what is being tested is the actual functionality of the system.**

This might seem obvious.

You might be thinking "duh, what else would you test if you didn't test the functionality of the system."

But, it turns out that you can test all kinds of things that aren't related to functionality, like performance, usability, resilience, security, scalability—I could go on and on, believe me.

So, functional testing is the kind of testing where you are really concerned with the system doing what it is supposed to do from a functional perspective.

If I put in this input and push this button, do I get this expected output?

I don't care how long it takes. I don't care if the screen flashes bright red and the computer starts to smoke, do I get my result?

EXPLORATORY TESTING

I like to make fun of exploratory testing and call it "lazy-ass testing."

It really pisses testers off when I do that.

But, there is definitely some legitimacy to the idea of exploratory testing and perhaps I am a bit too harsh and judgmental.

The idea behind exploratory testing—when done correctly—is that you have some guidelines and a basic plan of which application areas you are going to test and ways you are going to test them.

Then, you go about without actual test cases and explore the application, looking for things that might be wrong or behavior that is unexpected.

Oftentimes, exploratory testing sessions are recorded, so that if an error is found, the problem can be reproduced by retracing the steps taken by the exploratory tester.

While I'm generally not a huge advocate of this kind of testing, I do have to acknowledge its merits, as exploratory testing can often uncover bugs which no rational test case would have ever been designed to exploit.

OTHER FORMS OF TESTING

Truly we've only scratched the surface of all the different types and classifications of testing.

Many other forms of testing exist, including:

* Load testing- How an application performs under a heavy load
* Performance testing- Performance of the application based on certain scenarios
* Recovery testing- Recovery from error conditions or hardware issues
* Security testing- The security of the system
* Stress testing
* Usability testing

The list goes on and on.

I just wanted to cover some of the basics here which you'll hear about and see in everyday conversations as a software developer.

HEY JOHN

I'm a bit confused. Black-box testing sounds a whole lot like functional testing. What's the difference? Oh, and also the same question for regression testing versus automated testing. Aren't all automated tests essentially regression tests?

Ok, shhh… I'm about to tell you a little secret that, well, kind of pisses off QA people—I mean testers.

So. Many of these testing terms are basically the same thing.

Sometimes I feel like the whole testing profession feels the need to invent a bunch of terminology and add a bunch of complexity to something that is inherently simple.

Now, don't get me wrong, testing is important—and it does require skill to be good at it— but it's not all that complicated… really.

To address some of the specifics.

Basically, functional testing could be either white-box or black-box, but usually it's going to be black-box.

Black-box and white-box testing just refer to how the functional testing or other testing is done. It's really just a type of functional testing.

Are you looking at the code to give you hints about what to test or are you treating the whole thing like a mysterious black box?

Black-box testing is just the higher-level concept or idea of testing an application without being able to look at the internals to see how it's implemented.

If you are doing effective functional testing, you are probably doing it in a black-box way, although it's conceivable that looking at the code might give you an idea of some edge cases or special cases you might want to test which you might have missed otherwise.

For automated testing versus regression testing, again, we are dealing with a higher concept and implementation.

Regression testing is the concept. It's the idea that when something breaks—or before it does—you should create some set of tests that ensure the functionality of the system doesn't go backwards, or regress.

Automated tests serve this purpose really well since, well... they're automated.

So, pretty much all automated tests will be regression tests, but it is possible to have manually-run regression tests to make sure the software doesn't regress in functionality.

If you decide to become a tester and want to pass a job interview for a testing position, you should probably know all this stuff and be able to expound upon why exploratory testing is actually a valid way to test things and how user testing and acceptance testing are not the same things.

But, if you are a software developer, honestly, it's only important for you to have an idea of the concepts and what the vocabulary is, and to understand the real idea behind testing, which is risk reduction.

So, don't worry about all the semantics, and focus on the big ideas in this chapter. That's what is important.

THE TESTING PROCESS

Different organizations are going to have very different ideas of how testing should be done and what process should be followed.

You'll also see plenty of formal specifications produced by various testing organizations out there which cover the "testing process."

So, again, like a large amount of what I said about testing, the idea here is not to be prescriptive or to perfectly model the perfect testing process, but rather to give you an idea of what the testing process is like in general and what it entails.

I like the pragmatic approach to life—and testing.

Testing usually begins with the **development of some kind of test plan.**

How will things be tested?

What is our strategy for testing?

What kind of testing are we going to do?

What features are we going to test?

What is the schedule?

These are all questions that are generally answered in the test plan, or, if the test plan is not a formal document, the test planning for a project.

Next, **the tests are usually designed at a high level** based on the requirements or functionality of the system.

At this stage a tester might be coming up with **a list of general test cases** which will be run, what kinds of conditions will be tested, and coming up with what will be needed to perform the tests.

After that, the **tests are usually created and executed.**

Sometimes this occurs as a single step.

Sometimes tests are written in test management software first and executed later.

The results from the **test execution are recorded and evaluated** and any **bugs or defects are usually logged** into some kind of bug tracking system.

Bugs are prioritized and sent to developers to fix.

Fixed bugs are retested and this cycle continues until the software meets the quality standards criteria for shippable code.

And that's basically it.

Plan how to test, design the tests, write the tests, execute the tests, find bugs, fix bugs, release software.

HOW TESTING WORKS ON AGILE TEAMS

The standard process of testing tends to run into some problems on Agile teams (https://simpleprogrammer.com/cg28-agile) where new features are being coded and implemented every couple of weeks or so.

Many teams try to either strictly follow the standard testing process or completely throw it out the window instead of working it into the Agile lifecycle of software development.

Both of these approaches are wrong.

Instead, **the focus really has to change to developing the test cases and test scenarios up front,** before any code is even written and to shrink the test process into a smaller iteration, just like we do when we develop software in an Agile way.

This just means that we have to chop things up into smaller pieces and have a bit of a tighter feedback loop.

Instead of spending a large amount of time upfront creating a testing plan for the project and intricately designing test cases, teams have to run the testing process at the feature level.

Each feature should be treated like a mini-project and should be tested by a miniature version of the testing process, which begins before any code is even written.

In fact, ideally, the test cases are created before the code is written at all—or at least the test design, then the development of both the code and the test cases can happen simultaneously.

Another major consideration with Agile testing is automation.

Since new software is released on very short iterations, regression testing becomes more and more important, thus automated testing becomes even more critical.

In my perfect world of Agile testing (https://simpleprogrammer.com/cg28-different), automated tests are created before the code to implement the features is actually written—truly test driven development—but, this rarely happens in reality.

TESTING AND YOU, THE DEVELOPER

What about you, the software developer? What is your role in all this testing stuff?

Do you even have one?

Yes. Definitely.

One of the big failings of software development teams is not getting developers involved enough, or taking enough ownership for, testing and the quality of their own code.

As a software developer, you should be more concerned with quality than anyone else.

You can not have the mindset that QA will find the bugs in your code.

Instead, you should absolutely make it your responsibility to find and fix the bugs before your code goes to testing.

The reason is fairly simple. The further along in the development of software a bug is found, the more expensive it is to fix.

Think about it this way.

If you test your own code thoroughly and find a bug in that code, before you check it in and hand it over to QA, you can quickly fix that bug and perhaps it costs an extra hour of time.

If you take that same bug, and you don't take the time to find it yourself and fix it, the process might go something like this:

A tester runs a test which finds the bug in your code.

The tester re-runs the test to make sure the bug is valid.

The tester files a defect in the bug tracking software.

A development manager decides that the bug is severe enough for you to work on and the bug is assigned to you.

You try to recreate the defect, but it seems to work on your machine.

The tester reproduces the bug and puts more detailed steps in the bug report.

You finally are able to reproduce the bug and you fix it.

You update the bug report with the fix.

The tester goes back and checks that the bug is actually fixed and marks the defect as resolved.

That's a large amount of everyone's time to waste...

Not saying you're a lazy ass, but...

Perhaps you should take that extra 10 minutes to test your own code before checking it in.

You won't catch everything, but if you can even catch 10% of the bugs that would otherwise make it to QA, you'll be saving quite a bit of time, don't you think?

Ok, so by now, hopefully, you have a decent idea of what testing is, the purpose of testing, what kinds of testing can be done and your role in that whole process.

CHAPTER 29

TEST DRIVEN DEVELOPMENT AND UNIT TESTING

I have a love / hate relationship with test driven development and unit testing.

I've been both an ardent supporter of these "best practices," but I've also been more than skeptical of their use.

One of the big problems in software development is when developers—or sometimes managers—who mean well apply "best practices" simply because they are best practices (https://simpleprogrammer.com/cg29-wrong) **and don't understand their reason or actual use** (https://simpleprogrammer.com/cg29-principles)**.**

I remember working on one such software project where I was informed that the software we were going to be modifying had a huge number of unit tests—around 3,000.

Normally this is a good sign.

This probably means the developers on the project implemented other best practices as well, and there is going to be some semblance of structure or meaningful architecture within the code base.

I was excited to hear this news since it meant that my job as the mentor / coach for the development team was going to be easier. Since we already had unit tests in place, all I had to do was get the new team to maintain them and start writing their own.

I opened up my IDE and loaded the project into it.

It was a *big* project.

I saw a folder labeled "unit tests."

Great. Let's run them and see what happens.

It only took a few minutes and—much to my surprise—all the tests ran and everything was green. They all passed.

Now I really became skeptical. **Three thousand unit tests, and they all passed?**

What is going on here?

Most of the time when I am first pulled onto a development team to help coach them, there are a bunch of failing tests if there are any unit tests at all.

I decided to spot check one test at random.

At first glance, it seemed reasonable enough.

It wasn't the best, most explanative test I'd ever seen, but I could make out what it was doing.

But then I noticed something...

There was no assert.

(An assert statement is what you use in a test to actually test something. The assert statement asserts something is true or false or some condition is met, otherwise it fails. Without at least one assert statement there is pretty much no way the test can actually fail.)

Nothing was actually being tested (https://simpleprogrammer.com/cg29-ego).

The test had steps and those steps were running, but at the end of the test where it is supposed to check something, there was no check.

The "test" wasn't testing anything.

I opened up another test.

Worse.

The assert statement, which was testing something at some point, was commented out.

Wow, that's a great way to make a test pass; just comment out the code that's making it fail.

I checked test after test.

None of them were testing anything.

Three thousand tests and they were all worthless.

There is a huge difference between writing unit tests and understanding unit testing (https:// simpleprogrammer.com/cg29-unit) **and test-driven development.**

WHAT IS UNIT TESTING?

The basic idea of unit testing is to **write tests which exercise the smallest "unit" of code possible.**

Unit tests are typically written in the same programming language as the source code of the application itself and written to utilize that code directly.

Think of unit tests as **code that tests other code.**

When I use the word "test" here, I'm using it fairly liberally because unit tests aren't really tests. They don't test anything.

What I mean by this is that when you run a unit test, you don't typically find out that some code doesn't work.

It's when you *write* a unit test that you find that information out.

HEY JOHN

You just said those 3,000 unit tests were bad because they didn't have asserts or the asserts were commented out. Who cares if I'm only concerned about knowing the requirement at the time of writing? Or, should unit tests become regression tests?

Ah, so you are paying attention.

Astute observation... and yes, your unit tests should become regression tests.

One of the main reasons to write the unit tests, besides clarifying exactly what the code should do and finding it when it doesn't do that, is to make sure the code continues to do what it's supposed to do.

Essentially, unit tests become regression tests that make sure new changes in the code don't break the old functionality.

Think of unit tests kind of like those little supports you see on young trees that make sure they grow up straight and tall.

Just because you planted a tree straight up from the ground, doesn't mean it won't bend or go crooked over time.

It's the same with your code.

Unit tests can initially tell you that your code is planted straight up and then can help you keep it that way—even if some junior developer brings a downfall of heavy rain upon your fragile code.

More on this later...

Yes, the code could change later and that test could fail, so in that sense, a unit test is a regression test. In general, however, a unit test is not like a regular test where you have some steps you are going to execute and you see whether the software behaves correctly or not.

As a developer writing a unit test, **you discover whether the code does what it is supposed to or not while you are writing the unit test** because you are going to be continually modifying the code until the unit test passes.

Why would you write a unit test and not make sure that unit test passes?

When you think about it this way, unit testing is more about specifying absolute requirements for specific units of code at a very low level.

You can think of a unit test as an absolute specification.

The unit test specifies that under these conditions with this specific set of input, this is the output that I should get from this unit of code.

True unit testing tests the smallest cohesive unit of code possible, which in most programming languages—at least object oriented ones—is a class.

WHAT IS SOMETIMES CALLED UNIT TESTING?

Oftentimes, unit testing is confused with integration testing.

Some "unit tests" test more than one class or test larger units of code.

Plenty of developers will argue that these are still unit tests since they are white-box tests written in code at a low level.

You shouldn't argue with these people.

Just know in your mind that these are really integration tests and that true unit tests test the smallest unit of code possible in isolation.

Another thing that is often called unit testing—but isn't really anything at all—is writing unit tests that have no assert. In other words, unit tests that don't actually test anything.

Any test, unit test or not, should have some kind of check—we call it an assertion—at the end that determines whether it passes or fails.

A test that always passes is useless.

A test that always fails is useless.

THE VALUE OF UNIT TESTING

Why am I such a stickler on unit testing?

What is the harm in calling unit testing "real testing" and not testing the smallest unit in isolation?

So what if some of my tests don't have an assert? They are at least exercising the code.

Well, let me try and explain.

There are two major benefits, or reasons, to perform unit testing (https://simpleprogrammer.com /cg29-unit).

The first one is to **improve the design of the code.**

Remember how I said unit testing is not actually testing?

When you write proper unit tests where you force yourself to isolate the smallest unit of code, **you find problems in the design of that code.**

You might find it extremely difficult to isolate the class and not include its dependencies, and that might make you realize that your code is too tightly coupled.

You might find that the basic functionality you are trying to test is spread out across multiple units, and that might make you realize that your code is not cohesive enough.

You might find that you sit down to write a unit test and you realize—and believe me, this happens—that **you don't know what the code is supposed to do**, so you can't write a unit test for it.

And, of course, you might find an actual bug in the implementation of the code as the unit test forces you to think about some edge cases or test multiple inputs which you may not have accounted for.

By writing unit tests and strictly adhering to having them test the smallest units of code in isolation, you find all kinds of problems with that code and the design of those units.

In the software development lifecycle, unit testing is more of an appraisal activity than a testing one.

The second main purpose of unit testing is to **create an automated set of regression tests which can operate as a specification for the low level behavior of the software.**

What does that mean?

When you change shit, you don't break shit.

In that way unit tests are tests: regression tests.

But the purpose of unit testing is not to merely build these regression tests.

In the practical world, very few regressions are caught by unit tests since changing the unit of code you're testing almost always involves changing the unit test itself.

Regression testing is much more effective at the higher level as a black-box testing activity because, at that level, internal structure of the code could be changed while the external behavior is expected to remain the same.

Unit tests test the internal structure, so when that structure changes, the unit tests don't "fail." They become invalid and have to be changed, thrown out, or rewritten.

Now you know more about the true purpose of unit testing than most 10-year software development veterans.

WHAT IS TEST-DRIVEN DEVELOPMENT (TDD)?

Remember the chapter where we talked about software development methodologies, and the waterfall methodology often didn't work out practically because we never had complete specifications up front?

TDD is the idea that, before you write any code, you write a test that acts as a specification for exactly what that code is supposed to do.

This is an extremely powerful concept in software development, but is often misused (https://simpleprogrammer.com/cg29-views).

TDD usually means using unit tests to drive the creation of the production code being written, but it can be applied at any level.

For the purposes of this chapter, though, we are going to stick with the most common application: unit testing.

TDD flips things around so that instead of writing the code first and then writing unit tests to test that code (which we know isn't the case anyway), you are going to write the unit test first and then write just enough code to make that test pass.

In this way, the unit test is "driving" the development of the code.

This process is repeated over and over.

You write another test that defines more functionality of what the code is supposed to do.

You change the code or add code to make the test pass.

Finally, you refactor the code (https://simpleprogrammer.com/cg29-refactor)—or clean it up—to make it more succinct.

This is often called "Red, Green, Refactor" because at first the unit test fails (red), then code is written to make it pass (green), and finally the code is refactored.

WHAT IS THE PURPOSE OF TDD?

Just as unit testing itself can be a best practice that is misapplied, TDD can be as well.

It's very easy to call what you are doing TDD and to even follow the practice and not understand why you are doing it or the value—if any—it is providing.

The biggest value of TDD is that tests happen to make excellent specifications.

TDD is essentially the practice of writing unambiguous specifications, which can be automatically checked, before writing code.

Why are tests such great specifications?

Because **they don't lie.**

They don't tell you code should work one way and then after you spend two weeks pounding Mountain Dew and everything works, tell you it should actually work another way and "it's all wrong; that's not what I said at all."

Tests, if properly written, either pass or fail.

Tests specify in no uncertain terms exactly what should happen under a certain set of circumstances.

So, in that respect, we could say the purpose of TDD is to make sure we fully understand what we are implementing before we implement and that we "got it right."

If you sit down to do TDD and you can't figure out what the test should test, it means you need to go ask more questions.

The other value of TDD is in keeping the code lean and succinct.

Code is costly to maintain.

I often joke that the best programmer is the one who writes the least code or even finds ways to delete code (https://simpleprogrammer.com/cg29-best) because that programmer has found a surefire way to reduce errors and to decrease the maintenance cost of the application.

By utilizing TDD, you can be absolutely sure that you do not write any code that is not necessary since you will only ever write code to make tests pass.

There is a principle in software development called YAGNI, or you ain't going to need it.

TDD prevents YAGNI.

A TYPICAL TDD WORKFLOW

It can be a little difficult to understand TDD from a purely academic perspective, so let's explore what a sample TDD session (https://simpleprogrammer.com/cg29-example) might look like.

You sit down at your desk and quickly sketch out what you think will be a high-level design of a feature which allows a user to login to the application and change their password if they forget it.

You decide that you are going to first implement the login functionality by creating a class that will handle all the logic for doing the login process.

You open up your favorite editor and create a unit test, called "Empty login does not log user in."

You write the unit test code to create an instance of a Login class (which you haven't created yet).

Then, you write test code to call a method on the Login class that passes in an empty username and password.

Finally, you write an assertion, or assert, which asserts that the user is indeed not logged in.

You attempt to run the test, but it doesn't even compile because you don't have a Login class.

You remedy that situation by creating the Login class along with a method on that class for logging in and another for checking the status of a user to see if they are logged in.

You leave the functionality in this class and methods completely empty.

You run the test and this time it compiles, but quickly fails.

Now, you go back and implement just enough functionality to make the test pass.

In this case, it would mean always returning that the user is not logged in.

You run the test again, and now it passes.

On to the next test.

This time you decide to write a test called "User is logged in when user has valid username and password."

You write a unit test that creates an instance of the Login class and try to login with a username and password.

In the unit test, you write an assertion that the Login class should say the user is logged in.

You run this new test, and of course it fails because your Login class always returns that the user is not logged in.

You go back to your Login class and implement some code to check for the user being logged in.

In this case, you'll have to figure out how to keep this unit test isolated.

For now, the simplest way to make this work is to hardcode the username and password you used in your test and if it matches, return that the user is logged in.

You make that change, run both tests, and they both pass.

Now you look at the code you created, and see if there is a way you can refactor it to make it more simple.

So on you go, creating more tests, writing just enough code to make them pass, and then refactoring the code you wrote until there are no more test cases you can think of for the functionality you are trying to implement.

THESE ARE JUST THE BASICS

So, there you have it.

Those are the basics of TDD and unit testing—but they are just the basics (https://simpleprogrammer.com/cg29-basics).

TDD can get a bit more complex when you truly try and isolate units of code because code is connected together.

Very few classes exist in complete isolation.

Instead, they have dependencies, and those dependencies have dependencies and so on (https://simpleprogrammer.com/cg29-hard).

To handle situations like these, veteran TDDers make use of mocks, which can help you to isolate individual classes by mocking the functionality of dependencies with pre-setup values.

Since this is a basic overview of TDD and unit testing, we won't go into detail here about mocks and other TDD techniques (https://simpleprogrammer.com/cg29-mocks), but just be aware that what I presented in this chapter is a somewhat simplified view.

The idea is to give you the basic concepts and the principles behind TDD and unit testing, which hopefully you now have.

HEY JOHN

Does it ever make sense to go back and create unit tests for code that never had it in the first place?

Yeah, well... maybe.

That's the million dollar question.

You really have to ask yourself why you are doing it.

Are you doing it because it makes you feel all good inside and warm and fuzzy to have a bunch of unit tests for all your code?

Or... are you doing it because you think that creating those unit tests is likely to help you better understand the code, make it more robust against a bunch of changes you are going to introduce, or some equally valid reason.

Don't just create unit tests because "it's a best practice" or because "all code should have unit tests."

Try to at least be a little pragmatic and have a real reason for going back and creating unit tests—yes, I know this may challenge your OCD and completionist tendencies. Afterall, I only wrote this "Hey John" because one of my editors made a comment on this chapter asking this question and I feel like I must address every single point every editor makes.

We'll go to rehab together… someday… I promise.

HEY JOHN

Does it make sense to write unit tests without doing TDD? Do they go hand-in-hand?

Now you are just trying to get me riled up—but it's not going to work.

I'm not taking the bait.

But, I'll say this:

If you've read this chapter and agree with what I've said about what the purpose of unit tests are, you have to really question yourself if those purposes are severely compromised if you go back and write unit tests after the code is written.

Yes, in some cases they are still valid and serve as regression tests, but is it really a wise use of your time?

Would it be a wiser use of your time to spend a little more time and effort utilizing a TDD approach?

I don't want it to seem like I'm leading you here, because you have to really answer these questions for yourself.

I've found instances where TDD and unit testing made sense.

I've found instances where neither made sense.

And I've found instances where TDD didn't make sense, but going back and creating some unit tests did.

Just don't do things because "you're supposed to do them;" always be pragmatic.

Get it?

Good.

CHAPTER 30

SOURCE CONTROL

I've always had somewhat of a love / hate relationship with source control.

I learned fairly quickly in my software development career that, love it or hate it, **knowing your way around source control is a pretty important part of being a programmer.**

I was working on a small project at HP at the time with just one other developer.

We were working on a program to automate the testing of HP printers called AntEater.

It was a lovely morning and I was happily coding away when I decided that I needed to get the latest updates to the code.

I was working on a few files for a new feature I was building, and my teammate, Brian, had just checked in some changes.

Not wanting to be working with outdated code, I pulled down the latest changes to my machine.

I built the application and ran it to make sure everything was working.

The application launched, but something strange was happening on my computer.

The hard drive light kept flashing.

I could hear the whirr of the mechanical drive working hard.

It was doing something, but what?

Within minutes, an error dialog popped up on my screen followed by the dreaded blue screen of death.

My PC rebooted automatically, and **I was greeted with the message "non-system disk error."**

Umm, ok. Usually this meant your hard drive had crashed.

I contacted IT.

They took a look at my system and confirmed that something was really wrong. Probably the hard drive had been corrupted.

They reimaged my machine and the next day I had a brand new Windows installation.

I spent that day reinstalling and reconfiguring my development environment.

Finally, I had everything back in order, so I downloaded the latest source code for the application, along with the changes I had made on my branch, and fired up the app.

Once again, my hard drive light started flashing.

I tried to abort, but it was too late.

Seconds later, I was greeted by a reboot and a familiar message... "non-system disk error."

WTF?

What was going on?

I was pissed to say the least.

Finally it occurred to me.

I went over to Brian's desk and looked at the changes he had committed.

He had changed a variable in a C++ header file to be initialized to the value of "C:\temp."

He had done this so that the function he wrote would work, which had the app scan from temporary files and delete them at startup.

I had made a change in the same C++ header file, but I hadn't merged my change yet.

So, when I pulled down his latest code, I didn't get the newest header file that had the variable set to "C:\temp," but I did get the code that scanned through "tempFileLocation" and deleted everything there.

Since my variable wasn't initialized, it was defaulting to "C:\"—the root directory of my computer.

Every time I launched the app, it was recursively deleting all the files on my computer.

Source control can be so much fun.

WHAT IS SOURCE CONTROL?

Source control, or version control as it's sometimes called, is **a way to keep track of different versions of files and the source code of a software project. It coordinates the efforts of multiple developers who may all be working on the same sets of files.**

There are many versions and implementations of source control and source control systems, but they all have the same goal of **helping you to best manage the source code of your software development project.**

WHY IS IT IMPORTANT?

Back when I first started working as a software developer, there were plenty of teams who didn't use source control.

I've worked on multiple projects where **the source code for a multimillion dollar system resided on a shared network folder or a floppy disk** that was passed around.

Lord knows how many companies relying on this version of source control—sometimes called the sneakernet—went belly up when **someone mistakenly deleted the contents of the disk** or shared folder.

One of the main reasons source control is so important is because it mitigates this problem.

A team using a source control system is much less likely to "lose" their code.

Source control gives you a place to check in your code and keep it secure so that it can't be haphazardly deleted, and it allows you to keep track of changes so that if you accidentally delete some portion of the code or make a huge mistake, you can go back and fix it.

Ever saved multiple copies of a document on your computer with different dates in the title, so that you'd be able to go back to an earlier version if you needed to?

That's what source control can do for all the code in your application.

But source control is not just about making sure you don't lose your source code.

You could just back things up regularly to avoid that problem.

Source control also **helps you to be able to coordinate multiple developers working on the same set of files in a codebase.**

Without source control helping to manage the different changes developers are making, it's very easy for developers to overwrite each other's changes or be forced to wait until someone else is done editing a file before they can edit it.

A good source control system will allow you to work on even the same files simultaneously and then merge the changes together.

Source control also solved the problem of working on multiple versions of a software application's code base.

Suppose that you have an application that you have released to customers and it has some bugs in it that need to be fixed, but at the same time you are working on some new features for the next version of the application and those new features aren't quite ready yet.

Wouldn't it be nice if you could have multiple versions of the code?

For instance, one version could be the current released version where you make bug fixes, and another version could be where you develop your new features.

And wouldn't it be nice if you could apply the bug fixes to the version of the code that contains the new features, as well?

Source control gives you the power to do just that.

SOURCE CONTROL BASICS

There is quite a bit to know about source control—and you **certainly aren't going to become an expert just by reading about it**—but you can learn the basics.

In this next section, I'm going to give you a quick rundown of the basics of source control, followed by a few of the most common source control technologies out there, so that you can at least understand how source control generally works.

REPOSITORIES

One of the key concepts with just about all source control systems is the idea of a repository— it's basically **the place where all the code is stored.**

When you are working with source code, you'll be getting the code from the repository, working on it, and checking in your changes.

Other developers may also be doing the same.

The repository is the place where all that code comes together and where the code technically "lives."

Different source control systems have different concepts of what a repository is and might even have local repositories, but ultimately, for any codebase, there has to be one central location or repository that acts as the system of record.

CHECKING OUT CODE

When you want to get a local version of the code that you can modify, **you'll need to check out code from the repository.**

Older source control systems had you actually check out the code and lock the files, so only you could edit them.

Most source control systems today let you "check out" code by letting you pull down a local copy of that code onto your own machine or local repository.

This checked out code is your local copy, and changes that you make to it are only made on your machine or in your local repository.

It is only when you "check-in" or merge your code to the central repository that other developers see your changes.

Normally when you are working with source control, you'll check out a local copy of the code-base, implement new features, or make other changes to the code, and then when you are done, you'll check that code back in and handle any conflicts which may arise from multiple developers working on the same sections of code.

REVISIONS

Source control systems have a concept of revisions which are **the previous versions of a file contained within source control.**

So, for example, if we have a file called foo.bar that I first create and then you later modify and then I modify again sometime later down the road, the source control repository will contain three different versions of foo.bar:

- The first one I created
- The version after you modified it
- The final version after I modified it again

Why is this important?

Well, for a couple of reasons.

First of all, suppose I screwed up foo.bar and you want to revert back to the version that existed before I made my changes.

Since the file is in source control, **you can simply revert back to the previous revision** or check out the revision and pretend like my changes never even existed.

You could also **look at the revision history and compare the changes in the file over time to figure out how a file evolved** by seeing what changes happened at each revision and who made them.

(I like to call this finger-pointing.)

BRANCHING

One of the most misunderstood areas of source control is branching—or rather how to use branching correctly (https://simpleprogrammer.com/cg30-branching).

The concept, though, is fairly simple.

Most source control systems allow you to create a branch off of an existing codebase, in order to create a new codebase that can be independently evolved from its parent.

Wait, what? I thought you said this was simple, John.

Ok, think of your code like a tree.

You've got the trunk, and at some point you might have multiple branches which come off of that trunk.

What does this look like in reality?

Suppose you have a version of your software that you are working on, and you are ready to ship that version to customers and call it version 1, but… you still want to continue working on new features for version 2.

The problem is—even though you are an awesome coder—you know there are going to be at least a few bugs you are going to have to fix in version 1, which you are shipping to customers.

However, you don't want to start shipping them version 2 features when you give them bug fixes for version 1. (You are planning on charging them for an upgrade to version 2 later.)

So, what do you do?

Simple. **You branch the code.**

Once you are ready to ship version 1, instead of just shipping what is in the trunk, you create a new branch. You call this branch "version 1."

That's what you ship.

Then, you can make bug fixes on the version 1 branch and implement your new features on the trunk.

Only one problem...

What if you want to get those bug fixes into the trunk as well?

MERGING

Look how beautifully I set that one up.

The solution to your problem is merging.

What is merging, you may ask?

It's exactly what it sounds like.

You are going to merge the changes from one code line into another.

In our little software example above, we simply used a merge feature of our source control system to merge our version 1 branch changes to the trunk.

Merging allows us to take all the changes we made on the version 1 branch, after we had branched from the trunk, and merge them right into the trunk.

The merge would only go one direction, so we'd get all the changes from the version 1 branch into the trunk, but none of the new features we were working on in the trunk would go into the version 1 branch.

Just as we intended.

All is well and peaceful in the world, that is until we actually try to do the merge and we find that we have...

CONFLICTS

F$%^!, d%&$! What is this s&$*?!

These are the kinds of words frequently uttered when developers try to do the simple, straight-forward process of merging just a few simple changes back into the trunk.

Mostly this happens on Friday evening at 5:00 PM, when you only mean to do a quick merge and get the hell out of there.

You kick off the merge, put your coat on, text your friends to tell them where you are going to meet them for a relaxing evening of drinks and dinner, and quickly glance at your screen to see:

"CONFLICT (content): Merge conflict in simplefile.java
Automatic merge failed; fix conflicts and then commit the result."

Or some other such garbage.

The hours pass by as you stare at a bunch of "<<<<<" and ">>>>>" symbols in a file and try to make sense of it all.

I'm not going to lie; merge conflicts are... a bitch.

Most of the time, a good source control system will try to automatically merge simple changes made in one part of a file into another file, and it all works magically.

But... every so often, you make a change in one file on a branch, and some stupid idiot developer also makes a change in the same file on the same line—because he's an idiot—and manual intervention is required.

The computer has no way of knowing which change should override the other one, or if both changes should somehow be included or if there is some other way to resolve the conflict, so it's up to you.

Your Friday night is ruined.

Resolving merge conflicts and the intricacies of merging could be a whole other book by itself, so I'm not going to delve into the details here.

It's sufficient to know for now how merging basically works, and that when it doesn't, conflicts exist which have to be manually resolved. Oh, and not to do "simple merges really quickly" on Friday nights right before you are getting ready to leave—save that shit for Monday morning.

TECHNOLOGIES

Source control has a pretty long and somewhat interesting history, of which we are not going to discuss here, since I lied about the interesting part.

It's sufficient to say that **source control systems evolved from passing around the source code on a USB drive, to strategically copying entire folders of source control and renaming them V1, to the fairly complex systems we have today.**

Many wars were fought in source control land, and eventually two major factions emerged victorious: centralized source control and distributed.

Centralized is older. It doesn't have quite as much "bling," but it's a little simpler to understand and it does the job.

CVS and Subversion are two examples of centralized source control.

Distributed is newer. It's probably a bit shinier in most people's eyes and it's a bit more complicated, but more people are using it.

Git and Mercurial are two examples of distributed source control.

CENTRALIZED SOURCE CONTROL

With centralized source control, **you have one repository, which exists on a central server** that all developers working on the code utilize to get copies of the files they need and to check in changes they've made to files.

Each developer has a source control client that manages checking in and checking out code from the central repository.

All of the version history and revisions of the files are stored in the central repository.

The typical workflow for using centralized source control might look something like:

1. Update my local copy of the code line I'm working on from the repository.
2. Make my changes.
3. Commit my changes to the central repository (and deal with any conflicts).

DISTRIBUTED SOURCE CONTROL (DVCS)

The biggest difference with using distributed source control is that **each developer has a full copy of the entire repository on their own machine.**

Some really cool hipsters like to say that this means "there is no central repository, dude. It's like we just all have our own versions of the software, and no version is better than any others."

This is just plain wrong.

Yes, theoretically this is possible, but how the hell are you going to ship code and coordinate a project between multiple developers if you don't have some kind of system of record?

It's not going to happen.

If you think it will, you should probably start your own utopia or cult or something.

The reality of the situation is that, yes, each developer has their own complete copy of the repository, but y**ou still utilize some central version of the repository that acts as the system of record** or the master repository for the project.

When you work in a distributed source control system, you simply work locally and do everything you would with a central repository system, except it happens locally.

Essentially, this means you don't have to transfer as many files across the network, and you can work disconnected for a while.

Eventually, though, you've got to get changes that other people have made, and you've got to send your beautiful, precious changes out into the world to fend for themselves.

You do this by pulling and pushing.

With a DVCS, you can pull down changes to your local repository, and you can push changes you've made out to the master repository or any other repository you want—including your hipster, decentralized, every-repository-is-equal friend.

A QUICK RUNDOWN OF THE MOST POPULAR SOURCE CONTROL SYSTEMS

If you are reading this book in the future, this list will probably change.

There is always a new source control hotness.

But, for now, at the time of writing this book, I thought I'd give you a brief introduction to the most common source control systems you are likely to see in the wild.

Caution: it's brief.

CVS

No, it's not a drugstore. It's source control.

It's known as CVS or Concurrent Versions System (https://simpleprogrammer.com/cg30-cvs). (I've never called it by the full name; I actually had to look that up.)

What is it?

Well, I know some people will get pissed when I say this, but **in my opinion it's the precursor to Subversion.**

CVS is a centralized source control system, and it is fairly robust.

It's pretty powerful, but a bit slow.

Most organizations that were using CVS eventually switched to Subversion, but CVS still handles some things a little differently and some people prefer those differences.

Tagging and branching, for example, as well as rolling back commits are handled differently in CVS.

(If you don't know what tagging is, think of it as just giving a name or label to a version of the repository or codebase.)

CVS zealots will tell you CVS does it right, and Subversion does it wrong.

I don't really care all that much, so I just nod my head because I don't like getting stabbed with a fork.

SUBVERSION

Bias alert.

Subversion is probably the source control system I'm most familiar with.

I've taught courses on how to use it in a purely graphical manner (https://simpleprogrammer.com/cg30-svn), I've written blog posts about branching and merging strategies (https://simpleprogrammer.com/cg30-branching) using it, and I've managed SVN servers, repositories and source control strategies for pretty large development teams using the technology.

Does this mean I'm a huge fanboy and think everything else sucks?

No, not really.

As far as centralized source control systems go, I think Subversion is the best (https://simpleprogrammer.com/cg30-subversion)**, but it definitely has its set of shortcomings.**

Overall, though, it gets the job done and is fairly easy to use, so I like it.

GIT

Git has basically become synonymous with source control.

Ask an under-25 developer today what source control is and he or she will most likely say, "What, do you mean Git?"

There is a good reason for this.

Git is... well... pretty awesome.

Really, it is.

As far as source control software goes, Git does pretty much everything you want (https://simpleprogrammer.com/cg30-git).

It's extremely powerful.

The basics are fairly simple.

And it's quick, efficient, and universal.

Git even has a pretty large company which supports open source and managed hosting for Git projects called GitHub (https://simpleprogrammer.com/cg30-github).

Definitely worth checking out if you haven't already.

MERCURIAL

Mercurial is kind of like Git's evil twin brother.

Some people have said Git is like MacGyver, and Mercurial is like James Bond.

I'm not exactly sure what they are talking about—or what they are smoking—but I sort of get it.

Mercurial could be described as a little more elegant (https://simpleprogrammer.com/cg30-mercurial) **and polished than Git.**

Same basic idea—they are both distributed source control.

Same basic functionality and features.

But, in my experience, Mercurial is just a little bit easier to use and figure out whereas Git is a little more arcane, but there are more ways to combine and hack things together.

So, essentially I've just described Mercurial by comparing it to Git.

Hmm, well that will have to do.

If you use both, you'll see why.

It's sort of like one of those pointless religious war type thingies.

ANYTHING ELSE?

No, not really.

The main source control systems are pretty much these four with Git taking a huge—and I mean, HUGE—share of the market.

Yes, some people are off using other stuff and merrily humming along, but it's much more rare.

So, there you go, now you have the basics of source control.

Remember to commit early and to commit often.

Oh, and please use meaningful commit messages.

CHAPTER 31

CONTINUOUS INTEGRATION

There is something you need to know about me.

I'm a huge fan of continuous integration.

If you put me on a new software development team and you don't already have an automated build process and continuous integration set up, **you can pretty much bet that the first thing I am going to do is get all of that going.**

I love the idea of automation.

I love making things more efficient and automatic, whenever possible.

To me, that is what continuous integration represents.

It's taking that slow, painful, tedious, and error-prone process of building the software, running tests against it, getting it packaged up to be deployed, and making it automatic.

But it's much more than that.

Continuous integration, or CI as it's usually called, is also about **increasing the frequency in which code that individual developers are working on is merged together**, so you don't end up in the kind of **merge hell** I mentioned in the chapter on source control quite as often.

The sooner you are able to integrate, the less chance for integration hell and the faster you will find integration issues.

And finally, continuous integration **provides the whole team with feedback**—and fast.

When you are able to check in some code and know in two minutes whether that code compiles and whether you broke something in five—all while seeing the results in one central location—you've got a very fast and useful feedback cycle.

The faster the feedback cycle, the faster software can evolve, and the more the overall quality can be improved—an extremely important element in Agile development.

At this point, you may be thinking, "Yeah, John, it really sounds like you are trying to sell me this thing called CI, but what exactly is it?

I mean, it sounds good and all.

I like automation. I like feedback. I don't think I'd like integration hell.

"But what exactly is this CI you speak of?"

Well, I think the best way for you to understand continuous integration is for me to take you back in time to show you how things used to be done and how continuous integration evolved over time. Then, I'll finally take you through the workflow of a modern software development environment that has a good CI system up and running.

Let's begin the journey, shall we?

HOW BUILDING CODE USED TO WORK

I'm not super old, but **I'm old enough to have built software in a time before there were fancy tools for automating it.**

Early in my career—we are talking like early 2000s—it was pretty normal to work on a software development team where every single developer was responsible for figuring out how to create their own build of the software.

What do I mean by this?

Well, in any sufficiently large application, there are going to be quite a few components that may go into the build of the software being worked on.

There are, of course, going to be a large amount of source code files which must be compiled.

Often, there will be some other resources like external libraries which will need to exist on a developer's machine to build the final software solution.

And there may be additional steps involved before or after the code is compiled to get the finished product.

It used to be that when you worked as a developer, you'd get a copy of the source code. Some guru who had been working on the software for the last five years would show you the magical incantations you needed to do to build the software, and then you were on your own.

Individual developers developed their own ways of getting the software built on their machines.

When it was time to produce a build that was ready to be tested or deployed out to customers, one of the developers would sacrifice chickens, walk backwards in a circle, light candles around a pentagram, hit CTRL+SHIFT+F5, and out would pop a finished version of the software.

There were **a few big problems** with this way of developing and building software, though.

The biggest one was that since each developer was building the software on their own machines—and in slightly different ways—**there was a huge chance that two developers with identical versions of the code could produce two completely different versions of the software.**

How could this be, you might ask?

Plenty of things can go wrong when you don't have consistency, and everyone is following their own process of doing something.

Developers could have **different versions of external libraries installed** on their machines.

Developers could **think they have the same source code**, but actually **forget to get the latest files** from source control or **had inadvertently made a local change to a file**, which prevented the code from being updated.

The file or folder structure could be different, and that in turn could cause differences in how the software actually runs.

Plenty of things could go wrong.

The other major problem was that since developers were all building locally, if someone checked in some code that didn't even compile, no one would find out until they pulled down that code and tried to build the software.

This might not seem like a huge deal, but **it gets really fun when multiple developers check in bad code over a period of days or even weeks, and then when someone finally tries to build everything and finds out it's broken,** they have no idea what change or changes caused the issues.

Plus, I've worked at places where it literally took hours to just create a single build of the software.

Nothing worse than running a build on your machine for 4-5 hours and then finding out it's broken.

THEN BUILD SERVERS CAME ALONG

One of the early ways to solve these kinds of problems was **the introduction of build servers.**

The idea was that instead of having every developer build the software on their own machine, there would be **one central build server, which was configured correctly and had all the right versions of the libraries, etc.**

A developer could kick off a build on the build server, or the build server would automatically build the software every night.

At first, this started out as **weekly builds.**

So, you'd at least have some official weekly build of the software that combined all the changes from all the developers from that week together and was built in a uniform way.

One issue with the weekly build, though, was that often—especially with large teams—**there would be an integration hell problem when trying to get that weekly build created.**

Often, there would be a developer or IT person in charge of getting that weekly build to work, and they'd manually fix all the issues that were breaking the build and hunt down developers with conflicting changes to try and resolve them.

An improvement over no build server, but not by much.

Eventually, **the idea of nightly builds became popular.**

The idea was that if we integrated the code daily with the build server creating a new build every night, there would be less time for big issues to pile up and compound, and we could catch problems much earlier.

At first, this idea seemed crazy.

You wouldn't believe the amount of resistance I got the first time I ever suggested a nightly build at one of the companies I worked for.

But, eventually it became the norm, and it did solve quite a few problems.

Nightly builds from a central build server helped get everyone synced up and on the same page, so to speak, and if the nightly build broke, it was everyone's top priority to get it working again.

The idea of a nightly build pushed forward the need for actual automation of the build process itself.

This was very good.

In order to consistently build the software each night, we needed some automated way to get all the code together, compile it, and do any of the other steps required to create a working build.

This was the era of many scripts which were created in order to automate the process of building the software, at least on the build machine. It was still quite normal for developers to still have their own local build processes (https://simpleprogrammer.com/cg31-one).

Makefile scripts, which used to only compile the code, started to become more sophisticated to handle the full build process for a build server, and XML-based build automation tools like Ant were created and became popular.

Life was getting better, but **there were still major problems.**

As Agile was becoming more and more popular, and the idea of unit testing was gaining support, nightly builds that just compiled the code and packaged it up were not quite good enough.

We needed **shorter feedback cycles.**

The whole team could get derailed if someone checked in bad code, and we didn't find out about it until the next morning.

We needed some way to build the code, reliably, multiple times per day and to run some other code quality checks besides just "it compiles."

FINALLY, CONTINUOUS INTEGRATION

Nightly builds were a difficult pitch, but nothing compared to trying to get management to buy into continuous integration, or the idea of building the software every single time someone checked in new code.

Why would you want to do that? We have nightly builds.

I don't understand; you want to continuously build the code?

Wait a minute, let me get this straight. You want me to tell all the developers they need to check in their code multiple times a day? Are you kidding me?

There was a good amount of resistance, but slowly it was overcome as Agile became more popular. Continuous integration wasn't just a nice dream, but rather a must-have in order to actually have short enough feedback cycles to get work items completed on each iteration.

The major problem, though, **was how to do this.**

How could we actually build the code every time new code was checked into source control?

The answer was **continuous integration servers.**

Specific software was developed that could be run on a build server with the capability to detect source control changes, pull down the latest code, and run a build.

Pretty soon, developers were working to **reduce the build time of codebases**, so that the feedback could be even faster.

Now that we had this capability, it made sense to do more than just build the code.

Continuous integration evolved to incorporate running unit tests, and running code quality metrics like static code analyzers, which were all kicked off by an initial check in.

The biggest hurdle was—and still is for the most part—**getting developers to check in their code early and often**, so that we can get feedback fairly quickly.

Now, with CI in place, we can not only know within minutes whether a code change prevents the whole project from compiling, but we can also find out if any units tests were broken and even do things like run automated regression tests to look for breaking changes.

Ah, life is good.

A SAMPLE CONTINUOUS INTEGRATION WORKFLOW

Ok, so at this point, you probably have a decent idea of what continuous integration is by hearing about the problems it solved and how it evolved.

But you still might not quite "get it"—and that's ok.

Let's walk through a sample workflow using continuous integration, and then maybe it will click a little better.

CHECK IN CODE

The cycle starts with you checking in your code.

Of course, you've run the build on your local machine and run all the unit tests before you dare check in code to the main repository and risk breaking the build for everyone… right?

NEW BUILD IS KICKED OFF

The CI software sitting on the build server just detected a change to the source control branch it's monitoring.

It's your code! Oh goody!

The CI server kicks off a new build job.

CODE IS CHECKED OUT

The first thing the new build job does is to get the latest changes.

It pulls down your code changes—and any other ones on the branch—and puts them into its working directory.

CODE IS COMPILED

At this point, a build script of some sort is usually kicked off to actually compile and build the code.

The build script will run the commands to build the source code.

It will also link in any external libraries or anything else needed to compile the code.

If the code fails to compile, the build will stop right here, and an error will be reported.

This is called breaking the build—and it's bad.

I thought you said you compiled the code on your machine before checking it in?

Shame!

STATIC ANALYZERS ARE RUN

Assuming the code built correctly, static analyzers are run to measure certain code quality metrics.

If you don't know what these are, that's ok.

Basically, they are tools that can take a look at the code and look for possible errors or violations of best practices.

The results from these analyzers are stored to be reported when the build is finished.

Some builds can actually be set to fail if some threshold is not met for a code quality metric derived from the static analyzer.

HEY JOHN

What is a static code analyzer and what code quality metrics do they measure?

Ok, I said you didn't need to worry about this for now, but I can see that you are curious... that's good... real good man... real good.

Ahem, ok.

So, a static code analyzer is going to run against the source code and tell you a bunch of things about that code that will give you an idea of its "health" and even point out some things you might want to fix.

For example, back in my Java days I used to run a static code analyzer called PMD (https://simpleprogrammer.com/cg31-pmd). (The meaning of the name is somewhat a mystery.)

What this program would do is look for common problems in your Java code like unused variables, creating objects when it's not necessary, and a whole set of "bad practices" which could lead to errors or difficult-to-maintain code.

With this software, you could also configure and create your own rules, so that you could look for potential issues in the code.

Some static analyzers also give you information about the code; things like cyclomatic complexity (how many possible paths there are through your code), maintainability index, depth of inheritance, lines of code... all kinds of stuff.

Ultimately, you can use this information to fix potential issues in the code and gauge what is happening to the code.

Think of it as a proactive way to keep the code maintainable and stave off easily avoidable bugs and potential pitfalls.

UNIT TESTS ARE RUN

Assuming everything is still good, the CI job kicks off the unit tests.

The unit tests are run against the compiled code and the results are recorded for later.

Usually if any unit tests fail, this causes the whole build to fail.

(I highly recommend this approach, because once you start down the slippery slope of ignoring unit test failures, it will be pretty darn hard to climb back up that hill. Pretty soon everyone will just expect some unit tests to fail and if that happens, the unit tests themselves become kind of pointless.)

RESULTS ARE REPORTED

Finally, the results of the actual build are reported.

The report will contain data about whether the build passed or failed, how long it took to run, code quality metrics, unit tests run, and any other relevant data.

Documentation might also be auto-generated by the build at this point as well.

The results can be set up to be emailed out to the team—especially in the case of a failure—and most CI software programs have a web interface as well where anyone can see the results of the latest build.

SOFTWARE IS PACKAGED

Now the build software is packaged up into a form where it can be deployed or installed.

This usually involves taking the compiled code and any external resources or dependencies and packaging it up into whatever structure is necessary to have a deployable or installable unit.

For example, a file structure might be created that contains all the right files, and then the whole thing might be zipped up.

At this point, the build job may also apply some kind of tagging in source control to mark the version of the software.

CODE IS OPTIONALLY DEPLOYED (CONTINUOUS DEPLOYMENT)

This last step is optional—actually, I suppose that the previous step is optional as well.

But more teams are doing continuous deployment (https://simpleprogrammer.com /cg31-continuous) where they deploy the code directly into an environment for it to be tested— or, if they are really brave, right into production.

FINISHED

And that's it.

There are some variations in these steps, of course, and there may be some additional steps, but the **basic idea is to build the code, check for problems, and get the code ready for deployment all automatically whenever new code is checked in.**

This allows us to be able to know very quickly if a new change to the system caused an error, so that it can be fixed right away.

Even though I've breezed over all of this, I don't want to make it sound too simple.

Build engineers can spend quite a bit of time constructing a well-oiled continuous integration process, and there are all kinds of debates about how it should be done and what are the best practices for doing it.

CI SERVERS AND SOFTWARE

One critical component of continuous integration is CI software.

Without CI software, we'd have to write custom scripts and essentially program our own build servers.

Fortunately, many smart developers quickly realized the value of building CI software, which helps to automate most of the common tasks of continuous integration.

Most CI software works in a very similar manner, making it easy—or at least easier—to implement a workflow like the one I described above.

There are actually quite a few CI servers and software available, but I'm only going to highlight a few here that I have found to be the most commonly used at the time of writing this book.

JENKINS

Jenkins is pretty much my "go to" CI software (https://simpleprogrammer.com/cg31-jenkins).

It's a Java program which was initially created to do CI in Java environments, but it's become so popular and is so easy to use that it has expanded to become usable for just about any technology.

Jenkins is extremely easy to install and get running as it contains its own built-in webserver.

It also has a ton of plugins.

If you are trying to do something in Jenkins, there is a good chance someone has written a plugin to do it for you. That is one of the main reasons why I like and use Jenkins so much.

(I actually have a Pluralsight course that talks you through the Jenkins basics (https://simpleprogrammer.com/cg31-start).)

HUDSON

I'm going to spare you the drama of the big long ass story about the Hudson / Jenkins split and give you the short of it.

Before Jenkins came along, there was Hudson.

There were some fights, Jenkins split off from Hudson, and Hudson continued to be developed on its own.

Hudson is controlled by Oracle, and I personally don't think it's as good as Jenkins, since the creator of Hudson, Kohsuke Kawaguchi, and most of the original Hudson team, moved to Jenkins.

Honestly, I don't know if Hudson is still alive and being worked on.

Ok, ok, I got off my ass and checked. It looks like the last news from Hudson's site was on February 15th, 2016.

TRAVIS CI

Travis is another popular CI software, but it operates a little bit differently.

Travis CI is actually hosted and is provided as a service.

In other words, you don't install Travis CI; you sign up for it.

It's really designed to perform CI for projects hosted on GitHub.

Travis is gaining popularity since many projects are hosted in GitHub, and it's well-designed and easy to use.

Plus, it's nice to not have to maintain your own build server.

TFS

If you are working exclusively in a Microsoft shop, TFS (Team Foundation Server) does offer continuous integration support, but in my experience, it's pretty simplified and isn't robust enough to compete with some of the other, more popular offerings.

But, I suppose if you want something simple—and it has to be a Microsoft solution—this one could work for you.

HEY JOHN

Do you hate TFS? I love TFS, it's way more powerful than you say here. Dammit John. I don't like you anymore.

Look, look, I don't hate TFS. I don't even hate Microsoft—remember my favorite language is C#, right?

I just haven't used TFS all that much and when I did, it wasn't very good.

So, if you like TFS, great, keep using it.

If you are running a Microsoft shop, it's probably going to integrate perfectly into everything you are doing and work just great for you.

I just wasn't the biggest fan when I tried it.

TEAMCITY

TeamCity is another popular continuous integration server (https://simpleprogrammer.com/cg31-teamcity), which is created by the commercial company JetBrains.

It has a free version, but it is also a licensed product.

So, if you are looking for something with a little more professional support, this is a good option.

Many .NET teams use TeamCity for their CI needs.

MORE?

I've only given you a small sampling of some of the more popular options for CI servers, but there are quite a few in existence.

Check out this near complete and updated list (https://simpleprogrammer.com/cg31-compare) if you want to see all the options.

CHAPTER 32

DEBUGGING

As a software developer, I can guarantee you one thing for sure: **you are going to spend a great deal of time debugging code.**

There are certain constants in life which are unavoidable: death, taxes, and programmers creating bugs.

Since so much of your time will be spent debugging code, it's probably a good idea to be good at debugging, don't ya think?

Unfortunately, many developers—even highly experienced ones—tend to, well… suck at debugging.

There are plenty of developers who can whip through new features and sling code around like nobody's business, but **who cleans up the mess of bugs they leave behind?**

It's one thing to know how to write good code; it's another thing to know how to debug the ugliest code you've ever seen in your life—that stuff written by the legendary Bob who built the whole first version of the application in 48 hours in his basement, but was kind of an "odd" fellow.

Fortunately, debugging, like any other skill, is **something that can be learned.**

If you apply the right techniques and practice, you can become great at it.

Who knows? You might even enjoy it.

The key to debugging is realizing that it's all about mindset (https://simpleprogrammer.com /cg32-mindset).

It's about taking a systematic approach to the problem—not rushing it, and not expecting you can just find the problem, get in, and get out.

It's about staying calm and collected: attacking the problem from a logical and analytical perspective instead of an emotional one.

In this chapter, I'm going to lay out a systematic approach to debugging, which will help you avoid that dreaded debugger mindset and take your debugging skills to the next level.

And for a useful 1-page summary of this approach that you can review at a glance, download the Debugging Cheat Sheet that's included in the online resources (https:// simpleprogrammer.com/career-guide-toolkit) for this book.

WHAT IS DEBUGGING?

Before we dive deep, let's go shallow.

What exactly is debugging?

It seems pretty obvious, right?

You open up the debugger and you "debug" problems with the code.

Ah, but that is where you are wrong.

Debugging has nothing to do with the debugger.

Debugging has everything to do with **finding the source of a problem in a codebase, identifying the possible causes, testing out hypotheses** until the ultimate root cause is found, and then eventually **eliminating that cause** and **ensuring that it will never happen again.**

Ok, I suppose we could call that fixing bugs. Semantics.

The point is, debugging is more than fiddling around in a debugger and changing code until it seems to work.

FIRST RULE OF DEBUGGING: DON'T USE THE DEBUGGER

Ah, what's this you say?

A new bug for me to fix?

Oh, this is a hairy one?

Have no fear, sir. I will unleash the full power of my mental arsenal on this unholy terror.

With that mindset, you the programmer sit down at your desk.

You fire up the debugger.

Carefully you step through the code.

Time seems to blur, minutes turn into hours, hours into weeks.

You are an old man sitting at the keyboard, still in the same debugging session, but somehow you are "closer."

Your children have all grown. Your wife has left you.

The only thing that remains is... the bug.

The first thing most programmers do when they want to debug an issue in the code is to fire up the good old debugger and start looking around.

Wrong.

Don't do this.

The debugger should be your last resort.

When you fire up the debugger immediately, you are effectively saying, "I don't have any idea what is causing the issue, but I'm just going to look around and see."

It's like when your car breaks down and you don't know jack shit about cars, so you open up the hood and look for something wrong.

What are you looking for?

You don't even know.

Don't get me wrong.

The debugger is a wonderful and powerful tool.

Used properly, the debugger can help you solve all kinds of problems and can help you see what happens when your code is running.

It's not, however, the place to start, and **many bugs can be solved without ever touching the debugger.**

You see, just like Facebook or funny YouTube cat videos, the debugger has a way of sucking you in.

REPRODUCE THE ERROR

So, if you don't simply fire up the debugger to debug a problem, what do you do?

Well, I'm glad you asked.

The first thing any sane person should do is to **reproduce the bug to make sure that it is actually a bug** (https://simpleprogrammer.com/cg32-reproduce) and that you will be able to debug it.

One-hundred percent of problems that can't be reproduced can't be debugged.

So, **if you can't reproduce the problem, there ain't no point in debugging it.** Ya hear me?

Not only can you not debug a problem that can't be reproduced, but also, even if you did fix it, you can't verify it was fixed.

So, the very first thing you should do when you are trying to debug a bug is to make sure you can reproduce the bug yourself.

If you can't, go and get help.

If a tester filed the bug, get them to reproduce it for you.

If the bug is intermittent and can't be reliably reproduced, this means that you do not know the circumstances required to reproduce the problem.

There is no such thing as an intermittent problem.

If it is a problem, it can be reproduced; you just have to know how.

HEY JOHN

What about intermittent problems that my boss says I have to fix?

Ok, so your boss is demanding that you fix the problem.

They've seen it in production. Customers have seen it. It's definitely a problem.

The "I can't reproduce it" pushback is not working—they aren't buying it.

What do you do?

You still can't debug a problem that you can't reproduce.

But what you can do is gather more evidence.

Insert logging statements into the code. (Logging statements are just lines of code that put some output to the screen or a file so that you can track various things that happen in your application. Very useful for debugging.)

Gather as many details as possible about when the problem happens and under what conditions it happens.

Artificially recreate the environment and circumstances if you can.

Do not be tempted to throw in "fixes" for the problem that you can't recreate.

If you don't understand the problem enough to recreate it, you have a very, very low chance of accidentally fixing it by a guess, and you will have an extremely difficult time knowing if your fix even worked.

Find a way to reproduce the problem, even if it is only reproducible in production.

SIT AND THINK

After you can reproduce your issue, the next step is a step most software developers skip because they are so eager to solve the problem—but this step is crucial.

It's a really simple step.

Just sit and think.

Yes, that's right.

Think about the problem and what the possible causes could be.

Think about how the system works and what might bring about the odd behavior you're seeing.

You are going to be in a rush to jump into the code and into the debugger to start "looking at things," but before you start looking at things, **it's important to know what you are looking for and what things to look at.**

You'll likely come up with a few ideas or hypotheses about what might be causing the issue.

If you don't, be patient. Keep sitting and thinking.

Stand and walk around if it helps, but before you move on, you should at least have a few ideas that you want to test.

If you absolutely can't come up with anything, continue to resist firing up the debugger, and instead **take a browse through the source code** and see if you can gather a few more clues about how the system is supposed to work.

You should have at least **two or three good hypotheses** you can test before you move on from this step.

TEST YOUR HYPOTHESES

Ok, so you've got some good hypotheses, right?

The flux-capacitor is connected to the thingamabob, so if the voltage coming out of the whozitswatt is below grade... THE THINGAMABOB MUST BE CONFIGURED INCORRECTLY!

Err... something like that.

Ok, let's fire up the debugger and test our hypotheses! Yeah, man, let's do it!

No! Wrong.

Hold up there, young buck.

We don't need the debugger just yet.

Wait, what? How am I going to test my hypotheses if I can't use the debugger, you ask?

Unit tests.

Yes, that's right: unit tests.

Try to write a unit test to test your hypotheses.

If you think some part of the system isn't working correctly, write a unit test that you think will exploit the issue.

If you are right and you've found the problem, you can fix it right then and there, and now you will have a unit test in place to verify the fix and ensure it never happens again.

(Still make sure you try to reproduce the actual bug, though, before you call it fixed.)

If you are wrong and the unit test you write passes as expected, **you've just made the system a little more robust** by adding another unit test to the project (assuming your unit test actually has an assertion in it), and you've disproved one of your hypotheses.

Think of it as ratcheting up the problem space.

Every time you write a unit test and it passes, you are eliminating possibilities. (Assuming your unit test actually could fail. Make sure that any unit tests you write don't just pass under any conditions—this is a surprisingly easy blunder to make… trust me.) You are traversing through your debugging journey by closing and locking doors behind you as soon as you find out they are dead-ends.

If you've ever been lost for hours or days in a debugging session, you should immediately realize how valuable this is.

One of the reasons why the debugger is so bad is because **it can encourage us to revisit the same wrong corridors over and over again** as we check and recheck our assumptions, either forgetting what we already looked for or not trusting that we looked hard enough.

A unit test is like climbing a mountain and putting an anchor in place that makes sure you can't fall too far backwards.

Writing unit tests to test your hypotheses will also ensure that you aren't haphazardly looking around and trying things.

You have to have a specific assumption you are testing when you write a unit test in order to help debug a problem.

Now, I'm a realist.

I'm pragmatic.

I know that sometimes it will be extremely difficult or impossible to write a unit test to test a hypothesis.

In this case, it's ok to fire up the debugger, but only if you obey this one rule:

Have a specific purpose for doing it.

Know exactly what you are looking for and what you are checking when you use the debugger.

Don't merely go in there to look around.

I know it may seem like I'm being a bit anal and pedantic about this whole thing but trust me, there is a reason for it.

I want you to become a skilled debugger, and you are only going to get that way by being deliberate about how you debug.

CHECK YOUR ASSUMPTIONS

Most of the time, your hypotheses are not going to pan out.

That's just life.

If that's the case, the next best thing you can do is to check your assumptions about how things are working.

We typically assume that code is working a certain way or that some input or output must be some value.

Often we think, "Well, this can't possibly be happening. I'm looking at the code right here. There is no way it could be producing this output."

Often, we are wrong.

It happens to the best of us.

The best thing you can do with these assumptions is to check them.

And what's the best way to check them?

Yes, that's right. More unit tests.

Write some unit tests that check obvious things which "have to be working" along the workflow of the problem you are trying to debug.

Most of these tests should easily pass, and you'll say, "Duh."

But, every once in a while, you'll write a unit test to test some obvious assumption and the results will shock you.

Remember, if the answer to your problem was obvious, it wouldn't be a problem at all.

Once again, the pragmatist side of me has to tell you that, yes, it's ok to open up the debugger to check your assumptions as well.

But only after you've tried to check the assumptions using unit tests first.

Again, it's like climbing that mountain and putting in anchors along the way.

Avoid the debugger if you can, use it if you must, but, once again, only to validate or invalidate specific assumptions you have already formed.

DIVIDE AND CONQUER

I remember working on a really hairy bug with a printer that was incorrectly interpreting a print file written in the PostScript printing language.

I tried everything I could think of to debug the problem.

I tested all kinds of hypotheses.

Nothing panned out.

It seemed like the bug was some kind of combination of multiple commands in the print file, and I had no idea which ones it was.

So, what did I do?

Well, I cut the print file in half.

The bug was still there.

So, I cut it in half again.

It disappeared this time.

I tried the other half. Back again.

I kept hacking away at big chucks of the print file until I got the entire file down from several thousand lines of code to just five.

The five lines of code that, in that order, produced the bug.

Easy peasy.

Sometimes when you get stuck debugging, what you need to do is figure out a way to cut the problem in half—or take as big of a chunk out of it as possible.

Depending on the problem, this could look very different, but **try and think of ways you can eliminate a large amount of code** or remove a large amount of the system or variables and still reproduce the bug.

See if you can come up with tests which completely eliminate parts of the system for being responsible for the error.

Then do it again... and again.

If you keep hacking away, you'll likely find the critical components required to create the error, and then the problem can become relatively easy to solve.

IF YOU FIX IT, UNDERSTAND WHY

I'm going to give you one final piece of advice about debugging—although I'm sure I could write a whole book on the subject.

If you fix a problem, understand why what you did fixed it.

If you don't understand why what you did fixed the problem, you are not done yet.

You may have inadvertently caused a different problem, or—very likely—you haven't fixed your original problem.

Problems don't go away on their own.

If you didn't fix the problem, I can guarantee you it's not fixed. It's just hiding.

But if you did fix the problem, don't stop there. Explore a little deeper, and make sure you understand exactly what was going on that caused the problem in the first place and how what you did fixed it.

Too many software developers debug a problem by twiddling bits, the code apparently starts working, and they assume it is fixed without even knowing why.

This is a dangerous habit for many reasons.

As I mentioned above, **when you randomly tweak things in the system and change bits of code here and there, you could be causing all kinds of other problems which you aren't aware of.**

But, perhaps more than that, you are training yourself to be a shitty debugger.

You are developing the habit of messing with things until it works. No technique, no rigor.

You may get lucky sometimes, but you won't have a repeatable process or reliable skillset for debugging.

Not only should you understand what broke, why, and how you fixed it, but also you should verify the fix.

I know it seems like common knowledge, but I can't tell you how much time is wasted by programmers "fixing a problem," assuming the fix worked, and passing the code to QA only for QA to reproduce the problem and have it go back to the developer who has to start over at square one again.

It's a huge waste of time that can be prevented by taking an extra five minutes to verify that what you fixed is actually fixed.

In fact, don't just verify the fix; **write a regression test for the problem so that it never happens again.**

If you truly understand the problem you fixed, you should be able to write a unit test that exploits the issue, and then your fix should make that unit test pass.

Finally, **look for other instances of this same class of bug.**

Bugs tend to hang out together.

If you found something wrong with one assumption you made about the system or some incorrectly coded component, it's very likely that there are other issues which are also caused by that same problem.

Again, this is why it is so critical that you understand what the real problem was and why your solution fixed it.

If you know what happened and why, you can quickly figure out if there are likely to be other issues caused by the same underlying problem.

ART AND SCIENCE

Remember, debugging—like software development—is part art and part science.

You can only get good at debugging by practicing.

But practicing is not enough. You have to specifically, systematically debug, not just play around in the debugger.

Hopefully, I've given you a good overview of how to do that; now the rest is up to you.

CHAPTER 33

MAINTAINING CODE

When you first think about becoming a software developer, you probably have dreams of creating exciting new features, playing with new technologies, and writing some really cool and interesting code.

What you probably don't think about is working on a 10-year-old, crufty application written by some guy who left the company a long time ago, fixing the bugs he left behind.

The truth of the matter is that **you'll spend much more time over the course of your software development career maintaining code than you will writing new code.**

That's how life is. Just one of those things.

This fact doesn't mean, though, that you'll only be working on maintaining old VB6 applications written decades ago.

In fact, probably a large amount of the code you'll be maintaining is your own.

So, it's probably a good idea if you learn two things.

First, you'll need to know **how to properly maintain code** so that it doesn't get worse and worse over time until it finally falls apart.

And second, you'll need to learn **how to write good code that is easy to maintain**, so that developers who later have to maintain your code don't track you down, come to your house, and kill you in your sleep.

In this chapter, we are going to talk about why learning how to maintain code and write maintainable code is so important, and I'll give you some practical advice on how to do both of those things.

Sound good?

A MAJORITY OF YOUR CAREER WILL BE SPENT MAINTAINING CODE

I've already mentioned this, but it's worth mentioning again because it's so true.

In one form or another, you are going to be maintaining code.

New software gets created all the time, but every new software application is expected to have some sort of lifespan that is hopefully longer than the time it took to create.

This means that there will always be more old software out there than new software. (Unless we have a ridiculously high influx of new software and a bunch of old software dies off at the same time, but that is very unlikely to happen.)

Old software that is out there will constantly need to be improved and maintained.

Customers will find bugs that need to be fixed.

New features will need to be added, or existing features will need to be modified.

Production software is like a living, breathing organism, always growing and changing or slowly dying.

Why am I telling you this?

Do I just want to dash your hopes against the walls?

No, I want you to have **realistic expectations** of what you will be doing in your career as a software developer.

Oftentimes, eager, well-meaning hiring managers can paint a rosy picture of a job, telling you that you'll be working on designing and coding a brand new system from scratch using the latest technologies.

While some of your job might be doing this, more often than not, a majority of that job—no matter how good it sounds—will involve maintaining an existing system.

Again, it's just the way life works.

Does this mean you can never get a job where you can completely write a new system from scratch?

No, it definitely happens, but don't expect it all the time.

Even if you do, expect that at some point in time, you or someone else will have to maintain that code.

That's all.

GREAT DEVELOPERS WRITE MAINTAINABLE CODE

Now that you have your expectations properly set, I'm going to try to inspire you to write "the best darn maintainable code you can," because by gosh, it's just a swell thing to do.

One incontrovertible fact I have found during my many years of working as a software developer, and working with software developers, is that **great developers write highly maintainable code.**

In fact, I would say that the sole criteria I judge a programmer on is how maintainable their code is.

This might seem silly.

You might think I'm making this up just to make my point in this chapter.

But I'm telling you, it's true. Here's why.

Great developers know that **the majority of the life of any code they write will be spent in maintenance phase.**

Great developers know that **the most valuable code they write is code that lasts a long time** (https://simpleprogrammer.com/cg33-wrong) **and doesn't have to be scrapped and rewritten.**

Rather than being clever and as fast or efficient as possible, great developers optimize for maintainability.

They write **good, clean code** that can be **easily understood, modified, and maintained.**

They **create flexible designs** that are loosely coupled, so that if one thing changes in the system, it doesn't affect every other component of the system.

They take extra care to make sure what they do is **well documented** and as self-explanatory as possible.

They've spent enough time looking at someone else's code—or their own—and trying to maintain it that they know the best code they can write is the code that is the most maintainable.

THE BOY SCOUT RULE

One secret to being great at maintaining code is the Boy Scout Rule.

This rule originates from the Boy Scouts of America who emphasize a simple rule for camping:

"Leave the campground cleaner than you found it."

This is a great rule to apply to multiple areas of your life, but it's especially useful in software development.

Leave the code better than you found it.

It's really that simple.

When you are working on some code, perhaps fixing a bug or adding a new feature, try to leave that code in a slightly better state than it was when you found it.

It might mean writing an extra unit test to make the code a little more robust for the next developer who comes along and has to change something in it.

It might mean renaming some variables in the code to make the meaning more clear.

It might mean grouping some functionality into a method or procedure to reduce some redundancy in the code or to make it easier to understand.

It might even involve refactoring a large chunk of the code to implement a cleaner, more simple design.

As long as you are following this rule, the code will gradually get better over time—or at least the rate of entropy will decline severely.

This basic rule is the most simple secret for maintaining an existing codebase.

READABILITY IS OF UTMOST IMPORTANCE

One of the most important factors influencing the maintainability of code is its readability (https://simpleprogrammer.com/cg33-readable).

The more readable the code is, the easier it is to maintain that code.

The more cryptic and difficult to understand code is, the more difficult it is to maintain.

It's that plain and simple.

Too many developers try to write succinct and clever code.

While being succinct can be valuable, being terse and clever is an absolute recipe for disaster.

Why?

Because **code is read more than it is written** (https://simpleprogrammer.com/cg33-legacy).

Every time a programmer is trying to understand some workflow passing through your code so they in turn can add a new feature, modify an existing one, or troubleshoot a bug, they are going to need to understand what your code is doing.

The easier it is for them to understand, the easier it will be for them to make the correct changes to the system and the less time it will take.

If the code is obscure and difficult to understand, it's going to take extra time whenever another developer—or even yourself—has to examine and try to understand that code.

It is also highly likely that someone will misunderstand the code, and may then make an error when changing the code or another part of the system which uses that code, further degrading the system.

The fact of the matter is that **readable code is just easier to maintain**, period.

Therefore, when writing code that is meant to be maintained, strive for readability above all else.

REFACTOR CODE TO MAKE IT BETTER

We've already talked about the Boy Scout Rule, but let's dive a little deeper into what it means to "make code better."

How can you make code better?

A whole book could be written on the subject of refactoring—and several have been (https://simpleprogrammer.com/cg33-refactor)—but in this section, I'm going to introduce you to the basics, and you can practice and learn on your own.

Refactoring is essentially improving the design of existing code.

To me, refactoring means **making existing code more readable without changing its functionality.**

The "without changing its functionality" part is pretty important because you can't go around leaving code better than you found it if you are also changing the functionality.

You could be introducing bugs and making the code worse.

Not that you can't ever change functionality when you improve code, but that isn't the point of refactoring.

The point of refactoring is to take some existing code and make it even better.

"Better" could—and really, always should—mean more readable and maintainable.

However, it could also mean that you've reduced the total lines of code by eliminating some duplication or by organizing it in a different way.

It could mean that you've improved the overall architecture to make it more flexible and robust against further changes.

There are many ways to refactor code, but the big rule in refactoring is to not change functionality but to make the code better.

Refactoring and unit testing go hand-in-hand since it's difficult to know that you haven't changed the functionality of code if you have no way to test it.

It's a good idea to have some unit tests in place before you do refactoring, especially if it's a non-trivial change.

HEY JOHN

What about unit tests? Do I need to worry about maintaining them as well?

Do I really have to answer this?

Yes! An Empathetic Yes!

Especially unit tests.

Unit tests are code, and just like any code they need to be maintained.

In fact, you should take the utmost care in making your unit tests as maintainable as possible because:

- When one fails, you won't want to have to spend 30 minutes trying to figure out what that unit test was doing.
- You know for sure that as the code changes, the unit tests will also need to change.
- By the very nature of what a unit test is, there is going to be a great deal of duplication, which is a recipe for maintenance headaches.

I'll be 100% honest with you.

> Most software development projects that end up abandoning unit tests or any kind of automated tests do so for one major reason: they are unmaintainable.
>
> So, don't make that mistake.

Treat unit tests just like any production code and both write them to be maintained and maintain them.

Trust me on this one.

There are also some modern refactoring tools which can assist you and can pretty much guarantee that the refactorings won't change the functionality of the code.

Most modern IDEs have some of these tools baked in.

Think of it as rearranging a mathematics equation without altering its meaning.

You can always be sure that $4x = 8$ is the same as $2x = 4$ or $x = 2$.

You don't have to prove it.

AUTOMATION IS ESSENTIAL

It's really difficult to maintain software on which you have to manually build and manually run tests to make sure nothing breaks.

The faster you can make and test changes, the better the safety net you'll have, which will protect you from adding new bugs and errors to an existing codebase.

This is why automation is essential to increasing the maintainability of a software project.

Having an automated build, a continuous integration system, and automated tests make it incredibly simple to make changes to the code and quickly find out if you broke anything.

This quick cycle of feedback gives developers more confidence in their changes and also allows them to refactor the code, making it better without fear.

IF YOU WRITE COMMENTS, WRITE GOOD ONES

I'm not a huge fan of writing comments in code (https://simpleprogrammer.com/cg33-comments).

Yes, I know this is heresy.

But **I'd rather write clear, expressive code which is self-explanatory than write cryptic code which can only be understood when reading through the comments**—which, by the way, hopefully have been maintained along with the code.

I'd rather see you write clean, readable code than add a bunch of comments to the code which usually end up outdated.

But, **if you do write comments, make sure they are really good.**

Make sure the comments clearly explain something that is non-obvious and needs to be explained.

Cryptic comments are sometimes as bad, or worse, than cryptic code because you can at least figure out what cryptic code does. You can't really figure out what a cryptic comment might have meant.

Along with comments in the code, **make your commit messages as clear and helpful as possible** as well.

Clear messages also contribute to the maintainability of a codebase because commit messages give us a history of not just what happened to code over time, but why.

That why can be crucial when trying to understand some code or change that wasn't apparent, especially when it involves fixing a tricky bug.

RESOURCES FOR LEARNING TO WRITE MAINTAINABLE CODE

Maintaining code is tricky.

It involves quite a few skills, from writing clean code, to refactoring, to design and even infrastructure concerns like devops and automation.

I've decided to include **a list of some valuable resources** which can help you become better at both writing maintainable code and maintaining existing code that you didn't write.

Clean Code by Robert Martin (https://simpleprogrammer.com/cg33-clean) – I've mentioned this book a few times, but it's one of the best books about writing clean, readable code, and it also includes great information about design and refactoring for maintainability.

Code Complete by Steve McConnell (https://simpleprogrammer.com/cg33-complete) – Again, I've mentioned this book a few times already, but it's another great book about writing good, maintainable code. You'll find this book goes into some of the low-level, structural details of writing good, readable code. Read it.

Combined, *Clean Code* and *Code Complete* will give you a solid base and understanding of what makes good, clean, readable code and how to write and structure your code, so I highly recommend reading both books.

Working Effectively With Legacy Code by Michael Feathers (https://simpleprogrammer.com /cg33-effective) – This is a classic book about maintaining existing code. It dives pretty deep down into the nitty-gritty of legacy systems and how to deal with code that someone else wrote. Every software developer should read this book, since every software developer is likely to spend a majority of their time working with legacy code.

Refactoring by Martin Fowler (https://simpleprogrammer.com/cg33-refactor) – Another classic book which all software developers should read. This book goes over all the major refactorings you can do to restructure code without changing its functionality.

Well, there's the gist of it.

Just remember the Boy Scout Rule, and you'll do ok.

Oh, also, don't worry: you'll get plenty of practice maintaining code over the course of your software development career.

Good luck.

HEY JOHN

My team has a "style guide" which tells me how I should write my code and what it should look like. Should I follow it?

Yes, even if it's not optimal.

Here's why: uniformity trumps perfection.

Many teams have a style guide that says how you should name your variables, how you should indent your code and other such stylistic things.

These style guides might even be more prescriptive in telling you to structure your code in ways you don't think are the most readable or maintainable.

But, I would still follow them, or if you really disagree, make a good case for having the style guide changed.

Again, even if the formatting suggested in the style guide is not optimal for readability—in your opinion—overall, the readability of the entire codebase will be greatly improved by the uniformity a style guide provides.

So, choke on that pride a little if you have to, and conform.

You can show your non-conformity in other ways if you must, like wearing socks with your sandals or get a big ring with a skull on it that says "REBEL."

CHAPTER 34

JOBS AND JOB TITLES

I've been a software developer for over 15 years and I still don't know what to call myself.

Really.

You'll notice in this book I try to drop programmer and sometimes software engineer into some of the text, just for SEO (Search Engine Optimization), because **I honestly don't know of a single title I can use to describe software developers which everyone can universally agree on.**

(Although, I'm sure you've noticed by now that I'm pretty set on software developer. That's why I use it so much.)

Beyond trying to agree on a generalized name for developers, software developers, programmers, software engineers, coders, computer programmers, and the like, we've got to contend with job titles.

What the heck is the difference between a Senior Software Engineer and a Junior Software Engineer?

And how do they compare to Software Developer II and Software Development Engineer in Test?

This is some pretty confusing stuff.

Well, if all of this has confused you in the past—and the present—I'm here to tell you that you are not alone.

I'm still confused by all of this, but this chapter is my feeble attempt to sort it all out for the both of us and offer you some general guidance in terms of how these titles can affect you and your career.

JOB TITLES DON'T REALLY MATTER...

The first thing to know about job titles is that **they don't really matter.**

Why don't they matter?

Because there are a hundred different job titles across many different companies, and even when companies have the same job titles, their meaning within that company can greatly differ.

In one company Senior Software Engineer could be the title given to all standard development jobs.

In another company Senior Software Engineer could mean that you are the technical lead for an entire team of programmers.

In yet another company Senior Software Engineer could mean you are old.

So, when you read the name of a job title in this crazy world of technology, don't read too much into it (https://simpleprogrammer.com/cg34-title).

Instead, **read the job description and pay attention to the pay**—that is what really matters.

... BUT GET THE BEST ONE YOU CAN

With that said, the world at large doesn't know what I just told you.

As confused as you are about job titles, so is everyone else.

No one can figure out whether a Software Developer III is better than a Senior Development Engineer.

So, what do people go on?

What the job title sounds like.

Yes, it's silly, but if you can land the job title Senior Director of Software Development, that's probably going to get you a better next-job than Junior Developer will, even though you might be doing the exact same job at a company that only has two programmers on the team.

That means you should try and get the most prestigious title as possible.

What? What is that you say, John?

Are you really saying that I should play this stupid title game?

Yes. I know it's silly.

I know it's meaningless, but **executives play this little game all the time.**

Ever wondered how someone gets to become a CEO?

Simple. They play the "title swap game" until they reach the CEO title at a small, rinky-dink company, and then they trade up to a bigger company once they've got that title on their resume.

Again, I wouldn't put too much emphasis on this.

During an offer negotiation, **it makes sense to at least consider negotiating your title** to add more prestige to it. You don't have to emphasize it over other things, but you should ask for a better title.

You can also play this game when you get a promotion, or even in lieu of a promotion if you get turned down for a pay raise. (Hey, I know you can't pay me more right now, it's not in the budget, I get it, but could you at least change my title to Supreme Commander of the Secret Codes?)

SOME COMMON JOB TITLES

Let's talk about some of the most common job titles you are likely to encounter as a software developer.

First, we'll start with the obvious, **Software Developer.**

Nothing special here. You'll probably hear this one quite a bit—especially if you consume the content I produce.

I like this title because to me it's pretty descriptive and general enough to describe what most programmers do. They develop software.

Programmer. This one is interesting.

I actually prefer this one, because it's extremely simple and it describes the core of what we do. We program.

Yes, we develop software, but technically you could develop software without programming and coder is a bit too vague.

However, it seems a great majority of programmers are insulted by just being called programmers.

You don't get it man, they'll insist. Software development is more than just programming (https://simpleprogrammer.com/cg34-difference).

I'm an engineer. I gather requirements, talk to customers, design, architect, test, mold clay sculptures out of silly putty.

No, I get it. But primarily **what people hire you to do is to program. To write code.**

So, I'll have to be happy enough with my company being called Simple Programmer and I'll use the more complex phrase software developer and call it a day.

Next, you have **Software Engineer** and all of its many variants.

By the way, have you noticed that 90 percent of Software Engineers are Senior Software Engineers?

I'm ok with this title, but electrical engineers, mechanical engineers, structural engineers, and the like seem to lose their shit when they hear this title.

It kind of amuses me, but I'd rather avoid wasting my time continually arguing the point, so I generally avoid this term nowadays.

I'm not really a respecter of gatekeepers (https://simpleprogrammer.com /cg34-gatekeeper) and people who say "you have to be approved and meet some criteria to call yourself an engineer."

It's kind of like people who insist on being called doctor since they have a Ph.D., or put silly initials after their name even in completely social settings.

The only academic authority I R-E-S-P-E-C-T is called R-E-S-U-L-T-S.

For me, **not using "software engineer" isn't really about respecting the engineer part of the title**, it's more about when I think about engineering, I think about the older, waterfall way of developing software.

When I think "software development," to me that conveys the evolution of software—the Agile way—a bit more.

THE ONE JOB TITLE TO AVOID

With that said, there is one job title I would try to avoid if possible.

That is the job title of junior anything.

Junior Developer. Junior Software Developer. Junior Software Engineer.

Many programmers starting out thinking that they have to start out as junior developers (https://simpleprogrammer.com/cg34-first)—but it's just not true.

I've found that junior developer positions usually require a similar set of skills as a non-junior developer role, but pay much less.

Besides, guess where the most competition in the software developer job market is?

That's right. Junior developer.

If you are just getting started and don't have any real-world experience yet, you may not be able to get a senior software engineer position, but there is no reason why you can't get a regularly titled developer role.

The biggest problem with junior roles is that if you take a junior role, in about a year — or at the most, two — you'll likely be doing the same work as developers without the "junior" attached to their title, but you'll probably be paid significantly less.

So, instead of looking for junior roles, look for jobs with non-junior titles that simply require less experience or require a very specific set of skills which you specialize in.

It may actually be easier to land one of these jobs than a junior job, which every fresh college graduate will be competing for.

THE BASIC ROLES OR JOBS

Even though there are quite a few different job titles for software developers, there are really only about five different roles on the technical track of software development.

Most jobs will fall into one of these job roles or levels.

SDET (SOFTWARE DEVELOPMENT ENGINEER IN TEST)

You don't see this role in many small organizations, but larger companies like Microsoft like to hire developers first as SDETs.

A Software Development Engineer in Test is really just a software development role where you aren't writing production code, but are instead writing either code to test code or working on tools. (Tools for the team that is—usually things that make the development team's job easier.)

This role could also be called a tools developer or something similar.

You can think of this as a software development support role.

This is a good place to start, because if you work on writing automated tests (https://simpleprogrammer.com/cg34-selenium) or tools to help with testing, you'll gain a good understanding of the testing process—which can actually help you to become a better developer overall.

DEVELOPER (JUNIOR / REGULAR SIZE / SENIOR)

This is the standard software developer role.

Most developers are going to fall into this category of developers.

Here you are working on the actual product and writing code.

TEAM LEAD OR TECH LEAD

This is a step up the ladder from software developer.

In this role, you may be leading a team of developers, doing some management as well as development, will likely be contributing to the architecture of the code base, and perhaps doing code reviews and mentoring other developers.

Leads are also usually in charge of making important technical decisions about the project and perhaps interviewing developers, assigning tasks, or other responsibilities.

Leads are usually still writing code for most of their job, otherwise they'd be managers.

ARCHITECT

In this role a developer might not be writing code very much any more, but will still be very technically involved with the software.

An architect may design the entire system, attend meetings to decide on technologies and architecture, or even prototype experimental features or complete systems.

Large companies tend to have architect roles—especially for large software systems that require quite a bit of design and planning.

An architect might be responsible for the technical direction and ultimate implementation of an entire project.

DIRECTOR

This role is barely a software development role—and some people could argue that it isn't—but I decided to include it here since many software developers in large organizations end up in this role.

Some companies call this role a fellow or technical fellow.

Essentially in this role a software developer is a distinguished expert in the field and might be leading research, working as part of a think tank, or involved in very complex or high-profile projects.

A director-type role might also involve directing an entire organization of developers and making both technical and non-technical decisions as a director of software development.

BIG TECH COMPANY JOB TITLES

Job titles tend to get a little more formalized when dealing with larger corporations.

Most large tech companies like HP, Microsoft, Apple, etc., have a formal set of job titles and associated pay scales that go with them.

Knowing this information and understanding how this system works ahead of time can really help you with negotiations. It can help you to get raises or move up in the company.

It basically works like this.

Suppose you get a job at a big tech company.

Most likely, you'll be applying for a specific job title—let's say Software Development Engineer.

That job is associated with a level, which determines the pay, responsibilities and general qualifications/expectations of someone in that role.

Typically this level will be assigned a number, like 59.

That particular job title, Software Development Engineer, might be associated with a range of levels.

For example, Software Development Engineer might go from level 59-60.

At 61, the title might change to Software Development Engineer II.

At 63, the title might change to Senior Software Development Engineer.

Each level has a lower and upper pay range, so the actual level is much more important than the title itself.

If you get a job at one of these companies, you want to get in at the highest level possible, so that you can have the highest possible pay band.

It would be better to get in at a higher level than a higher salary, if given the option, because over time the software developers at the same level who are lower on the pay band for that level are more likely to get raises.

The company's Human Resources office tends to want to get everyone at the same level to near the same amount of pay.

Typically in these large corporations, a raise would just be a salary increase within the same level, but a promotion would be a raise to a higher level.

In most of these companies the pay bands themselves are kept somewhat secret—although you can find the information if you look hard enough—but the titles and level progressions are usually provided by HR.

You can also usually find a set of requirements that define what makes a software developer a certain level.

We'll talk more about this in later chapters, when we discuss getting raises and promotions, but **you should always know what the requirements of the level above you are and the level above that.**

Shoot to fulfill all the requirements of the level that is two above you and you'll have a much easier time getting a promotion.

You'll also notice that **some of the highest levels usually require you to be an industry leader and have an influence beyond your company.**

This is one of the reasons why I stress creating a blog (https://simpleprogrammer.com/cg34 -blog) and building your personal brand (https://simpleprogrammer.com/cg34-marketyourself) so much.

If you ever want to be a technical fellow or similar role and reach the highest ladder levels, you need to be well-known in your specific niche within the software development industry.

THAT'S QUITE A BIT ABOUT JOB TITLES

Yeah, I know—especially when I said they don't matter.

But, the simple fact is that even though the job titles themselves don't matter in the industry as a whole, **they certainly can matter within an individual company.**

So, my best advice to you is to not worry too much about a job title across companies, but to try and figure out what a job title means within a company and more importantly, to understand the job itself.

And if you really don't like any of the jobs titles you've been given, you can always start your own company and call yourself whatever you like—that's what I did.

CHAPTER 35

TYPES OF WORK

True story.

I almost deleted this chapter from the outline of the book.

Really. I looked at it and said, "types of work," what does that mean?

At first I was thinking that I meant the kinds of jobs you could have as a software developer and I recall already covering most of that in earlier sections of the book.

But then it hit me. Duh.

Software developers do a lot more than just write code (https://simpleprogrammer.com /cg35-right).

There are quite a few different "types of work" that software developers do.

And guess what?

You need to know about them.

I mean, I couldn't exactly call this section of the book "What You Need to Know About Software Development" if I didn't actually tell you **what you were going to do all day at your job.**

Heck, you might get the crazy idea that you'll spend all day coding.

Imagine how disappointed you would be if you showed up at that corporate gig all ready to spend eight hours writing code like a madman only to find out **you might only get to actually write real code a few hours a day.**

That's what this chapter is about—a reality check.

If a software developer doesn't write code all day, what, indeed, does a software developer actually do all day?

Let's find out.

WRITING CODE

Wait, what? I thought you just said software developers don't write code all day?

Yes. That's right. But **they do write some code.**

I mean, would you really call yourself a programmer if you didn't actually program? It's just not as much as you think—at least most days.

You can definitely end up going on a code writing binge and code like a madman for several days and nights, living on Mountain Dew and Hot Pockets. (I have to throw the cliché into every book I write.)

But, in general, most days, you do not just simply write code. There will be many days where you don't write any code at all.

Those are sad days, but necessary.

The general rule is, the smaller the company you work for (https://simpleprogrammer.com /cg35-bigsmall), **the more code you are likely to write in a given day.**

The bigger the company, the more overhead there is going to be, and the less time you'll spend writing code. That's just life.

But, you'll definitely spend some time writing code.

I won't explain what writing code entails, because if you don't know, well... I'm not sure I can help you.

FIXING BUGS

Ha! Sucker!

You thought you were going to write a bunch of new code and use the latest and greatest JavaScript framework, but instead you are fixing bugs.

Sometimes you get to write new code, **but more often than not, you get to fix bugs in old code**—again, life.

Software developers write code. That code is not perfect. It has bugs in it.

Someone has to fix them. That someone is you.

Check out the chapter on debugging to learn more about how to do this effectively, but just know that a decent portion of the time you will spend working in code during the day will be spent fixing bugs, both your own and others.

DESIGN AND ARCHITECTURE

This is actually a pretty fun non-coding part of being a programmer, because you get to use your brain, draw on a whiteboard, and argue with people.

For some reason, programmers really like to argue with people and to yell.

True story. I was once accused of throwing a chair at a Quality Assurance person.

I didn't actually throw a chair.

I accidentally knocked it over while having a heated discussion.

But, you know how rumors are.

There is a pretty good chance, that, as a software developer you'll spend some amount of time working with your team—or by yourself—to develop the architecture or design of the system you are working on.

Most software developers don't just jump straight into the code and start coding something up.

Ahem. Let me correct that.

Most great software developers don't just jump straight into the code and start coding something up.

Instead, they spend some time designing out what they'll be coding ahead of time and arguing with other nearby developers about why one way of doing something is .01 percent better than another way.

You'll spend a good amount of time working on some kind of design or architecture activity in your tenure as a software professional.

MEETINGS

Yes, I hate them too, but sometimes they are necessary.

I was pretty notorious for skipping meetings as a software developer, when I didn't find them important.

I still do that.

I don't like to waste my time.

But, the truth of the matter is that no matter how much you despise meetings and try to avoid them, you'll likely get sucked into at least one or two during your software development career, perhaps even a daily or weekly one.

You are just going to have to get used to it and realize it's all part of the job.

You might wonder why a software developer would need to go to any kind of meeting at all.

Well, sometimes I do, too. But there are actually some legit reasons.

If you are following a process like Scrum, it's important to have a planning meeting to plan out and estimate the work which will be done in the Sprint.

Retrospective and review meetings are also important for demonstrating work, getting feedback, and making improvements.

Sometimes important project-level decisions need to be made and having a developer in that meeting, who understands the technology, can be an important part of making the right decisions.

All in all, expect to at least spend some time in meetings in your life as a developer.

LEARNING

I often get asked if software developers should be paid to learn (https://simpleprogrammer.com /cg35-onthejob) or if they should do it on their own time.

The answer is "yes."

You should be learning while at work, but you should also be doing it on your own time (https://simpleprogrammer.com/cg35-tensteps).

It's pretty naive to think you can work at a software development job and not spend at least some of that time learning.

When I worked as a software developer, **I would spend the first 30 minutes of my day browsing software development blogs and keeping myself up to date.**

Doing this allowed me to do my job better and to better understand the industry.

In fact, **one of the first—and most important—interview questions I ask potential candidates is how they stay up to date.**

I'm actually looking to hear that they dedicate a certain amount of time each day to reading and learning to keep their skills sharp and get a heartbeat on the industry at large.

You'll also need to learn on the fly when you encounter a difficult problem at work, which will be pretty often.

You'll spend quite a bit of time at work Googling for answers to your questions, reading tutorials, and even going through books to help you solve a problem, design a solution, or learn to use a new technology in your job.

Some software development environments actively encourage learning, while others try to milk developers for every ounce of productivity they can and tell you to "learn on your own time."

Good software developers can't do their jobs without constantly learning, so learn you will.

EXPERIMENTING AND EXPLORING

This is sort of learning, but a bit more than that.

In order to do your job effectively, you'll find that you need to spend a large amount of time reading through existing code in the codebase to understand what is going on and to know where and how to make changes.

You'll also find that you need to just "try some things."

You'll want to write up a sample program to try and use a new API or technology that you are going to utilize to implement a new feature or fix a bug.

You'll want to play around a bit with technologies and tools to figure out what will work best for the problem you are trying to solve and to get familiar with them.

You'll likely prototype certain features or functionality before you implement it in production code.

Expect to spend a good amount of time doing these things, especially when working on large systems with complex codebases or when implementing new features with new or unproven technologies you may not be familiar with.

TESTING

At the very least, you'll spend a good deal of time testing your own code. Or you might help out by testing in general or working on writing automated tests.

Testing is an integral part of software development (https://simpleprogrammer.com /cg35-testing) **and good software developers make sure they test their code before they check it in and distribute it.**

See the chapter on testing for more about testing in general.

Some software developers really hate the idea of testing–they think it is beneath them.

They think it is their job to write the code and then the testers' job to test it.

This isn't true at all.

You, as a software developer, should be responsible for the quality of your own code.

You should spend the extra time to test, to the best of your ability, your own code to make sure it works correctly.

Only after you've tested the code, should it go to QA for further testing, after you've found—and fixed—all the bugs you can.

THINKING

I swear, sometimes software development is more thinking than anything else.

I often sit at my desk for long stretches of time, apparently doing nothing, but really just thinking, thinking, thinking about how to solve my problem or how to structure my code.

In fact, **you really should spend at least three times more time thinking about the code you are about to write as you do actually writing it.**

It's that old saying, "measure twice, cut once."

Even though code is highly malleable, it still pays to get it as close to right as you can, the first time.

You can save yourself hours of rewriting and debugging if you spend a few extra minutes thinking about a solution—and thinking it all the way through—before you implement it.

It can be tempting to think that thinking isn't productive and that it is a waste of time just because you can't see tangible results from it.

I fall into this trap all the time.

If you feel this way, sometimes it helps to have a notebook that you write your thoughts in as you are thinking about solutions to your problem, giving you a physical artifact of your thinking

And it can give you something to fall back on when you wonder why you did something a certain way and can't remember the thought process that got you there.

I'd probably be willing to go on record to say that the most effective software developers will spend more time in their day thinking than anything else. And I guess I just did.

INTERACT WITH CUSTOMERS / STAKEHOLDERS

This can suck. I know.

And you might not be good at it.

But you are going to have to do it and you might as well get good at it.

Start by reading *How to Win Friends and Influence People* (https://simpleprogrammer.com /cg35-influence), and if you haven't read my book *Soft Skills: The Software Developer's Life Manual* (https://simpleprogrammer.com/cg35-lifemanual), you should probably do that, too.

But why, why John, do I have to talk to customers and stakeholders?

Can't I just sit in my cubicle and write code and let the business people deal with everyone else?

Yes, you can.

You can absolutely do that.

But **you are going to extremely limit your career and your potential.**

We no longer live in a world where software developers are valuable just because they can write code.

The skill of writing code is being commoditized.

You can find coders all over the world who can write code for cheap.

The value of a software developer today is not just their ability to write code, but to communicate and translate the requirements of the business or customer into the ultimate technical solution.

If you want to be a good developer, **you are going to need to understand the requirements of the system you are building.**

That means you are going to have to talk to customers or stakeholders and understand the problem domain and the problem you are trying to solve for them.

This is especially important in an Agile environment where you are constantly iterating on the software you are building.

Expect to spend some time each day, or at least each week, talking to customers or key stakeholders and actually communicating.

TRAINING / MENTORING

The biggest value of an experienced software developer, for a team, is not his or her individual ability to write code.

Yes, a really good programmer can do the work of perhaps as many as 10 not-so-good programmers, but the impact is still limited in comparison to the effect a really good developer can have on raising the ability of the entire development team.

As you gain experience and become better at your job, you'll spend more and more of your time training and mentoring other developers.

This is a good thing, although sometimes it can make you feel not productive and make you yearn to write more code.

But it is very rewarding to know that your contributions to a team and to the community extend beyond your personal abilities to write code.

AND THAT'S IT...

Well, mostly.

There may be some other jobs you have to do as a software developer, depending on where you work, like setting up servers and perhaps even selling to customers, but we've covered most of the basics here.

And that actually brings us to the end of this section of the book, so now it's time to get to work.

In the next section, we'll be focusing on how to survive and thrive in the work environment of a typical software developer.

Journey on.

SECTION 4

WORKING AS A DEVELOPER

"It's just a job. Grass grows, birds fly, waves pound the sand. I beat people up."
—Muhammad Ali

Your job as a software developer entails much more than just writing code.

In fact, the primary success that you see in your long-term career will be more influenced by soft-skill factors like how you get along with your coworkers, how well you communicate your ideas, deal with your boss, ask for raises, handle performance reviews and possibly even how you dress, rather than the kind of code you write.

That doesn't mean you can get away with being a bad-code-writing-brown-nosing-yes-man (or woman), but it does mean that you have to pay careful attention to the social dynamics involved in working in the technology field.

This section is all about navigating that complex and sometimes chaotic work environment, filled with reclusive coworkers, overbearing asshole bosses, demanding clients, and even a few bigots of various sorts thrown in here and there.

Oh, and you'll also need to figure out that life / work balance thing everyone likes to talk about.

It can be challenging to deal with annoying coworkers, but it's worth the investment to learn how, because you'll likely see them more than you do your own family.

The same could be said for bosses.

I've had my share of unbearably idiotic or micromanaging ones in my day, and I know how much of a pain this can be.

So, again it's essential that you know how to deal with these kinds of difficult people—especially when they are in positions of power.

And when it's time for that yearly or quarterly review, do you know the best way to ace the review and get that raise or promotion you've been dreaming about?

Don't worry, I've got that covered, but it might involve paying attention to how you dress—covered as well—and getting into a leadership position—also covered.

Finally, the world is not always a fair and hospitable place.

The tech world is no exception—in fact, sometimes it's a bit more harsh in some regards.

So, what should you do if you feel like you are the victim of prejudice or how should you approach the delicate topic of women in tech, whether you are a man or a woman?

Yes, I've waded knee-deep in the mud to answer those questions, because the only thing I'm afraid of is dealing with QA—also covered.

So, fair warning this section is going to get messy.

You might want to put on your poncho and pull up your undies.

I could have written this section in a completely politically correct way that leaves everyone feeling happy and nice, but that really won't do you much good in the work environment you'll likely face, so instead I just gave it to you raw.

So, ready or not, here we go...

CHAPTER 36

DEALING WITH COWORKERS

I can recall one of the worst coworkers I ever had the pleasure of dealing with.

His name was Sam, and he stunk.

No, I mean literally.

He didn't wear deodorant.

Not sure if he ever showered.

His breath stunk.

He got right up in your face when he talked to you—and talked to you he did, in the most abrasive way possible.

It's like he had no understanding of normal human interactions.

He would brag incessantly.

He would immediately declare your ideas as inferior to his.

He would say "indeed" far too often and used $5 words to make himself sound more educated than you, because he believed he was.

At first I thought I would have to quit my job, because I just couldn't deal with him and he was constantly in my face.

But then I realized a few things about old Sam.

Despite all his faults, underneath it all, he was actually a pretty nice guy.

Not only that, he was actually quite intelligent.

He was very critical, but at least he was honest.

While other people would shine you on, Sam would give you the truth, whether you liked it or not.

His lack of tact could be a good thing, if you developed some thick skin and knew how to handle it.

So, I decided to change my approach.

Instead of trying to change Sam, I accepted him.

I actually praised and acknowledged him for his strengths, which few people had done in the past.

He responded with a loyalty you couldn't even imagine.

Even though Sam still wasn't someone I would necessarily call a friend, he was not only a coworker I could deal with, but one who actually acted as an ally, by helping support my ideas.

In your job as software developer, you'll encounter plenty of your own Sams (https://simpleprogrammer.com/cg36-coworkers).

You'll also encounter plenty of friendly people who you naturally get along with.

You may even encounter the toxic person who, no matter what you do, will always spell trouble, and who you should generally avoid as much as possible.

It's important to know how to deal with all of these kinds of coworkers because, by definition, you'll be working with them almost every day.

You can be the best programmer in the world, but if you can't figure out how to get along with your coworkers, you are not only going to have a miserable time at work, you probably won't be all that productive either.

This chapter is about learning how to deal with coworkers—both the difficult and the easy ones.

FIRST IMPRESSIONS COUNT

It's really difficult to change the way people perceive you after you've met them, so when dealing with people who will likely make up a relatively large portion of your life, **it's probably a good idea to make a good first impression.**

Now, I realize that for you it may already be too late.

But you can always make a good first impression for your next job. Or you can try and remake your first impression at an existing job by doing a complete 180 and resetting people's impressions of you. (Difficult, but not impossible.)

When you first come into a new work environment, you want to make sure that you don't come off as inferior or not qualified for the job.

Being confident in your skills is really important, because many times what your coworkers think of you will inform the decision your manager makes regarding your career advancement.

So, even though humility is a virtue, **don't be timid and acquiescent just because you are the new guy or gal.**

You don't want to be forever labeled and thought of as the new guy.

We all know coworkers who have worked at the same job for several years and are still thought of as the new guy, because that was everyone's first impression of them and it stuck.

But don't be cocky and arrogant either.

Instead, **aim for a mix of confidence and curiosity** (https://simpleprogrammer.com /cg36-cocky).

You know what you are capable of and are secure in your abilities, but you are at a new job and respect the experience of your coworkers who have been there longer.

One of the best ways to pull this off is to **ask plenty of intelligent questions**—especially if someone is training you.

You also want to be especially careful about how you dress and behave during your first few days on the job.

Just because you can dress casually, doesn't mean you should.

Dress one or two notches higher than what you would normally wear in that work environment for your first week, so that you give off a more professional impression.

Also **make sure you are a bit more outgoing and friendly.**

Say "hello" to everyone you meet, and try to **use their first names** when you greet them.

Doing all of these things will help you create a good first impression which will go a long way in starting off on the right foot with your coworkers.

BE AS HELPFUL AS POSSIBLE

One thing that has always served me well in my career and ensured that I made plenty of allies wherever I worked was **my willingness to help my fellow employees.**

Your attitude at work should not be combative or competitive–although there is nothing wrong with a little healthy competition at times—but helpful and supportive instead.

You really don't want to get into situations where your coworkers are trying to bring you down or make you look bad all the time.

Some people are going to do that no matter what you do—we'll address that in a bit—but, **for the most part, if you are seen as a helpful person, people will respond in kind.**

Being willing to help coworkers with their problems will also benefit you, because you'll look much smarter than you are.

You'll **gain a reputation for being a "go to" person on your team**, which will help you greatly if you are ever trying to get a team lead position or promotion.

Overall though, being helpful is just a good idea in general. It disarms combative coworkers, nets you more overall experience, and generally makes people see you in a positive light, which leads to less overall problems and a better work environment.

AVOID DRAMA

Even if you make a great first impression and you are the most helpful person on your team, you are likely going to face some drama at the workplace.

Where there are humans, there is drama.

It simply is a consequence of social environments.

But just because there is drama, doesn't mean you have to get all caught up in it.

Do not allow bullshit into your life.

If you have drama, you have allowed bullshit in. It's as simple as that.

Really, it is.

You are in control of what you allow into your life and what you choose to invest your emotional and physical energy in.

When someone comes your way looking to start some drama, all you have to do is not encourage or acknowledge it (https://simpleprogrammer.com/cg36-drama).

Don't get caught up in the gossip.

When someone talks behind someone else's back, just reply by saying something nice about that person.

When a rumor is going around, don't even listen to it—certainly don't spread it.

Just do your job and change the subject to something work-related.

When you hear the conversation of the room buzzing with the pre-drama buzz, it's a great time to throw on those headphones and start typing away.

This is especially true when coworkers are trying to create drama around or about you.

So, someone doesn't like you and they've said something nasty about you?

Big deal. Ignore it. Move on.

Drama doesn't add anything positive to your life. Getting involved in drama has ended many programming careers, just because an otherwise smart software developer couldn't mind their own business and stay out of it.

BUT DON'T AVOID CONFLICT

Drama is unnecessary, but conflict isn't.

Wherever there are people working together to achieve a goal, there will be some form of conflict.

I think this, you think that, you think I am stupid, I think you are a moron, therefore we have conflict.

Some amount of conflict is healthy. It's healthy in any kind of relationship.

People don't always agree.

They have differing points of view, different world views, etc.

Conflict, if resolved properly, is beneficial, because it should result in a better outcome than either you or I could produce with our own limited thinking.

So, don't avoid conflict (https://simpleprogrammer.com/cg36-conflict).

If you disagree with someone's suggestion, be tactful, but state your opinion.

Conflict can become drama, but it doesn't have to as long as it is resolved properly.

Try to keep your cool and don't get upset.

Conflict shouldn't become personal.

If it does, you might need to cool off and leave the situation until you can re-engage with your coworker in a peaceful, constructive way.

Your goal should be to **find the best solution to the problem, not to prove you are right or smarter than your coworker or that their idea is dumb.**

You may also need to get into conflict if a coworker is violating your personal boundaries.

Read the book *Boundaries* (https://simpleprogrammer.com/cg36-boundaries) to get a good understanding of what constitutes reasonable personal boundaries, and how to deal with people who violate those boundaries.

In these cases, you can still engage in healthy conflict by letting your coworker know when something they are doing or saying to you is not ok.

This can be done in a friendly, but firm way that doesn't attack the other person, but clearly defines what your personal boundary is.

Conflict isn't fun, but if you avoid it, it can blow up into drama and repressed anger or resentment which will poison your relationships at work and at home.

With that said, you should always strive to avoid arguments.

Conflict can be resolved without resorting to arguments, especially about subjects not related to work.

(We'll get to two of those in a second.)

The difference between a healthy conflict being resolved and an argument is mainly intent.

If you are seeking to prove yourself right and your opponent wrong, it's an argument.

If you are genuinely looking to find a place of mutual understanding and respect to resolve differing views as best you can, it's a healthy resolution of conflict.

Dale Carnegie said it best when he said:

> *"I have come to the conclusion that there is only one way under*
> *high heaven to get the best of an argument—and that is to avoid it.*
> *Avoid it as you would avoid rattlesnakes and earthquakes."*

POLITICS AND RELIGION

Speaking of arguments, let's talk about politics and religion (https://simpleprogrammer.com /cg36-politics).

Oh, and we could throw in a healthy dose of sex in there, too.

Or perhaps not.

Not at work. **Just don't do it.**

If you want to find an argument and create animosity like you've never seen before, go ahead and bring up one of these topics.

People have extremely strong views on these subjects.

People are generally very narrowly-minded on these subjects.

People get very emotional about these subjects.

But, most importantly, these subjects don't in any way help you get your job done or contribute to a strong working environment.

Even if you think a coworker is likely to agree with you on one of these subjects, it's best not to talk about them, because:

1. They might not agree

2. Other coworkers, who don't agree, are likely to overhear the conversation and get involved or silently seethe at their desks, just waiting for the opportunity to bring you down.

Trust me, **nothing good can come of it.**

You can also be branded as a troublemaker or rabble-rouser when word gets around that you are the source of the political unrest at the office.

I've seen many well-respected and intelligent programmers be escorted out of the building with a cardboard box, because they couldn't keep their highly-charged opinions to themselves.

Save these conversations for the dinner table where they belong.

COWORKERS WHO DON'T WORK

In just about every work environment there is that one guy or gal who seems to never actually get any work done.

They are a deadweight on the team and everyone knows it.

You are working hard at your desk, kicking ass and taking names, and **they are just sitting there browsing the web** and posting political messages on Facebook.

It can be infuriating.

You feel the urge to slap them and drag them into the boss's office with the declaration that they are a slacker and should be fired.

Don't do it.

In fact, don't do anything.

This person has a rope, and they'll eventually hang themselves (https://simpleprogrammer.com /cg36-nowork), if you let them.

You worry about you.

Get your work done.

Be as productive as possible.

Don't worry about what other people do or don't do.

The best way you can deal with one of these kinds of people is to be so productive yourself that the contrast becomes so apparent that your boss can't help but notice who the slacker is.

The worst thing you can do is tattle on them, which makes you look petty and gives them a chance to defend themselves.

For one thing, you could be wrong about your assessment and they could pull out a notebook documenting everything they've done every single day for the past year—now making you look like the slacker.

For another thing, they could be on the job because of some form of nepotism that you aren't aware of.

You don't want to go and report the CEO's nephew to your boss, because guess who's going to win that conflict and guess who is going to get fired?

Instead, **just shut up and do your own work as best as you can.**

These issues have a way of resolving themselves, given enough time.

If you do want to do anything, offer to help this person.

That's right.

Reach out and **ask if they need some help.**

See if you can **inspire them with your work ethic.**

See if you can **motivate them** and get them to care about doing a good job.

You'd be surprised what a little encouragement can do.

HEY JOHN

What if they are actually worse than dead weight? What if they are actually bringing the team down or are completely incompetent—not just lazy?

I'll point you to an article I wrote called "7 Things Your Boss Doesn't Understand About Software Development," (https://simpleprogrammer.com/cg36-boss) but I'll quote the relevant part here:

Let's face it; we've all worked with programmers who actually ended up hurting the team more than helping them.

There is a huge variation in ability and skill level in the field of software development.

In fact, some software developers are so bad at their job that every line of code they write actually ends up costing the company more time and money.

These kinds of developers should probably be paying the company instead of the other way around.

It might be obvious to you, but you might be wondering why your boss doesn't realize that Joe is actually a complete loser and needs to be fired, because he seems to have the opposite of the Midas touch. Everything he touches turns to crap.

If you have a boss who doesn't seem to understand that some of your team is actually worse than dead weight, what can you do?

Well, most software developers are afraid of coming off like a tattletale and don't want to report a coworker for being a lazy, incompetent ass—I totally get it.

But… you have to do it anyway. That's right. If someone is actually hurting the team, it absolutely is your job to let your manager know.

I know it's an uncomfortable situation to be in, but if you don't report blatant incompetence, you are incompetent as well. You are an incompetence accomplice and I'll make you wear a red letter.

Just be sure to phrase things nicely and drop some hints that will lead to more investigation.

You might say something along the lines of:

"Hey, I don't like to do this kind of thing, but I feel that if I were in your shoes, I would want to know if someone was directly handicapping the team. So I feel that it is my duty to inform you of something that I've been observing.

Now, these are just my observations, so definitely check them with other team members and your own experience, but…"

> *Or, if you prefer a less subtle approach:*
>
> *"Hey! Joe is a jackass. He sucks at writing code and he's slow. In fact,
> his only redeeming quality is that he is slow, because he can only eff
> things up at a snail's pace. You should definitely shit-can him."*

This make seem like a contradiction that flies in the face of what I said earlier in this chapter, but there is a huge difference between being lazy and not working hard and actually being harmful and destructive to the team.

Let lazy people seal their own fate, but incompetence which is bringing down the entire team needs to be dealt with—even if there are some potential consequences for yourself.

COWORKERS WHO TALK TOO MUCH

Here is another situation many of us face.

You want to get your work done.

You want to be polite and social.

But, there is just this one dude, who's really friendly, but he just won't shut up.

You sit down to do your work and there he is popping his head over the cubicle wall wanting to talk about who you think will win the election.

You come back from work and there he is again, in your cubicle waiting for you so he can discuss the newest developments in his ongoing feud with his neighbor.

You are even giving him all the signals that you are busy and that he should go on and go back to work.

You repeatedly look at your watch.

You reach for your headphones.

You even swivel your chair to face your monitor and put your hands on the keyboard, but **he just doesn't shut up.**

So what do you do?

There are quite a few ways to handle this situation, but one easy way that has the advantage of cutting out quite a few potential distractions is to **set aside a focus time and make clear rules around it.**

I've used the Pomodoro™ technique myself for working in a focused manner (https://simpleprogrammer.com/cg36-kanban).

In fact, as I'm writing this very chapter, there is a 25-minute timer ticking down, during which I am 100 percent focused on writing this book and am not tolerating any distractions at all.

You don't necessarily have to use the Pomodoro™ technique.

What is important is that you have some way to designate focused time when you don't want to be interrupted.

In the past, I've done something as simple as creating a little hanging sign (https://simpleprogrammer.com/cg36-pomodoro) that on one side says "feel free to interrupt," and the other side says "focusing, please don't interrupt."

I simply explained to my boss and coworkers that I read a study showing that context switching caused by interruptions causes a huge loss in productivity, so I am trying an experiment to increase my productivity.

Then I explained to them the sign and said I knew it was silly, but would they please humor my attempts to be more productive.

No one argued or had any problems with it.

And it worked like a charm.

Mr. Talk-too-much got the hint and I didn't even have to confront him.

My productivity actually did skyrocket, since I wasn't being interrupted all the time.

So, I highly recommend doing something similar, not just to solve this one problem, but to increase your overall productivity.

Multitasking and interruptions really do cause huge productivity hits.

Alas, if this technique doesn't work, or you refuse to try it, the next thing I'd recommend is pretty obvious, but it takes some courage.

Remember how I said not to avoid conflicts?

This is one of those times.

Simply confront Mr. Talk-a-lot and tell him that you are there to work and that you'd appreciate it if he didn't talk to you about non-work related stuff at work.

Tell him you are weird and you know this is a strange request, but that you just have a difficult time working when you are distracted and you are easily distracted.

Make it seem like a defect you have. Not that he's an ignorant ass who talks too much and doesn't work enough and can't take any hints.

TOXIC PEOPLE

I really can't end this chapter without talking about the kind of coworkers who are the worst... no make that, are impossible to deal with.

I call them toxic people.

Some people you can't help no matter what, and you should just avoid them all together.

Some people just seem to always have bad things happen to them. They carry around five suitcases full of baggage and drama, and always seem to be the helpless victim who just can't catch a break.

You can identify these people by the string of dead bodies they leave behind.

They have bad attitudes, can't be reasoned with, and just do everything they can to make their lives and the lives of the people around them a living hell.

They can't get along with their coworkers.

They can't get along with their families.

Even their own dog thinks they are an asshole.

The danger of these kinds of people is that you feel bad for them and you want to help them.

It seems like they are just really unlucky and that they've been dealt a crap hand.

But whether fate has any part or not in their predicament, it's not up to you to decide.

It's best that you just avoid them altogether.

If you have to interact with them, keep your interactions as brief as possible.

If you can avoid them completely, do it.

If you are on a team with one of these people and you constantly have to interact with them, actually consider switching teams or even switching jobs.

I know this seems somewhat extreme, but trust me on this one, do what Morpheus told Neo to do when he saw an agent in the Matrix: RUN.

WHAT ABOUT X?

I realize this short chapter in dealing with coworkers is not enough to cover all situations.

I've tried to outline the most common situations and pragmatic general advice, but arguably a whole book could be written on the subject.

Rather than write one, I'll refer you to what I think is the quintessential book on dealing with people—which I'll do many times throughout this book—*How to Win Friends and Influence People* (https://simpleprogrammer.com/cg36-influence) by Dale Carnegie.

Speaking of dealing with people?

How about your boss?

Don't worry, we'll cover that tricky topic next.

CHAPTER 37

DEALING WITH YOUR BOSS

Unless you work in a flat-hierarchy company like GitHub or Valve, or you've gone rogue and work for yourself, you'll no doubt have to contend with that beast of a creature also known as "your boss."

If you are super politically correct or feel like you need to be the only one in control of your own destiny, and no one can tell you what to do, you might also refer to this person as a manager.

Regardless of the name, **we all report to someone**—or at least most of us do—if we work in the regular workforce.

Learning to effectively deal with your coworkers is definitely important for your well-being and job satisfaction, but **learning to deal with your boss can mean the difference between getting fired and/or losing your sanity and climbing the corporate ladder, snagging promotions all along the way.**

Having worked on both sides of the table, both being the boss and reporting to the boss, I am going to give you some tools to help you first understand your boss and how you can interact with him or her, and then some tips for dealing with those difficult kinds of bosses we all have to face from time to time.

Let's dive right in.

UNDERSTANDING YOUR BOSS

It's always a good idea to observe a wild animal from a distance before trying to interact with it, especially if it has sharp claws and teeth and is known to be aggressive.

In the same vein, it's important to understand your boss and to know both what motivates your boss and what he cares about in order to better understand how you should deal with this potentially lethal specimen.

Too many employees fail to interact properly with their bosses, not because they are trying to be difficult, but because they just don't get it (https://simpleprogrammer.com /cg37-frustrate).

They haven't looked at the world through the eyes of their boss. They don't know what is really expected of them and how to tell good from bad as seen through their boss's perspective.

To really understand your boss, you need to understand what bosses are measured on, and it's not the same things as what you are measured on.

A good boss is measured on how well the people under him perform and how he is able to manage and report on their activities.

Think about it.

If you owned a company that employed a bunch of software developers and you were going to hire a boss to manage those pesky, unruly developers, **what would you judge the performance of this boss on? What would you expect this person to do?**

What would make it worth it to you to pay this person money to be the boss?

Probably you'd want this boss to make sure that the work was getting done and that it was being done efficiently.

You'd probably want this boss to report to you about what was going on and to let you know whether projects were on track or not.

You'd probably want this person to **keep everything running smoothly and handle any issues** that might reduce the efficiency of the team.

These are the metrics your boss is likely judged on.

If you want to know how to become more valuable to your boss, you want to focus on making your boss's job easier in these areas.

Now, let's talk a bit about what your boss actually cares about.

This time think about it from his perspective.

If you were the boss and you were being judged by some of the criteria we talked about, what would you care about and how would you want employees under you to act?

The main thing you'd probably care about is status, or information.

You'd probably want to know **how the project is doing, what work is being done, how the schedule looks,** and **any major issues surfacing** which could throw things off.

You'd probably also care about **the efficiency of the team.**

You'd want to know that each person working for you is doing a good job and contributing to the overall success of the team.

It would probably be important for you to not have to hunt all of this information down, but instead have it reported to you.

You'd want your team to operate as autonomously as possible, solving as many issues as possible without you having to intervene.

You definitely wouldn't want them making mountains out of molehills.

Ideally, **you'd like every person working under you to figure out what needs to be done, do it** without being told, and keep you informed on the progress, all the while not creating any political drama.

That would make your job easier and you could spend more time watching YouTube videos and golfing.

THE ONUS IS ON YOU

The reason we are starting here in regards to dealing with your boss is because **the real onus is on you.**

It's important to understand power dynamics and fairness.

In the real world here, certain people have more power than others and life, well... it isn't exactly what I'd call fair.

Your boss might be a jerk—a real asshole (https://simpleprogrammer.com/cg37-toxic)**—but that doesn't matter, because he has the power and you don't.**

That means it's up to you to get along with him and not the other way around.

It's important to not forget that.

It's important to respect that position of authority or, if you just can't do it, leave.

Because that is how the world works and trying to fight reality is not a very effective strategy.

You have to figure out how to effectively deal with your boss, even a bad one.

It starts with you.

WHAT MAKES YOUR BOSS'S JOB EASIER?

Based on what we talked about above, you can probably guess that there are a few ways you can help to make your boss's job easier.

One of the best things you can do is to start by **anticipating the needs of your boss.**

Try to figure out what your boss is going to want and perhaps what things are high priority to your boss and then try to take care of those things right away.

This could be best described as **getting shit done without having to be asked.**

As a boss myself, I know that if I have someone working for me who figures out what needs to be done and what I am concerned about and takes care of that before I even have a chance to ask them to, they are extremely valuable.

They've both saved me a large amount of time and potential headache, and have proven themselves trustworthy.

I don't have to spend my time managing them, because **they manage themselves.**

One less employee to worry about.

I can leave Joe alone and know that Joe will do his thing and produce results, because Joe is able to anticipate my needs, sometimes before I am even aware of them.

I need to hire more Joes and put Joe in charge of more stuff.

What else makes your boss's job easier?

How about reporting?

One of the big responsibilities of your boss is to know what is going on so that he can report that information further up the chain and so he can diffuse potential problems before they grow and really slow down the team.

You can make that part of the job easier by self-reporting exactly what you did each day (https://simpleprogrammer.com/cg37-report) along with any other important information that your boss would find useful.

It's such a simple thing, but I **am amazed how many software developers fail to create a weekly report each week detailing out what they worked on during the week** and giving summaries of progress and any potential issues.

I started creating weekly reports at every job I worked at fairly early in my career and it was one of the best decisions I ever made.

Not only did it make my bosses happy and make me look good, but it was an iron-clad defense against any accusations of me not pulling my share. Plus it was great supporting material when I argued for why I deserved a promotion.

Finally, I'd say that you can make your boss's job much easier by actively taking responsibility for the team.

Too many software developers like to point fingers and play the blame game.

In the end, whose fault it is doesn't really matter.

If you are doing a kickass job and Bob is faltering and not getting his work done, the whole project is in jeopardy.

Your boss might care who is at fault when the project fails, but I guarantee he's going to be more concerned about getting the project back on track and getting the work done.

That means you can make his job easier by taking the same attitude and not only taking responsibility for yourself, but also **taking responsibility for the other members of your team and the team as a whole.**

Step up and be the developer who makes sure that everything is running smoothly and what needs to get done is being done.

If it's not getting done, step in. Offer help. Take on more responsibility.

In short, **be the person your boss can count on to resolve problems and move the project forward, and you'll be regarded as an extremely valuable asset.**

This also happens to be a great way to get promoted to a team lead position or to move up the ranks.

We'll talk about that more in later chapters.

BAD BOSSES

Isn't there a movie about bad bosses?

Yes, I think there is.

I've worked for some really good bosses in my career, but I've also worked for some horrible ones as well.

And, like I said, the onus is on you, so good boss or bad, you've got to figure out how to deal with them or how to find a new job.

In the next section, I'm going to go over the most common types of bad bosses and a few ways I recommend you deal with them. Hang on tight, this ride is about to get bumpy.

MICROMANAGER

This type of boss is probably the most common of the bad boss types and potentially the most annoying.

A micromanager tells you what to do, then he tells you how to do it, then he watches you do it, then he tells you how you did it wrong, and then he asks you about every single detail about what you did, again telling you how you did it wrong.

Your micromanaging boss doesn't seem to trust you.

He gives you a task and immediately follows up on it like you are a five-year-old who may or may not have actually brushed their teeth and needs mommy or daddy to check to see if the toothbrush is actually wet.

A micromanaging boss can be extremely difficult to deal with, because you feel like he is always breathing down your neck, nothing is ever good enough, and you are just a robot doing the work, unable and not allowed to use your own brain.

I worked with a micromanaging boss who was so extreme that he'd actually check to see what tools I had installed on my computer and ask me to remove certain ones.

So, how do you deal with this kind of boss?

There are a few things you can do.

The first thing is to try to gain their trust by doing what we talked about above in regards to making your boss's job easier.

If you self-report and volunteer information, you won't be quizzed about it as much.

Do what needs to be done without having to be asked, but in this case make sure you report on what you are planning on doing.

Nothing freaks out a micromanager more than not knowing what is going on.

Doing those things is going to help, but it might not cure the problem, so here's another idea.

I stole this one from a book I read called *The Art of the Deal* (https://simpleprogrammer.com /cg37-deal) by Donald Trump—quite an interesting book, actually. Anyway, he was actually the micromanager, along with his wife, for a hotel he invested in.

The other investor in the deal was getting tired of all the questions and micromanaging that Trump was doing, so he fired the guy who was running the hotel and instead hired a very welcoming manager who would gladly address any issues Trump or his wife brought up.

In fact, this gentleman took it one step further.

He called Trump to ask his input on every single decision made at the hotel, from how the carpet should be cleaned to what pillows to use.

As you can imagine Trump eventually got fed up with this constant badgering and told the gentleman not to bother him with this nonsense anymore and to run the hotel how he saw fit.

You can employ a similar strategy with a micromanaging boss of your own by engaging in a bit of information warfare.

Overreport information and ask for input on everything that you are doing.

Be a pain in the ass by **giving your micromanaging boss more details than he can handle** until he asks you to just get it done and report the results back.

Sometimes the best way to "fight" someone is to be like a Judo practitioner and not fight them at all, but instead just let their own momentum take them down.

BROWBEATER

We see less of this type of boss in the United States—although it still exists, unfortunately.

From the emails I get from software developers in India, I understand that this kind of boss is almost the norm there, sadly.

A browbeater is someone who verbally abuses you and intimidates you into doing what they want.

A browbeating boss works to get you to submit to his authority through the use of the tools of fear and abuse.

A browbeater is a bully.

If you are in a situation where your boss is browbeater, I'm going to be honest with you, you are in a very bad situation.

I'm all for being tough and eating shit when you have to (https://simpleprogrammer.com /cg37-eating), but you might want to strongly consider getting out of the situation completely and finding another job.

If you are going to hang on though, you are going to need to be tough and set clear and absolute boundaries as firmly as you can.

It might be a good idea to read the *Boundaries* book (https://simpleprogrammer.com /cg37-boundaries) I mentioned in earlier chapters for some background and reference.

The best way to deal with a browbeater—if you must—is to take a stand and not tolerate abusive language or behavior.

You should not allow anyone to talk to you in a demeaning manner, call you names, curse at you, or especially get physical with you (again, this appears to be more common in places like India, not so much in the U.S. and Europe).

As soon as one of these boundaries is crossed, **speak up and say in no uncertain terms "do not speak to me like that."**

Don't make threats, don't say you are going to call HR or get a lawyer, just clearly define when something is unacceptable in as calm of a manner as possible.

If they refuse, make fun of you, ask you what you are going to do about it, or engage in some further form of abuse, leave.

You always have the power to engage with someone or not engage with them.

Understand that doing this might get you fired or may mean walking off the job, but it is the best course of action if you are going to remain in this kind of environment.

Your only other alternative is to continue to tolerate the abuse until it progresses to the point where you can't take it anymore, at which point you'll be looking for a new job anyway (and perhaps facing criminal charges).

But, in all honesty, just like in the schoolyard, **most bullies back down when they are confronted.**

Bullies rely on the fact that victims are afraid to stand up to them, and it's the same with browbeating bosses.

Besides, if you do have to leave the situation, your browbeating boss will have to explain to his boss or bosses why you left.

If you remained calm and collected and didn't do anything inappropriate such as hurl back insults in response, he'll have to outright lie to explain the situation.

If there are witnesses, you'll be easily vindicated.

Another thing you should do when dealing with a browbeating boss is to document everything.

Document conversations, instances of abuse, exactly what was said by whom and when.

If you get into an HR or legal battle and you have everything documented, you'll increase the chances of a favorable outcome for you tremendously.

Honestly though, I don't think anyone should ever have to tolerate a work environment where they are being abused by a boss or coworker.

I am pragmatic though, and I understand that we can get ourselves into what I call squeeze situations where we have very limited options and may have to endure what would otherwise be intolerable.

If you are in one of those situations, or you are just "eating shit" because the opportunity is so good and you are biding your time, and you absolutely don't want to risk losing your job, there is one other alternative.

You could just develop a really thick skin and not take any of the abuse seriously.

Just laugh it off.

Do your job, don't take anything personally, and bide your time.

Most people can't actually remain disconnected and detached enough from the situation to actually do this, so I really, really don't recommend it.

Caution here though: don't just play pretend.

You may tell yourself that you don't care and are laughing it off while all the while it's providing a lot of stress and unhappiness that can manifest itself in the form of sickness, depression and more.

So, if you are going to be all Zen and tranquil actually be it—don't try and fake it.

IGNORAMUS

We've all worked for these kinds of bosses before.

A boss who you just can't understand how they could have possibly gotten to where they are (https://simpleprogrammer.com/cg37-noclue).

A boss that makes you wonder how they even have the intelligence to tie their shoelaces in the morning.

Yet there he is, presiding over you. Telling you what to do.

Perhaps the Peter Principle was involved, perhaps nepotism or sheer dumb luck, but it doesn't matter, because this dude, with rocks where his brain belongs, is your boss and now you have to deal with him, so how do you do it?

Honestly, **I'd rather have a dumb boss than a micromanager or browbeater.**

But before we get into dealing with this so-called idiot, perhaps we should take a moment to determine if that is really the case.

It's really easy to look at someone else who doesn't agree with you or sees things differently than you and think they are dumb, when in fact they may actually be smarter than you give them credit for.

It's sort of like armchair quarterbacking (https://simpleprogrammer.com/cg37-armchair).

Don't just assume your boss is dumb.

Not only is it likely not entirely true, but it's a bad general attitude to have. Whether your boss isn't quite the sharpest tool in the shed or not, it doesn't change the fact that this person is your boss and you have to report to him.

I'm going to talk about some ways to deal with a boss who, perhaps, is not as intelligent in the same way that you are—but **just know that there are all kinds of intelligence and your assessment could be wrong.**

One of the biggest conflicts in dealing with less-than-intelligent bosses is that they sometimes ask you to do things that make no sense, or they make decisions which are just plain wrong.

Most software developer's initial reactions to these conflicts is to come out shooting and blast their bosses with all the arguments and reasons why what they are suggesting is wrong and why you know what you are talking about.

This approach has the same effect as putting a cat on a leash and trying to drag them in the direction you want to go.

They are going to bring out their claws, sink them right down into your crotch and hiss at you.

Instead of taking this direct, combative, I'm-smarter-than-you approach, **try using your superior intellect to your advantage.**

Try asking some intelligent questions which will lead your boss in the correct direction, without being combative.

For example, suppose your pointy-haired boss says, "Hey, we should just make the changes directly in production so that we can get them done faster."

Instead of slapping him repeatedly, perhaps you could engage in a dialogue akin to this:

"That's definitely a solution that would get the code deployed faster, but I wonder if there are any possible drawbacks?"

"What do you mean drawbacks? We'll ship the code faster."

"Well, what would happen if we introduced a bug that wiped out some customer's data, and since we went straight to production, we didn't even realize it?"

"That's not possible, is it? Hmm, what if we tested it first?"

"Yes, excellent idea! I agree with you, we should set up some kind of a staging server, so we can test the changes before we put them into production."

"Ok, go do that instead then. Gosh, I'm pretty smart."

"Yes… yes, you are… boss."

It takes a bit of humility to use this approach, but it's much more effective than trying to argue your point logically with someone who may not understand the logic.

It's also a good idea, in general, to t**ry to explain everything as simply as possible**, so that you don't confuse your boss and cause him to become frustrated with you or just ignore what you are saying altogether.

If your boss isn't highly technical, **don't speak in complex technical terms** to him.

Instead, dumb things down.

Make extensive use of analogies which your boss is likely to understand.

If he's a football jock, try to explain things in terms of football.

Try to find something your boss does understand and explain things using that metaphor in order to increase understanding, build rapport, and get your points across.

Again, perhaps your boss really is intelligent, but you just think he's dumb because he's intelligent in a different way than you.

Sometimes software engineers and highly technical people assume people who understand business or people more than they understand technology are dumb, when in fact they are quite brilliant.

They just don't understand computer programming or computer programmers (https://simpleprogrammer.com/cg37-noclue).

So, figure out a way to speak your boss's language and put things in terms that he will understand.

Finally, **fight incompetence with supreme competence.**

Be really good at your job and do it well.

Be an ally to your boss, like a wise vizier to a dim-witted sultan.

Or a shrewd royal chancellor advising a less than capable monarch.

Don't directly challenge your emperor—in fact, at times actually play dumb yourself—but, become indispensable.

Consider giving your boss the credit, while you yield the true power though his utter dependency on you.

Now your doe-eyed boss has become an advantage instead of a handicap.

SLAVE DRIVER

The last kind of evil boss you may encounter in your quest, is the muscle-bound, tunic-wearing, bloodthirsty creature known as the slave driver.

A slave driving boss works you, and works you some more.

He's never quite satisfied with the heroic efforts you've shown so far and always expects you to take on more tasks, do them faster, and work more hours.

The slave driving boss is trying to milk every employee for every ounce of productivity he can get out of them until they finally burn out or throw in the towel voluntarily.

"Umm… yeah. I'm going to need you to come in on Saturday… yeah."

What do you do with a boss like this?

Here is another case for clear boundaries.

You need to define, upfront, how many hours you are willing to work for your ruthless overseer.

Don't get suckered into the trap of working long hours every day and coming in every weekend just because your boss is a lunatic and everyone else is doing it.

Be firm and say that you have other responsibilities that you need to take care of, and that while you are at work, you'll work hard and get your job done, but you won't be sacrificing your family and other commitments to work unpaid overtime.

And then do work hard. Work extremely hard!

Be so focused and so productive when you are at work that even though you only work eight-hour days, you get more work done than those poor hapless fools being suckered into working 12 and 14-hour days and coming in on the weekends.

You need to show a slave driving boss that he's going to get good—in fact, great—work out of you, but it's going to be on your terms, not his.

I know this is easier said than done.

You might be reading this in disbelief, thinking I'm all talk, but throughout almost my entire career as a software developer, I adopted this policy of working 40 hours a week, except for dire emergencies, and I always got promoted and never had any problems.

I simply went home at 5 p.m. every day and I didn't come in on weekends.

But when I was at work, I worked hard.

Yes, **in some work environments you might get fired for not working ridiculous amounts of overtime.**

Yes, sometimes you do need to work extra hours or even come in on weekends, but that should be the exception, not the rule.

You'll live a much better and happier life if you decide that you are going to adopt a policy that prevents you from being abused in this manner.

For a slave-driving boss, you should also **make sure that you are sending detailed weekly reports** showing exactly what you worked on during the week and proving your productivity.

If you can show yourself to be a self-motivated, highly productive worker, your boss is less likely to breathe down your neck.

You'll also want to **avoid the trap of committing to impossible schedules.**

Often an overzealous, productivity-squeezing boss, will try to get you to commit to ridiculous schedules which can't possibly be achieved without copious amounts of overtime.

Push back and don't sandbag the job, but give as realistic and honest of an estimate as you can.

I've often used the language "from the data I have I think it will take at least X amount of time, but I can't give you an absolute certain answer. What I can do is work as diligently as possible, give you frequent updates on my progress and revise the estimations as frequently as you would like."

This is a way of not committing to a time period, but committing instead to a process in which you are making the fastest progress possible and constantly providing more and more accurate estimations as time goes on.

Overall though, when dealing with this kind of boss, make sure you set clear boundaries and do not let yourself get taken advantage of.

It can be difficult to initially establish these boundaries, but once they are established, you will find that they will hold up pretty well and life will be much easier.

YOU DON'T ALWAYS GET TO CHOOSE YOUR BOSS

Well, hopefully you've gained a bit of perspective on dealing with your boss—good or bad.

You don't always get to choose your boss, so it's pretty important to learn how to deal with bosses of all kinds.

If your boss is really horrible and you can't get along with him though, I'd strongly consider looking for a new job. There are some battles that just aren't worth fighting in life.

CHAPTER 38

WORKING WITH QA

It's a bit humorous and somewhat unexpected, but **for many software developers, one of the most difficult parts of their jobs is dealing with QA**, quality assurance… yes, those dreaded… testers.

In a previous chapter, we talked about testing and laid out the basics of what it is and how it's done.

But just because you understand testing doesn't mean you understand testers.

So, that is what this short chapter is about.

It's about you, as a developer, and how you can deal with testers and QA in general.

QA IS NOT THE ENEMY

It's important to start out this chapter by letting you in on a little secret… QA is not the enemy.

I know it may seem that way.

I know things are set up that way.

I mean, here you are making stuff, building features, kicking ass, getting shit done, and there is QA over there picking their noses, making sneering comments, reading the latest post on sticky minds, and—oh yeah—breaking your code.

But, are they really breaking your code?

Is it really QA's fault that the code you wrote has bugs in it and that they are trying to find those bugs?

It's not.

It's your fault, or it's no one's fault, if you like to be one of those "let's not blame anyone" type of people. (But it is really your fault.)

Anyway, the point is you are actually on **the same team** (https://simpleprogrammer.com/cg38-agile).

You actually have **the same end goal**: to produce high-quality working software.

Yes, it can seem at times that you are enemies because it seems that your goals conflict.

And I'm not going to say that there aren't testers who aren't hell bent on breaking your code and making sure it doesn't ship.

There are plenty of QA people who forget that the goal is to actually create working software, not to prevent any software from ever being released. We'll get to them a little later.

But, in general, you have to recognize that **it is not you versus them.**

Because if you start that battle and make it you versus them, you are going to have a really difficult time trying to do your job.

Whatever notions you have of QA being the enemy, get rid of them now.

It's not going to help you, it's only going to hurt you in your software development career.

Oh, and I'm talking from personal experience on this one.

Trust me, I've had many epic battles with testers over the years.

I've even being accused of throwing a chair—utter nonsense.

KNOW WHAT YOU ARE BEING TESTED ON

Here is where most QA/developer conflicts start:

"Hey, what the heck, this isn't a bug."

"Yes it is, your code doesn't sort non-alpha characters correctly."

"It's not supposed to. That's not a valid test. The feature works."

"Well, it should. It's a bug."

"No, it's not a bug. I'm going to throw this f—— chair at you, mother f——!"

What we have here is a failure to communicate.

No, really. That's all it is.

Problems like this one can be resolved extremely easily, simply by **talking to QA *before* you write any code** and agreeing, together, on what is going to be tested.

In that situation, a five-minute conversation could have prevented a perfectly good chair from being destroyed.

If I—ahem, I mean the software developer involved in this "incident"—had talked with this ass—I mean tester—ahead of time, and simply discussed what was going to be tested, then the software developer would know that they should make their code handle the sorting of non-alpha characters.

Or, they could have disputed it before writing the code, before any ego was invested, and the conversation could have been much more civilized.

You wouldn't take a test in school without knowing what you are going to be tested on first, right?

I mean, I don't think very many lawyers walk into the bar exam without knowing exactly what is going to be on the test.

It's not like they sit down to take the exam and say, "I have no idea what is going to be on this test, but let's just hope it's what I studied."

So, **don't write code that will be tested without knowing in which way and on what criteria it is going to be tested.** Duh.

HEY JOHN

Isn't it really the project manager's responsibility to define the requirements, NOT the tester's? If I follow the spec I was given, what gives?

I agree. Wouldn't it be nice if it worked that way.

Unfortunately, when your college professor gives you a test, he doesn't always give you a test based solely on the content from the textbook.

The best strategy to pass an exam is to study for the exam.

Want to get a near-perfect score on your SATs?

Don't go and study a bunch of random vocabulary, mathematics or whatever else SHOULD be on the test.

Instead, go take an SAT prep course and study the actual test itself.

Yes, I know software is different and the testers shouldn't be setting the requirements, but they do help define them and they are the ones who are going to be writing the exam.

So, if you think the test is being written incorrectly, find out ahead of time.

"I was just following the spec" is not a very good excuse.

TEST YOUR OWN STUFF FIRST

I briefly covered this in the chapter "Testing and QA Basics," but I'm going to mention this again since it's so important.

Test your own stuff first.

QA is not a babysitter who tests your code for you so that you don't have to.

QA is a **last defense** before your code goes out and wreaks havoc on your customers.

Don't expect testers to find your bugs, expect them to validate that your code works.

In fact, good testers often call what they do verification, not testing.

(Oh, don't get me started on this. I went to a QA conference one time and I was lectured for hours on the difference between verification and manual testing.)

Anyway, **it's your responsibility to test your code before you hand it over to QA.**

When I say this, some software developers get annoyed and ask me, "What is a tester's job if I have to test my own code anyway? What good are they?"

It's a fair question, and in some organizations testers exist solely to run manual tests, but in general, a tester's main value is coming up with what should be tested and thinking about all the ways things could break or use cases which haven't been thought of.

Think of it this way.

Anyone can come up with the basic scenarios of how an obvious feature should work.

You should be testing all of those basic, obvious scenarios before you hand your code over to QA.

But a good tester might try running some of the not-so-obvious scenarios and corner cases which you might not have thought of.

(Of course, I still recommend that you run even those tests. Just talk to QA before you actually write your code so you can get an idea of what some of those not-so-obvious scenarios might be.)

The point is that the basic use cases, and anything you know is going to be tested, should work.

Testers should never waste their time finding bugs in your code which you could have easily caught yourself (https://simpleprogrammer.com/cg38-sniff).

Which brings us to the next point.

AVOID THE BUG/FIX CYCLE

The big reason for working with QA in this way has less to do with whose job something is and more to do with increasing the overall efficiency of the team.

As much as possible, we want to avoid the cycle of finding bugs, fixing bugs, verifying the bugs are fixed.

It takes a large amount of time and resources for a bug report to get filed, get assigned to a developer, be reproduced, fixed, sent back to QA, verified to be fixed, and then logged as fixed.

We want to avoid going through all that time and overhead as much as possible.

That is one of them main reasons you should test your own stuff.

If you find the bug before you even send the code to QA to be tested, you cut most of the steps out of that loop.

But... there is another way to shorten this loop.

Try to work directly with QA to fix any bugs as they find them rather than them filing a bug report and going through that whole formal process.

One simple way to do this is to ask the tester who is going to test your code to come over to your desk, run through a few scenarios, and look at what you built before you even check it in.

You could also put the code on a development server or give them some other way to access it.

Or, if it has already reached QA officially, you can go over to their desk and watch them execute some of the tests or ask them to let you know if they find anything, so you can figure out if you can do a quick fix for it instead of filing a bug.

Sometimes, an official bug report needs to be logged, and then it makes sense to track the bugs, prioritize them, and go through that whole process.

But, in general, if you can avoid that bug/fix cycle as much as possible, you are going to save the development project quite a bit of time.

HELP WITH AUTOMATION

Most testers are not software developers.

Even the ones who know how to write some code probably aren't as good at writing code and architecting a system as you are (https://simpleprogrammer.com/cg38-sucks).

Yet, many software development organizations want to have their testers automate their testing efforts.

As a software developer, this can be extremely frustrating when you get bug reports on code that you know works, but some automated test failed because it wasn't properly written or designed.

You should step in before this happens and help with creating automated tests, and especially with creating a test automation framework.

This is one area where you can be a huge benefit to QA. It is a great opportunity to bring the testers and developers closer, which can greatly reduce conflict and the me versus them attitude.

WHAT ABOUT THAT ONE ASSHAT?

Ok, so you are trying to get along with QA.

You are testing your own stuff first, you are making sure you know what is going to be tested before you even write your code, you even took the entire QA team out to lunch to show them how you aren't such a bad guy.

But **there's this one QA dude—this asshat—who just seems to be gunning for you.**

No matter what you do or how friendly you are, he just seems to be hell bent on proving that your code sucks, derailing the project, and finding as many bugs as possible, whether they are relevant or not.

What do you do?

Warning: what I am about to say is not politically correct and it's going to piss some people off, but it's the truth.

Look, here's the deal.

Let's be honest.

Sometimes—not all the time—people who are in QA feel inferior to developers. (Or perhaps they are just not good at testing and look for any bug they can find because of job security.)

In the back of their head, they feel like they just couldn't hack it as a developer, and they settled for a job as a tester.

Now, don't get me wrong, this doesn't describe every person in QA, but it does describe some people in QA and, most likely, that asshat you are struggling with.

One way of dealing with this feeling of inadequacy is to try to bring down other people, especially developers they are envious of, in order to make themselves feel smarter and better.

I've seen this pattern enough times to know that it is fairly common.

And, in my experience, I've found that **one of the best ways to deal with this kind of problem is to swallow a little of your pride and frustration and acknowledge the intelligence of your colleague.**

It's not easy to compliment someone who is purposely dishing out abuse at you, but it is the higher road.

I've found that in many cases, this person is just looking for some validation and acknowledgment, and once you give it to them, they are like a puppy following you around and wagging their tail.

A little genuine and sincere praise can go a very long way—remember that.

And if your efforts still fail, at least you'll know you've done what you can.

CHAPTER 39

WORK / LIFE BALANCE

Here I sit, on a plane, getting ready to write a chapter about work/life balance, and **I've already slipped into one of the habits that I'm about to condemn.**

I'm trying to figure out how to start this chapter, trying to will myself to type it, and I'm thinking of it as "work," a thorn in my side, interrupting me from my "life."

I've allowed my mind to shift from: "I get to do this" to "I must get this done so that I can enjoy the rest of my day."

I've made the cardinal sin of allowing work to become "work," and that is the formula for misery.

You see, work/life balance is about a mindset, not about a specific formula of how many hours you should devote to the office, how much time you should take to decompress, and how much time you should spend with your family or doing what you want.

To achieve true work/life balance—at least how I see it—is to not achieve it at all, but to blur the lines so well that everything becomes "life."

To make a subtle shift of focus from two heavily-compartmentalized concepts, making them become one.

To stop trying to balance work and life, and instead to seek to live a balanced life in general.

In this chapter, we'll explore the myth of work/life balance, and then focus on some key concepts to living a balanced life—to live the life you *want* to live, rather than the one you *have* to.

WORK/LIFE BALANCE IS A MYTH

Far too many software developers I know—and people in general—tend to have two separate lives.

One life is their work life, which they sometimes enjoy, mostly tolerate, and quite often dread.

The other life is their "life" life, where they play with their kids, socialize with friends, play video games, run, bike, hike—whatever they enjoy—and there just never seems to be enough time for it.

Other software developers I know have no "life," instead they work, work, work, and keep telling themselves that someday they'll actually live their life.

They've actually put their lives on hold until they achieve this goal or that, or even until they retire.

That's when they can do what they want.

It's at that time they can actually live their life.

Sadly, I have to admit, that was me, for a large portion of my life.

I always had the dream of retiring early (https://simpleprogrammer.com/cg39-secret), so that I could really live my life.

The fact that the day of early retirement did come, and I am still working and writing this book, should alert you to the fallacy of my thinking.

The problem is that **work/life balance is a myth.**

The very concept requires you to compartmentalize your life, to say that these hours are for working and these hours or days belong to living, and ne'r the two should meet.

Let's just consider this from a practical perspective.

You and I, we both have the same number of hours in the day—along with everyone else.

We've all got 24 hours and we've got seven days a week.

If you take a typical work day and you subtract out eight hours for sleeping, you've got 16 left.

Now take out the eight hours for working and we'll throw an hour commute time in there as well for good me—oh wait, what's that you say? You work more than eight hours?

Oh, ok. Fine then. Let's be realistic and take out 10 hours for working and commuting to work?

Happy now?

You shouldn't be, because **that just leaves you with six hours.**

Six hours every day to get ready for work in the morning, eat your breakfast and dinner, watch the evening news, play with the kids, relax, and do whatever else you like to do with your "life."

Six hours a day where you get to live your "life" life.

That's not much.

That's not much of a life at all.

Oh wait though, I've forgotten the most important part: the weekends.

Yes, the glorious weekends, in which you get a full 48 hours—and on the lucky occasion of a three-day weekend, 72 hours—of pure, unadulterated, heavenly bliss. (Aside from the sleeping you have to do between your partying, but I don't want to completely ruin your fantasy just yet.)

And for how many years do you expect to do this?

Perhaps 40 or more?

So, you are going to spend your "life" only "living" six hours a day plus weekends for the next 40 or so years?

Again, doesn't sound like much of a life.

I don't know about you, but I'd rather live my full life to the fullest, all the time.

That's why **compartmentalizing your life is toxic.**

When you make the distinction between work and life, and love one and dread the other, you are robbing yourself of any chance of having a life full of enjoyment, enrichment, and purpose.

The truth is, your work is as much part of your life as anything else.

We have to stop thinking in terms of work/life balance and **start thinking in terms of quality of life.**

What is the kind of life you want to live? What is important to you?

Those are the important questions to ask yourself.

Once you can answer those questions, you can start to figure out how to design your life, including work, the way you want it to be, instead of trying to fit your life into the hours you have left over outside of work.

OVERTIME IS RARELY BENEFICIAL

Even though I said that work/life balance is a myth, that doesn't mean there isn't such a thing as working too much.

I see far too many eager software developers spending ridiculous amounts of time at the office (https://simpleprogrammer.com/cg39-work)**, with the belief that putting in all these hours is going to help them advance their career.**

While it's true that working overtime may help you climb the corporate ladder, especially in a work environment where it is expected, in most cases **it's not going to make as big of an impact on your career as you would think.**

More importantly, **it's going to greatly reduce the quality of your life.**

I'm all for working hard, but I'd rather work hard for myself rather than making someone else rich.

Excessive overtime often comes at a high price with very little reward, so try and avoid this trap.

My advice: work 40 and that's it.

The only exception is the very rare occasion where there **truly is an emergency** and the extra hours really will make a difference.

Most work/life balance issues are solved by this single piece of advice.

BUT THAT'S NO EXCUSE FOR NOT WORKING HARD

Don't get me wrong though, I'm not saying to slack off.

In fact, far from it.

I work quite a few hours, and I always have (https://simpleprogrammer.com/cg39-sixteen).

But when I did work a regular job, I gave my employer his 40 and then I gave the rest to myself.

When I worked a job for someone else, I worked hard.

I did the best job I could.

They got their money's worth for my 40 hours—I made sure of it (https://simpleprogrammer.com /cg39-waste).

I didn't give them my entire life.

I didn't sit back and relax when I was off from work; I worked even more, but I worked for myself.

Sometimes people would say I had no life, because I worked so much.

But that's not quite true.

Part of integrating your life and removing the distinction between work and life is to realize that sometimes you don't need balance, you need seasons instead (https:// simpleprogrammer.com/cg39-seasons)**.**

There were seasons where my life mostly consisted of working.

Working for someone else for the 40 and then working for myself the rest of the time.

I put in 70, sometimes 80-hour work weeks, but it was a season of my life where I was willing to make that sacrifice to get to where I wanted to be and to reach my goals.

I wasn't concerned about balance, because I saw my life, whether I was working or playing video games, as my life.

I was making the choices I wanted to make so I could enjoy my life 24-hours a day, even though it was often quite a bit of hard work.

The important thing is to know what price you have to pay, and then be willing to pay that price (https://simpleprogrammer.com/cg39-price).

You can have anything in life—**you can have any kind of life you want—if you are willing to pay the price for it.**

Again, that's not work. It is life.

Life involves work—sometimes really hard work.

Think in terms of seasons instead of balance.

Oh yeah, and after my season of work was done, I took a season of living on the beach in Maui for a couple of months where I didn't work much at all.

But whether I was surfing or coding, I still considered my life one whole integrated life which I was choosing to live, not being forced to live or begging for scraps for.

PAY YOURSELF FIRST

One way to make sure that you have control over your life is to **make sure to pay yourself first with your time.**

Again, so many of us go to work for our employer and then give ourselves the leftover time.

Often when we live our lives this way, we feel like we need more work/life balance, because we are not setting the direction of our lives and using our most valuable asset, time, effectively.

Wake up an hour earlier each morning and dedicate that time to you.

Spend your first, freshest hour on yourself and your ambitions.

Perhaps it's starting that side business, building up your physical fitness, or even getting good at playing an instrument.

I suppose it could even be playing video games—if that is what you want to do with your life.

But, just like my dad used to say about my paycheck, **pay yourself first.**

When you live your life this way, you won't feel like you are getting robbed and living your real life in leftover spaces.

If you need more time, take more time.

Wake up two hours early.

Wake up at 4 a.m. if you have to and spend your most productive hours of the day on you.

MAKE TAKING CARE OF YOURSELF YOUR PRIORITY

This brings me to another point.

Before you take care of anyone else, before you give, make sure you get.

I know this sounds greedy, selfish, and quite unlike what your Sunday school teacher taught you, but the truth is that you can only give what you already have.

If you aren't taking care of yourself and meeting your needs, if you aren't personally growing and developing as a person (https://simpleprogrammer.com/cg39-personal)**, you aren't going to be very useful to the people around you.**

On my calendar every single day from 3 to 5 p.m. is "workout."

I never miss it.

When I say never, I mean never.

Some days I may have to reschedule it, but I almost never do that.

Pretty much every single day, I am either lifting weights or running from 3 to 5.

That is my personal, physical development time.

I also spend that time listening to audiobooks, so I develop mentally as well.

In fact, I spend a great deal of time on personal development, because **I want to live as close as possible to my full potential.**

Doing so ensures the quality of my life improves every day and it gives me the ability to contribute more to society and the people around me.

My "greed" enables me to be much more generous than I would be able to be without it.

I'm selfish with my time, so I can give more valuable time to those around me, and I can be more effective at everything I do.

One sure formula for bitterness and resentment is to give to other people, when you yourself are lacking.

Put your own oxygen mask on before you help someone else with theirs.

HEY JOHN

That's great and all. I'm really happy for you that you get to take two months off in Maui and work out for two hours a day... really, I'm mean that's great, but what about those of us who, oh, I donno, can't do that?

Ah, I see what's happening here.

Don't take this the wrong way, but you've got a mild-to-heavy case of "self deception" going on here.

Do you think I always had the freedom to do whatever I wanted with my life?

Do you think I was never chained to my desk, sitting in a cubicle?

Yes, of course I was, but guess what? Even when I was working for someone else... even when I was "part of the system," I had freedom. I just didn't realize it—and you have that freedom too.

We are ultimately responsible for our lives and what we choose to do with them.

No one is putting a gun to your head and telling you what to do—unless they are, in which case do it.

But what I mean is that no one is telling you that you have to go to work everyday or that you even have to have a job at all; you choose to work because you like the paycheck.

I'm not saying it's a good choice to be a homeless bum, but you need to realize it IS a choice.

It's a choice you are making—just like everything else in your life.

You might say, "I can't take two hours to work out every day and take care of myself."

Fine. You don't have to, but just realize that it's a choice you are making. You are prioritizing something else over two-hour workout sessions.

In most cases, that's probably a good choice, but it's essential to recognize it is a choice.

There are plenty of amateur triatheletes who hold down regular 40 to 50 hour jobs and still train for two hours a day because it's a huge priority for them. They are making a choice.

Perhaps it doesn't make sense for you to spend that much time working out. Again, totally fine, but perhaps you can watch one less hour of TV or give something else up so that you can work out at least one hour a day.

Or maybe working out isn't important to you at all—that's cool as well.

Again, the point is, it's your choice—and bringing it back to seasons—there are going to be different choices you make at different seasons of your life, based on your goals in life.

Just try to avoid self-deception, telling yourself that you don't have a choice—as if it's out of your control.

You always have a choice.

There is always some level of sacrifice in achieving what you want in life.

What is the price you are willing to pay?

That's always the question.

Oh, and when I was in that "season" of my life where I was working 70 to 80 hour work weeks, I was waking my ass up early every morning and either running or lifting weights for an hour, every single day!

So, don't tell me you can't afford the time, just be honest and tell me it's not worth it to you.

I'm not special. Anyone can do what I've done with my life—if they are willing to pay the same price.

Are you?

CAREFULLY CHOOSE YOUR RELATIONSHIPS

One of the reasons so many software developers, and people in general, struggle with work/life balance is the number of relationships they try to maintain.

The more relationships you try to maintain in your life, the less time you are going to feel you have, because it takes time and effort to maintain all of these relationships.

It's good to have many friends, but it's better to have a few good friends, especially if they are aligned with your professional and personal goals.

Carefully culling your relationships and only keeping the ones that are most valuable and important to you can free up a large amount of your time and give you more time to spend with the people you really want to spend time with.

Maintaining fewer, stronger relationships will make the overall quality of your life better without requiring a larger social time commitment.

This is especially important if you are in a season of your life where you are working very hard to get ahead in your career, build your own business, or take on some other time-consuming challenge.

Not only do you gain the benefit of having a better work/life balance by getting more value out of your social life, but by carefully selecting your friends and which relationships you want to maintain or invest in, you can better direct the course of your own life.

Jim Rohn is famous for saying "you are the average of the five people you hang around the most," (https://simpleprogrammer.com/cg39-friends) and I believe this is absolutely true.

So many of us hang around and maintain relationships with people—and sometimes family members (https://simpleprogrammer.com/cg39-family)—who constantly bring us down instead of lift us up.

Life is too short to waste your time with these people.

It doesn't mean you have to cut them out of your life completely, but you can always demote them from friend to acquaintance status.

The more you improve the quality of the time of your non-working life, the less need you'll feel for work/life balance.

The more closely your relationships align with your professional and personal goals, the more integrated your life will be.

LIVE IN THE PRESENT

The final piece of advice I'd offer you on work/life balance–or rather dispelling the need for it— is to **live in the present moment.**

So many of us spend most of our thoughts in the past or the future; we don't realize that **life is now**, and life is passing us by.

It's very easy to put your life on hold, always looking to "really live your life" at some point in the future.

So many times I've heard people say, just like I've said myself, "I'll really live my life once I achieve this, once the kids grow up, once I get a better job, reach this financial goal, etc."

Well, life is now.

Life is always now.

You can't live in the future anymore than you can live in the past.

Unless you change your thinking and stop putting off your life and begin really living it, when that someday comes, you'll find yourself longing for the next someday.

Some people live their entire lives waiting for their lives to begin (https://simpleprogrammer.com/cg39-waiting).

This is not a dress rehearsal; your life is now, in this very present moment.

So stop putting off "living your life" and start doing it now.

That doesn't mean you adopt the YOLO (you only live once) philosophy and live completely for the present moment, neglecting your future.

It does mean that **you have to stop seeing your days and your life as something you get through** in order to get to some point where you can finally enjoy yourself.

You and I have the capacity to fully enjoy every moment of our lives.

Again, this is another reason why I believe the work/life balance myth is so toxic.

It tells us that we have work, which we just tolerate and we have life, which we enjoy.

Instead, **make the most of every moment of your life**, whether you are at work, doing something you don't particularly enjoy doing, or you are at home engaged in your favorite hobby or socializing with friends and family.

An excellent book on the topic is *The Power of Now* (https://simpleprogrammer.com/cg39-now) by Eckhart Tolle.

It's a bit of a strange book, so don't say I didn't warn you. You don't have to agree with all of the author's philosophies on life and spiritual beliefs, but it has some great wisdom in it and some practical advice for living in the now.

TRUE WORK/LIFE BALANCE

Remember, you'll only achieve true work/life balance when you stop trying to achieve it, and instead **focus on just living your life as fully as possible.**

And you can only do that if you are willing to take the time and put in the effort to actively decide what kind of life you want to live, and then take the actions required to make it a reality.

Take care of yourself, choose your relationships carefully, and live as much as possible in the present moment, and you'll find your life doesn't need "balance," because you'll find joy and fulfillment in whatever you are doing.

If you take one thing away from this book, take this.

CHAPTER 40

WORKING ON A TEAM

One of the most common interview questions software developers get asked is whether or not they consider themselves a good team player.

Although this question is a bit generic and overused, it's asked for a very good reason: team-work is important.

Most of your career as a programmer will be spent working with other people on a team.

We've already talked about how to get along with your coworkers, but there is a different dynamic when those coworkers are actually fellow members of a team.

Highly-functional teams can be more effective than the abilities of all the individuals combined.

This is called synergy.

Ineffective teams can be less effective than the least effective person on the team (https://simpleprogrammer.com/cg40-fable).

This is called "you are all getting fired and the project is doomed, so you'd better start looking for another job."

All it takes is one bad apple to spoil the bunch.

This chapter is about making sure you are not the bad apple.

TEAMS SUCCEED OR FAIL TOGETHER

The first thing to understand about teams is that **teams fail or succeed together** (https://simpleprogrammer.com/cg40-team).

You've heard there is no "i" in team, but the truth is much more than that.

Any team where the members of that team feel like they are in competition, or where one member can succeed while the others fail or vice versa, is going to immediately be in jeopardy, because **it is human nature to serve our own best interests first.**

When teams have their fates tied together, and failure or success is at the team level—not the individual level—the best interests of every member of that team is the same as the best interests of the team.

We live in the real world and I realize that doesn't always happen. You may not even have control over how the success or failure of your team is determined.

Your boss or organization may have put you on a team where each member is rated individually and the whole "we are in this together" attitude is difficult to maintain.

That doesn't mean there is nothing you can do about it.

You can be the one to step up and suggest that the team would be more effective if the team members were bound to similar fates and success was derived at the team level.

You can unofficially carry this attitude in how you operate on the team.

You can set the example by acting and speaking in such a way as to indicate that you believe that the overall success of the team is more important than the success of any individual on the team.

You can choose to exhibit the team spirit by slowing down to help a fallen teammate rather than taking the gold medal for yourself.

One person's influence and example can be powerful.

TEAMS HAVE COMMON OBJECTIVES

Not only are teams' fates tied together through success and failure, but **good teams have common objectives.**

One of the biggest problems I see with software development teams is that they, too, widely disperse tasks (https://simpleprogrammer.com/cg40-speed) **among the team members.**

Far too many teams adopt a divide-and-conquer approach instead of a swarm-and-destroy approach.

Don't get me wrong: too many cooks can spoil the broth, but it's ideal to have a team work together as much as possible.

Not only does working together help enhance the feeling of a unified fate, but it can often bring about more synergistic outcomes.

If everyone on a team is working in isolation on their own tasks, and not actually working together, there isn't much teamwork happening.

Sure, there may be a common, larger, objective of getting the project done or completing the assigned work for the week, but the actual benefits of having a team are not being realized.

Again, real world. I know.

You may not have direct control over the objectives of your team.

You can still influence them.

One of the things you can do as a software developer on your team is to **make sure that you don't pick up new work when you can contribute to work that is already in progress** by another team member.

HEY JOHN

This is a great idea, but what if members of my team don't want to collaborate?

Well, you can't really force someone to collaborate with you, but you can offer them some help—just don't make it sound like they need help.

For example, suppose you are looking for the next bit of work to do and see that Joe is working on developing a new feature, so you say to Joe "hey, do you need any help with that new feature, before I move onto something else?"

Joe is pretty cool.

Joe is pretty confident—he doesn't need anyone's help.

So, what does Joe say?

Joe says "no, it's cool. I got it man."

On the other hand, suppose you approach Joe like this:

"Hey Joe, I know you probably can handle feature X by yourself and don't need my help, but I'd like to work with you if possible, both so that I can expand my skillset a bit and understand this feature. Also, so I don't start on a new task before we get this one finished. Is there anything at all I can do to help you?"

Now Joe doesn't feel threatened and like you are asking if he "needs your help."

Now Joe is much more likely to be willing to collaborate.

You could even approach Joe and just suggest that the work will go faster if the two of you work together, or that you like working with Joe, or you'd like to learn how Joe does things because he's really good at X.

> Ultimately, though, if Joe doesn't want to work with you, you can't really force collaboration.
>
> But, at least give it a good try.

In an Agile development environment, this means not picking up a new backlog to work on by yourself, but instead to go and find team members working on a backlog already and help them complete that backlog before moving on to the next.

In the Kanban style of software development (https://simpleprogrammer.com/cg40-kanban), this is known as limiting the WIP, or work in progress, and it's an effective technique to get more backlogs flowing through the pipeline faster.

TAKE RESPONSIBILITY FOR THE TEAM

Not everyone on a team is going to understand the idea of what makes a good team and what teamwork is, but that doesn't prevent you from doing what you can to help make the team succeed.

It's tempting to focus on your own goals and objectives and put those of the team secondary.

In fact, **many software developers erroneously believe that by looking out for number one, they'll be doing the best thing they can for their career.**

This is rarely the case.

Although individual performance is important, most software development managers are more concerned about the overall performance of the team.

It does no good to be the all-star MVP player on the lowest-ranked football team in the league.

Sure, everyone will know how great you are, but your team will still lose, which means you will still lose.

An individual can only do so much.

Even the best software developer has a maximum amount of effectiveness he can produce by writing his own code or doing his own job.

An exceptional software developer is a developer who makes everyone else around him better, and improves the ability of his entire team.

If you really want to get noticed and be the kind of software developer everyone wants to hire and have on their team, be the kind of software developer who cares more about the ability and performance of the entire team rather than your own.

This involves **taking responsibility** for things you may not have direct control over, and it's not easy.

Jerry doesn't work. He just sits at his desk all day and watches cat videos on the internet (https://simpleprogrammer.com/cg40-coworkers).

You could say "Screw Jerry," and do your work as best as possible and just let Jerry fail to get anything done.

But what does that do to the team?

Again, you might perform great as an individual programmer, ignoring lazy Jerry, but when the status of the project is reported and all your work is done but the objective for the team is not met because Jerry didn't pull his weight, your victory is going to be quite empty, isn't it?

Instead, even if you aren't asked, even if you aren't the team lead or manager, take responsibility for the whole team—including Jerry.

That doesn't mean that you have to go over to Jerry's desk and call him a lazy asshole, but it does mean that perhaps you should go over to Jerry's desk and ask him what's wrong or if there is anything you can help him with.

It might mean that you have to encourage Jerry and other team members by reminding them you are counting on them and so is everyone else.

It might mean that you have to go out of your way to mentor other developers and help them bring their skills up to par.

Taking responsibility for the team is not an easy task, but it can make a huge difference on not just the team itself, but your career.

If you are known as the kind of software developer who not only gets their work done and does a great job at it, but also brings up the performance of the entire team, you'll never have a problem finding a good job, and you'll not be overlooked for promotions.

COMMUNICATE AND COLLABORATE

As a software developer, it's easy to adopt the attitude of just tell me what you want done, leave me alone, and I'll do it (https://simpleprogrammer.com/cg40-difficult).

It's easy to hide in your cave and crank out some code by yourself, finally emerging when it's all done and tested—you did test it, right?

But being part of a team means communicating and collaborating.

To be an effective team member, you need to be an effective communicator.

You need to let other team members know what you are working on and any issues you are encountering so that you can benefit from and contribute to the collective knowledge and ability of the team.

Really, that's the whole point of having a team.

It's not difficult to do, but you have to develop the habit.

Instead of working solo, try to work with other team members as much as possible.

Yes, I know you could code up that feature much faster by yourself and that Fred is going to slow you down, but by working with the less-experienced Fred, you'll be bringing up his skill level, even if it slows you down a little.

And Fred, although less experienced, may see things differently than you do, and may notice something obvious which you overlooked, saving you hours of time.

BE HONEST, BUT USE TACT

One of the worst kinds of teams is a team where everyone is exceedingly polite and no one ever directly opposes anyone else's opinions.

It's human nature to try and avoid conflict as much as possible, but a healthy team—like a healthy relationship—has some degree of good conflict.

If you want to be a valuable member of a team, you can't go around blowing smoke up everyone's asses.

When something is wrong, or you have a differing opinion, you need to state it.

When a team member isn't pulling his weight and it's slowing down the team, or another team member is causing disruption, which is preventing the team from reaching its objectives, you can't stand idly by and think, "it's not my problem."

It is your problem.

It's everyone on the team's problem.

Remember, **teams succeed or fail together.**

So, be honest.

Say what is on your mind.

Don't mind your own business.

But use tact—please.

The same message can be communicated in a variety of ways.

Healthy conflict comes from communicating opposing ideas or dealing with issues in ways that don't directly personally attack the other person.

Before you say something, think about how it will sound.

Think about how you would feel if a team member said to you what you are about to say.

Tread carefully. Words can do a large amount of harm.

They can also do good, so choose to use them for good.

Remember, plenty of software developers can write code, fix bugs, and develop software in isolation, but if you really want to be as **effective as possible**, and you really want to have a successful career as a software developer, you need to learn to work on a team.

CHAPTER 41

SELLING YOUR IDEAS

I often hear complaints about how **the software development world is not a meritocracy.**

Plenty of upset and well-meaning software developers will rant on and on about how **the loudest voice is the one heard**, and how that's just not right.

While I understand the sentiment, I can't say that I agree, for a couple of reasons.

First off, **it's not about being the loudest, it's about selling your ideas.**

There are software developers who can sell their ideas effectively and those who can't.

Those who can't don't matter.

I know that's harsh, but it's reality.

The reality of the situation is that you can be the most genius software developer in the world with the best ideas and plan, but if you are quiet, don't speak up, and don't sell your ideas, it doesn't really matter now, does it?

Which brings me to the second point.

Those "loudmouth" programmers who drown out the voices of their more reserved, quiet compatriots are actually more valuable—much more valuable.

Why?

Because they actually **make things happen.**

Software developers who are good at selling their ideas are effective, because they actually create an effect.

It's true they might not have the best ideas and the quiet developer sitting in the corner might have a better one, but the quiet developer sitting in the corner isn't effective, because he's not actually able to turn his wonderful ideas into reality.

I'd rather eat a peanut butter and jelly sandwich than a vaporware steak.

In this chapter we are going to talk about why learning to sell your ideas is so important, and then I'm going to tell you exactly how to do it.

WHY SELLING YOUR IDEAS IS IMPORTANT

It should be pretty clear by now that a software developer who is able to sell his ideas is more effective and more valuable on a team, but **you still might not be convinced that breaking out of your shell and becoming more assertive is the right move for you.**

You might be thinking that you are fine playing second fiddle and you'll just offer your ideas when you are asked directly.

It's a nice idea, but it's just not practical.

Wherever you work, there is going to be at least one loud mouth with plenty of ideas.

Now, those ideas might be good, or they might not be. That's irrelevant.

The point is that you are not going to be effective and make an impact if you can't hold your own against this kind of person.

The truth is, **your advice is going to be directly solicited very rarely** unless you are known for having sold your previous ideas in the past.

Again, why is this important?

If you want to advance in your career, you need to be seen as a software developer who has good ideas and makes things happen.

Effective software developers get promoted, not the ones who just have the good ideas, but the ones who are able to rally the troops around their ideas and actually get them implemented.

And even if you didn't care about career advancement—I doubt you'd be reading this book if you didn't—you'd still probably like to have at least some control of your fate.

What am I trying to say here?

I'll put it pretty simply.

If you can't sell your ideas, you are going to have to do what the loudmouthed idiot programmer who doesn't know jack shit is suggesting.

I don't know about you, but I can't stand working in that kind of environment.

So, like it or not, you better learn to sell your ideas.

Fortunately, **it's not as difficult as you might think.**

There are a few simple rules and techniques anyone can use to be more effective at pitching.

DON'T ARGUE

The cardinal rule of selling your ideas is not to get into arguments.

When you are arguing, you aren't convincing anyone of anything (https://simpleprogrammer.com /cg41-arguing).

If you push on me, I am going to plant my feet into the ground and push back at you as hard as I can.

This is basic human nature.

If you want to sell your ideas to someone, you can't stuff those ideas down their throats.

Never directly oppose or contradict someone—this is a surefire recipe for an argument.

Instead, try to...

BE PERSUASIVE

There are many good ways to be persuasive.

There are lots of books on being persuasive (https://simpleprogrammer.com/cg41-influence), so I won't launch into a full-out coverage of the topic, but I want to give you a few suggestions.

(By the way, learning to be persuasive is not the same thing as being manipulative, although the two can be linked. Being persuasive is an extremely valuable skill that you'll find helpful in just about any situation. I'd highly invest in learning how to be more persuasive.)

One of the best and simple ways to be persuasive is to simply try and find some common ground.

Arguments are about finding differences, persuasiveness is about finding commonality.

I often have the best results being persuasive when I try to show someone with an opposing view that we are basically saying the same thing.

I look for commonalities—especially in intent—and **I try to focus on those and how what I am suggesting or saying aligns with what they are already proposing or serves their core purpose.**

The better you can bridge the gap, the smaller the leap you'll need people to make in order for them to come over to your side.

You can also **take your idea and reframe it** (https://simpleprogrammer.com/cg41-pitch) in a way that will be more palatable to your audience.

Reframing can be extremely powerful.

The right frame can present the exact same idea in a totally different light.

There is a huge difference between being for gun control and being anti-gun.

Framing makes all the difference.

Think about your audience and what their frame of reference is, and make your idea fit that frame.

Suppose your boss is concerned about the schedule of a project and you want to sell him your idea that you should use this new, shiny framework in the application, because it will result in better, more maintainable code.

Don't talk about better and more maintainable code.

Your boss doesn't care about that. He might even get the impression that whenever someone talks about more maintainable code, it's going to take longer to develop.

Instead, talk about how switching to this new framework will cut down development time and will help the project to be finished much faster.

The frame has to fit the audience.

LEADING

Another great way to get people to buy into your idea is to **lead them in the direction of the idea without giving it to them straight out.**

Let them discover the idea themselves.

You are only going to act as a guide, gently nudging them in the direction you want them to go.

The famous philosopher Socrates often used this approach. Sometimes it's known as the Socratic method.

Utilize carefully-worded questions to lead your audience down the path that ultimately leads to your idea.

People are much more likely to buy into ideas they have discovered or thought of themselves.

You might have to give up some of the pride and credit for the idea if you lead people to it by asking questions, but you'll get a much higher buy-in than by just giving them the answers.

COMMUNICATE CLEARLY

If you want to sell your ideas effectively, it certainly pays to be a good communicator.

It's well worth the investment in time and effort to improve your communication skills, both written and verbal.

The more clearly and simply you can communicate your ideas, the more likely people will be to buy into them.

Try to be short and to the point, and use analogous examples with which your audience can easily relate.

Very few people buy into an idea they don't understand (https://simpleprogrammer.com /cg41-nontech).

Even if people buy into your idea at a surface level, if they don't understand it, it won't really do you much good since it won't have much effect and it may face opposition down the road.

Far too many times I thought I effectively communicated my idea and got the proper buy-in, only to be confronted later with statements like, "What do you think you are doing? Who gave you permission to do that?"

So, **make sure that you are clear in what you are communicating**, and brush up on your communication skills so that you can present your ideas as effectively as possible.

Starting a blog that you update regularly (https://simpleprogrammer.com/lp/create-your -blog-1/) is a great way to practice and improve your written communication.

Attending a group like Toastmasters and giving presentations whenever you can will help you with your speaking and presentation skills.

BORROW AUTHORITY

One technique I used when I was first starting my software development career, and didn't have a large amount of credibility or experience, was to **draw on someone else's authority to sell my ideas.**

Oftentimes you can come across as arrogant, naive, or a know-it-all when you try to present ideas that are contrary to the current way of doing things.

You often face huge resistance in getting people to buy into something, just because you are suggesting it.

Who are you to say this is the "right" way to do things?

Instead of relying on your nonexistent authority or experience, borrow someone else's.

Try citing a book you read, or saying, "It's not my idea, it's <insert famous author here>'s idea."

Now your opposition will have to argue with someone who does have a large amount of credibility.

They can't simply call the idea stupid or uninformed, although they may still oppose it.

CREATE AUTHORITY

While borrowing someone else's authority can be useful and effective, in the long run it makes much more sense and is more beneficial to create your own authority.

Surprisingly, there are some pretty simple and easy ways to do it.

One of the easiest things you can do is **publish your writing or ideas somewhere on the internet.**

I originally started the Simple Programmer (https://simpleprogrammer.com/cg41-homepage) blog specifically for this purpose.

I was tired of arguing and trying to convince people my ideas were good. They didn't listen because I didn't have any real authority.

So I started writing about some of the ideas I had and putting them into my blog at https://simpleprogrammer.com.

My coworkers and bosses ended up reading my blog posts and somehow, just because the words were written on the blog, they seemed to carry more authority.

This authority increased further when people commented on the blog posts agreeing with me, or the blog posts were shared around and read by thousands of developers.

I'd also often reference a blog post I wrote a while back when talking about some idea or during a discussion where I was trying to sell my point of view.

By always having blog posts to reference, **I could quickly establish that what I was saying wasn't off the cuff, but that I had given considerable thought to it**, enough to have written a whole blog post.

HEY JOHN

How do I get my boss and coworkers to read my blog?

Don't worry, they'll read it, trust me.

If you start blogging, word will get around, and your boss and coworkers will end up reading it—curiosity trumps all.

It also doesn't hurt to do what I mentioned earlier and throw out references to a blog post you wrote in an email or other communication with your team, when discussing a relevant issue.

At one company I worked for, my boss would actually jokingly ask me if I had a blog post about a subject we were discussing, because so often I did.

Just be careful how you mention your blog and the tone you use.

Not as easy, but even more effective is to publish a book.

There is something about being a published author (https://simpleprogrammer.com /cg41-lifemanual) **that gives you a certain authority and prestige that can't be achieved elsewhere.**

Being able to say you wrote the book on the subject really carries disproportionately more weight than it should.

After all, anyone can write a book.

Just writing a book doesn't necessarily mean you know what you are talking about, but people assume it does.

Finally, **you can create authority simply by just speaking authoritatively.**

Too many people speak in ways that makes them sound unsure or wishy-washy.

They often do this because they don't want to sound arrogant or they are trying to hedge their bets in case they can't win people over to their side.

Don't do this.

If you are going to speak, speak with conviction—always.

Strong convictions, loosely held, is the name of the game (https://simpleprogrammer.com /cg41-conviction).

You reserve the right to change your mind later down the road, but for now, based on the best of your ability and what you know, you are going to speak your mind and you are going to do it with conviction.

You can win many people over to your ideas, simply by earnestly believing in them and speaking with conviction and enthusiasm when you do.

EDUCATE

One of the most effective ways to sell any idea is through education.

Educating people establishes authority and credibility, and makes them much more receptive to what you have to say.

Don't come right out and try to convince someone of your ideas on test-driven development (TDD) and why they should be doing it.

Instead, do a presentation on TDD.

Educate your audience about what TDD is and how it works and how it should be done.

Educate your audience about other tools for doing TDD and about books they can read to learn more about TDD.

Give them a bunch of value and information first, then ask for their buy-in.

They'll be much more receptive and open to being convinced when you take this approach rather than by just trying to convince them that TDD is good and you should be doing it on your project.

IT TAKES PRACTICE

Don't stress too much about selling your ideas.

Like anything, it's going to take practice to get good at it.

But keep trying.

Practice the techniques in this chapter, and don't be afraid to express your ideas and share them.

Eventually you'll become more effective.

And remember, even the best idea sellers can't always sell their ideas, but it's always worth giving it a shot.

CHAPTER 42

HOW TO DRESS

Software development teams, especially on the west coast of the United States, seem to have the loosest dress code of just about any profession.

I remember working for a small startup company and being introduced to **a guy who didn't wear shoes.**

At first I thought it was a one-time thing, or perhaps he had temporarily taken his shoes off for some purpose.

After a few weeks it was apparent, **the dude just didn't wear shoes to work.**

Strange, but not shocking—not for software developers.

I've been in plenty of development environments where there was basically an anything goes dress code.

No shirt, no shoes?

Fine. Whatever you like, just don't break the build.

But **just because you can wear anything you want, should you?**

That's the question of this chapter.

And while I've been guilty of less than professional dress myself, my answer to that question is a firm no.

Years of experience and careful observation, as well as my own missteps, have taught me that **how you dress and the image you present to the world matter.**

Even if you are just a code monkey.

APPEARANCE MATTERS

Here's the thing, we are all just *Barbie girls living in a Barbie world.*

It's true, it's fantastic, my boyfriend… erhmm…

Well, you get the idea.

The point is that **people will, and do, judge you by your appearance.**

How do I know?

Well, I've been an overweight slob with unkempt hair and a less-than-GQ sense of clothing style (https://simpleprogrammer.com/cg42-slobjohn), and I've been a six-pack donning, bleached white teeth model (https://simpleprogrammer.com/cg42-cooljohn).

(I literally worked for a modeling agency. Although I never quite got famous. You may have seen me in the fall bridal catalogue for a department store, though.)

Did I get treated differently in both of those cases? You bet!

Was I the same person underneath?

Now that is a matter of debate, because **what you wear can actually influence how you act—** but, we'll get to that a bit later.

Basically, I was the same person.

Everyone is prejudiced (https://simpleprogrammer.com/cg42-race).

Everyone engages in stereotyping.

I know that liberal media and a bunch of people holding signs on the street want you to believe this is a bad and horrible thing, and you should be ashamed of yourself for doing it, but that's not true.

The truth is, our ability to stereotype is a survival advantage.

Our brains can look at surface level details, quickly assess situations, and make snap judgments that can save our lives.

We don't have to sit and think about whether that lion we just caught out of our peripheral vision looks like he has a hungry, evil, or peaceful grin on his face and what we should do about it.

We instantly pick up that he looks menacing and quite dangerous and aggressive and that we probably shouldn't hang around.

It's this exact same mechanism which tells us that dude walking down the street, heavily tatted up and looking like a gangster, might not be the best guy to stop and ask directions. In fact, perhaps we might be in the wrong neighborhood.

HEY JOHN

Now, wait a minute, I can't agree with that. No offense dude, but you kinda sound like a bigot and maybe even a racist.

Look here's the thing. I'm not saying this person might not be a great guy.

I know a lot of tatted up dudes who look like gangsters and are really great people—hell, some of my good friends fit that category.

But, here's the thing:

This guy CHOSE how to dress.

He CHOSE to get tattoos and to look like a gangster.

He didn't accidentally throw on some clothes, sag his pants and whoops, walk into a tattoo parlor and get that teardrop tattooed next to his eye.

> He himself, most likely has a really good idea of what his image portrays, because he CHOSE it.
>
> Let's not forget that.

Now, can we be wrong?

Yes. Absolutely.

In many cases our stereotypes are completely wrong and actually do us harm.

But the fact is that as human beings, we receive so much input through our senses in a day that we have to have some mechanism in place to make snap judgments, which we hold in place until they are proven otherwise.

It allows us to navigate our world successfully without stopping to think about every single thing we see or hear.

We don't even notice we are doing it.

The problem is that **once we form a snap judgment, it's not that easily dispelled.**

And even when we know we are judging a book by its cover and being influenced by stereo-types, that hardwiring of our brain, which bypasses our analytical mind, is still intact and it's still sending us signals.

So, why am I telling you this?

Am I trying to tell you that you are a racist, stereotyping, prejudiced person and so am I and it's all ok?

No. Not at all.

I just want you to **face the reality that judging people by appearances is something that everyone does** and that we can only partially control.

So even though you want to be valued for your brain and your brilliant coding skills, and you don't think anything besides your ability should matter, the truth is how you look and how you dress does actually matter. You can either fight a hopeless battle against that or you can face reality and learn to deal with it.

And believe me, as someone who likes to wear shorts and flip-flops, I'm with you man, but let's face reality together, shall we?

DRESS TWO LEVELS ABOVE

The most simple, straightforward advice I can give you about how to dress in the workplace to be as successful as possible is to **simply dress two levels above your current position** (https://simpleprogrammer.com/cg42-dress).

Don't dress in the kind of style your boss does, dress like his boss dresses.

While it may be perfectly acceptable to wear shorts and a t-shirt at work, and while doing so might not actually hurt you, it's very, very unlikely to actually help you.

Some people might complain if you dress up when everyone else is dressing down, but there is an instinctual, stereotyping response that is going to influence those people, and they're probably not aware of it at all.

That is why, regardless of the flak you get, you should still err on the side of dressing more formally rather than less.

A person will say that you are too dressed up and that clothes don't matter here or that this environment is laid back, but they will still view you as more professional and of higher status, regardless of what they are saying.

Still don't believe me?

Try this mental experiment.

Imagine a police officer, dressed in uniform.

Now imagine this police officer in many different contexts and environments, but still dressed in a full police officer uniform.

No matter how you picture them, no matter what they say or what they do, **that uniform is still going to influence how you see them.**

You can say it doesn't, but it does.

That's why it's a good, general rule to dress two levels above your current position.

People will see you the same way you see that police officer, no matter how hard they try not to.

The "uniform" will lend you professionalism and status beyond your current level.

For a deep dive on what your software developer's "uniform" should look like, download the free "what software developers should wear" guide and suggested wardrobe list (https://simpleprogrammer.com/career-guide-toolkit).

FOLLOW THE LEADER

What is two levels above your current position?

How do you even know what that looks like?

What if there aren't two levels above your position?

When in doubt, follow the leader.

Take a look and observe what the executive team running your company or what the CEO is wearing.

What kind of attire do the really successful and high up people wear?

Try to match their style as much as possible and it will look like you belong there.

Remember how important perception and stereotyping is.

The idea here is to create a positive stereotype that will cause you to be perceived as someone of a higher status than what you currently are.

When review time comes around, or upper management is trying to figure out who to move into a higher-level position, you are going to seem like you just fit the part.

Think about what someone means when they say that someone "seems presidential."

There is some quality about them that makes them look the part.

Dress for the part you are auditioning for.

HEY JOHN

What if the big boss walks around the office in shorts and bare feet?

First off, he probably doesn't.

Not if we are talking about a large corporation or medium-to-large-sized business where there are actually ranks to move up.

And, in that case, ignore what he's doing and seriously think about the image he's presenting to you.

He's probably not making you feel like he's in charge and knows what he's doing.

Now, there are exceptions of course.

But, hey even when you see someone like Mark Zuckerberg in the news, don't you kind of get the impression that he's still just a "kid" who started Facebook?

Even though he's worth billions of dollars?

-Yeah, but he's successful, so that disproves your point, doesn't it?

No, not exactly.

Think about it this way: no one promoted Zuckerberg to CEO of HIS company.

He made Facebook.

If you start your own Facebook, you can dress however you like.

The question is always how you want to be perceived.

The best way to do that is to look at who is already in the role and mimic their style and to some degree, their behavior.

CHARISMA AND CONTRADICTION

Just because you are planning on mimicking the general style of your higher ups, doesn't mean you can't and shouldn't add your own style and personal flair.

When I was an actor, my acting coach told me something I'll never forget when I was having difficulty playing a certain role.

He said, "**the reason why you don't seem authentic is that people are contradictions.** You can't just act angry, you have to be angry and happy at the same time. You have to be sad, but excited. Real people, likeable people, are contradictions."

I immediately realized he was right.

I thought about how I could bring out that contradiction in the part I was playing by expressing two seemingly opposite or unrelated emotions at the same time and BAM, there it was.

What I've come to realize from this idea is that **contradictions actually can help us to create charisma** (https://simpleprogrammer.com/cg42-tattoos).

Take me, for instance.

I'm really not your typical programmer at all.

I'm 6'3", 220 pounds, and at about eight percent body fat (https://simpleprogrammer.com /cg42-fitness).

I look like a weightlifter or a professional wrestler, but I talk a bit like a philosopher or self-help guru, and I think like a programmer.

I've got a bunch of different contradictions going on, which makes me much more interesting than if I was just a "what you see is what you get" kind of guy.

Does that make sense?

You can apply the same thinking to your own personal style to be able to enhance your charisma, which will make you more likable and ultimately more successful in your career and any social interactions.

How?

By **dressing, to some degree, the opposite of what your natural appearance is.**

Let's say that you just happen to have one of those natural looks where you look like an accountant or actuary.

You've got the face for it, you've got the glasses, you've got skinny arms, your mannerisms are very reserved, your voice is soft and timid.

If you wear a plain button-up shirt with a single pocket and some slacks, you are going to look even more like that image.

But what happens if you get a tattoo?

What happens if you grow out a beard with a soul patch and rock a leather vest with some motorcycle boots?

All of a sudden you've created quite a contradiction.

Now I don't quite have you figured out when I see you.

You sort of seem like that timid accountant-like fellow, but you look like you might smack me in the face with a chain. I need to figure out what you are about.

You are... interesting.

That's a fairly extreme example, and you might not want to go that far, but I want to make sure you get the idea.

Contradiction is good. Contradiction is interesting.

Contradiction = charisma.

(Fair warning: Create contradiction and some people will hate your guts. It actually goes along with the charisma territory. The more people love you, the more other people will hate you. But, it's much better than not being noticed at all.)

Carefully think about your image and traits and see how you can offset them by creating contradictions.

If you have a naturally scary demeanor and you are being negatively stereotyped as a "thug," fair or not, don't try and fight it. Instead, contradict it.

Dress to the nines.

Wear a nice suit to work.

Work on your speech so that you speak eloquently.

Make it so that when people see you, they have to take a second look, because their stereo-typing circuitry seems to be broken.

DRESS TO... CHANGE YOUR PERSONALITY?

Can how you dress actually affect how you act?

You bet ya, it can.

Try wearing a tank top and putting a hat on backward and see how differently you act and feel versus wearing a full tuxedo and a top hat.

What we wear affects what we think about ourselves, influences how we act, and can even change our personalities.

That is why it is a very bad idea to lounge around in your pajamas or sweat pants when you are feeling depressed.

It will only make you feel more depressed.

Want to act and feel more professional at work?

Dress more professional.

Even if the dress code says you can wear flip-flops and cut-off shorts, and you don't care about climbing up that corporate ladder, you might still want to consider how your dress will affect how you feel and how you act.

STATUS SYMBOLS

What about status symbols like an expensive watch, designer clothes, an expensive car, etc.?

Do these things actually help you get ahead in your career?

I had serious doubts about it.

To be honest, I still do, because I don't think it's a good investment to play the status symbols game for most software developers, but I defer you to someone who's much "richer" than me and who has actually tested the theory, Neil Patel.

Check out this post he wrote called "How Spending $162,301.42 on Clothes Made Me $692,500." (https://simpleprogrammer.com/cg42-spending).

In his article, he goes on to say that in everyday situations, the expensive clothes aren't extremely beneficial, but **in business meetings and networking, there seemed to be a large effect.**

I think this one is very situational, and I wouldn't get carried away here.

Don't go into serious debt maxing out your credit cards and mortgaging your house to get a bunch of status symbols, thinking it will be a good investment (or bring you happiness).

But a few key indicators of wealth or success could be beneficial.

For me, the jury's still out on this one (https://simpleprogrammer.com/cg42-dress).

I'm convinced that status symbols do work, but I'm just not convinced about the return on investment for software developers and other tech professionals.

Although I have heard from some highly-paid consultants that what they drive to client meetings and how they dress can greatly increase their business—especially when they are dealing with high level executives.

My advice?

If you are meeting with the CEO of Salesforce or IBM, rent an expensive suit and an expensive car for the day, then you can get the benefit without the monthly payments.

HAIR, MAKEUP AND BASIC HYGIENE

Before we move on, let's talk briefly about some things that should be a bit obvious, but are worth talking about, nonetheless.

First of all, **it should go without saying that if you look like a million bucks, but smell like a bum, the smell will win out.**

I recently met with a very expensive image consultant who charges $300/hour and she said the very first and most powerful perception we have is smell.

So, yes, dress well, but don't neglect basic hygiene.

Make sure you take a shower, wash behind your ears, brush your teeth, trim nose hairs, all that jazz.

It's also not a bad idea to consider skincare—even for men—as that can make a big difference in your appearance.

Finally, let's talk about hair and makeup.

For guys, it's a good idea to have a good cut. Make an appointment to get your haircut about every two weeks at least.

For men and women both, learn to style your hair. Again, small time investment, but can make a big impact.

And for women, here is what one woman told me about hair and makeup:

> "As a woman, I notice I am treated with a lot more respect, especially by other women, when I have my makeup done. I think women should consider taking the time to do their hair / makeup (even if it means having to learn how) because it will affect how they are treated both in and out of the workplace."

Couldn't have said it better than that.

WHAT IF I DON'T CARE?

Whenever I talk about dressing up and how you should dress two levels higher than your current position, some people inevitably say "I don't care."

I don't care about dressing to impress.

I don't care about moving up the corporate ladder.

I don't want to be an executive.

I just want to do my job, increase my skills as a programmer, and be as successful at writing code as I can.

Well, if you don't care, then don't.

I'm not going to try and convince you.

I'm just giving you some advice about how to use stereotyping and perceptions that people are going to have of you to your advantage.

You don't have to apply this advice.

You can be completely successful without it.

You can make it as a programmer wearing shorts and t-shirts and even get promoted into senior development positions.

So, if you really don't care, don't.

I mean it.

But if you do, this is a fairly easy-to-control ingredient to success that you can easily apply to your career.

The choice is up to you.

HEY JOHN

I get what you're saying and I care, but I want to be myself too. How do I implement this and still feel like myself and who I want to be?

You can still be yourself and look good.

You can always take your own personal style and take it up a notch.

I just hired a very expensive image consultant—actually two—to help me do that myself.

I'm a pretty buff dude and I wear tank tops a lot, but it's not exactly the look that says "successful."

I was doing myself a bit of a disservice by not taking the time to really cultivate my appearance and image. It took an outsider's view for me to realize that.

So, what did I do?

Well, I hired an expert and they gave me some advice on my style and helped me find clothes that were still clearly me, but helped create the image of a better version of me.

You can do the same.

And you might even want to hire an expert. Not all of us have the fashion sense to do this on our own, and sometimes we do need that outside, objective opinion.

CHAPTER 43

ACING THE REVIEW PROCESS

The review process.

Ah, such good memories...

Such bad memories...

Such... bullshit.

Yeah, you know it's true.

Most review processes are exactly that: bullshit.

Let's just go ahead and adjust these goals to match what you actually did instead of what we decided to set as goals six months ago.

Can't give you a perfect review, so let me see if I can think of some area that could use some improvement.

Rate yourself—we'll get to this one a little later.

Even though you and I know that most review processes are shams, **it's still important to learn how to master that sham**, so you can get raises and have a good employee file.

This chapter is about how, but first, a story.

HOW I TURNED MY REVIEW AROUND

Once upon a time, I worked for a very corporate company called HP (https://simpleprogrammer.com/cg43-hewlett), or Hewlett Packard.

This company utilized a stack ranking system for their review process.

We'll talk about it more in a bit, but basically it's like grading on a curve.

Only so many people can get the highest ranking, so many people can get the middle, and some poor suckers—whether they deserve it or not—have to get the poor ratings.

In this particular year, **I had kicked ass.**

Really.

I had read about 15 technical books, had earned 5 Microsoft Certifications (https://simpleprogrammer.com/cg43-certification), formed and led a brand new team, produced several new tools for the development environment, and was a key player in bringing a new .NET architecture to printers. Not only that, but I had exceeded all the objectives I had set out to achieve on the "goals for next year" section of my previous performance review.

I was ready to get the highest rating possible and possibly a promotion.

I filled out my portion of the review paperwork, wrote down what I accomplished, set out my goals for next year, and then had my review meeting with my manager.

I had already been checking in with him periodically, so I was pretty sure nothing was going to be a shock.

The meeting went well, and he was impressed with what I had accomplished.

I waited patiently—well, not exactly patiently—to find out what my rating would be.

The next week, when all the reviews were done, I logged in to check my rating.

HOLY CRAP!

I was ranked at below average. One level from the bottom ranking.

I almost fell over in my chair.

There had to be a mistake.

I scheduled a meeting to ask my boss about it.

He confessed that since I had recently received a promotion and I was at the higher-end of my payscale, he was getting pressured to rank some of the other developers at the top so they could balance things out a bit.

He emphasized that if it were up to him, I'd get the highest rating possible, but they could only give out one of those rankings, and only with that ranking could they give a promotion to another developer, so they had to make some tough choices.

I was not happy.

He told me that I could appeal the rating and he'd see what he could do, but I needed to provide some documentation showing why I thought it was not a fair ranking and how I had exceeded all my objectives.

I spent the next day taking all the highlights from my weekly reports and sorting through the "kudos" folder I had created in my Outlook email program.

I looked at the requirements publicly stated for each ranking.

I took all this and put it together in a several page document, **listing about 50 accomplishments I had achieved over the course of that year**, 10 of the most impressive kudos emails I had received from managers, coworkers, and stakeholders, and a detailed point-by-point list of every objective in my performance review and how I had exceeded it.

Oh, and I also included documentation and emails where I had been checking in every week with my boss asking if I was on target and if there was anything at all I needed to work on and improve.

My case was airtight.

At this point you are probably expecting the typical "but it didn't matter" ending.

Well, that's not what happened.

The next week, when I came into work, on my desk was the revised employee review.

I had now been ranked at the top of the stack, and was offered a job title promotion and a significant pay bump.

I had accomplished the impossible.

How?

Let's talk about that.

CHECK IN AHEAD OF TIME

Your annual review should not be the first time you and your boss have a discussion to talk about how you are doing and where you need to improve.

In fact, **if anything on your annual review or anything your boss says about your annual review is a shock to you, you've already messed up.**

I don't like to leave things to chance, and I'm not a fan of surprises, either.

Once you've created your plan for the year and outlined your goals and areas to work on, **you should be checking in with your boss on how you are progressing**, at least once every two weeks, and preferably once a week.

You should ask point blank how you are doing and if there is anything, anything at all, that you are doing that could use improvement.

If there is something, work on it and then show progress during the next "check in."

If there isn't anything, confirm it.

Say, "So, what you are saying is that right now I'm 100 percent on track to meet all the objectives for this year and there is absolutely nothing you think I need to work on to improve?"

"Just want to make sure I've got that straight."

Document this.

Note the date and the time and exactly what was said.

If you are really smart, you'll send an email asking that question after having the face-to-face meeting.

It's called CYA. I'll let you figure out the acronym.

By doing this, you'll be accomplishing a few key things.

First of all, **you'll be giving yourself the opportunity to fix any actual or perceived deficiencies** before the actual review.

Second, you'll be **leaning on the consistency principle** to ensure there are no surprises in your review.

People are very strongly compelled to be consistent with what they've said or done in the past.

(You can read about this in Robert Cialdini's famous book *Influence: The Psychology of Persuasion* (https://simpleprogrammer.com/cg43-influence).)

If your boss says you are doing a great job and there is nothing you can improve on now, he's going to be much more compelled to say the same thing at review time.

Finally, you are creating extremely compelling evidence that you are doing everything you can in case you ever need it.

HAVE CLEAR GOALS, MAKE THEM KNOWN

What is your objective or goal for your review?

Are you looking to get a promotion?

To get a perfect review score?

Perhaps you are trying to overcome a weakness on last year's review and this year you want it to be a strength?

Whatever your goal is, figure it out and make it known.

Tell your boss what you are trying to accomplish in terms of your review.

Make it well known and then ask what you need to do to achieve it.

Document the response.

Write that down.

If you can get it via email, even better.

Once you've said "according to the HR role descriptions, a Software Engineer IV needs to be able to do X and, blah, blah, blah..."

And you've told your boss you'd like to be promoted to a Software Engineer IV, you are doing X to get there, and asked him what would make it clear that you were there at your next review...

And he's told you.

And you've documented it.

Then, you've got something you can almost take to the bank.

Just do what was agreed upon and make it known that is what you are doing; if you now meet those requirements, at review time you are going to have a really good case for getting what you want.

It really is that simple.

TRACK AND DOCUMENT YOUR PROGRESS

This is key.

I've said it many times, but **make sure you document everything**, especially your progress.

You should already be creating weekly reports which detail the high-level things you've done each day and summarize the highlights of your week.

But you shouldn't stop there.

Document the books you've read (https://simpleprogrammer.com/cg43-books), **any trainings you've attended or given, anything that shows improvement and progress towards your goals.**

Look at your previous review and objectives for the year.

Document everything you can that shows you are meeting those objectives and/or moving towards them.

Again, this is not rocket science.

It's actually common sense, but still so many software developers get blindsided by reviews.

You'll find in life that most people don't document things, but if you ever get into an argument or a legal case with someone who does—oh boy.

Be that guy or gal.

BUILD YOUR CASE

Part of the reason why you want to document everything is to build up your case for getting high marks on a review or ultimately getting that promotion.

Take the documentation you have about progressing towards your goals, and what your boss indicated you needed to do and how you are doing it, and combine it with everything else you need to build an airtight case.

Pretend you are a lawyer.

Gather emails where people have praised you.

When someone gives you kudos, ask them to send you an email.

I used to keep a kudos folder in my email for storing all the good emails I received from people throughout the year.

This is all good evidence that supports your case.

Your boss, and especially his higher-ups, aren't going to know about all the great things you've been doing. You have to tell them.

So, do it.

Don't be afraid to brag here.

When you walk into the review, it should be with a casefile worth of material that even the toughest jury couldn't ignore.

APPEAL, IF YOU NEED TO

I did just about everything I'm recommending here and I still got screwed.

But guess what? I didn't give up.

Especially in a big corporation, HR doesn't expect you to put up a fight.

They have their BS stack ranking systems that they know are BS.

They have a fake review process and job-level descriptions that serve to provide some semblance of fairness and order, but they really don't mean anything.

That is, until you challenge it with evidence.

What I did at HP was unheard of.

No one changes their rating on a review.

Yet, I did it—and it was easy.

Because **I had the evidence to back up my case** and no one had any evidence to show otherwise.

Maybe someone could have assembled some kind of evidence against me, showing how I indeed did not meet the expectations or how I didn't meet some objective, but it would have been quite a bit of work.

It was much easier to find some other sucker who wouldn't fight so hard, give him the lower ranking, and give me what I wanted.

So, **don't be afraid to appeal the decision.**

Just make sure you have ample evidence to back up your appeal, or you will just seem like a whiner.

Kapesh?

THE RATE YOURSELF TRAP

One of the most infamous review traps is the one where you "get to" rate yourself.

How the heck do you handle this situation?

Do you give yourself all perfect ratings and risk seeming like a narcissistic jerk?

Do you humbly rate yourself lower than you really deserve, hoping that your boss will correct you and lift you higher?

Do you honestly try and rate yourself from an unbiased perspective? Ha, as if that were possible.

Really, what do you do?

First of all, **if you can refuse to rate yourself, do it.**

Simply say that you can't reasonably rate yourself in an unbiased way—no one can—and that anything you put down would not be accurate.

If that fails, which, honestly, most likely it will, then here is what I think is the best strategy:

Rate yourself as highly as possible in all areas but your weakest one and give yourself one mark below perfect there.

The reasoning behind this is simple.

If you are being asked to rate yourself, why would you want to purposely do yourself harm? (Even politicians get to plead the fifth.)

It doesn't make any sense at all.

There is no possible benefit from you giving yourself a low rating.

Best case, your boss says "you deserve higher than that," worst case he believes you.

Instead, you should try to rate yourself as highly as possible.

Worst case, your boss says "don't you think that's a little high?"

To which you reply "you asked me to rate myself."

Best case, he believes you.

I don't know about you, but I don't like harming myself (https://simpleprogrammer.com/cg43-harm).

You give me a gun and tell me to pick somewhere to shoot myself, I'm going to aim at the empty space right between my toes.

If I thought you could get away with it, I'd say rate yourself completely perfect—I'm actually still on the fence on this one.

But, I think you'll do better by giving yourself at least one less-than-perfect mark, because it will make your self-rating more believable.

For the record, **I absolutely hate self-ranking and peer ranking.**

Both are extremely biased and only present you with situations that can harm and not help you.

PEER RANKING

I wasn't planning about talking about peer ranking, but since I just mentioned it above, let's take a real quick second to discuss.

So, peer ranking...

What should you do?

If you are forced to do this communist, rat-on-your-friends tactic, refuse to be part of the gestapo by simply rating all your peers as perfectly as possible.

Yes, you heard me right.

Give them all perfect reviews and say plenty of good things about them.

Nothing good can come of giving your peers bad ratings.

At best, they get demoted or fired, which is highly unlikely.

At worst, they find out about it, they become your boss or team lead and make your life hell, your boss thinks you are an ass, everyone thinks you are an ass, and you have to quit and look for another job because you've created a hostile work environment for yourself.

So, even if your peers suck and deserve to be fired, unless you are the actual boss in charge of firing, don't be the sucker who brings them down.

HEY JOHN

What you are saying seems... a bit unethical to me. Isn't it dishonest to not rate yourself and your peers... honestly?

I want to make it very clear about why I am advocating what some people might deem dishonest practices when it comes to self-rating and peer-rating.

Why don't I say, just rate yourself and your peers as honestly as possible?

I completely understand the sentiment, and I'd like to advocate that approach, but I have a problem.

I think self-ratings and peer-ratings are bullshit on every level.

It's not fair to put people into situations where they have to stab themselves or the people next to them.

And **whatever you put down isn't going to mean jack anyway.**

> It's like one of those fake psychological tests where they see how much you'll zap someone with fake electricity when you think that it's real.
>
> If I thought self-and-peer ratings were fair—or that they could be fair and unbiased without the potential for extremely negative repercussions—I'd be all for filling them out honestly.
>
> Rather than marching out into the street and protesting these kind of reviews, I advocate doing the next best thing. I choose a more passive-resistance approach.
>
> Take away their power by subverting the system.
>
> Don't stab yourself or your friend.
>
> Feel free to disagree.

STACKED RANKING

I dislike stacked ranking almost as much as I dislike peer reviews, but stacked ranking is just a fact of life at some corporations and we have to deal with it.

I have found that lately more and more corporations are getting rid of the stacked ranking programs.

The idea behind stacked ranking is fairly simple, and actually makes some sense.

Essentially, you take all employees and you figure out the top 10 percent of the high achievers, the 80 percent that are average, and the 10 percent that are the worst.

You promote and reward the top 10 percent and you fire the bottom 10 percent.

There are a few problems with this approach, though.

The biggest one is that most HR departments and managers don't actually give the rankings based on performance, but rather on other motivations.

So, instead of actually ranking the top 10 percent at the top ranking, they pick based on politics, pay scales, and other factors.

And since there are only so many "top slots" to go around, managers and departments tend to horse trade over those slots, and again, the ranking is determined more by politics than performance.

Don't get me wrong, I think it's a great system in theory—I'm all for firing the bottom 10 percent of any company—but, in practice it leads to all kinds of problems.

The point here is not to complain about the stacked ranking system though; it's to tell you what to do about it.

Obviously, what **you want to do is stay out of the bottom 10 percent and preferably get into the top 10 percent.**

The best way to do this is to, again, **have ample evidence to back up your case** that you are an overachiever at the company.

HEY JOHN

You keep calling me an "overachiever," but I'm not one. Do I still do this?

It's about time we mentioned ethics and integrity.

I've been kind of assuming you have them, but I realize that you might be reading what I am saying in some of these chapters and interpreting them as tactics that can be applied to manipulate your way to success.

I'm not advocating that at all—in fact, it may work in the short run, but in the long run eventually it will catch up to you… karma is a bitch.

I believe 100% in having both integrity and a strong set of ethics that guide you.

If you are not an "overachiever"—or even an "achiever"—your first step is to become one.

Tactics and techniques are not made to take the place of hard work and effort.

> You have to actually do the effort to get rewarded for it.
>
> I'm just showing you how to have the best chance of getting rewarded for it.

Next up: make sure that you know what is going on politically.

How many employees are in your group?

How many top rankings are there?

Try to figure out who you are competing against and any political movements that might be underway.

You might need to make friends with managers in other groups or teams if they share the ranking slots with your boss and determine together how to distribute their slots.

Also, be aware of the HR policy on how they assign the rankings.

There should be a written definition of how the ranking system works.

You want to make sure that you clearly demonstrate what is needed to have the top 10 percent ranking in your review.

Knowledge is your ally here.

It also doesn't hurt to **let your boss know that you are aiming for a top ranking.**

This will create extra pressure on him in any political situation where he might have been tempted to throw you under the bus.

Ultimately though, regardless of what you do, you might… get screwed.

It's true.

In that case, appeal.

But, even then, you can't guarantee a positive outcome.

Just do the best you can, **make the best case possible**, and understand that there are some things you just can't control.

Good luck!

CHAPTER 44

DEALING WITH PREJUDICE

I wish I didn't have to write a chapter on this subject, but I do, because although we'd like to believe that we've moved beyond racism, intolerance, and other forms of bigotry in the workplace, the truth is we haven't.

It still exists. It's still a problem.

It likely always will be.

I don't mean this to paint a glum picture of the software development world (https://simpleprogrammer.com/cg44-darkside).

There are more good, honest, non-prejudiced software developers and managers out there than there are bad ones.

For the most part, we live in a time of opportunity—for all people—like never before.

The world, in general, is more accepting of different cultures, races, religions, sexes and just about anything else you can think of than ever before.

But... there are still problems.

And as much as I'd like to tell you how the world needs to change and what should be done about these situations, I'm a realist.

And the realist in me says that we might not like how things are, and we can do our part to change and affect what we can, but at the end of the day, **we have to learn how to adapt and deal with our current environment.**

That's what this chapter is about.

It's not about what is wrong and how society can fix it.

It's about what you can do.

It's about **how you can deal with prejudice if and when you encounter it.**

It's about **how you can respond and rise above the people who try to hold you down.**

It's about **choosing to control what you can control, accepting what you cannot change, and not inadvertently becoming part of the problem, by having grace for all people**, even the "bad" ones.

ACCEPT THAT PEOPLE HAVE UNCONSCIOUS PREJUDICES AND STEREOTYPES

We talked about this a bit in the chapter on "How to Dress," so I won't beat a dead horse here, but **it's important to know and realize that everyone—including you—has some deep-seated prejudices** and relies on stereotypes.

Again, the point of this chapter is not to judge or to say what is right or wrong, but to tell you how to effectively deal with this fact.

The best way to deal with other people's prejudices, especially when they are against you, is to accept them.

By accept them, I don't necessarily mean tolerate them. There are certainly instances where you need to assert yourself and respond.

By accept them, what I am really trying to say is that **you need to realize that no matter who you are, someone is going to have some prejudice against you** for some reason that is out of your control.

You need to accept this fact.

You need to expect that this is the case, otherwise you'll always be in shock, outrage, and disbelief.

But if you come into situations–especially in the workplace—expecting and understanding that there will always be some level of prejudice and that everyone has some, you'll be much better prepared to handle it.

Again, when I say "accept" I'm not trying to tell you it's not a problem, I'm just trying to tell you to face and see reality clearly, so you can respond appropriately.

GIVE YOURSELF THE BEST CHANCE FOR AVOIDING PREJUDICE

I know what I am about to tell you isn't a popular opinion.

Some people might label me as an enabler of abuse and intolerance. (Kind of ironic, don't ya think?)

But, like I said, this chapter is about being effective, about what you can actually do to make your life and career better in an imperfect world filled with imperfect people.

It's not about changing the world to shape our desired reality.

With that said, **often the best way to avoid prejudice is to be aware of it enough to actually change how you present yourself to other people** who you think may be prejudiced against you—especially unconsciously.

Let's pick an easy example.

How about your name?

Depending on different contexts, **your name can invoke unconscious—and unfortunately, sometimes conscious—prejudice against you.**

In the U.S. at the time of writing this book, if you happen to have the name "John Smith," "James Robert," or something similar, you probably don't have to worry at all about someone in a workplace being prejudiced against you just based on your name.

But if your name is "Fatima Jones" or "Tamicka Mohammad," you might have more of an issue.

I know this isn't politically correct, but let's just be honest here.

On the flip side, I had the chance to visit China recently and I can tell you with a large amount of confidence, that if your name is "John Smith" or "James Robert" there, or in Japan, you are probably going to experience some prejudice as well.

I'm using both of these examples so you can see it's context-based.

Different people are going to experience different kinds of prejudice in different contexts and environments. It doesn't matter who you are, I can find a place where people will be prejudiced against you based on your name alone.

So, what can you do about it?

Well—and I'm actually not kidding about this—**you can legally change your name** or go by a nickname.

I know it can feel like you shouldn't have to do that or even that it's wrong to do that, but I'm talking about being practical here.

If you have a name that you know is likely to invoke prejudice against you, which is a better strategy? Try to get other people not to be prejudiced against your name, or change your name so that you don't have the problem in the first place?

This is actually a fairly common thing for book authors and actors to do.

I know plenty of software developers who have done it as well.

Heck, I considered it, because my last name is Sonmez.

I've always wanted to have a screen name of "Vince De'Leon."

It's too late now though, since too many people know my name, but I'm sure that some people are immediately prejudiced against me because of my name.

The point is, it's just a name. It's not you.

If you feel like changing your name is going to help you avoid prejudice, do it.

If you don't want to, don't, but at least accept that you may experience some prejudice because of it.

Don't expect the world to work how you want it to.

The same goes for how you dress, the accent you speak with, and the vocabulary you use.

The most pragmatic advice I can give you is to **take an honest assessment of yourself in relation to the context of the work environment you'll be working in, and try to figure out what things about you or how you present yourself are likely to invoke negative stereotypes or prejudice.**

Then, figure out which of those things you can alter to reduce that prejudice without sacrificing the core of who you are.

Don't get me wrong, I'm not saying be ashamed of your name or your heritage or your skin color or hair color or religion or whatever it is.

I'm just asking you to assess what you can change or how you can present yourself to reduce prejudice against you.

There are quite a few simple things you can do that do not involve sacrificing your integrity or changing the core of who you are.

Let me give you a few examples.

Many intelligent people in the U.S. who have southern accents, for instance, choose to hire voice coaches to help them get rid of their accent.

Having a southern accent doesn't mean you aren't intelligent, but there is a stereotype of a southern accent in the U.S. that is not always positive.

Tattoos can work against you, but can be covered up or removed.

Some racial prejudices can be overcome or reduced simply by dressing a bit more professionally, reducing accents, and altering vocabulary.

Even looking good—for example, being a bodybuilder or an attractive woman—can cause you issues, but clothing choice can negate some of those stereotypes.

Now, there are some things that you know might negatively affect you and you don't want to change them. That's perfectly fine. I totally understand.

I'm just giving you some suggestions about what you could do.

Ultimately, it's up to you.

Again, I know this chapter is going to rub some people the wrong way. I get that.

But **ask yourself if what I am telling you is a pragmatic way for you to deal with prejudices against you or not.**

Am I trying to say prejudice is ok and make an excuse for it, or am I trying to give you some practical advice for avoiding it in the first place?

DON'T SEGREGATE YOURSELF

One mistake I often see in workplaces where there is some amount of prejudice is self-segregation of people who are experiencing some degree of prejudice.

Don't do this.

Don't "find your people," form a big group, and only hang out with them.

This will only serve to create more prejudice, and will likely make you actually look like you are exhibiting prejudice.

In the spirit of throwing all political correctness out the window, I'll tell you this story.

Once upon a time, I was working a government contract with a bunch of other contractors, of which a good percentage were Indian.

The Indian contractors would self-segregate.

They'd hang around each other and go to lunch together every day.

Then there was me.

I got right in the middle of it.

I'd jump in and invite myself to their lunches.

I'd be right there talking shop with them.

I was an honorary Indian guy—even though I have no Indian ethnicity at all.

Other contractors would frequently have issues with the Indian contractors—not me.

The Indian contractors would frequently have issues with the non-Indian contractors—not me.

I could see things from both sides and I was well-liked by Indians and non-Indians.

Eventually, I started inviting other non-Indian contractors to go to lunch with us as well.

I greatly reduced the amount of prejudice that I would have had to deal with, and I was in position to reduce the prejudice the Indian contractors had to deal with, because I broke up the self-segregation and I included everyone, starting with myself.

As someone in a leadership position on the contract, I could see how the self-segregation was hurting the project.

It's not always as easy to see it from the inside.

I do this everywhere I go.

You'll often see me hanging out with the strangest groups of people, because I'm not afraid to get in there and mix it up.

As a result, I don't receive much prejudice at all.

So, my advice to you is to **get in there, mix it up, talk to people, and interact with people who aren't "your people."**

Most people look for people who share commonalities with them and self-segregate into those groups, whether it be by race, religion, ethnicity, or some other divisor.

As a result, they experience more prejudice.

Don't do that. Be brave. Expand your tribe.

HAVE CONFIDENCE IN YOURSELF

By far the best way to combat prejudice is to **not let it influence what you think of yourself.**

If you hold yourself and your own abilities in high regard, it will be difficult for someone who tries to disparage you in some way to have any effect.

Yes, I know this is easier said than done. When you feel like people are unfairly discriminating against you, or threatening you unfairly based on some bias or stereotype, it can be difficult to go on your merry way, but the more self-confidence you develop, the easier it will be.

You can't change other people.

You can't change how they think.

You can't directly change how they feel about you or act towards you.

But **you *can* change you.**

You can become stronger and more resilient.

If you are willing, you can develop your self-confidence (https://simpleprogrammer.com/cg44-confidence) to the point where when people make racist remarks or come at you with prejudice, it doesn't even matter, because you know what you are capable of and you can overcome the disadvantages they are trying to put on you.

There is great power in taking away the power of would-be oppressors by simply being so confident in your own abilities and who you are that what they say or think doesn't matter.

One of the people I admire the most in history is a man by the name of Frederick Douglass.

Here's a quote from him, relevant to our discussion:

> *"The limits of tyrants are prescribed by the endurance of those whom they oppose."*

Frederick Douglass was a slave who escaped his master, became a free man, and helped other slaves escape.

He was a great man, not just because of what he did, but because of what he thought and what he said.

He didn't allow his condition or the prejudice and racism around him to define him. He rejected it outright.

Here's a quote from the Frederick Douglass Wikipedia entry about his time as a slave:

> *"In 1833, Thomas Auld took Douglass back from Hugh ("[a]s a means of punishing Hugh," Douglass later wrote). Thomas Auld sent Douglass to work for Edward Covey, a poor farmer who had a reputation as a "slave-breaker." He whipped Douglass regularly, and nearly broke him psychologically. The sixteen-year-old Douglass finally rebelled against the beatings, however, and fought back. After Douglass won a physical confrontation, Covey never tried to beat him again."*

Why do I like Frederick Douglass so much?

Simple. At no point did Frederick consider himself a helpless victim (https://simpleprogrammer. com/cg44-victim).

His response was always to ignore you or to fight you, never to acquiesce.

IGNORE AS MUCH OF IT AS YOU CAN

I'm reading a book right now by Mark Manson with a pretty controversial title, *The Subtle Art of Not Giving a Fuck* (https://simpleprogrammer.com/cg44-subtle).

In the book, Mark says that one of the biggest problems with society and people in general is that they, as he would put it, **give a fuck about too many things.**

Far too many things.

I'm not trying to make light of discrimination, prejudice, sexism, racism, bigotry, and all the other ills that plague our society—these are real problems—but on an individual level, **do we really have to care so much about these things?**

I'm not Hispanic, but plenty of people think I am.

I don't get a large amount of discrimination or prejudice for it, but I do get some.

You know what my default response is?

Nothing.

I simply ignore it.

As Mark Manson would say, "no fucks given."

So, you think I'm less intelligent because of some stereotype you have of me.

So, you dislike me and want to treat me poorly.

So what?

I simply don't care (https://simpleprogrammer.com/cg44-noexcuse).

I simply go on with my day and treat your ignorance as what it is, ignorance.

People say stupid things.

People say hurtful things.

Sometimes out of malice, but **mostly out of ignorance.**

Heck, half of this chapter—or more—could offend you.

If **you choose** to let it.

Or you can simply ignore it and move on with your life.

Prejudice happens. Injustice happens.

It happens every day.

It shouldn't happen, and when it crosses the line, you certainly have to deal with it, but **your default mode should be to ignore it.**

Pick the hills you are willing to die on very carefully.

I realize this viewpoint isn't very politically correct and you might not like it, but guess what?

I don't care.

I've got too many important things to worry about and do with my life than to waste time and emotional energy caring about stuff that doesn't really matter.

I'd rather be pragmatic than offended.

REPORT WHAT YOU CAN'T IGNORE

With that said, **not everything can be ignored.**

There are times when you must stand up for yourself and you can't be tolerant of someone's ignorance, because, pragmatically speaking, it does affect you in a serious way.

If someone in your workplace is hurling racist insults at you and actively discriminating against you, I'm not suggesting you stand idly by and ignore them.

That's a bit different than saying culturally insensitive things or making inappropriate jokes or some other things that might be "offensive," but don't actually harm you.

If you are being treated very unfairly by a boss or someone in a position of power because of your race, sex, religion, sexual preference, etc., and it's actually affecting your career, the answer is not to get a thick skin, it's to report them.

You've got to be the judge, and say clearly when enough is enough.

You have to have clear boundaries (https://simpleprogrammer.com/cg44-boundaries)—what you will and will not tolerate.

It's a personal decision, but I'd encourage you to **be as pragmatic as possible and to err on the side of thick-skinned** versus hypersensitive, because fighting battles all the time is going to wear you out emotionally, physically, psychologically and won't be worth it in the long run.

But, when that line is crossed, and you can't ignore it, here is what you do.

Start by documenting things.

Write down what was said, what happened, who did it, where it took place, and when.

Keep very detailed notes so that it is apparent that you aren't making things up, causing trouble for trouble's sake, and that there is a clear pattern of inexcusable behavior.

Again, **don't crucify someone for a single slip-up**—unless it's a severe violation like some form of physical or sexual assault—but, if you need to report someone, make sure you have evidence.

Once you have the evidence you need, **try and handle the issue on your own**, if possible.

Confront the person, tell them what boundary they have crossed, why it isn't acceptable, and tell them to stop.

Don't threaten, don't intimidate, don't lecture or beg.

Simply be clear and firm with the boundary they crossed and that **you will not tolerate it.**

If they don't comply, then it is time to go to HR or the higher ups and bring your evidence with you.

If the problem isn't resolved there, you may want to seek legal council and/or remove yourself from the environment completely.

PREJUDICE SUCKS

Believe me, I know.

I've been the target of it.

I've seen other people affected by it.

I hope you can understand that in this chapter, **I'm not trying to turn a deaf ear to it, excuse it,** or dismiss it in any form.

What I am trying to do is **give you pragmatic advice for dealing with it.**

In life, I've found that being a martyr for a cause is rarely effective.

It's much more effective to be successful, gain influence and respect, and then use that influence to make an impact on the world.

Holding a picket sign rarely makes a difference.

I'd much rather further my cause by **proving naysayers wrong** than by telling them they are wrong.

CHAPTER 45

BEING IN A LEADERSHIP POSITION

On one of my 10-mile runs a couple of weeks ago, I was listening to the audio version of a book called *Extreme Ownership: How U.S. Navy SEALS Lead and Win* (https://simpleprogrammer.com /cg45-seal).

It's a book about leadership and the principles learned from some of the most important and difficult positions: combat leadership.

In the book, one of the authors, Jocko Willink, says, "**There are no bad teams, only bad leaders.**"

In fact, he dedicates a whole chapter to this idea.

He gives an example of a grueling Navy SEALS training exercise where teams of "boat crews" compete against each other in very harsh conditions to beat out other boat crews in a race.

It involves six-man teams carrying heavy boats on their heads up hills, and then racing across the water.

In his example, one of the boat crews was falling behind and finishing dead last every time.

Another boat crew was dominating just about every race.

He decided to switch the leaders from the crews to see what would happen.

When he did this, the boat crew that was finishing last ended up eventually finishing first, and the crew that was finishing first ended up finishing second.

This is the power and responsibility of an effective leader.

An effective leader—one who takes extreme ownership, as Willink suggests—is not only able to make their team succeed, but leaves such an impact on their team that even when they are replaced the team is still a winner.

This chapter is all about how to become that kind of leader.

The kind of leader who **inspires, motivates, and pushes their team so that success is all but guaranteed.**

Not the kind of leader who is simply given a title of "leader," but one who doesn't need a formal designation of authority to command respect, foster cooperation, and inspire the best performance possible.

WHAT IS LEADERSHIP?

Let's start off by talking about what exactly leadership is.

Leadership is not a title or a position.

Leadership is something **you do** and exemplify.

You can be told that you are the leader.

You can be given the official title.

You can be put in charge of a team.

But no one, **no one, can *make* you a leader.**

You have to do that yourself.

You have to own it.

Leadership is all about getting people to follow you into your vision of the future, to go the direction you are going, to follow the path you have set out.

That means you have to walk the path first.

Leadership is about being in front, not pushing from behind.

No job title, no official designation, no mandate from on high can make you a leader, because compliance is not the goal. Buy-in—full support—is.

You can temporarily control someone's actions with force or authority, but **leadership seeks to win their hearts and minds**, and in turn, inspire loyalty rather than fear.

HOW TO LEAD EFFECTIVELY

There is only one way to lead effectively, and that is **by example.**

The best leaders do what they ask of their team first.

They are willing to sacrifice and go the extra mile to pave the way for the people they are trying to lead.

Even without an official title, you can lead people if you are willing to set an example for them to follow.

If you want your team to do test-driven development (https://simpleprogrammer.com /cg45-views) and write unit tests before they write any production code, don't just tell them to do it, do it yourself first.

If you want your team to write better commit messages when they check code into source control, you better be doing it first, and be doing a damn good job of it.

Want your team to treat each other with respect, avoid arguments, and cooperate?

You should know what to do by now.

Oftentimes, leading by example means doing jobs that are "beneath you."

Too many "leaders" want to sit in their ivory towers and command their troops from above.

To be a true leader who leads by example, you have to be willing to get in the front lines and lead from the battlefield.

Take on some of the difficult and boring tasks that no one wants to do on your team.

Show them the kind of quality you can bring to even the most monotonous task.

LEAD IN ALL AREAS

A good leader is someone you look up to in multiple areas, not just their main discipline.

What I mean by this is that it's great that you are an excellent programmer and that you can write the cleanest code anyone has ever seen, but that is just one area in which you must lead (https://simpleprogrammer.com/cg45-lead).

You should lead in every area you want your team to follow.

Do you want your team to have a good work ethic?

To be motivated?

Develop good communication and soft skills?

You've got to be exemplifying your best in each of the areas you want your team to excel in.

If you want to know the behavior and habits of a team, you have to look no further than their leader.

Teams tend to take on many of their leader's traits, especially over time.

So, if you are constantly late for work, take long lunches, and spend a good amount of time surfing the internet instead of working, you can expect your team members to do the same.

If you make crude jokes, frequently get into arguments, grumble and complain about your higher ups and/or don't treat people professionally, you should expect that same kind of behavior from your team.

As a leader, you must...

HOLD YOURSELF TO A HIGHER LEVEL OF ACCOUNTABILITY

This means that whatever you expect your team to do, you have to expect that same thing from yourself and more.

I consider my role at Simple Programmer (https://simpleprogrammer.com/cg45-homepage), and especially my YouTube channel (https://simpleprogrammer.com/cg45-youtube) to be one of leadership.

I want to inspire and lead people to perform and do their best.

I want to teach people how to reach their true potential and to never give up, no matter how difficult things get.

So, what do I do?

I set standards for myself far higher than what is expected and far beyond the goals I am trying to inspire people to reach.

I hold myself to an exceptionally high level of accountability.

On the work side, I work in a focused and diligent manner and I never, ever give up.

I try to get more work done in a week than most people think is humanly possible.

On a given week, I produce several blog posts, 18 YouTube videos, several podcasts, and do plenty of other work.

On the fitness side, I try to push myself harder than anyone I know.

I run 40 miles every week, lift weights for six hours, fast until 5 p.m. every day, and I maintain sub-10 percent bodyfat levels.

If I'm going to ask you to do something, I'm going to not only have done it, but have done the 10x more difficult version of it (https://simpleprogrammer.com/cg45-ten).

If I ask you to run a mile, I'm going to run 10 first.

If you want to lead people, don't just lead them by example. Truly inspire them by showing them what is possible by going the extra mile—or 10.

Think about the best leaders you have known.

Think about the people who inspired you the most.

Did they just do the minimum, or did you feel like they did much more than they were asking you to do?

When supplies are low, a good leader gives his rations to his team, not because he is self-sacrificing and selfless, but because he wants them to see that even without food the battle can be fought and won.

A good leader inspires people, because they think to themselves, "If he can do that, then surely I can do this."

YOU ARE RESPONSIBLE FOR THE TEAM

In the chapter, "Working on a Team," I talked about the idea that you should try to take as much responsibility for the team as possible. As a leader, this idea isn't optional.

As a leader, you and you alone are responsible for the performance of the team.

As a leader, there is no one to blame but yourself.

To lead effectively, you must take full ownership for your team and everything your team does.

You cannot pass the buck or play the blame game.

The blame is always yours.

If your team fails, it is your fault and your fault alone.

You will lead and inspire the team much more effectively when they know that they have 100 percent freedom to do what you are asking them to do, because you will hold yourself responsible for the outcome.

That doesn't mean that team members don't screw up.

It doesn't mean that team members can't throw a wrench in your plans, or even completely foul them up, but it does mean that when that happens, **it's still your fault and your responsibility.**

It's your fault, because you could have **trained that team member better.**

It's your fault, because you could have made sure that the team member **better understood and bought into the plan.**

It's your fault, because if you did all those things and you knew that team member still wasn't on board, **you could have kicked them officially off-board** and removed them from the team.

Remember, your most important job as the leader of a team (https://simpleprogrammer.com /cg45-great) is to make as many people around you as successful as possible.

You have to take responsibility, not only for your own mistakes, but for the mistakes made by everyone else on your team.

A good leader is responsible when things go wrong, but gives all the credit to the team when success is achieved.

TRUST YOUR TEAM, DELEGATE

Even the best leaders can only do so much by themselves.

Some leaders recognize they are ultimately responsible for the team, so their response is to simply do everything themselves.

They figure if they are responsible for it, they need to make sure it's done correctly, and the only way to do that is to do it themselves.

This kind of attitude creates a team that is completely dependent on the leader and can't function on its own.

"How should we solve this problem?"

"I don't know, we need to ask James."

"Well, James is out to lunch."

"Ok, guess we can't do anything until he comes back."

No. Wrong!

You don't want that scenario to play out on your team, so you need to make sure you trust your team well enough to delegate tasks and responsibility for them, although you'll still be ultimately accountable.

But how can I trust they'll do it right?

You can never be 100-percent sure, but there are a few things you can do to reduce the instance of screwups.

The first thing is to **make your mission and intent as clear and simple as possible.**

As long as the members of your team know what you are ultimately trying to accomplish and what is important—the overall vision—they can make decisions on their own on how to achieve those ends.

The idea is to **tell team members what the objective is without telling them how to do it,** or making them run every little decision by you.

You can also have a **clear operating procedure** that anyone can follow to get certain types of tasks done.

Flowcharts or checklists work extremely well here.

Currently at Simple Programmer, I have team members doing jobs that I thought only I could do.

I decided that I would start documenting the process I used to do the task, the decisions I had to make along the way, and the reasons for making those decisions one way or another.

Pretty soon, I had a process document that anyone could pick up and run with.

Now we have a Wiki with all of our processes and delegation is very easy to do.

Don't forget training.

The first time you ask someone to do a task, even if the process is documented, there are likely going to be issues. That is ok.

Go over the work, tell them what mistakes to correct and why they are mistakes, and then have them correct them.

That's the best way to do training.

If your team is aligned and understands the mission, has a process to follow, and is well-trained, it's not that difficult to trust them to get things done—even the things you think you could only do yourself.

To be an effective leader you have to be able to delegate. This fact becomes even more important as you rise up the ranks and lead larger and larger teams.

You will have to groom and train leaders who will lead their own teams, and you will have to put significant trust in them.

One word of caution, though.

There is a difference between delegation and abdication.

Delegating a task or responsibility means giving it to someone else to do, but still ultimately owning it and being responsible for it.

Abdicating means chucking it over the wall and saying "you handle it."

Make sure that when you delegate tasks, you still take ownership for them and check over the results. Don't just assume it will be done—and done correctly— and then think, "It's not my fault, I assigned Bob to do it."

Leadership doesn't work that way.

LEAD ON!

As you can see, leadership isn't exactly easy.

To be a leader, you are going to have to make a number of sacrifices. Much will be expected from you.

But there is a certain reward and satisfaction in knowing that you have inspired people to be their greatest.

Being a leader is not for everyone, but if you do take on that burden—and honor—hopefully this chapter has equipped and prepared you just a little bit better to do it.

CHAPTER 46

GETTING A RAISE OR PROMOTION

Hey John, didn't you already write this chapter?

Yes, I recall that you wrote a chapter telling me how to ace my review process.

Shouldn't that get me a raise or a promotion?

If I ace my review process?

Huh?

What gives, man?

Sheesh, you ask a lot of questions.

Hold your horses, calm down a bit and I'll tell you.

You see, **many software developers erroneously think that if they get a good review, they'll get a raise or promotion.**

While sometimes this is the case, it's usually not.

More often than not, I hear programmers tell me about how they got the highest marks they could, yet a raise or promotion "just wasn't in the budget."

Or worse yet—ok, maybe not worse, but more insulting—they get a peanut-level raise of a few measly percent that doesn't even keep up with inflation.

Yes, it's important to ace your review, but **just acing your review alone won't get you that big raise or promotion you're after.**

You'll have to be a bit more strategic and plan things out a little more carefully if you really want to make the big bucks.

And that is what this chapter is about, making the big bucks.

Well maybe not about making the big bucks, but getting a hefty raise or promotion—one to write home to your mom about.

As we get started, I should mention that there are a lot of parallels between negotiating your salary and getting a raise—so you'll definitely want to have your copy of the Software Developer's Negotiation Checklist (https://simpleprogrammer.com/career-guide-toolkit) nearby for easy reference.

ALWAYS CHOOSE RESPONSIBILITY OVER PAY

Before we can talk about how to get a raise or promotion, let's talk about whether you should go for a raise or a promotion.

Which is better: more money or a bigger title?

More moolah or more responsibility?

It seems like an obvious answer, right?

I'll take the cash, Bob.

Bob, SHOW ME THE MONEY!

But, no. That is actually the wrong answer.

See, it's like this.

I've only watched two episodes of House of Cards (https://simpleprogrammer.com /cg46-cards), but I remember that the main character—I believe he's played by Kevin Spacey— said something that was so true.

"Such a waste of talent. He chose money over power—in this town, a mistake nearly everyone makes. Money is the McMansion in Sarasota that starts falling apart after 10 years. Power is the old stone building that stands for centuries."

It's the same thing with responsibility.

Responsibility is power, for all intents and purposes.

The thing is, if you chase responsibility, money will follow.

You can always trade responsibility—read: power—for money.

Think of it this way: would you rather get a job at a Fortune 500 company where you get paid what a CEO gets paid, or get paid what the janitor gets paid but get the actual title of CEO?

In the short term, the money makes sense.

But what happens after you lose that job? (https://simpleprogrammer.com/cg46-fired)

You can try to tell the next company you apply for that you were making $300,000 a year at your last job, but they'll just laugh at you.

Yet, if you've been the CEO of a Fortune 500 company, imagine how you could parlay that into cash at a later date.

The point is that when you are going after something, you need to be going after positions of power, which roughly translates to more responsibility.

Take every opportunity you can to be put in charge of something, even if it is a shit job.

It doesn't matter.

You want to grow and expand your fiefdom by gaining more and more responsibility.

Look for some undeveloped swampland that no one wants to touch, take it over, get your hands dirty, and build a theme park out of it—heck, that's what Walt Disney did.

Find those areas that no one wants, those projects that no one will touch, and take them over. Then, make them shine.

I promise you, if you keep getting promoted and increasing your responsibility within any organization, the pay will eventually catch up with you.

TAKE INITIATIVE

Some people seem to think "paying your dues" means that you clock in and clock out every day, day after day, and get your work done. Then after some magical amount of time, the "dues fairy" will strike you on the head with the "dues wand" and you'll suddenly be rewarded for your efforts.

Nope. Sorry, it don't work that way, brah.

If you want to get a raise, if you want to get that promotion, you gotta do more—much more—than what is asked of you.

You've got to go out there and make things happen, not wait for things to happen to you.

It's called taking initiative.

Let those other people in the diner wait patiently for the ketchup to come out of the bottle. I'm gonna stick a straw in the bottle and suck that ketchup right out of there.

The point is, **a promotion or raise is not going to come to you because you simply deserve it.**

You are going to have to get out there and be aggressive.

You are going to have to tell your boss that you want to get a raise or promotion.

You are going to have to actively take steps to get what you want.

You have to make your own opportunity.

Most of the rest of this chapter will focus on ways you can do that.

Ways that you can not just sit at your desk and do your work, and even do a good job of it, but to do more, to become more.

INVEST IN YOUR EDUCATION

One of the first initiative-taking things you can do is to invest in your education.

When was the last time you read a book? (https://simpleprogrammer.com/cg46-books)

I suppose if you got this far in this book, you are probably one of the overachievers in this area, or I'm an extremely awesome and entertaining writer and you just can't wait to see what I am going to say next.

Hint: it's the second one.

But, seriously, **buy more books** (https://simpleprogrammer.com/cg46-ultimate) **and read them.**

Always be reading some kind of technical book, every single day.

I used to read a technical book for 30 minutes a day.

I'd call this "treadmill time," because I'd do it while walking on a treadmill (https://simpleprogrammer.com/cg46-treadmill).

Don't just read books, but do online courses—and actually complete them.

Attend seminars or conferences or live training classes.

Go back and complete your degree, or get another degree.

Hire a personal career coach (https://simpleprogrammer.com/cg46-coaching) to mentor you.

Don't be afraid to spend some money to make more money.

I've heard it said that you should reinvest 10 percent of what you make back into yourself as personal development.

I'm not sure if I invest 10 percent exactly, but **I've invested tens of thousands of dollars in my personal development over the years.**

Not only will this make you more valuable and more effective, but a marked increase in education is one of the most effective bullets in the "give-me-a-raise" gun.

(That doesn't sound right. Not sure I should use the term give-me-a-raise gun, but you know what? I'm going with it. Oorah!)

Anyway, I think you get my point.

If your boss asks why you should get a raise or promotion and you say, "Well, when you hired me I had an eighth grade education, but now I have my Ph.D.," it's pretty difficult to argue that you aren't worth more money or deserve a title upgrade.

MAKE YOUR GOALS KNOWN

I used to practice what is called covert communication.

This was my basic strategy.

Suppose I wanted you to do something for me. I wouldn't say to you, "Hey, I'd really like to have some of that Kit Kat bar you have there. Can you snap me off a piece?"

Nope, instead what I would do is this: I'd go "humph."

Then—in a masterful stroke—I'd sigh and look at you, making my eyes just slightly bigger.

If you still didn't get the message, I'd humph again.

Guess how effective this covert communication strategy was?

Pretty much zero effective. All it would do is piss people off.

Often people would know what I wanted—that tasty, crunchy Kit Kat bar—but they'd often ignore me just to spite me.

If you want something, ask for it.

When I sold you this book, I didn't beat around the bush and try to drop hints that you should buy my book.

No, I said, "This is a fucking awesome book! Buy it now! It's fucking awesome!"

If you want your boss to give you a raise or a promotion, just ask for it.

Just say "Hey dude, look man, I've been here a while and guess what, man? I want a raise dammit. Give me a raise."

Well, don't put it quite that way, but tell your boss directly, in no uncertain terms, that you want a raise or a promotion and it is your goal to get one.

Oh, and you do this BEFORE the review—well before the review.

Not during, not after.

I promise you, the raise or promotion is mostly decided well before you sit down for the formal review.

In fact, many times the entire review process is a sham designed to give the person who has already been slotted for that raise or promotion that raise or promotion.

You don't have to ask for the raise or promotion right away. In fact, don't do this.

Instead, plant the seed.

Tell your boss that's what your goal is.

Tell him what you plan to do to achieve the goal.

Ask him what else you need to do or what he would suggest for you to reach this goal by your next review.

If he says "it's not possible," respond with, "if it were possible, or if there was only a small chance and it required a huge effort, what would I need to do?"

If you can get him to answer that question and you can do whatever herculean task he asks you to do, you are going to get the raise, buddy—and then you are going to take me out to a nice steak dinner.

HEY JOHN

What do I do if they tell me I deserve a raise and they'd give me one but it's not in the budget or that the company is having financial problems or cutting back right now? What if the company just had layoffs—do I still ask for a raise?

I'll start with the last question, since it's the easiest:

Yes, you still ask for a raise! If the company just had layoffs it means they have a lot more money to spend than they did before there were layoffs.

It may seem a bit counterintuitive, but here's the thing; when we perceive something as valuable enough, we'll do anything to either get it or keep it.

Your boss might say you deserve a raise, but the company doesn't have the budget right now, the company's having financial problems, we should start seeing less of each other, yada, yada, yada.

But, what he's really saying is that you aren't valuable enough for the company to do what is needed to keep you and to keep you happy.

Honestly, most of the time this is bullshit anyway.

Companies are always financially strapped, there is never enough money in the budget.

Don't buy that hogwash.

Just realize it's a clear message that you haven't conveyed enough value for your boss or your company to overcome whatever obstacles are necessary—financial, political and otherwise—to keep you from leaving.

Let me put it this way:

You like your kid right? (Ok, but let's pretend like you do.)

If you were in Venezuela and some Venezuelan kidnappers had your kid and wanted like $10,000 to get your kid back, would you say, "Oh sorry, it's not in the budget right now?" or "Man, I would, but I'm financially strapped?"

No, you'd be selling your car, calling your friends and relatives, mortgaging your house. Whatever you needed to do to get that cash.

MAKE YOURSELF VALUABLE OUTSIDE YOUR COMPANY

One of the best ways to increase your value inside a company is to **increase your value outside the company.**

There is only so much you can do to build your brand and reputation inside your current company and position.

In fact, it's often difficult to change first impressions and to grow inside a company.

It's kind of like how your family will always see you as that goofy 11-year-old version of yourself no matter how old you are.

The solution is to **get out there and market yourself** (https://simpleprogrammer.com /cg46-marketyourself): **build your personal brand.**

You want to create some sense of external pressure where your employer realizes how valuable you are because other people, outside the company, realize how valuable you are.

When your boss hears you on a podcast, sees that you've published a book, or hears someone else talking about an article you wrote, your value goes up.

You are finally not that goofy 11-year-old kid.

We'll talk about the specifics of how to increase your value outside the company and market yourself in the next section of this book.

I've actually found learning how to market yourself to be so important that I built an entire course called, "How to Market Yourself as a Software Developer" (https:// simpleprogrammer.com/cg46-marketyourself).

In general though, you want to do things that are going to increase your reputation and overall notoriety in the software development industry, especially in your particular specialty.

If people outside your company think you are valuable, people inside your company will think you are valuable, and it will be much easier to get that raise or promotion.

BECOME AN ASSET

If you can prove to me that you can make me more money than it costs me to have you on my payroll, I'll hire you on the spot.

Most smart employers would—it's just common sense.

Yet, many software developers forget that the primary reason they are being paid a salary at all is not because they are smart or because of the skills they have, it's because they make their employer money. Moolah.

You need to make the company money.

If you want to get paid more money, the equation is pretty simple: make the company more money.

As an employee, it's easy to get disconnected from the business world and economics of the company you are working for and forget that ultimately you are part of, and contribute to, the bottom line.

Try to figure out how.

Try to figure out how what you are doing directly impacts the revenue your company makes.

Then try to figure out how you can increase that bottom line.

What can you do that you know is going to make the company more money?

I know software developers who figured out a brand new product they could create for their employer. They penned deals where not only did they get a raise, but they got a royalty percentage from the new product.

You have to think outside the box here. Think like an entrepreneur or business person.

You can be an intrapreneur in the company you work for.

When you go in for a raise, the best argument you could possibly make is that you are making the company more money.

HEY JOHN

What about making the argument for how you are saving the company money? Is that just as valuable?

Nope, and I'll tell you why.

Two reasons:

1. It's much more difficult to prove.

2. It's just not as noticeable.

How are you going to show that you are saving the company money?

In most cases, it's pretty difficult to do.

It's much easier to show how you are making the company money—that's a much less subjective thing to show.

Think of it this way; how many war heroes do you know?

How about people who are famous for preventing wars or preventing gigantic catastrophes?

Surgeons save lives, but what about the doctor preaching preventative medicine?

I'm sure he's probably saved even more lives than most surgeons, it's just that it's much more difficult to prove and it's not very glorious.

So, unless you've got some really compelling proof of how you are saving the company money—like you've automated some process that was costing the company $1,000,000 a year and now it costs $0—it's going to be much better to show your boss how you are making the company fistfuls of cash.

Also: consider reframing savings into earnings if you can. If I were selling people on refinancing a loan, I wouldn't say, you could say "$200" a month on your mortgage. I'd say, "We'll put an extra $200 in your pocket every month."

Show how you increased the bottom line and how much the company is benefiting from your work, and you'll have a very solid argument.

Think of it this way.

If I'm your boss and you walk into my office and you show some compelling evidence that suggests you are making the company $1 million dollars a year in revenue, do you think I am going to refuse your request for a $10,000 raise?

Maybe, but it's much, much less likely.

ASK FOR A SPECIFIC NUMBER

Here is the thing; if you ask for a raise, ask for a specific number.

Ask for exactly what you want.

It's very difficult to negotiate and get what you want, when what you want is "more."

More sounds greedy.

More is undefined.

Your definition of more is different than mine.

When my wife asks me if I want some more Toll House pie, her definition of more is another small slice. Mine is the rest of the pie please, oh and put whip cream on top and some ice cream on the side.

Before you even go into your boss's office to ask for a raise, know exactly what number you are going to ask for.

Do your homework and calculate what that number is.

Then, do more homework and come up with the reasoning and calculations which give you some evidence to support why the number you are asking for is what you should be paid.

You are much more likely to get what you ask for when you are specific and can provide evidence to back up your number.

DON'T MAKE THREATS

One of the worst ways to try to get a raise or a promotion is to threaten that you are going to leave.

Sometimes, if you are a key player on a project and the company can't afford to lose you right now, they'll give in and meet your demands, but your victory is likely only temporary.

Why temporary?

Well, let's think about a scenario for a minute.

Suppose you come into my office and you tell me how you are going to this other job where they will pay you more if you don't get a raise.

I'm a bit stuck, because I don't want you to quit on the spot, since I don't have a replacement for you and you are a critical resource to completing the project on time.

But, I'm a bit annoyed. More than a bit.

You've put me in a spot.

You aren't telling me you deserve a raise because you are more valuable than you were before, or based on some other compelling evidence, but instead, you are taking advantage of the bind I would be in if I had to replace a key player on the project this late in the game.

So, I realize that I don't have much of a choice and reluctantly agree to your demands—because that is what they are.

But guess what I do?

I start looking for your replacement immediately.

I can't have someone on my team whom I can't trust.

When I'm on the front line, I want someone who is watching my back.

I don't want someone who might fragg me with friendly fire. That's not cool.

You've moved yourself, in my mind, from the asset category to the liability category.

You are now a liability to the team, and an expensive one at that.

When you ask for the raise or promotion, just ask for it.

Don't make threats, don't say you are going to leave (https://simpleprogrammer.com /cg46-nothreats).

If you've made yourself valuable outside the company like we talked about, your boss is going to know that refusing your request may very well cause you to look elsewhere.

But there is a huge difference between making a wise business decision and carefully coming to your own conclusion, and being given an ultimatum.

No one likes an ultimatum.

DON'T TALK ABOUT WHY YOU NEED THE MONEY

I know this is going to seem kind of hard to believe, but **no one cares about your sad sob story or how poor you are.**

Really, no one cares.

They may pretend to care and toss you a sympathy bone, but underneath it all, they are much more concerned about themselves and their own problems.

You are very unlikely to get a raise out of pity.

Of all the reasons to give a raise or promotion to someone, pity is perhaps the last.

I want to give you a raise because you are doing a kickass job and you are making me money.

I don't want to give you a raise because your neighbor just bought a new car and you realized how old your car is and you've been racking up debt and you are barely making it, so you need more money.

Yet, so many software developers go and ask for raises and when asked why, they talk about how they have a new baby or they just bought a house or some other thing that no one in the world cares about besides themselves.

Don't do that.

Talk about the business case.

Talk about why you deserve the money, not why you NEED the money.

(Oh, and make sure you actually DO deserve the money.)

IF ALL ELSE FAILS, GO ELSEWHERE

So, you've executed everything in this chapter to a "T."

You've made yourself more valuable, invested in your education, set up the business case for why you should get a raise or promotion, and you've even taken on huge amounts of responsibility without being asked—all on your own initiative.

But, when you ask for a raise or promotion, your pointy-haired boss just says "no."

That's ok. At least you tried.

Honestly, the best way to get a raise or promotion is usually to go somewhere else.

It's true.

I advanced my own career more by strategically hopping from jobs than I did just staying in one place.

I'm not saying you should become a software developer hobo or transient, but you might strongly want to consider making a move every two or three years to another company where you can get a bigger salary, better title and more growth opportunities.

It's often easier to move up in a company from the outside than it is from the inside.

In fact, I've actually left a company, worked somewhere else, and then came back to the original company in a much higher position. From the emails I get from software developers, I'm not the only one.

Oftentimes it's difficult for people who work with you every day to see how much you've grown and increased your skills and abilities. The simple truth of it is, if you want to get paid what you are worth, you may have to go somewhere else where people don't have preconceived notions.

So, if you've tried everything else and you still can't get that raise or promotion, it might just be time to move on.

CHAPTER 47

WOMEN IN TECH

Oh boy.

That's probably what you thought when you saw the title of this chapter.

That's what I'm thinking right now.

When I originally wrote the outline for this book, there was no chapter titled "Women in Tech."

But, after doing this .NET Rocks podcast interview (https://simpleprogrammer.com /cg47-netrocks), I got a tweet that said, "Loved it. @jsonmez, you should include a Women in Tech chapter in your new book."

And this tweet was from a woman, mind you.

I thought to myself, "What do I really have to lose?"

And then I imagined an angry mob chasing me with pitchforks, but since I'm a guy who cares more about truth and helping people than about danger—and I'm a bit stupid—I decided to write it anyway.

The goal of this chapter is pretty simple.

I want to talk, honestly, about women in technology; how they are perceived, what the stereotypes and stigmas surrounding them are, and why I honestly think that so many men do really stupid things like send death threats and make comments about rape.

By understanding and really taking an honest look at these things, we can begin to move past them, because you can't change reality until you honestly look at it, as painful and sometimes politically incorrect as it may be.

I also want to give **some real, practical advice to both women and men on dealing with the topic of women in technology**, in a way that is beneficial to both sexes.

Now, you might be asking what makes me "qualified" to speak on this subject.

Or perhaps you have the mistaken belief that just because I am a man that I don't even have the right to have an opinion on women in technology.

Well, the answer is, **I don't need to be "qualified" to offer my opinion on this subject, based on personal observations, experience, and coaching both male and female software developers.**

And, really, just like the rest of this book, that's all it is—that's all any of this book is—my opinion.

I don't really see how my opinion on this matter really differs that much from my opinion on how to negotiate a salary, deal with QA, or learn a programming language.

If you wanted a book on facts, you probably should have picked up a history book or a biography.

With that said, let's dive into the fascinating topic of women in technology.

STEREOTYPES AND STIGMAS

I've addressed the idea of stereotypes several times in this book so far, and that is because **I truly believe we need to be upfront and honest about the stereotypes that exist**, and the fact that all of us have them, if we want to be able to overcome them, or at the very least work around them.

Women in technology are stereotyped.

Many men—and some women—often assume that a female programmer is not going to be as technically competent.

A woman in technology can also be thought of as either not as passionate or dedicated as a man, or seen as a geeky anomaly who isn't very feminine, but hangs with the guys and plays Zelda.

Women are often thought to be good testers, but not taken as seriously in software developer roles.

Of course none of these stereotypes are universally true, but it's important to be aware of them, whether you are a woman in technology needing to know what you'll likely face, or a man in technology needing to understand that you may hold these views and they may not be correct.

(I could write an entire essay on how forced diversity often increases and reinforces these negative stereotypes, but the goal of this chapter is pragmatic action you can take, not political advice.)

The point is, some women in technology will fit these stereotypes, but that doesn't mean that all—or even most—do.

There are plenty of technically-competent female software developers who are just as passionate about programming and technology as any guy, and are not "guy-like" in nature.

WHY GUYS HARASS WOMEN

Ok, so we've taken a look at what I think are the most common stereotypes women face in the technology world, but let's talk a little bit about the social stigma that gets applied to some women, or, why guys harass women.

And it does happen.

I've known enough honest, non-attention seeking women in technology to know that guys do send pictures of their anatomy, threaten to sexually assault women, actually do sexually assault them at conferences, and even send death threats.

But... before I get into why I think some guys engage in this absolutely horrid behavior, I want to say that not all guys do this and that it is a very, very small minority who can make the environment seem worse than it is.

In general, from my experience, most men in the technology industry are supportive, welcoming, and even protective of women in the technology field—although the protective bit can be overdone and cause its own problems.

With that said, let's dive into male psychology.

Am I a psychologist?

No, but I've spent enough time reading emails from guys writing into my YouTube channel (https://simpleprogrammer.com/cg47-youtube), and coaching them. And being a guy, I understand a pretty good deal of male psychology, especially when it comes to women.

Getting back to stereotypes, many male software developers come from a background of being a nerd or dork.

They were picked on and bullied in school, socially awkward, flabbergasted around girls, and rejected quite often.

For many male software developers, these conditions drove them deeper and deeper into technology as both an escape and a way to prove themselves worthy to society.

These men **harbor a deep-seated resentment towards cool guys, jocks and especially, especially, those girls that they wanted, but couldn't have**—the ones that rejected them.

What happens when all of a sudden in their "safe," mostly male, environment of programming and technology, where they have become the "alpha male" based on their intellectual prowess, a woman enters, especially a good-looking one?

All of a sudden, they are back in high school.

All of a sudden, their "alpha male" status is challenged because the rules change.

They can't "pretend" to be an "alpha male" just based on intellectual superiority.

Now that there is a female in the room, the dynamics have shifted.

Rejection—in fact, all the rejection from their life—is staring them in the face.

So, how do they react to this?

How do they respond?

They secretly hate.

They seethe with anger and jealousy.

This woman represents everything they wanted but could not have, all the bullying and rejection they faced, and the torment they went through.

What do they do?

In public, they smile and bend over backwards to be nice to her, trying to win her affection and approval, since it represents the acceptance and approval of all their past rejections.

But of course that doesn't work, **because that desperate, needy behavior is not attractive** (https://simpleprogrammer.com/cg47-niceguy) and never wins anyone's approval.

So, out of frustration, in private and anonymously, they type that nasty email.

They make threats.

They send inappropriate pictures.

They lash out in any way they can, taking their rage out on the wrong target.

I could go on and write an entire volume about this subject alone, but I think you get the point.

I'm not justifying this behavior or giving an excuse for it in any way, I'm just trying to help you understand it, because it is so misunderstood.

ADVICE TO WOMEN

In the next sections of this chapter, I'm going to address men and women separately.

First, I'm going to give some advice to women, based on my experience.

Remember, **my own perspective is limited because I'm not a woman in technology**. I'm a guy, but I'll try to do my best.

And one more word of caution.

Remember, I'm approaching this from a pragmatic perspective of what you can do, not what is wrong with society and how it needs to be fixed.

This advice is geared towards how you can best deal with and navigate the technology world as it is, not how you, or I, or anyone else wants it to be—there is a huge difference.

TRY NOT TO LOOK FOR REASONS TO BE OFFENDED

No, I'm not victim blaming.

I really despise that phrase anyway, because it's a great label to put on people so you don't have to hear their ideas and you can talk over them.

But **I do think it's practical, for not just women, but really anyone in the software development field to grow a thick skin.**

If you go around and look for reasons to be offended, you'll find them—trust me.

It's like going out in the wrong neighborhood at night and looking for trouble.

If you look for it, you will find it.

Plenty of guys will says inappropriate things.

They will make offensive comments and jokes.

They will do silly, childish stuff, that you should just ignore, because **it's not worth the fight**, it's honestly not a big deal, and you don't want to get a stigma attached to you that causes everyone to walk on eggshells around you all the time.

Like I said, there are plenty of reasons you can be offended, and you can find them pretty easily.

But I would personally suggest making that list of things very, very small.

The less you let things affect you, the fewer things will affect you, and that makes for a much less stressful life.

There are some women in technology who have made it their mission to find and call out any kind of behavior they deem inappropriate or offensive— embarrassing people, stirring up trouble, and not really advancing their cause at all.

I'm not saying we don't need social activists and reform, but **we need to deal with real issues, in the right way**, not jump at every perceived slight or slightly inappropriate joke.

With that said...

DON'T IGNORE REAL ISSUES, THOUGH

There are times when growing a thick skin and turning your head or ignoring grossly inappropriate behavior is not the right thing to do.

I've been a whistleblower myself, when I witnessed a woman at one of the environments I worked at being blatantly sexually harassed by her superior (https://simpleprogrammer.com/cg47-harassed).

It wasn't the easiest thing to do, and it didn't exactly boost my career, but I reported this person to HR and made sure that the harassment stopped.

If you see or experience something that you know is just not right or acceptable, I suggest you do the same.

I'm only saying to tolerate the minor offenses or unintentional behavior that can be easily ignored.

If someone is blatantly or intentionally harassing, discriminating, touching, or doing something else wildly inappropriate and offensive to you or someone else, do not ignore it.

Go find someone to report the behavior to and/or confront that person.

I know that one of the difficulties with actually taking action against completely inappropriate behavior is the possible negative repercussions it can have on your career, or even that it can make the problem worse.

And that is exactly why I suggest, from a pragmatic standpoint, overlooking things that are slightly offensive—it's just not worth the fight.

You've got to decide where that line is for you, and when someone crosses it, you have a choice to be a victim, or to be the kind of person who will not allow themselves to be victimized.

Sometimes it's a difficult choice.

Sometimes there are real consequences for not allowing someone to victimize you.

But sometimes it has to be done anyway.

I leave it to you to decide where that line is.

DON'T TRY TO BE ONE OF THE GUYS

There is nothing wrong with being a software developer, or being involved in some other technology-related field, and still being a woman.

Being a 100-percent, unapologetic, I-like-shopping-and-shoes woman.

Don't get me wrong, you can still be a woman and not like either of those things, but what I am saying is that **you don't have to act like a guy to be a woman in technology.**

You can still be that 100-percent-feminine woman that you are—if you are—and not only can you be, but you should be.

I know this can be easily misinterpreted, but I mean this in the nicest, most sincere way.

I mean that trying to "fit in with the guys" by being one of the guys is a bad strategy and it actually hurts the team and environment.

The problem with changing who you are to fit in, is that you lose who you are.

And who you are as a woman in technology is valuable.

Your viewpoints, your softening of a masculine environment, the way you see the world and interact with it differently, are valuable.

By trying to fit in with the guys, much of that value is lost, and it reinforces some of the behavior that you probably aren't going to like.

Maybe I'm a bit old-school, but I don't think guys should treat women like guys.

I think when guys start treating women like guys, they start losing respect for them.

And I think if we trace the loss of respect to actions, we get some pretty bad actions.

But, ah, I promised to be pragmatic, and here I have gone off a little into the theoretical.

Let's bring it back to you.

If you act like one of the guys, you'll probably be treated like one of the guys, and you probably won't like that.

You'll also be sacrificing much of what makes you, you—and you probably won't like that either.

And quite honestly, you'll never be accepted as one of the guys, because you are simply NOT one of the guys.

You'll feel this rejection, and it will probably hurt, to be honest.

So, don't do it.

Be a woman, be yourself.

Yes, you'll have your own set of issues to deal with that could be alleviated to some degree by pretending to be one of the guys, but in the long run figuring out how to be 100-percent authentic to who you are and how you work in technology will be a better choice than sacrificing who you are to make things easier.

USE YOUR ADVANTAGES

If you ever had dreams of me tightening up the knot in my tie and writing a chapter in a politically correct tone, I'm sure you've abandoned them by now.

So it should come as no surprise to you that **I'm going to bluntly honest here.**

Women have certain advantages over men, especially in male-dominated environments like technology, and they should use them.

Now, don't get me wrong. I'm not saying you should, for lack of better a term, "sleep your way to the top."

I'm really not suggesting that at all or anything that even slightly resembles doing that.

But I am suggesting that, all other things being equal, **I'd rather hire an attractive woman to work on my team than a hairy, sweaty, hasn't-showered-in-three-days man.**

Gasp! How could I say that?

Really, how could I put down on paper something that we all already know, but we aren't allowed to say?

Remember how I told you I wouldn't be politically correct and I'd be extremely pragmatic?

Well, there you have it.

This whole section could simply be summed up by "if you got it, use it."

That's all I'm saying.

And it's not just looks; it's womanly charm and eloquence as well.

A feminine woman who knows how to "turn it on" a bit has a power strong enough to conquer just about any man.

Take a look at Cleopatra and Mark Antony or Josephine's control over Napoleon (https://simpleprogrammer.com/cg47-art).

History is littered with examples of the awesome power of the feminine mystique.

Again, I'm not saying to manipulate and deceive, but I'm just saying that **there is nothing wrong with using an advantage that you have.**

You've got enough disadvantages in a technology workplace that you should have no problem leveling the playing field a little bit.

HEY JOHN

Could you maybe elaborate on exactly what is appropriate to "flaunt" and use and what isn't? I don't want to get fired. Also, aren't there other guys out there in the workplace who resent women because they say women do these things in the workplace to gain an unfair advantage? And John, what if I just don't want to? Why should I have to take advantage?

Fair enough, I stepped into that one, didn't I?

First of all, don't do anything that makes you feel uncomfortable.

And don't feel like you have to do anything.

I'm just saying here that if you know how to "turn it on," there's no reason not to, and if you don't know how and you want to figure out how, I've got no objection to it either.

Just don't take it too far.

Don't be "that girl."

Don't make it look like you are seeking attention or that you need validation, unless you want to be perceived that way.

I could try to tell you want is appropriate to "flaunt" and what isn't, but it's too subjective and what works for one woman might not work for another.

You are going to have to use your womanly intuition here.

As for the guys who resent women because they "do these things in the workplace."

I wouldn't worry about them. They are going to resent you pretty much no matter what you do.

That's just how they are.

Don't modify your behavior just to suit these people, but at the same time, like I said earlier in the chapter, don't do anything that would be considered "sleeping your way to the top."

Your own merits and ability should be your primary value at the workplace; your womanly advantages are just icing on the cake.

And like I said, if any or if all of this makes you uncomfortable or you just blatantly don't agree with it, by all means, don't do it.

It's 100% your choice.

NEGOTIATE

Speaking of leveling the playing field, **one of the areas where men have historically done better in the workplace is with negotiations.**

I don't mean that in any kind of derogatory way, just trying to address the truth so we can learn from it.

I'm not sure if there is a pervasive problem with pay differences between men and women or if a large portion of it can be chalked up to the fact that men are more likely to negotiate, and negotiate harder, than women are.

If you are still having trouble digesting that last sentence because you can't believe I would say that when so many studies show it to be true, let me remind you about pragmatism.

Can you affect whether or not women are unfairly discriminated against, as far as pay goes, in the workplace?

Not really.

I mean, you can if you stage a million-woman march, have a large platform, and a good deal of money, but for all practical purposes, you can't.

But can you do something about your pay—you individually?

Yes, you can.

So, let's talk about that.

(Oh, and sidenote, if every woman does something to improve her pay—from a purely pragmatic perspective—guess what happens on the larger scale? That's right; problem solved.)

All this is to lead up to say what was already in the section title, which is to negotiate and learn to negotiate better.

The best book I know on how to negotiate is one called *Never Split the Difference* (https://simpleprogrammer.com/cg47-split).

Read that book, read my chapter on salary negotiations (https://simpleprogrammer.com /cg47-negotiate), and the next time you are given a job offer or are trying to get a raise, negotiate.

This is one time where it might make sense to try to be one of the guys, although using your advantages may also be an ace up your sleeve here as well.

There are some perceptions that a woman playing "hardball" isn't a woman.

I don't think that is true at all.

I've been on the other end of a woman playing "hardball" plenty of times in my life and I have never thought she wasn't a woman.

So don't be afraid to get in there and "mix it up."

Negotiate.

HEY JOHN

Let's be real here. The perception isn't that she's not a woman. It's that she's a bitch. Men think women who play hardball are bitches.

Look, you said it, I didn't say that at all.

(Well, actually it wasn't you necessarily, but you probably thought it and an actual reviewer of this book—who is a woman—really did say this, so that's close enough.)

Yes, I can see how that perception may be true, but so what?

There are plenty of people who think I'm a misogynistic, racist, bigot, homophobic asshole.

If I let that stop me from doing what I'm doing in life, you certainly wouldn't be reading this book—and definitely not this chapter.

I, personally, respect a woman who can play "hardball" during negotiations. I don't see it as any different than when a man does it—in fact, I gain more respect for a woman doing it because I find that fewer do.

I would say though, that you can't play "hardball" all the time.

If you are walking around with a chip on your shoulder, and proud of the fact that you're a "ball crusher," constantly trying to crush as many balls as possible, it's going to come off as always trying to prove something and perhaps as being a bitch—as my reviewer so eloquently put it.

A strong, confident woman doesn't have to constantly prove herself, but she knows when to play hardball and when to back off and use some feminine energy to get things done.

It's the yin and the yang.

The same goes for a man.

A guy who plays hardball all the time isn't going to be perceived very well at all either.

But, ultimately, it comes down to what I first said.

People are going to think bad things about you no matter what you do; you can't control that.

Don't try to please other people and worry about what they think of you. Do what you feel is right.

Ignore the haters.

ADVICE TO MEN

Alright guys, it's your turn.

I can speak a little more freely here since I'm actually a guy and one who's worked with women in the technology workplace many times.

I know that working with women in the workplace can be difficult.

It can be a bit awkward and intimidating.

You might not know how to act.

The political and social justice warriors may have made you so afraid of being part of the "rape culture" that you are afraid to do or say anything.

You might want to ignore the issue and put "feminist" on your Twitter profile, so people will just leave you alone.

It doesn't work like that.

There is no easy way out.

So, let's get into it.

DON'T PATRONIZE

One of the first solutions that most men devise to deal with women in technology is to try to be overly nice to them.

It's a sensible strategy.

It actually probably comes 50 percent from a good place of actually wanting to be supportive and help women in technology because you think they are valuable and frankly you'd like to see more of them, and 50 percent from fear.

The strategy is wrong though, because it results in creating a feeling and environment of patronization.

(Wow, I can't believe patronization is an actual word.)

Anyway, if you don't know what patronizing is, here's the definition:

pa·tron·ize
verb

1. treat with an apparent kindness that betrays a feeling of superiority.

""She's a good-hearted girl," he said in a patronizing voice."

Synonyms: treat condescendingly, condescend to, look down on, talk down to, put down, treat like a child, treat with disdain

"don't patronize me!"

Yeah... I know. Whoops. Didn't mean to do that.

But, you did, I did, we all did, it's ok.

We just have to learn to stop doing it, because it's not helping.

I'm not saying to not be nice, helpful and supportive.

Even perhaps to show a little extra consideration to women working in technology, who may appreciate a little welcoming kindness in a mostly male-dominated field.

The key is to do it in a way that doesn't say "Hey, you aren't as smart as me or as good of a programmer, so I need to help you."

(As one female reviewer of the book said "Don't treat me like a freakin' kitten. You can quote me on that.")

Don't bend over backwards trying to be overly nice.

Don't become the personal defender of all women in technology and decide you need to aggressively attack anyone who is displaying any chauvinist characteristics.

This kind of behavior does come off as patronizing and it only makes the environment more difficult for women, not better.

I'll give you an example from the classic book, *Ender's Game* (https://simpleprogrammer.com /cg47-enders).

Early on in the book, when the main character, Ender, is leaving his family and joining a group of other soldiers who are going to be heading to a training camp called Battle School, the instructor in charge, Graff, singles out Ender and appears to be showing him some favoritism.

Can you guess how the other boys reacted?

They slapped him in the back of the head as they got out of their seats and passed by him.

This happens quite a bit when there is a blow-up about some women-in-technology incident online.

A bunch of well-meaning guys rush to the defense and it ends up creating more hostility and resentment and now something that was a small issue blows up into something much larger.

I'm not saying don't step in if someone is verbally or physically harassing a woman—I'm right there with you on that one—but, I am saying, **don't try to be the defender that fights people's battles when they don't need help.**

Not only is that patronizing, but it makes the situation worse for them.

HEY JOHN

As a woman, how do I deal with those patronizing guys? The ones who go over the top, think I need extra help and treat me like I'm slow? How do I establish that, when I'm just as good as they are or maybe even have a higher role? And what about the exact opposite? The jerk who is trying to protect his turf and hides information?

Have you ever heard the expression: the cream rises to the top?

Just like it's difficult to hide incompetence, it's also difficult to hide competence.

What most people do when they feel threatened is to react—defensively.

Your natural instinct might be to prove yourself. "Hey, I don't need your help! Don't treat me like a little baby. I can program circles around you."

That actually has the opposite effect.

I was listening to a dating coach for women, Matthew Hussey—don't ask—anyway, he said something that resonated with me.

He said that a first-level woman is helpless and "needs help from a man."

A second-level woman can do it herself and says, "I don't need your help, I can do it myself." Which is better.

But a third-level woman recognizes that sometimes it's fun to have a little help and sometimes it's nice when other people do things for you. She's not threatened by someone trying to help her because she's confident enough to know she can do it herself, but it's much more fun when someone else does it for you.

The point isn't to let guys write your code or do your work for you, it's just that there is much more strength in not getting all bent out of shape and defending yourself.

If a guy wants to patronize you, let him. It's not a big deal. He's the one who's ignorant.

Besides, he's probably trying to be nice or do what he thinks is right.

Show some graciousness and let him act like an idiot, because you are confident enough to know that you don't really need his help.

Eventually, he'll figure it out.

Like I said, cream always rises to the top.

He'll realize that he's been showing a Nascar driver how to use the stick shift and he'll feel stupid.

But, it won't be you making him feel stupid—and that's the difference.

And about the guy trying to protect his turf and hiding information, there's just not much you can do about that.

That problem exists regardless of whether you are a man or a woman—although, some guys may purposely exhibit that behavior specifically because they feel threatened by you.

Again, let them.

Give them enough rope and they'll eventually hang themselves.

Just do the best you can to get the information you need and do your job. Try to ignore the behavior as much as possible.

If it becomes a big enough issue where you can't do your job, then go ahead and go over his head and talk to his boss. Really, that's about all you can do.

Just keep your poise and "Keep Calm and Carry On," as the British would say.

WOMEN ARE NOT GUYS

Even though women want to be treated equally in the workplace, it doesn't mean they want to be treated the same.

Equal and the same are not synonymous.

Equal means to have the same value.

The same means not taking into account a person's differences.

If you have kids, you might love them equally, but you don't treat them "the same."

You don't treat a 5-year-old and a 10-year-old the same.

You don't treat a girl and a boy the same.

Don't treat women in technology the same as you treat guys.

Again, I'm a bit old-school in this regard, but I believe that men, **real men, should treat women like women, regardless of the environment.**

That means not palling around with them and making crude jokes and slapping them on the back like you might do with your guy friends.

It doesn't mean not being friendly.

It doesn't mean not including them in social activities or as equal members of the team.

It just means altering your behavior to show a little respect.

For lack of a better term, to **act like a gentleman.**

Not a chauvinist, not a white knight, but just a gentleman who understands that there are differences between men and women, and that one should pay attention and pay respect to those differences.

DON'T TAKE YOUR RELATIONSHIP FRUSTRATIONS OUT ON WOMEN

Women are not the enemy.

I realize that many of you reading this have been hurt and rejected by women.

Believe me, I get it. I understand.

I realize that you may think that women like jerks and treat nice guys (https://simpleprogrammer.com/cg47-niceguy) poorly and that makes you angry, because you feel like you deserve better.

Again, I get that—I don't agree with it (https://simpleprogrammer.com/cg47-better), and I'm not going to get into why here—but I get it.

Regardless, you shouldn't let those feelings and frustrations spill over into your professional life.

(In fact, you should really not let them spill over anywhere, and you should find a way to deal with them, but again, this isn't the place to cover that.)

It's important to realize that women have just as much right to be programmers or software developers as you do.

And they are here to stay.

Get used to it.

And don't hide behind anonymity either.

Bullying and harassing online behind a pseudonym is just plain cowardice.

At least have the guts to say or do what you are going to do with your real name attached.

This book—and this chapter—might piss off quite a few people, but I'm still using my name.

JUST ACT NORMAL

Honestly, **the best advice I can give overall is to just act normal.**

Really.

Don't bend over backwards being overly nice, walking on eggshells.

Don't be a jerk and harass women.

Just be a cool, normal guy and treat everyone equally with respect.

Again, not the same, but equal.

Women don't want special treatment, they don't need you to defend them, and they don't need you to be a jerk either.

I know it can be difficult to "act normal," but the best thing you can do is to just not make a big deal out of the whole thing.

It's really not even a big deal.

So there are women programmers, big deal.

As long as you have that attitude, you'll be fine.

Sure, you'll make mistakes, but it doesn't matter, because that is all part of being and acting normal.

I SINCERELY HOPE THIS HELPS

Like I said at the beginning of this chapter, I'm not a woman.

I'm a man, giving my advice based on my experience, trying to do what I can to give the most pragmatic guidance that I can.

I'm not perfect.

You may not agree with me.

Heck, you may not even like me, but I'm hoping that you can at least get something from this chapter that will help you.

SECTION 5

ADVANCING YOUR CAREER

"Advancement only comes with habitually doing more than you are asked."
—Gary Ryan Blair

If you just do what you are supposed to do, you may survive as a software developer, you may even have a great career, but don't expect exceptional results.

If you are fine with mediocre, you might want to skip this section—really.

So many people have an illusion, this ridiculous dream that someday they are going to be famous or rich—or both.

They dream that it will magically happen.

Almost as if they have some magical fairy godmother who will someday make all their wishes and dreams come true.

I'm sorry to be the one to break the news to you, but the only things guaranteed in life are death and taxes—everything else you have to work for.

So, yes, there is work involved in advancing your career as a software developer, but the good news is, you don't have to kill yourself to do it.

Consistency and commitment—and knowing what to do—are much more important than just hard work by itself.

In this section, I'll take you through everything I know about advancing your career as a software developer.

We'll talk about the importance of building a reputation or personal brand and how to do it through networking, groups, blogging, speaking, conferences and more.

We'll also talk about how to keep your skills up-to-date so that you don't fall behind and how to decide what to learn.

Should you become a generalist or a specialist?

Should you get certifications?

We'll walk through the different career paths you can embark upon and how to advance along them.

And we'll even cover some auxiliary topics that can help you advance not just in your job, but all around as a software developer, like starting a business of your own, freelancing, creating a side project and even what books you should be reading.

If you are ready to leave mediocre in the dust and see what it really takes to turn your dreams into reality, kiss your fairy godmother goodbye, throw on those overalls, clear your throat and let's get started.

CHAPTER 48

CREATING A REPUTATION

One of the most important things you can possibly do in your software development career, more important than learning the newest programming language or JavaScript framework, is to **build a solid reputation.**

Being a good programmer and having a high degree of technical competency is great, but it will only take you so far.

If you really want to excel, if you really want to take your career to the next level, you'll need to learn how to build a solid reputation—how to market yourself and build a personal brand— that will open up the doors of opportunity that are locked to everyone else.

How do I know this?

I spent most of my software development career relatively unknown — ok, completely unknown.

I worked hard to develop my technical skills.

I spent a good deal of time honing my craft, reading book after book about software development, reading blogs, learning new technologies, and practicing what I had already learned.

I taught and mentored other software developers on my team.

I did everything I could to improve myself in the best way I knew how as a software developer.

Now, I'm not going to tell you I didn't have any success. Of course I did.

I had a decent career.

I struggled from time to time to land jobs, but overall I got some pretty good jobs and opportunities, though nothing major.

I quickly hit "the glass ceiling."

The point where I couldn't really make more money as a software developer and there wasn't much I could do about it, or so I thought.

Then I started my blog, Simple Programmer (https://simpleprogrammer.com/cg48-homepage).

The initial idea was just to blog about topics that I felt certain software developers were making more complex than they really were in order to make themselves seem smarter and more valuable.

That's why I called the blog "Making the Complex Simple."

But as I started writing and **more and more people started reading the blog**, something interesting happened.

When I attended Code Camps and events, some people would know who I was, or they'd at least be familiar with my blog.

I started contacting some popular podcasts with the offer to be interviewed for their show, and more people started to know who I was.

Pretty soon I started getting job offers, and not just from spammy recruiters via email.

And then one day, when I was sitting at my desk, I got a call from a company who just wanted to **hire me on the spot.**

No interview, nothing.

All their developers were readers of my blog and had heard my podcasts or taken some of my Pluralsight courses (https://simpleprogrammer.com/cg48-pluralsight).

I didn't think that was possible.

I had never heard of being offered a job without an interview.

Things only increased from there.

I focused on actively building my brand and marketing myself—in fact, I started teaching other programmers how to do it—and suddenly my head was crashing right through that glass ceiling.

So many opportunities came my way that I had never even imagined.

Fast forward to today, where **literally the decision to start my blog made me millions of dollars**, allowed me to "retire early," and led me to the business that is Simple Programmer.

Now, you don't have to go down the same road I did—not everyone wants to retire early and become an entrepreneur—but wouldn't you like to get your dream job?

Wouldn't you like to get paid more money?

Wouldn't you like, just once, to read an article in a popular software development magazine that you wrote?

Wouldn't that be cool?

Good. In this chapter, I'll show you how.

THE BENEFITS OF BEING "FAMOUS"

Before we get into how to build your reputation as a software developer, let's talk a little bit about the benefits of being well-known.

Consider, for example, the difference between a really good chef and a celebrity chef.

A really good chef can make a decent amount of money.

But a famous chef, who is on TV, **makes a shit-ton of money.**

Why?

Does it really have to do with how good that chef is?

Really, ask yourself if the chef that makes $1 million a year is 10 times better than the chef who makes $100,000 a year.

Do you think that is even possible?

I mean, I'm for gourmet eating and I love food, but food is food.

It can only taste so good.

So if the difference isn't skill, what is the difference?

That's right. Reputation. Fame. Essentially, being well-known.

You could look at a similar phenomenon with musicians, actors, plastic surgeons, lawyers, real estate agents, you name it.

The point is, you get unequal rewards for having a reputation.

You get paid more than what your skills deserve.

This is a good thing—a very good thing—if you can achieve it.

But not only do you get paid more if you have a reputation—if you are "famous."

You get people coming to you, jobs coming to you, opportunities coming to you, instead of having to go out and chase them.

This is really good.

STYLE + SUBSTANCE

I, unfortunately, named one of my flagship courses on building a reputation and a personal brand for software developers, "How to Market Yourself as a Software Developer." (https://simpleprogrammer.com/cg48-marketyourself)

Why do I say this naming is unfortunate?

Because, at the time, **I didn't realize how opposed many software developers are** (https://simpleprogrammer.com/cg48-criticism) **to self-promotion and the idea of any kind of marketing**, especially marketing themselves.

That doesn't mean that the course isn't valuable or it didn't sell well—I've sold hundreds of copies of it and it's taught many software developers how to build that "fame" we've been talking about—but if I had named it a little better, I probably wouldn't have produced as much of the knee-jerk reaction that many programmers have when they hear the word "marketing."

But regardless of how other developers may respond, you've got to get over that.

You have to realize that self-promotion, building a brand, and marketing are not bad things.

It's all in how you do it that counts.

There is this formula I often quote which looks something like this:

Skills * Marketing = $$$

You could rewrite it to:

Substance * Style = $$$

Or:

Programming Ability * Reputation = $$$

A friend of mine, Jason Roberts, coined a similar phrase which defines this phenomenon called "Luck Surface Area." (https://simpleprogrammer.com/cg48-surface)

It's basically the idea that you can be the best programmer in the world, but if you are sitting alone in your basement and no one knows it but you, it doesn't really matter. You aren't going to have much of an impact.

But if you can get out there and promote yourself a bit—we'll talk about how shortly—you can achieve phenomenal results.

In fact, you don't have to be the best programmer in the world. I'm not.

I'm not the "best" at anything, but what I am is "well-known." (At least in the programming world.)

I'd rather have a medium amount of skill and a huge reputation than a huge amount of skill and no reputation.

You can't focus on just being "great."

624 || THE COMPLETE SOFTWARE DEVELOPERS CAREER GUIDE

That's not a very profitable career strategy.

On my wall I've got a framed poster that has two dimensions: talk and work (https://simpleprogrammer.com/cg48-poster).

There are three combinations of the dimensions:

1. High talk, no work = Charlatan
2. No talk, high work = Martyr
3. High talk, high work = Hustler

Be a hustler.

HEY JOHN

But I want to be the best in something. I don't want to have a "medium amount of skill."

Great, awesome, even better.

Everything I'm saying will be magnified even more by being the best at something, or if not the best, at least really, really skilled. (Just like Derek Zoolander is really, really good looking—if you don't get it it's ok.)

My point is, that if you have to choose one, it's more pragmatic and beneficial to have a medium skill with a huge reputation than a high skill with a medium reputation.

The reputation part of the equation carries more weight.

I know that might rub you the wrong way, but that's the way the world works. I didn't invent it. I just observe it and report it here.

CREATING A PERSONAL BRAND

Sold yet?

Good; let's move on.

Before you can promote anything, **you've got to know what you are promoting.**

If you want style + substance, you have to have style.

So, how do you get style?

What is style?

It looks quite a bit like what the cool kids these days are calling **a personal brand.**

A personal brand is just like any commercial brand, except it's a brand that represents you (https://simpleprogrammer.com/cg48-easy).

The first thing you need to do when you create your personal brand is to **define what it is that you want to be known for.**

And you can only pick one thing at a time.

That's what makes it so difficult.

(We'll talk more about how to do this in the chapter on specialization.)

For now, let's just say that you need to come up with the simple elevator pitch that you'll give people—a one-liner, if you will—that represents you and your brand.

If I ask you what you do, what do you say?

Do you ramble on about the 100 technologies and programming languages you know, or do you have a simple way to describe yourself—your brand—that people will remember, so that when they introduce you to someone else they say, "Hey this is Joe, he's the guy who teaches people how to create animations in Android."

When I'm at an entrepreneur-type conference or event and people ask what I do, I say, **"I teach software developers how to be cool."**

That's essentially what my current brand is built around.

It's personal growth for software developers.

That's it.

Simple Programmer represents that.

Branding starts with **a clear, simple, and concise message.**

Who you are and what you represent.

From there, you go forward and actually create a logo, pick a set of colors that you consistently use, get a headshot that you consistently use, etc.

HEY JOHN

Do I really need all this if I just want to be an employee?

No, you don't have to do any of this at all.

But, I'll ask you this… why the heck not?

I mean, don't you think having a logo, a clear consistent message, a good personal brand and a really good headshot will improve your chances of getting a really good job and being much more respected in the industry?

I know this can seem like a lot of stuff to do, but just take it one step at a time.

It's important to cultivate your career and your personal brand and image, because over the long-haul these little details can really add up.

You may have picked up from that last sentence the other two components of a brand.

In case you weren't paying attention, **the first one is your message.**

The second one is visuals.

This is your logo, colors, etc.

And **the third one is consistency.**

Without consistency in message and visuals, it all falls apart.

If you want to have a brand and not just a flavor of the week, you have to be consistent.

So pick something and stick with it.

Even though people tend to focus on visuals when message is way more important, you should start with your message.

HOW TO BECOME "WELL-KNOWN"

Ok, so I lied.

There is one more thing you need for a brand of any kind.

You see, you could have a fantastic brand.

You could have a clear, concise, targeted message.

You could have a kick-ass logo of a frog holding a flaming sword on it.

And you could be consistent everywhere you apply your brand's message and visuals.

But... if you don't have **repeated exposure**, it doesn't matter. It's not a brand.

People have to see and hear about your brand, and they have to see and hear it more than once.

In fact, I'd say it takes about four-to-five exposures to a brand before someone recognizes it and says, "Hey, I know that guy."

So, you've got to get out there and get in front of people.

You've got to get your name out there.

"Well, sheesh John, how do I do that?," you ask?

Since I don't want to repeat myself and I've already produced a large amount of content about this topic, I'm going to just give you a quick rundown here.

If you want, you can fill in the gaps either through my section on marketing yourself in my *Soft Skills: The Software Developer's Life Manual* (https://simpleprogrammer.com /cg48-lifemanual) **book or "How to Market Yourself as a Software Developer"** (https:// simpleprogrammer.com/cg48-marketyourself) **course.**

The basic strategy is to **start with one channel or medium, learn how to master it and systematize it so that you can be extremely prolific** and effective on that channel, and then expand so that you are essentially everywhere.

Let's break that down.

Suppose you said I'm going to start getting my name out there by starting a blog (https:/simple programmer.com/cg48-createblog) and writing blog posts.

That would be the channel you've decided to master.

So, you create your blog (check out my free course on how to do that (https://simpleprogrammer.com /cg48-blog)) and you start writing.

Eventually you develop a system for writing effective blog posts.

Perhaps you develop the system to the point where you can actually just do the writing and have someone else edit the post, schedule it, add images, etc. (hmm… why does this sound so familiar?)

Then **you use that system to become very prolific**, and you start going from one blog post a week to three posts a week.

Now you are starting to really get your name out there.

From there you expand and you decide to move to a few more channels.

You start a YouTube channel, start reaching out to software developer podcasts (https:// simpleprogrammer.com/cg48-podcast) to be interviewed, perhaps write for a software development magazine, and submit to speak at some software development conferences.

Now your brand is getting out there through repeated exposure.

Now, wherever anyone goes in your space, they find you or hear of you or see you.

Do this for long enough and be consistent, and over time you will become "well-known."

Maybe not "I want to take off my underwear and throw them at you" famous (this hasn't happened to me yet), but you'll build up enough of a reputation to increase your luck surface area tremendously.

Here is a list of ideas or channels you can use to get your name out there:

* Your own blog
* Guest posting for other people's blogs
* Writing a book
* Writing magazine articles
* Getting on someone else's podcast
* Creating your own podcast
* Creating a YouTube channel
* Being a really active Twitter or other social media user
* Speaking at local user groups and code camps
* Speaking at large developer conferences
* Creating a popular open source project

CREATE VALUE FOR OTHERS

Here's the thing: just doing all of this stuff and wanting to be famous isn't going to make you famous.

I know I said it would, and I know I lied before when I told you all you needed was a cool logo and a message, but I lied again.

You see, **the perfect brand and all the self-promotion in the world won't amount to anything if it's not all based on this one important thing**, this one important principle or idea: create value for others.

And preferably free value.

90 percent of what I do, I give away for free and 10 percent I charge for.

My focus is giving people as much value as possible so that they'll not only consume my message, but spread it.

I want people to say, "Hey, that Simple Programmer dude, John Sonomez, or whatever his name is, he's a cool dude, you should check out his stuff. I got a job and a girlfriend because of him."

The best possible marketing you can do is to add value to other people's lives.

Be known as a giver.

Be the kind of person who other people want to be around and associate with because they feel like when they are around you they are benefiting.

So many companies and brands fail because they try to milk their customers for whatever they can.

They try to *extract* value instead of *inject* value.

I promise you that if you are injecting value and making a real difference in people's lives, and doing it on a consistent basis, you will reap the rewards of doing so.

One of my favorite quotes of all time says:

> *"You can get everything in life you want if you will just*
> *help enough other people get what they want."*
> –Zig Ziglar, *Secrets of Closing the Sale* (1984)
> (https://simpleprogrammer.com/cg48-closing)

So, whatever you are doing, first think about how it will create value for others.

IT TAKES TIME

Finally, you have to realize **this is not something you are going to achieve overnight.**

In fact, it's going to take you a very long time to really see any noticeable results of your actions to create reputation.

That's one of the reasons why **you had better start now.**

Oftentimes, new software developers or people just getting into software development tell me that they aren't ready to start a blog or start building a reputation, because they don't know enough yet.

You'll never "know enough."

You have to get started before you are ready because there is a large lead time before you see any results.

Even if you are new to programming, you have something to offer.

You can share your journey as you learn to program and other people will find that useful.

You can pick a specialization to go deep on and share the journey as you take yourself from novice to expert on a subject.

That journey has immense value for others who are looking to do the same.

So, start early—before you are ready—and be patient.

It's going to take time, but you are going to get results if you keep at it.

The problem is many software developers start a blog and write blog posts for about a year, see no results, and give up.

You've got to be willing to stick it out longer than that if you want to have success.

It might take you two or three years, or even five years, but **if you keep pushing forward, you'll eventually get there.**

Most people never achieve anything great in life because they give up too soon.

Don't be one of them.

CHAPTER 49

NETWORKING AND GROUPS

I have to be completely honest with you.

I really HATE the word networking.

I detest it.

The reason why is simple: **most people do it in completely the wrong way.**

When most programmers ask me about networking, what they are really asking about is **how they can use people to get what they want.**

I'm not about that at all—in fact, my personal philosophy—and the one I firmly believe you have to have for true success—is to figure out how you can give as many people as possible what they want... or even better, what they need.

Still, networking can be extremely valuable and essential to advancing your career (https://simpleprogrammer.com/cg49-reach) *if* you do it correctly.

That's what we are going to talk about in this chapter: networking. Doing it both the wrong way and the right way. And one of the best ways to network as a software developer, is by joining software development groups.

THE WRONG WAY TO NETWORK

I've already alluded to this, but let's start our talk about networking by talking about the wrong way to network.

You see, **most software developers only start worrying about networking or trying to network at all when they need something**—usually a new job.

But that is the absolute worst time and wrong way to build a network.

Building a network takes time.

Trying to rush the process and do it quickly results in you reeking of desperation and coming off as a sleazy moocher, trying to be nice to people so that you can extract something from them.

You have to invest in your network before you can take any value from your network.

That is why networking takes time and can't be rushed.

If you are looking for a new job because you just lost your old one, and you think, "Wow, this is a great time to network. I'd better network so I can get a new job," you are doing it wrong.

Everyone you meet and try to network with will immediately smell a rat.

They'll rightly guess that you aren't really interested in them and meeting or helping them, but that you are trying to get something from them.

This will have the opposite effect of what you are trying to accomplish.

It's not just the time component, though, that leads many software developers down the wrong path of networking; it's also the approach.

The point of networking is not to throw as many business cards as you can into as many people's faces as possible.

That scattershot approach will build extremely shallow relationships which won't amount to much.

Networking is also not a time where you tell as many people as you can your entire life story and how great you are.

But if these are all the wrong ways to network, what are the right ways, you might ask?

THE RIGHT WAY TO NETWORK

Networking is about something that should be a recurring theme in this section of the book–that's right, **creating value for others.**

The right approach to building a network is building relationships (https://simpleprogrammer.com /cg49-healthy).

And just like romantic relationships, real business and professional relationships can't be rushed. That's why networking takes time and you can't just do it quickly when you need a job.

Imagine if you met a person you'd like to pursue a romantic relationship with and on the first date, you asked them to marry you.

That probably wouldn't go over too well, yet many software developers want to approach networking in exactly that manner.

Instead, think about the long game.

Think about networking as planting a large number of little seeds that you are going to water and nurture until they grow into large plants that eventually produce fruit.

You can't rush that process, and you have to be deliberate.

The best way to plant and nurture these seeds is to give first.

You have to invest in your network and the people in your network.

When you meet someone at a conference or a group, don't think about what they can do for you—even if you really, really need a job right now.

Instead, **focus the entire conversation on what you can do for them.**

Try to be as helpful as possible.

Listen carefully and use **active listening skills** to figure out if there is some way you can help this person directly, or if there is someone else you know that you could introduce them to which would benefit them.

You give, give, give value and that's how you build a network.

You **become the kind of person who people want to be around** and want to know because of the value you create for them.

You can create this value in many ways.

It could just be your super positive attitude.

It could be the connections you have, which helps them grow their network.

It could be your skills, or even just your ability to listen and really hear them.

In order to truly give value, you are going to need to go deep.

Don't be one of those guys handing everyone you see a business card and chatting with them for three seconds.

Instead, **take the time to really talk to the people you come in contact with**, whether it be at a party, conference, meetup, or some other event.

Sure, you'll meet fewer people in total, but you'll actually be planting the seeds of relationships and growing a well-rooted network, not a phony, I've-met-all-these-people-but-I've-only-talk-ed-to-them-for-two-seconds one.

Oh, and if you are having trouble knowing what to say when you meet people, or how to talk to them, there's a simple tactic: ask them questions about themselves.

There is one subject everyone loves to talk about: themselves.

Too many people make the mistake of trying to network by trying to get random people to listen to stories about who they are and what they do, instead of talking about what those other people care about, which is...

Say it with me...

THEMSELVES.

So, just ask questions that let the other person talk about... themselves... and you'll be good to go.

There is an excellent example of this in Dale Carnegie's classic book, *How to Win Friends and Influence People* (https://simpleprogrammer.com/cg49-influence), where he does just that and is lauded as an excellent conversationalist.

Oh, and read that book if you haven't already.

In fact, read it more than once.

WHERE TO NETWORK

Ok, so you are a master networker.

You are a combination of the Pied Piper and a snake charmer all rolled into one.

You can "work a room" like no one's business.

The only problem is, you don't have a room.

Where do you actually go to network?

The short answer is: everywhere.

You should always be networking.

Always start conversations with people and build relationships.

Say "hi" to everyone you meet, whether you are in an elevator or sitting at the bar on a business trip, or just standing in line at Starbucks.

You never know who you'll meet and what they might have to offer to your growing network.

But let's get specific, because if you are trying to grow a specific kind of network, you need to meet specific kinds of people.

The easiest and best thing to do in this case is to **find groups of people who are interested in what you are interested in.**

I'd highly suggest using the site Meetup.com (https://simpleprogrammer.com/cg49-meetup) to find local groups on just about any kind of topic you can think of.

Use Meetup to find software development groups in your area, and then attend those groups and you'll have plenty of networking opportunities.

Just make sure you don't show up at one meeting and expect to build your network because now you are looking for a job.

Attend whatever groups you are interested in regularly, and you will definitely grow a network.

Be willing to put in the time.

Another great place to network are conferences and code camps.

Code camps are almost always free and are usually local, yearly events that attract a large crowd of software developers, college students and recruiters.

Software development conferences, although sometimes expensive, are also great places to meet new people and pick up some training as well—although I only go for the networking opportunities (https://simpleprogrammer.com/cg49-conference).

When you are at a conference or code camp, walk around and talk to people, attend different sessions, and talk to the speakers.

I almost always go up to the speaker of any session I attend afterwards or later when I see them and thank them for their presentation and give them a few good compliments about it.

Being a frequent speaker myself, I know how nice it can be to have someone tell you that you did a good job, so I try to think about how I could talk to a speaker in a way that would make me feel good if I were in their position.

Speakers at these kinds of events are often great people to have in your network. Many people are intimidated to talk to them, so this is an excellent opportunity if you are willing to take advantage of it.

Also **consider what is known as the "hallway track"** as another great way to network at these kinds of events.

I often skip sessions altogether and just hang out in the hallways at conferences and talk to the other people hanging out in the hallways.

Sometimes all I do is go to a conference to do just that.

You should also **try to attend as many social events as possible**, especially at conferences or code camps.

Go to the after party or the dinners.

These are great chances to meet people when there is less of a crowd and you're in a more social atmosphere.

I'd also recommend **not drinking**—even if everyone else is.

Trust me on this one.

HEY JOHN

But, I like drinking, besides, it breaks the ice.

Yes, I know drinking can be fun.

And, yes, I know it can make it easier to talk to people, but it's a bad idea and here's why:

It's a crutch.

I'll tell you the same thing I tell to the guys I coach on dating and meeting women.

Drinking is a crutch. If you can't talk to people without having a few drinks, you'll never really develop the skills, confidence and charisma to be both a genuinely good conversationalist and to get over your shyness and social anxiety.

I'm not a teetotaler from a moral or ethical standpoint, but from a practical, pragmatic one.

If you rely on crutches, you'll never develop real skill.

Plus, everyone thinks they are the bee's knees when they're drinking—believe me I do—but, usually everyone else thinks you are an idiot.

It's true. Ask around.

Also, **consider hackathons** and other events which might be hosted in your area.

Hackathons are marathon-like coding events where teams come together to "hack out" a complete prototype product in 24 to 48 hours, or sometimes longer.

Because of the close working conditions and reliance on teamwork, these are really good opportunities to meet other programmers, designers and entrepreneurs, plus they are a lot of fun!

HOSTING AND CREATING GROUPS

Do you really want to take your networking mojo to the next level?

Want to get your black belt in networking?

Consider being the host of a group or starting your own event.

By far, the best networker I know is a buddy of mine, Dan Martell (https://simpleprogrammer.com /cg49-martell).

He's a serial startup founder most famous for creating Clarity.fm, which billionaire entrepreneur Mark Cuban, invested in.

Dan knows everyone.

When I meet new people, I almost always eventually ask them if they know Dan Martell and the answer is almost always "yes."

It's crazy.

So how does he do it?

Well, one of the tactics I've seen him execute the most is something he calls "founders' dinners."

Every time he travels to a city, **he puts together a dinner event and invites all the most prestigious people in the area** whom he would like to meet.

At first this might seem silly, why would they go to his dinner?

But all those people are usually also interested in networking, and so if someone is hosting a dinner with all the most prestigious people in an area, all of those people are going to be interested in attending to meet the other prestigious people.

Think about it.

And if the host can show pictures from past events and talk about the kind of people who attended them, they've got a pretty compelling offer.

The beauty of Dan's founders' dinners is that since he's the one hosting the event, **he gets to meet everyone and they are all appreciative to him for putting on the event.**

He's created value for them.

Now, you don't have to do exactly what Dan does, but there is no reason why you can't organize your own event or group in your area.

Just model what you are doing after other successful groups or events.

Sure, maybe no one will come, or it might take time to build a group of any size, but if you really want to up your networking game, I can't think of a better way, so you might as well give it a shot.

And if you aren't quite ready to host your own event or start your own group, **consider volunteering for an event or group that someone else has created.**

I know that organizers are always looking for volunteers, especially at large, free events like code camps.

Go ahead and volunteer, and you'll get exclusive access to the organizers of the events or groups and probably many of the high profile attendees.

You'll also learn the ropes if you want to create your own group or event in the future.

NETWORKING ISN'T DIFFICULT

It just takes time and patience, and you have to shift the focus from you to the people you are networking with.

It takes time to build up a large network.

It doesn't happen overnight.

You shouldn't just start when you need a job.

Having a large and valuable network is a fantastic asset for advancing your career—and your life in general.

I've heard it said that your network is your net worth, and I've found that statement to be more true than most people would imagine.

CHAPTER 50

KEEPING YOUR SKILLS UP TO DATE

It's a wild world of ever-changing technology.

What was new and hot yesterday is old and crufty today.

Dinosaurs actively roam the halls of software development organizations, and you don't want to be one of them (https://simpleprogrammer.com/cg50-lose).

The key to not going the way of the Dodo Bird is to **keep your skills up to date.**

You don't have to learn every new-fangled technology and programming language that comes along—in fact, that would be impossible—but you do have to keep your skills sharp.

So, how do you do it?

NO PLAN IS A PLAN, JUST A SHITTY ONE

It all begins with a plan (https://simpleprogrammer.com/cg50-planning).

If you don't have a plan for how you are going to keep your programming skills up to date and you don't have a plan to advance your career, **it's just not going to happen.**

As someone who does a considerable amount of personal training and coaching, I can't tell you how many times someone has told me that they are going to lose weight and get in shape.

When I ask them "how?" They say, "Oh, I'll cut back on the calories and exercise more."

NO. WRONG.

That is not a plan, or if it is, it's a shitty one.

You need a real plan that you can follow and track so you know if you are off course or not.

A good plan is specific.

If you ask me how I am going to lose weight or get in shape, I'm going to say something like this:

"First of all, I'm not going to lose weight. I am going to work on losing fat while maintaining lean body mass. I will do this by cutting my calories to a 500-calorie deficit per day, eating a mostly ketogenic diet, running four-times a week to increase fat oxidation, and lifting three-times a week to keep as much lean muscle mass as possible."

Then I'll drone on for another hour explaining the intricate details of my plan (https://simpleprogrammer.com/cg50-fitness).

That's a plan.

See the difference?

You need to develop your own plan for how you are going to advance your career and keep your skills up to date.

To start, make sure to grab your copy of the Software Developer's Skills Assessment in the digital toolkit that's included with this book (https://simpleprogrammer.com/career-guide-toolkit). Use this self-diagnostic to figure out which skills you most need to shore up.

The rest of this chapter will give you some ideas of what you can incorporate into your plan, but ultimately it's up to you.

READING BLOGS

I've found that one of the best ways to stay up-to-date in the programming world is to read programming blogs every morning for about 30 minutes or so.

Throughout my career, I've had a changing list of software development blogs which I've read for the first 30 minutes of my day.

To some degree, this allows other people to do much of the work for you.

By reading other software developer's blogs, **you gain insights into what is new and what is important in the programming community**, and you might even learn a thing or two as well.

Usually if something is important, you'll find someone blogging about it.

Blogs also provide you the opportunity to read about some of the difficult problems in your particular area of the software development world and what the solutions are to those problems without having to struggle through them yourself.

READING BOOKS

You should always be working your way through at least one technical book.

I used to read a technical book for 30 minutes each day while I walked on the treadmill (https://simpleprogrammer.com/cg50-treadmill).

At that pace, I'd get through one to two technical books each month.

Reading that many books each year ensured that my skills were constantly up to date and that I was improving as a technical professional.

Now, just reading books cover-to-cover isn't the best way to learn, but getting in the habit of reading and working your way through new technical books all the time is a great way to broaden the base of your programming knowledge and stay current on technology.

For this kind of reading, **try to pick books that you will benefit the most from or that will have a lasting value.**

Picking books which are directly relevant to what you are currently working on is a great choice, because you'll have immediate, applicable value.

Picking books about software development methodologies or design patterns (https://simpleprogrammer.com/cg50-books) **and architecture are also good, timeless choices.**

This book, along with my *Soft Skills: The Software Developer's Life Manual* (https://simpleprogrammer.com/cg50-lifemanual), were specifically designed to be as timeless as possible, because I wanted to write the kind of books that had long-lasting value—the kind of books that I would like to read.

That doesn't mean you should never read books on new technologies, but make sure if you do, you also spend time actually learning by doing, not just reading.

HEY JOHN

What's the best place to get started? Should I read the technical books specific to my job first, or the timeless books on writing quality code first?

Ah, the old chicken-or-the-egg problem.

You should definitely read a mix of both, but realize that you'll get the most long-term benefit from timeless books on code quality and self-development, because those books will be based on principles that will likely be universal and last a very long time.

Here's how I would play this game if I were you.

If you are working with a specific technology and you are spending a large amount of your time using it during the day, you should probably prioritize learning about that specific technology, because it could save you hours a day or make you much more efficient.

In that case, investing immediately in technical skills is going to have a very high return for you.

Even if you end up switching jobs later and essentially have "wasted the time" learning a skill, or getting better at a skill you no longer use, you will have probably gained enough benefit from the time you put in initially to make it worth it.

On the other hand, if you are fairly proficient at what you are doing and you are just looking for a new technical skill to pick up, you might be better offer prioritizing timeless books on writing quality code and personal development books which will benefit you more in the long run.

PICKING A NEW THING TO LEARN

Always be learning something new.

I don't care how skilled you are or how much education you have, there is always something new to learn.

Have a plan for what you are going to learn next, so that when you finish learning one thing you can move on to the next thing.

Evaluate your current skills and where you want to go, then decide what new things you should learn and what priority and order you are going to learn them in.

I always have a list of the books I want to read and I keep it up to date (https://simpleprogrammer.com/cg50-read) so that I always know what book I should read next.

This list helps me make sure that I don't waste my time and that I **only read high-quality books.**

Do the same with the skills in your programming career.

Decide what technologies, programming languages or frameworks would benefit you most and put them on a list of things to learn.

Then make sure you are always working your way down that list.

You'll be amazed how many new skills you can pick up in just a year's time if you are constantly devoting a dedicated amount of time each week to learning something new.

You may even want to schedule this time each week explicitly on your calendar.

One word of caution, though: **don't learn things you aren't ever going to use.**

HEY JOHN

In my current job I need to know X. But I'm really more interested in Y. Should I be reading the books that will help me in my current job or will help me learn the skills I am actually interested in?

So, there is some value in learning things that you want to move into or that you are interested in, but aren't using yet.

But, there is also some risk.

If you spend a large amount of time learning something you are never going to use—especially if it's highly technical—you run the risk of making a very bad investment of your time (and effort.)

Of course some people will argue that learning a new programming language that you aren't actually going to use will make you better at a programming language you are using because it will cause you to think about things in a different way.

And there is the argument as well that sometimes learning things for fun is… well… fun.

I can't disagree with either of those things, but I would say to at least try to have some secondary benefit from what you are learning, both so you can learn it better by applying it and so that it reduces the risk of being a total waste of time.

Creating a side project or even a personal project is a good way to do this. (More on this in the "Side Projects" chapter.)

I'll conclude with one final point to consider on this matter.

As human beings, we are really bad at predicting the future.

> It's usually a bad bet in software development to prematurely optimize and it's also usually a bad bet in life.
>
> I only say this because I've been bitten by this particular animal more than once.
>
> Several times in my career I've invested a significant amount of time learning something I thought I would use, only to find that I never used it at all and pretty much all that time was a waste.

Be strategic in what you decide to learn.

I know many developers who binge-watch Pluralsight courses (https://simpleprogrammer.com /cg50-pluralsight), read through technical books and learn programming languages without any real purpose in mind.

This kind of extra knowledge is not bad, but because it is unfocused and doesn't move them towards their goals, much of it is wasted effort.

If I spent months learning a new programming language that I'll never use, it doesn't really help me much in advancing my career or reaching my goals.

Sure, I might learn a little and it might broaden my perspective, but that same time would have probably been better spent learning something that I will actually use.

LEARNING QUICKLY

If you want to stay sharp, you have to keep on learning.

Like I said earlier, technology is moving at an extremely rapid clip in today's environment and I don't think it's going to slow down anytime soon.

If you are going to spend so much time learning, **don't you think it's worth investing some time in learning how to learn better?**

How to learn quickly?

I used to approach learning in a haphazard manner, until I made the goal to create 30 Pluralsight courses (https://simpleprogrammer.com/cg50-pluralsight) in a single year.

In order to produce that much content and to learn many technologies, programming languages, and frameworks in that short period of time, **I needed to develop a system for learning quickly.**

So, I took everything I knew about learning and what was working best and I actually made it into a system.

I call it "10 Steps to Learn Anything Quickly," (https://simpleprogrammer.com/cg50-10steps) and if you read my *Soft Skills: The Software Developer's Life Manual* (https://simpleprogrammer. com/cg50-lifemanual) book, you've probably already been introduced to it.

You don't have to use my system, but you do need to have some system for learning quickly.

You can even take parts of my system and combine it with your own, but you need some strategy for learning quickly if you want to stay ahead.

I'd encourage you to take the time to really invest in learning how to learn since it is a skill that will be valuable to you for the rest of your life.

ATTENDING EVENTS

Another great way to stay up to date and pick up the highlight reels of what is new and note-worthy in the ever-changing field of software development is to **attend events.**

These events can be conferences or code camps, but they can also be less formal meetups, or even events that companies like Microsoft put on to showcase their new technologies.

You can spend a day at an event, watch a few presentations, and gain a really good under-standing of how a new technology or tool works or how it can be applied, without having to read a whole book or slog your way through tutorials.

There is something about seeing someone demonstrate a technology live and watching them show you code examples that tends to make things "click" much faster than some other mediums.

When I was a big .NET developer, I'd often attend the Microsoft events for developers in my area, which would have five or six presentations on new technologies or tools for developers.

I found that I could get a really good gist for what was new and important and the basics of those technologies in just a day, because it was a highly-curated amount of information.

READING THE NEWS

Normally I'm against reading the news.

I honestly think that, for the most part, **it's a huge waste of time.**

Most of the news out there doesn't really affect your daily life in any significant way.

I try to avoid information that I can't act on or that doesn't matter in my life.

The exception to this is, of course, technology news, especially when it's related to programming.

It's not a bad idea to scan sites like Hacker News (https://simpleprogrammer.com/cg50-hacker) or Proggit (https://simpleprogrammer.com/cg50-proggit), or to subscribe to technology or programming related news feeds.

I like to utilize these sites to get a pulse on what is happening in the programming world.

Usually I can see trends, like an increase in people writing about a specific programming language or technology, which can help me to plan for the future and see where I might need to shift my own career course.

You can definitely waste a large amount of time reading the news—even technology news—so, **make sure you timebox this kind of activity.** Specific news feeds on what you are interested in can be a great way to stay up to date on what is going on in the field.

CODE—A LOT

Finally, I'll state what should be the most obvious way to keep your programming skills up to date: program.

And do it a lot.

I'll talk about this more in the Side Projects chapter, but **you should always have some kind of side project you are working on.**

The more you code, the less likely your coding skills will become rusty.

Seems like common sense, but you'd be amazed by how many software developers end up getting into situations where they feel their skills are out of date, and when asked how often they code, they say "not much."

So, make sure you are dedicating some time each week, or preferably each day, to actually writing code.

John Resig wrote an excellent article on the subject called "Write Code Every Day." (https://simpleprogrammer.com/cg50-everyday)

One great way to do this is to be always working on small projects.

You can combine a few of the ideas in this chapter together by picking out something new to learn and working on a small project with that technology or programming language.

Just make sure that the projects are small enough that you actually complete them.

One of the best decisions I made in my life was to start finishing every single project I undertook.

I became a finisher (https://simpleprogrammer.com/cg50-finisher) and it made a huge difference in my career and life in general.

DON'T GET TOO COMFORTABLE

Remember, no matter how secure you might feel in your current job or environment, it's important to not get too comfortable.

I know programmers who worked for the same company for over 20 years, so they decided not to invest in keeping their skills up to date.

They just kind of relaxed and thought that they'd be ok, since they had job security and there was no need to learn anything new.

And then, when unexpected layoffs happened and they were suddenly thrust into a workforce where they were 20 years behind in skills and knowledge, they quickly realized the error of their ways.

Don't let that happen to you.

Make an active plan to keep your skills up to date.

CHAPTER 51

GENERALIST VS. SPECIALIST

I don't even need an outline to write this chapter.

Of all the topics I talk about, this is perhaps one of the most exhausted; continually asked about, questioned, and evaluated.

I've talked about this topic so much that I dedicated an entire YouTube playlist to all the videos I've done on the topic (https://simpleprogrammer.com/cg51-niching), and that list is continually growing.

What am I talking about?

The age-old debate of whether or not you should become a specialist or a generalist.

Should you become a "jack-of-all-trades" and a "full-stack developer," or should you specialize in one or two areas of software development and "go deep?"

Well, it turns out this is sort of a false dichotomy.

The real answer is both.

Let's find out why.

THE POWER OF SPECIALIZATION

Before we get into the debate, I want to start off by showing you **just how important and beneficial specialization is.**

Let's suppose that you were on trial for a murder.

Yes, a murder.

You didn't do it—I know you didn't—but you still need to prove your innocence.

What do you do?

Do you hire a lawyer who is good at tax law, divorce law, real estate law and criminal law?

Or, do you hire a lawyer who specializes in criminal law, specifically defending people who are convicted of murder?

I don't know about you, but if the rest of my life is on the line, I'm going to choose the specialist every time.

Many people say they want or value a generalist, and they think they do, but when it comes down to it, they pick a specialist every time.

I'll give you another example.

I wanted to get some crown molding done throughout my house, because I am pimp like that.

Anyway, I was looking for carpenters or contractors to do the crown molding when I came across this one company who specialized in crown molding. In fact, the name of their company was Kings of Crown.

All they did was install crown molding.

That is all they did.

Who do you think I chose?

Did I want to take a chance on a carpenter or contractor who did some crown molding, or did I want to call the crown molding "experts" and get the sure thing?

That's not to say there isn't any value in having a broad base of knowledge, or being a generalist to some degree (there are times when I'm looking for a general handyman), but it is extremely valuable to be a specialist of some kind—or at least to market yourself that way.

Think about it this way.

Do you think that fictional murder trial lawyer knows about other areas of law other than murder trials?

Of course he does.

He might actually be pretty good in multiple areas of law and have knowledge in several fields.

But **he advertises himself as a murder lawyer, because he understands the power of specialization.**

The same for those crown molding guys.

Don't you think they could probably handle other carpentry jobs?

Of course they could, but they choose to specialize because it's much more profitable to do so.

(By the way, even businesses themselves greatly benefit from specialization (https://simpleprogrammer.com/cg51-built).)

IN ORDER TO SPECIALIZE, YOU HAVE TO HAVE A BROAD BASE

One thing that many software developers don't understand is that **just about all specialists are also generalists, but no generalists are specialists.**

What do I mean by this?

I mean that, usually, in order to acquire the skills of a specialist, a great deal of general knowledge is required and accumulated along the way.

It's very difficult to be a good specialist without also building a broad base of general knowledge about your field.

My brother-in-law is studying to become an oral surgeon.

In order for him to do that, he had to first go through dental school and become a dentist.

Now, he's not going to be doing general dentistry very often, but to him, filling a cavity or doing some general dentistry work is cake.

He's probably better than most generalist dentists, simply because he had to learn all that and more in order to become an oral surgeon.

That doesn't mean that every specialist is a good generalist, or that they keep their skills up to date, but in general (ha ha) you'll find most specialists generally do. (How do you like that sentence?)

This is all to say that specializing does not preclude you from being a generalist also, it just gives you more options and makes you more valuable.

IT'S ALL ABOUT THE T-SHAPED KNOWLEDGE

What you really want to strive for is what is known as T-shaped knowledge.

It means that you have a broad base of knowledge in your field, and then you **have at least one area of deep, specialized knowledge or skill.**

As a software developer, you should strive to be well-versed in best practices, algorithms, data structures, different architectures, front-end, back-end, databases, etc.

(Basically, everything we covered in the section of this book titled "What You Need to Know About Software Development.")

But, **you should also pick at least one area where you are going to go deep.**

You need to pick some specialization that will set you apart from the masses and greatly increase your value.

When you build up your personal brand and market yourself (https://simpleprogrammer.com /cg51-marketyourself), you are going to use this specialization to do it.

If you want to make waves, you need a small enough pond.

In the HUGE pond of software development, being a generalist will make it more difficult to even make ripples, at least at first.

So, yes, work on being a well-rounded software developer.

Develop a broad base of knowledge and grow that base, little by little, year after year.

But also pick some specialization that you will dive into and become a master at.

Eventually, you can even have a "comb-shaped knowledge," where you have multiple deep specialties, like Elon Musk (https://simpleprogrammer.com/cg51-elon).

But start with one.

BUT EVERYONE SAYS THEY ARE LOOKING FOR GENERALISTS

I know, I know, every job description says that they are looking for good software developers who can wear many hats or work with the "full stack" or can be a jack-of-all-trades.

They want you to possess every skill under the sun.

It's all a lie, I tell you.

A big fat lie.

I guarantee you, if you have the exact skills that are required for a job, if you are an expert in the framework or technology that company is using, they are going to be much more likely to hire you than a generalist.

What companies are really saying when they say they want someone who is a generalist, is that **they want someone who is adaptable and can learn quickly.**

The fear is that they'll hire someone who can only do one thing, so they try to safeguard against that by making the job description state that experience with their framework or technology stack is not necessary, even though that's not completely true.

Don't get me wrong, it's not an intentional lie.

I do believe hiring managers honestly *think* they want generalists, but like I said, **what they really want is someone who is versatile and flexible.**

You can still be that and be a specialist.

And like I said before, your best bet is to sort of be both.

Get that T-shaped knowledge so that you do have a broad base, but go deep in one area so that you can be the expert in the exact technology or skillset that matches the job you apply for.

YOU CAN'T EVEN BE A GENERALIST TODAY

It's not really possible.

The field of software development and technology is so large, and changing so rapidly, that you can't know it all.

Yes, you can have a broad base of knowledge.

Yes, you can understand fundamental principles.

But, no, **you just can't understand enough about everything that exists out there to really call yourself a generalist anymore.**

Even if you are a "full stack" developer, you are going to have to pick a stack or two. You can't know them all and be effective by any real measure.

It's not just computer science and programming where this phenomenon is occurring either.

Every major profession is moving towards more and more value on specialization.

Consider how large medicine is today.

Generalist doctors have trouble diagnosing underlying illnesses and problems because there are just too many possibilities.

Accountants, lawyers, financial analysts and just about every kind of engineer have to specialize to be effective, because knowledge domains are growing to such large extents.

BUT WHAT IF I SPECIALIZE IN THE WRONG THING?

Then specialize in something else.

It's not that big of a deal.

One of my good friends, John Papa (https://simpleprogrammer.com/cg51-johnpapa), specialized in a Microsoft technology called Silverlight.

And then Silverlight was axed by Microsoft and it's now as dead as a doorknob.

But did John throw his hands up in the air, give up and decide to live in his car?

No. Because he was already a specialist, he had built up a reputation and a following.

He just shifted and pivoted to another specialty that was closely related.

Now John is a specialist at developer SPA (Single Page Applications), and he's doing even better than he was before.

Far too many software developers I talk to are so afraid of picking the wrong thing to specialize in (https://simpleprogrammer.com/cg51-unsure) that they don't specialize in anything.

They remain stagnant in their careers for years, paralyzed by fear, always considering the "what ifs."

Don't do that; **just pick something and go with it.**

It's a much better choice than doing nothing, and you can always change course and switch directions later on if you need to.

Plus, you'll find that once you learn how to go deep into one specialization, the next one is much easier.

Many skills that don't seem transferable, are, and developing the ability to "go deep" is valuable in itself.

SO, WHAT SHOULD YOU DO?

Regardless of where you are in your career, **pick some kind of specialization to pursue.**

Don't worry if it's not the "right" or final one.

Start with one, **build your personal brand around it,** and decide to go deep.

HEY JOHN

Should I choose a specialty based on my interests or on what I'm doing for my current employer?

This is a tough one.

Some things to consider:

If you specialize in something other than what you are currently working on in your day-to-day job, it's going to be very difficult to get the time to build the expertise you need and to find the depth required to really specialize.

It's certainly possible. I know some people who are doing it. I've done it myself in the past, but just realize it's going to be a somewhat difficult path.

However, it is a good way to switch into something new, possibly something you really want to do.

If you can find something to specialize in that you currently are working on at your day-to-day job or that you can incorporate into it, you are going to get a double benefit from that specialization.

If you don't have any strong feelings either way, I'd go this route.

Finally, you might be best off switching jobs into what you want to specialize in so that you can work on it all day.

Perhaps start off learning your desired specialization and building a reputation around it in the mornings before work and/or in the evenings, and when you have enough traction, jump to a new job that will use that specialty.

Err on the side of picking something too small and specific rather than too broad.

Don't be a C# developer: be a C# developer specializing in a specific C# framework, or technology or even technology stack.

Try to go as small and detailed as you can. You can always branch out and expand later.

My friend Adrian Rosebrock is a very successful software developer and entrepreneur who specializes in a specific Python library for computer vision (https://simpleprogrammer.com/cg51-adrian).

You wouldn't believe how successful he has been with this particular niche, even though it's extremely small and focused.

At the same time, **work on building up your general knowledge of software development—** your broad base.

Learn how to write good code.

Learn about the underlying principles and technologies that may manifest themselves in many ways, but really are never changing at the core.

You either want to learn things that are deeply focused and directly in your specialty, or broad enough to be widely applicable and somewhat timeless.

Don't try and learn a bunch of different programming languages and frameworks that you will likely never use.

Following this approach, you'll set yourself apart and set yourself up for success.

CHAPTER 52

SPEAKING AND CONFERENCES

Software development conferences provide many opportunities to advance your career as a software developer.

Attending conferences can be a great networking opportunity (https://simpleprogrammer.com /cg52-conference), as we discussed in the chapter on networking, but they are also **great places to learn from some of the most advanced programmers in the field.**

But if you really want to gain the maximum benefit from software development conferences, you'll have to become a speaker.

As a speaker, you'll be building your personal brand, networking with other speakers and conference hosts, and perhaps even drumming up some side business or consulting gigs.

I know all this may seem overwhelming.

But don't worry.

The purpose of this chapter is to **give you some guidance on how to navigate the world of software development conferences and—if you choose—to get started speaking** at smaller events and eventually, conferences.

ATTENDING CONFERENCES

As I mentioned before, just attending conferences—even without speaking at them—can be extremely beneficial.

I personally think all software developers looking to advance their career should attend **at least one software development conference each year.**

Spending a few days just focused on learning and networking is extremely valuable.

One of the great things about conferences is that they take you out of your normal environment and force you to focus for a few days.

Every time I go to a conference, whether I'm speaking or not, I walk away from the experience with a huge number of new connections and new ideas, and I'm usually pretty fired up.

BUT CONFERENCES ARE EXPENSIVE

It's true, many are.

But there are also plenty of reasonably priced ones as well.

Search around and look for events that might be happening in your area.

Oftentimes, you can use sites like Lanyrd.com (https://simpleprogrammer.com/cg52-lanyrd) or Eventbrite (https://simpleprogrammer.com/cg52-eventbrite) to find conferences you might be interested in attending.

Also, depending on where you work, **you may be able to get your boss to pay for your trip to a conference.**

It's usually not that tough of a sell to convince your boss to let you go to one conference a year, especially if you emphasize the training aspect of it.

Try to appeal to how much you'll learn and the information you'll bring back with you from the conference.

One good tactic is to **offer to put together a training for all the other developers on your team based on what you learned from the conference.**

This makes it so your boss can look at the cost of sending you to a conference and divide it by the number of software developers on your team to come up with a much smaller overall training cost.

Finally, **consider speaking.**

We'll talk about this more later on in this chapter.

But usually **when you speak at a conference, you get in free and even have your travel paid for** (https://simpleprogrammer.com/cg52-oredev).

So, if you really want to attend conferences and can't afford it, speaking is great option.

WHAT TO DO AT A CONFERENCE

Ok, so you are going to a conference, but what do you do when you get there?

How do you make the most of it?

It actually starts before you even get to the conference.

The first thing you should do is look at the conference schedule and plan your agenda.

What sessions do you want to attend?

Which speakers are you interested in hearing?

Take some time to plan out what your agenda is ahead of time so that you know what to do when you get there.

You may also want to consider showing up a day or so early and either attending a pre-conference event or even hosting one yourself.

Usually there are unofficial dinners and events before or after conferences, which afford you a great networking opportunity with smaller crowds and potentially some time to speak with speakers at the conference or organizers directly.

It's also not a bad idea to figure out who is going to the conference and who you might want to meet.

Oftentimes, I'll find there are specific people I'd like to meet who happen to either be attending or speaking at a conference I am going to.

In many cases, I'll offer to buy them dinner, set up a quick meetup over coffee, or just make a note that I need to try and bump into them while I am there.

This just about covers your "pre-conference game."

What about at the conference itself?

I'd highly encourage you to **utilize the time you have there as much as possible by talking to as many people as you can.**

HEY JOHN

How do I just go up to someone I don't know and start talking to them?

Honestly, you just do it.

Yes, I know it may be scary.

Yes, I know you might not know what to say or you might be afraid that you'll say something stupid.

But, it's an acquired skill that will only develop over time if you make a concerted effort to practice it and the fear won't go away by itself.

You'll only become a better—and less fearful—conversationalist by having conversations.

But, what do you say, you ask?

Really, it doesn't matter that much since at conferences like these you will have so much in common with everyone you meet, and there will be plenty to talk about, but if you are really unsure of how to start a conversation, here are a few quick tips:

1. Try complimenting them on something they are wearing or something unique about them. It's always a good conversation starter, because people like talking about themselves and they usually like compliments as well.

2. Try asking open-ended questions—questions that don't have just "yes" or "no" answers—especially about themselves. "Why are you here? What's your story? What did you get out of the last talk?" (Just don't ask them all at once.)

3. Just simply go up and introduce yourself. I know this seems lame, but it's super easy to do and at an event, like a conference, it's really all you need to do.

4. Comment on some common experience or what is happening around you. "Hey, wow, that guy with the bright red top hat. I was going to wear mine, but it was in the wash."

But, like I said. The most important thing is just to practice and to get into the habit of opening up conversations with people wherever you are.

Don't sit there working on your laptop.

You can do that on the plane ride over or on your trip back.

Maximize your networking opportunities by talking to as many people as you can and attending as many events as you can.

Have some business cards to give out and have an "elevator pitch" worked out so you can say who you are and what you do in two to three sentences max.

Apply the networking techniques we talked about in "Networking and Groups."

SPEAKING

Personally, **I think every software developer should try their hand at speaking.**

I know it might make you nervous and uncomfortable, but if you can learn to get over that initial discomfort and conquer the fear of public speaking, there are huge benefits.

One of the biggest benefits is **building up your reputation.**

Being known as a conference speaker can open up a huge amount of opportunity to you in your software development career.

In the chapter,"Creating a Reputation," we talked about getting your name out there, and this is a great way to do it.

Being known as a speaker, or even speaking at just a few events, is kind of like being a book author (https://simpleprogrammer.com/cg52-lifemanual).

It gives you a certain prestige, which sets you a bit apart and can greatly increase your perceived value.

Plus, it's just a great way to get people to know about you.

It's perhaps not as effective as having a successful blog or podcast, simply because you don't reach as many people, but **you impact the people you do reach much more because of the personal nature of the medium.**

Aside from just building up your reputation, speaking can be a great way to build or even create a freelance or consulting business as a software developer.

I know several software developers who bill hundreds of dollars an hour (https://simpleprogrammer.com/cg52-bill) **and their main source of business is the speaking they do at various software development conferences each year.**

Speaking at conferences provides you a unique opportunity to get in front of potential clients and demonstrate your knowledge as an expert they may want to hire.

HEY JOHN

Is it okay to advertise that I'm available for consulting or is it best to wait for it to come up?

If you speak at a conference or event, you shouldn't have to advertise your services directly, but you should instead mention a few successful clients or case studies in your presentation, if you really want to be the most effective at pitching your services.

Make sure your audience is aware that you are a consultant and do provide consulting in the area you are talking about and that your clients have had success using you.

I'm all for making strong and direct sales pitches, but in this context, a less direct approach is likely to yield you better results.

You can also finish up with saying something along the lines of "if you have any other questions or if there is anything I can help you with, please don't hesitate to reach out and contact me" and then provide your contact information.

This is a good way to get potential leads.

You would be amazed at how much business you can drum up just by speaking at a few events each year.

Plus, if you enjoy travel, **speaking is a great way to experience it at a discounted price in a way that also benefits your career.**

Speaking has afforded me the opportunity to visit many countries around the world.

Just this year, I spent three weeks in China (https://simpleprogrammer.com/cg52-china) and most of that trip was paid for simply because I was invited to speak at a conference there.

GETTING STARTED SPEAKING

So you are all fired up.

You want to travel the world.

You want to meet new people and start a consulting business.

You want to get out there and speak at software development conferences.

Great!

Unfortunately, **you can't just volunteer to speak at most software development confer-ences**—especially if you have no experience and are relatively unknown.

So, how do you get started?

Well, just like everything in life, **you have to start small.**

You aren't going to be keynoting large software development conferences if you haven't at least spoken at smaller ones.

And you probably aren't going to speak at smaller software development conferences if you don't have any experience speaking in general.

The first thing you need to do is get experience.

One of the best places to start is at your current workplace.

Offer to give a presentation to your team on something new you are learning.

You might even consider offering a brown bag style lunch where you deliver a talk or training during lunch time.

Don't even worry about being a good public speaker—that will come in time.

Just prepare your presentation and do your best to deliver it.

You are going to have to suck a lot if you ever want to get good at something (https:// simpleprogrammer.com/cg52-crappy), so you might as well get good at sucking.

670 || THE COMPLETE SOFTWARE DEVELOPERS CAREER GUIDE

A good move up from giving a few presentations at work is to **give a talk at a code camp or user group** like the ones you can find on Meetup.

Code camps allow just about anyone to register to give a talk, so they are a great place to get some experience speaking in front of people you don't know.

Another great option you can pursue at the same time is to join Toastmasters (https://simpleprogrammer.com/cg52-toastmasters).

Toastmasters is an international organization with clubs all around the world, and possibly many in your area, dedicated to helping people become better public speakers and to giving opportunities for people to practice speaking in public.

I joined Toastmasters this year (2016), and I can tell you that **it's an extremely supportive and encouraging environment.**

I'd highly recommend it.

Once you are ready to move up to the big game, you'll likely need to submit abstracts to software development conferences.

Usually conferences have a call for speakers where they officially ask speakers to submit an abstract about what they want to talk about and perhaps some video of them speaking or a list of events they've previously spoken at.

Unfortunately, as much as conference organizers deny it and claim to be a meritocracy, it's just not true.

It's still a "good ol' boys" club for the most part.

That means **you'll need to develop relationships and build a reputation** if you want to be able to speak at bigger events or even be asked to speak at a conference.

But, if you have some experience and write a really good abstract, it can certainly help you break into the circuit.

I'd recommend getting someone to film you giving a talk at a smaller event, so that you can submit that along with your abstract.

Frequently, event organizers are afraid to accept first time or unknown speakers because they don't know if you can actually do it or if you'll just freeze up on stage.

Anything you can do to assuage this fear is going to help you get selected.

Also, when you are getting started you want to submit as many abstracts as possible.

If you can talk to the conference organizers ahead of time and ask them about what kind of talks they are looking for and what makes a good abstract, do it.

OVERCOMING STAGE FRIGHT

You know what is scary?

Getting up in front of a bunch of people you don't know, and have them all stare at you while you try to speak to them about something.

It's true. It's ok to admit it.

It is scary—well, at least at first.

The first time I got up on a stage to deliver a talk, I was trying to be calm and confident, but my voice kept trembling—completely out of my control.

My armpits were sweating and making huge sweat stains on my shirt.

It was awful.

I was just glad to be done with it.

Then I did it again and I had pretty much the same result.

Still trembling voice, still sweating like a pig.

And again, and again.

But guess what?

About the fourth or fifth time I delivered a talk in front of crowd, I didn't feel quite as nervous.

Somehow, magically my voice held.

Somehow, I didn't drench the stage in sweat.

Somehow, I actually felt a little confident, perhaps a little energized.

What was once terrifying was just a bit frightening.

And now, when I get up on stage, **I absolutely love it.**

I feel most alive when I'm delivering a talk to a large audience.

I honestly can't think of a better feeling.

But what changed?

How did I go from being afraid to get on stage to confident and actually enjoying myself?

To be honest, **the biggest thing was time and experience.**

Fear tends to be caused by the unknown.

The first time we get on stage, we don't know what is going to happen.

We don't know what it is going to be like.

We aren't sure if people will like us, or boo us, or what will happen.

But if you keep getting on stage and giving talks, eventually most of that mystery disappears.

You realize that even though you may not have given your best performance, no one booed you, no one threw rotten eggs at you… you survived.

So if you want to get over stage fright, **you have to get out there and do it.**

Don't wait for courage to come or for you not to be afraid.

That won't happen; **courage is acting in spite of fear, not in absence of it** (https://simpleprogrammer.com/cg52-softskills).

Have some courage and get out there and be willing to mess up.

Don't be afraid to look like an idiot (https://simpleprogrammer.com/cg52-idiot)—we all do from time to time.

That's how you get better.

SOME PRACTICAL TIPS

I like a good pep talk as much as anyone, but practical tips are often more useful, so here are few.

First, **do it at least five times.**

Get on stage and give a talk at least five times before you decide it's not for you.

Oh, and these five times don't really count.

Just get up there and do it; don't worry about the outcome.

If, after five times you decide it's not for you, then fine, at least you tried. But don't give up until you've at least been on stage giving a talk five times.

Second, **when you get into a room to give a talk, show up about 10 minutes early.**

Instead of messing with your mic or pacing the stage, go to the front rows of the audience, introduce yourself and shake hands.

Now, when you get on stage, you are going to have at least a few people in the audience who you know or at least have met, and they are going to be rooting for you.

It's an honor for the speaker to come up and talk to you.

It makes you feel special.

Those people who you just met will reciprocate by paying extra attention to what you are saying and will positively encourage you.

If you start to get nervous on stage or feel your heart rate start to rise, just take a look down at the front row, where there will be smiling, encouraging faces.

I don't really need this trick anymore, but I still do it every time.

Finally, **prepare and practice.**

The more you know about a subject and the more prepared you are, the less nervous you will be.

When someone asks you about your favorite TV show or movie or video game, are you nervous?

No.

You have plenty to talk about, you might even be gushing.

But if someone asks you about nuclear physics and you are not a nuclear physicist or don't have really strange reading habits, you are probably going to be a bit more nervous.

So, make sure you know your material well and you've practiced it quite a bit.

Get in front of the mirror and deliver your talk, timing yourself.

Use a video camera and record yourself, and then watch it.

PREPARING TALKS AND SLIDES

I tend to prefer to give talks with no slides or as few slides as possible.

If your topic is highly technical and involves quite a bit of code, this won't be possible, but you can still work on making things simple and easy to follow.

You should strive to convey only a few key points in a talk, and they should all be based around one big idea.

If you use slides, try to make them **as simple as possible.**

Do not make slides with many bullet points full of text, and then read the bullet points during your talk.

Your slides should provide additional information or visualizations which enhance your talk, not repeat the content in it.

Simplicity is key—and so is being entertaining.

You can't teach someone if you don't entertain them.

Your job as a presenter is always to entertain first and educate second.

It's impossible to teach someone when you don't have their attention, and you won't have their attention if you don't keep them entertained.

So make sure your talk is not boring, that it's simple enough to follow, and that it is entertaining in some way.

It could be a few funny cat pictures, it could be a few jokes or stories.

There are many ways to entertain.

Rather than trying to give you a whole treatise on how to prepare a talk and create slides for it, I'm going to give you two books for reference.

The first one is called *Presentation Zen* (https://simpleprogrammer.com/cg52-zen).

I highly recommend this book for learning what makes a good, simple presentation.

Your slide deck and your audience will thank you for reading this book.

Second, I'd recommend Dale Carnegie's excellent book, *The Art of Public Speaking* (https://simpleprogrammer.com/cg52-art).

It's a classic book about public speaking, where I first heard the idea of:

Tell them what you are going to tell them, tell them, and then tell them what you told them.

PAID SPEAKING

If you speak enough, or you become famous enough, or you are aggressive enough to advertise your "speaking services," **you might get the opportunity to actually get paid to speak. Imagine that.**

When I first started speaking, I was honored just to get a chance to speak at an event.

But after time—especially after my first book came out (https://simpleprogrammer.com /cg52-lifemanual)—I started getting quite a few speaking requests and realized I needed to start charging money if I was going to spend all the time and effort required to go out and speak somewhere.

And don't be mistaken, **there is quite a bit of time and effort involved.**

You have to book plane tickets, show up somewhere, spend usually two or three days at an event or traveling, prepare your talk, rehearse your talk, give your talk and then talk to people afterwards about your talk.

Plenty of logistics and time required.

After I realized this and realized how little time I had to spare in the year, I started asking for speaking fees.

At first I would ask for travel and expense reimbursement and $2,500.

Then I started asking for $5,000.

Now, at least at the time of writing this book, my standard fee is $10,000.

I know many public speakers who charge a great deal more than that.

The famous author and creator of Dilbert, in his excellent book *How to Fail at Almost Everything and Still Win Big* (https://simpleprogrammer.com/cg52-fail), said that his highest speaking fee was $100,000.

So, yes, you can actually make quite a bit of money being paid to speak.

Now, usually if you are going to be paid to speak at a software development conference, it is going to be for a keynote spot.

You usually don't apply for those, someone invites you to speak.

So, you need to build up a reputation or be a well-known speaker in order to be able to even get into that game.

There are also often speaking opportunities at private company events.

I've been asked to speak to software developers at corporate events where they have specifically put aside a budget to have a famous or semi-famous speaker come in to give a talk.

Caution: **if you really want to pursue paid speaking, you might not want to speak for free or submit to conferences too often.**

I know this seems a bit backwards, but let me explain.

Once, a long time ago, when I was an "actor" taking acting lessons in Santa Monica, California, my acting coach told me something that has stuck with me because it applies to many different situations.

He told me to never sign up to be an extra.

He said, "I know you think it's a good way to make some extra money and you'll get on the set of real productions and get in front of casting directors, but if you ever want to be an A-list player or have a leading role, don't do it."

He went on to say that **once they see you as an extra, you'll always be an extra.**

It's very difficult to convince someone to pay you a large sum of money and take you seriously if you are or have been willing to work for free or even for peanuts..

You don't want to compete with every speaker out there who submits for every conference and hopes they get selected to speak for free or for peanuts.

Instead, if you are really serious about being a professional speaker, **turn down most free speaking requests, build up a solid reputation and charge from the beginning.**

HEY JOHN

But how do I go from speaking at code camps to speaking at large conferences for a fee?

Let's be honest, it's not going to be easy and most people are not successful at it.

It's certainly the long-game approach.

> The key is reputation and patience.
>
> You have to build up your reputation enough, using the other techniques in this section, to be a desirable enough speaker that people want to pay you to speak.
>
> It may take a long time or not happen at all.
>
> You can always go the free route and submit for conference speaking opportunities, like most developers do, but if you want to eventually be a paid speaker, my opinion—and my acting coach's opinion—is that you're better off charging from the start.

That's how you set yourself apart and don't have to compete with the masses.

GET OUT THERE AND DO IT

If you've never been to a software development conference, find a good one, book some tickets, and go.

If you have any interest in speaking, pick a topic, make some slides, and do it.

Your life isn't going to change if you don't take steps to change or improve it.

Yes, I know it's scary.

It's scary just going to a conference if you've never been, but when you regularly do the things that scare you, they eventually become routine.

I never thought I'd go to conferences or speak on stages, but I've done it so many times now that it's become natural—even exciting.

Most importantly though, overcoming those fears, doing those things that made me feel the most uncomfortable at first, were the very things that improved my career—and my life—the most.

So, take a chance.

What do you really have to lose?

CHAPTER 53

CREATING A BLOG

I honestly think one of the best possible things you can do for your software development career is to start a blog—and regularly update it.

I have to admit I'm a little bit biased.

After all, **you probably wouldn't be reading this book and I probably wouldn't be writing it, if one day in late 2009, I hadn't decided to create the blog named "Simple Programmer: Making the Complex Simple."** (https://simpleprogrammer.com/cg53-homepage)

I had no idea what I was doing.

I had no ambitions.

I just wanted to share my thoughts and my experiences, mostly with my work team, since I knew they would likely read my blog.

But I kept writing, week after week.

And then things started to happen.

Amazingly, **people actually started to read what I was writing**—not many people, but there were enough that I started to notice, and then people started to notice me.

I started getting job offers and opportunities.

Eventually I took one opportunity to create some online courses (https://simpleprogrammer.com/cg53-pluralsight) for a small—at the time—company called Pluralsight.

In three years time, I ended up creating 55 courses for Pluralsight and making literally a few million dollars in royalties.

I got invited to speak on podcasts and at conferences and events.

The readership of Simple Programmer grew and grew, and eventually that little bit of affiliate income I was generating from recommending Amazon products in my blog posts also grew.

I launched my first product, "How to Market Yourself as a Software Developer," (https://simpleprogrammer.com/cg53-marketyourself) to my growing audience at Simple Programmer and it was a huge success.

Eventually, **I quit my full-time job** and started to work on Simple Programmer full time.

My little blog from 2009 was providing me a full-time income.

Today, that blog is still growing.

Today, Simple Programmer **employs three people full time**, and many part-time contractors.

Simple Programmer has become a real business, has allowed me to **travel the world** (https://simpleprogrammer.com/cg53-travel)**, meet people I'd never thought I'd meet, and make a real positive impact on people's lives.**

It all started from a blog and a simple message to make the complex simple.

I'm not special: if I can do it, so can you.

The journey may not be easy, but in this chapter, I'll share with you what I know.

WHY A BLOG IS STILL YOUR BEST CHOICE

Today, I get more traffic to my YouTube channel (https://simpleprogrammer.com/cg53-youtube) each day than I do to my Simple Programmer blog.

But **I still think blogging is the best choice for most software developers** (although, you should consider YouTube as well).

The reason why is simple: **it's low barrier to entry and it's extremely effective.**

For a long time people have been ringing the death knell of blogging and saying that it's dead because too many people are blogging and there are too many blogs out there, but it's just not true.

Yes, there are quite a few blogs out there now, but most of them don't have many posts and are not regularly maintained.

If you blog regularly and consistently, it's almost guaranteed that someone searching for your name on the internet will find your blog.

This is going to enhance your reputation for any recruiter, employer, or possible customer, just by virtue of you having a blog that is regularly updated.

Countless students of my blogging course (https://simpleprogrammer.com/cg53-blog) have emailed me to tell me about how having a blog got them a better job, either because a potential employer saw their blog and decided to hire them, or they received an invitation to apply for a job from someone who came across their blog.

And the best part is, it's so easy.

Anyone can create a blog and have one up and running in five minutes or less (https://simpleprogrammer.com/cg53-5minutes).

Yes, you still have to do the work for writing blog posts on a regular basis, but anyone can get good at doing that with just a little bit of practice over time.

Think of a blog as an advertisement for you that works all day and night without you having to do anything other than feed it every once in awhile.

Aside from the external opportunities blogging offers you, it offers some great personal development opportunities as well.

I don't think there is any better way to improve your communication skills than writing.

Writing teaches you to organize your thoughts clearly in a way that other people can understand.

The more you write, the better of a communicator you'll become in general.

Blogging also helps you keep track of your own career and progress, as well as provides some historical documentation and reference material which you can look back on to see how you solved a particular problem in the past.

I'm always searching my own blog for answers to current problems that I know I've solved or talked about in the past.

Every software developer should have their own blog: it's like a lightsaber for a Jedi.

HOW TO CREATE A BLOG

Alright, so you are convinced you need a blog, great!

But how do you actually create one?

(I'm going to cover some of the basics here, but I'd highly recommend you sign up for my free blogging course (https://simpleprogrammer.com/cg53-blog) *for some step-by-step details and a complete walkthrough of creating your blog.)*

My first advice is not to create one... well, I mean not to create one yourself.

Many software developers are tempted to create their own blog, from scratch, and not use an off-the-shelf solution.

This is a bad—nay, horrible—idea.

Here's why.

The point of blogging is not to exercise your ability to write blogging software, which is more difficult than you think.

The point of blogging is to build your reputation, get your name out there, and record your ideas, not to increase your development skills.

It's not that there is anything necessarily wrong with creating your own blog, but doing so is going to **waste a large amount of time that you could be using to write and actually publish your blog posts.** If you never finish the project of creating your own blog—which is highly likely—you'll never have a blog.

Plus, the commercial blogging software out there is extremely good, widely used and supported, and has a huge number of plugins and integrations which you could never write on your own.

In fact, **I'd highly recommend you use WordPress as your blogging platform**, since it is the most dominant software in the blogging space and as a result, has the largest number of plugins and extensibility points.

I use WordPress for all of my websites, because it is that flexible and easy to use.

Creating your blog with WordPress is **extremely easy.**

The first thing you need is a host.

I recommend either using Bluehost (https://simpleprogrammer.com/cg53-bluehost) or WP Engine (https://simpleprogrammer.com/cg53-wpengine) if you are just starting out.

Currently, Simple Programmer runs on a Digital Ocean (https://simpleprogrammer.com /cg53-ocean) droplet that is specially configured, but I have a Linux admin who handles all of the maintenance for that system.

I wouldn't recommend going the route I am using until you really need the performance, which you won't until you have huge traffic spikes.

Bluehost (https://simpleprogrammer.com/cg53-bluehost) is a good choice if you are looking to save money initially, and you don't anticipate a huge amount of traffic.

WP Engine (https://simpleprogrammer.com/cg53-wpengine) is a bit more robust and scalable, so it can handle heavier loads, but is a bit more expensive.

Once you've picked your host, you need to get your blogging software installed.

For Bluehost (https://simpleprogrammer.com/cg53-bluehost), it's an extremely simple process. Just a few clicks.

For WP Engine (https://simpleprogrammer.com/cg53-wpengine), it's even easier, since you already get WordPress installed when you set up your account.

If you use a solution like Digital Ocean (https://simpleprogrammer.com/cg53-ocean), you may have to manually install WordPress yourself or use a snapshot image that they provide with it preinstalled. (Although, remember you'll have to maintain an entirely virtual server.)

I'd highly recommend registering your own custom domain to go with your new blog.

Don't just use the default one a blog hosting provider will give you since you will want to build what is known as pagerank or domain authority for your domain.

Your pagerank and domain authority will influence how much traffic you get from search engines later on, so it is very much worth the small investment of registering your own domain.

You should be able to get your actual blog set up in just a few hours, so don't delay the process: take action right away.

In fact, if you've been procrastinating on starting your blog, finish this chapter, then **put the book down** and do it today. You'll be glad you did and it's not that difficult to do.

PICKING A THEME

One of the first things you'll want to do when you start your blog—probably even before you pick your domain name—is to **pick the theme of your blog.**

When I say theme here, **I don't mean WordPress theme.** (Although if you'd like a recommendation on where to get a WordPress theme, I recommend and use Thrive Themes (https://simpleprogrammer.com/cg53-thrive).)

But, let's get back on topic. What I mean is, **what is your blog about?**

How are you going to describe your blog and what are you going to focus on?

This is essentially the same as your specialization or niche (https://simpleprogrammer.com/cg53-niching).

You want to make the theme of your blog very focused and small initially. You can always expand it later.

So for example, you might create a blog all about using the ListView control in Android.

This might seem like an extremely small and narrow topic, but I guarantee you that you can come up with hundreds of posts about using the ListView control and how to customize it and other closely related topics.

By picking an extremely narrow focus like that, you'll be able to dominate that space much more easily and be able to grow at a faster rate.

It would be much easier to become known as the expert on the Android ListView control than it would be to be known as the expert on the C# or Java or Agile development.

So **try and pick a very narrow focus for the theme for your blog**, but not so small that you can't come up with at least 50 ideas for posts around that theme.

You can also make your theme a bit unique by taking a different angle on a broader subject.

Making a blog about C# would be a bit too broad and not narrowly focused enough, but if you made a blog about C# where the theme is funny and informative C# stories, where you explained some C# concept using a funny story and perhaps a comic strip, that would be an excellent theme for a blog.

You can also combine multiple things together.

I have a podcast (now a bit defunct) called "Get Up and Code." (https://simpleprogrammer.com /cg53-getup)

The podcast was about the intersection between programming and fitness.

Either of those topics is too broad for a theme, but together, they create a much smaller niche that is tightly focused.

The key thing to think about is **what kind of theme can you pick for your blog where you can be known for being number one in the world** for a particular topic or niche.

Brainstorm a list of possible themes and pick the most promising ones where you feel like you can dominate that particular niche and be number one.

If I asked you what is the number one blog in the world for teaching software developers soft skills, what would you say?

Hopefully, you'd say Simple Programmer.

HOW TO BLOG

Blogging is both easier and more difficult than it looks.

It's easier, because all you have to do is write and then publish what you write.

It's more difficult because **writing is difficult.**

Even if you are an experienced writer, writing can be a challenge.

I'm standing here at my desk, typing this chapter, and my head is constantly filled with doubts about what I am writing.

Is this sentence good?

Am I going the right direction with this chapter?

Why do my wrists hurt?

Ultimately though, **you just have to do it.**

Everything you write won't be good.

When you first start writing, you'll probably find that you suck (https://simpleprogrammer.com /cg53-crappy)—that's ok.

Eventually you'll get better.

You have to trust the process (https://simpleprogrammer.com/cg53-trust).

I do have a few tips that will help you to write your blog posts and make them as effective as possible, though.

First of all, **make sure you know what you are going to write before you write it.**

I highly recommend having a list of topics you are going to write about. When you sit down to write a blog post, pick one of those topics and start writing.

For this book, I outlined the entire book and decided on all the chapters before I started writing anything.

Now when I get up in the morning and start writing, I know exactly what I'm supposed to write about.

I don't spend hours wasting time trying to come up with a topic.

I do the same thing for my blog posts—well, most of the time.

One of the best ways to beat procrastination is to know what you are supposed to do.

When you know what you are supposed to do, you are much less likely to procrastinate.

Next, I'd recommend that **if you need to do research, you do it all up front.**

It's much easier to write on a topic in which you are well-versed.

So go and explore the topic and do the research before you sit down to write.

If your piece is an opinion piece, you might not need any research, but you might want to sit down and gather your thoughts on the subject or even discuss it with someone.

Some of my best blog posts come from conversations—or even arguments—I've had with someone about a topic the night before.

You'll also want to **create some kind of an outline before you start writing.**

I find it useful to come up with a rough outline of the different sections of the blog post or book chapter I am going to write before I sit down to write it.

This very chapter started from an outline in which I decided what major points I was going to cover.

This will give some structure to your posts. Plus, it's encouraging to know that you need to write about this topic, followed by that topic, then that topic and then you are done.

You will also want to decide what kind of blog post you are going to write.

Here are some of the common types of blog posts you could pick:

- How-to post showing how to do something.
- Opinion post where you are expressing your opinion about a technology, framework, programming language, etc.
- Opinion post where you are talking about a general concept or methodology and why it is good or bad.
- News or current event where you report about something that happened or is going on.
- Review, where you review a product or service.
- Expert roundup where you get opinions from different experts on a topic.
- Technology or news roundup where you round up a bunch of news or other posts on a topic, or daily or weekly posts about some subject.
- Interview, where you interview someone and write it out as a post.
- Resource, where you create a resource or guide about some technology, framework or tool.
- Explainer post where you explain a topic to your audience so that they can understand it better.

And this list is by no means comprehensive.

There are hundreds of types of blog posts you could write.

Try to keep your posts on topic, though.

When you are first starting out, no one wants to know about your personal life and what you did today.

Once you build up an audience, some personal posts may interest them, but try to stay on topic as much as possible.

The key thing is that you just do it.

Give it your best shot.

It doesn't have to be perfect.

It doesn't have to be a work of art.

Just write something and post it. Get 'er done!

THE POWER OF CONSISTENCY

If you want to be a successful blogger, **the most important thing you can do is be consistent.**

I don't know any successful bloggers who don't consistently produce content, but I know plenty of unsuccessful bloggers who very rarely update their blog and don't have a consistent posting schedule.

Consistency is key.

Pick some kind of schedule and stick to it.

Don't make it optional.

Don't blog only when you feel like it.

Pretend you work for a newspaper which has a deadline that has to be met and you have to publish your post, ready or not.

In fact, treat it like a real deadline and **put in your calendar the exact time and date that each post is due to be published and the exact time and date you are going to write your posts.**

If you know you have to have your blog post published at 10am every Monday and you've set a specific time on your calendar each week to write the post, you are much more likely to be consistent.

In the long run, consistency beats out every other factor (https://simpleprogrammer.com /cg53-heroics).

Trust me, there are going to be days and weeks where you just don't feel like blogging at all.

You are going to have times when you aren't seeing any results from your blogging and it is going to seem pointless and worthless.

You have to keep going anyway.

Discipline is doing what you are supposed to do whether you feel like it or not.

And you need to have discipline to keep writing and to do it consistently.

In time, results will come. Most people are not patient or consistent enough to wait for results, and that is why most people fail to get what they want out of life.

Remember that.

GETTING TRAFFIC

It's not fun creating a blog that never gets read.

When I first started my blog at Simple Programmer, I'm pretty sure the three or four views I got each day were from my mom and perhaps a random coworker who was just curious what I was up to.

But **I kept writing** and I kept posting blog posts and eventually traffic came.

Were there some things I did to increase the traffic specifically?

Sure, there were a few things, but overall the most important factors were consistency and time, and we've already covered consistency.

Over the life of your blog, most of your traffic will likely come from search engines—to be more specific, from Google.

It used to be possible to game the search engines and stuff a bunch of keywords into your web pages or create a bunch of dummy links to your site (backlinks), that would cause your page and site to rank higher in Google searches.

Long gone are those days.

Not to say that you can't do any kind of search engine optimization (SEO), but I wouldn't waste a huge amount of time on these efforts, at least not at first.

The key thing is to create good content that people will want to share and link to.

If you keep creating good content, not only will people share that content and link to it from their sites, but they'll bookmark your site and keep coming back for more.

There is no shortcut here, though; it just takes time.

The more blog posts you have out there and the more time they sit out there, the more likely it is going to be that you are going to have a least one post that goes "viral" and gets spread and shared quite a bit.

These viral posts increase your overall traffic permanently, as they are a signal to search engines that your blog is an authority on a subject and has good content.

I'd recommend writing a few "epic" posts on your blog that will be so good that people can't help but share them.

Create a few ultimate guides or posts that you consider the best resource on whatever topic you are writing about.

For example, I have an extremely popular post that I keep updated called "**The Ultimate List of Developer Podcasts**." (https://simpleprogrammer.com/cg53-podcast)

This one post gets me 150 to 300 new visitors each day.

Plenty of people link to it, tweet about it and share it, because it is really the best resource out there for software development and programming podcasts.

Another good strategy that is only effective when you are first starting out, is to **comment on other people's software development blogs.**

This strategy won't bring you a huge amount of traffic, but it can get you a few visitors a day and can start to get you some general exposure as people click on your profile or a link you provide and go back to your site.

A popular blogger might even read one of your articles and like it enough to link to it on one of his posts, which would get you more traffic and a nice backlink.

You have to be careful with this tactic though, because you don't want to just spam other people's blogs, otherwise you'll have the opposite effect and you'll likely just have your comments deleted anyway.

Only add real, valuable comments which actually contribute to the post, and if you link back to your site, you'd better have a really good reason to do so.

You should, of course, share your posts on social media and do some basic SEO.

If your blog is a WordPress blog, you can find SEO plugins like Yoast SEO which will do most of the SEO work for you.

HEY JOHN

Can you explain what SEO is?

Sure, SEO means search engine optimization, which basically means optimizing what you write so it's more likely to be suggested by results in search engines like Google.

There is a whole industry based around SEO, because for most websites, the largest source of traffic they'll ever get is from Google searches. If you can optimize your content to rank highly for popular search terms, you'll… well, you'll have a lot of traffic.

The only problem is, SEO is an arms race with Google.

As people try and "game" SEO to trick Google into ranking their pages higher for certain search terms, Google is constantly tweaking their own algorithms to prevent people from manipulating the results.

Google's goal is the have the most relevant and valuable content surface for each search term so that the data they provide is more valuable to the end user.

So, yes there are some things you can do to explicitly try and "trick" Google and there are some valid things you can do to give Google hints about your content, but overall the best long-term strategy is going to be to write the kind of quality content that is naturally going to rise to the top of search results because it is truly valuable.

Overall, **what is going to matter most in getting traffic is writing high-quality posts, often, consistently, and over a long period of time.**

FINDING YOUR VOICE

One of the biggest mistakes I've found with new bloggers and writers, in general, is that **they try to present everything as if they were writing an academic paper or news report.**

It's dry and bland and lacks any kind of character or spunk.

It's ok to try and sound professional, but **a writer without a unique and individual voice is just going to be boring as hell.**

Think about this book.

If you've read this far, you've no doubt been exposed to my voice in the writing.

I'm not just telling you facts—or opinions, in my case—**I'm presenting them in a unique way that is hopefully entertaining, but definitely is identifiable as my voice.**

Now, I'm no Hemingway or C.S. Lewis.

I've got plenty that I can improve in my writing, but for the most part, I've found my voice.

That's what you have to do—if you actually want people to read your stuff.

Finding your voice isn't easy, though.

You have to be willing to try things out and go to different extremes until you settle on what fits you best.

And your voice will change at times, depending on your mood and what you are talking about.

Some of the chapters I wrote in this book were much more "spunky," others were a bit more on the dry side, but you should have gained some overarching kind of feel for who I am based on the way most of the chapters in this book were written.

Your voice in writing is who you are.

Someone reading your posts shouldn't just learn how to create an Android application using the latest Java framework, they should also get an idea of who you are as a writer and what your personality is.

That's what makes writing interesting.

As much as humans are interested in technology, they are much more interested in people.

People magazine will always outsell MSDN magazine—I promise.

So, **don't be afraid to insert some personality into your writing.**

Give it a little "spunk."

It's ok to have an opinion.

It's even ok to have bad grammar—if it serves your purpose.

Try a few different shoes and see which one fits.

Try writing like you talk.

Try writing in different styles and express yourself in different ways.

Try throwing the word "fuck" into your writing and see how that feels.

Shake things up.

I find that one of the best ways to find your natural range is to **go to one extreme and then the other, pushing the envelope in both directions.**

You'll settle down where you feel most comfortable, which is usually somewhere in the middle, but with the capability to go to either extreme at any time.

And remember, this is a process.

I've written millions of words and I'm still going through this process myself.

I'll always be searching for my voice—and you will, too.

At first it will be difficult to find, but one day you'll write a post and you'll think "Damn, that was fricken sweet," or "Shucks, that was a golly swell post," or "Hot dog, I rock!" or "I felt that conveyed my sentiments very precisely."

Get it?

HEY JOHN

How do I deal with the "trolls" and "haters" who say negative things about my writing or post negative comments on my content?

Ah, yes the trolls.

Those people who have such critical opinions of what you are doing, but don't seem to be producing anything themselves.

There are plenty of ways to deal with trolls and haters, that range from ignoring them, to calling them out, to directly combating them with indisputable facts and figures, and even replying with your own absurdity to compliment theirs. (I've done all of these things.)

But for the most part, the most effective thing to do is to ignore them.

No matter what you do—especially if it is of any value or consequence—you are going to have haters and people who want to disparage you and make you feel bad.

Rather than being angry at these people and letting them discourage you in any way, you should feel sorry for them.

One human being does not lash out and attempt to destroy the work of another human being unless that first human being is in some kind of great pain themselves.

Most of the time when someone is attacking you or your work it is more about them than it is about you.

Perhaps, what you've said or even the very fact that you've done something with your life and produced something threatens them in some way.

Perhaps, they are just having a bad day—or a bad life—and they are just crying out for help in the only way they know how; like a child looking for any form of attention that the world will give them.

Regardless, however you decide to handle the situation, don't let them take you down.

Keep doing what you are doing, don't take it personal, stay calm, and carry on.

KEEP WRITING

I can only fit so much in this short chapter on blogging.

I'm sure I could fill an entire book on the subject (https://simpleprogrammer.com/cg53-blogging).

So, I tried to give you what I think are some of the **most important ideas and concepts** to get you started and keep you going.

However, I want to leave you with one final piece of advice: **keep writing.**

Writing is not easy (https://simpleprogrammer.com/cg53-writing).

It's not always fun.

Famous author, poet, and screenwriter Dorothy Parker, when asked if she enjoyed writing said, "I enjoy having *written*."

Despite how bad you might suck, how painful it feels and how much you think you just aren't a writer and no one will possibly read what you wrote, **do it anyway and keep doing it.**

In time, you will improve.

You will get better.

And if you keep at it long enough, the reward will come.

In high school I was in every advanced placement class they offered, except for one: AP English.

I did AP Calculus as a sophomore, I took AP U.S. History, AP Biology, AP Chemistry, AP European History, but I was not allowed into the AP English class.

To put it bluntly, **I sucked at writing.**

Or rather, I sucked at writing the way people wanted me to write.

But, here I am now, in many respects, writing for a living, having published one extremely successful book (https://simpleprogrammer.com/cg53-lifemanual) and pounding out another.

My first blog post was horrible.

The next few just as bad.

But the one I wrote last week... well, it's halfway decent and it's getting better all the time.

If I can do it, you can do it. All you have to do is keep writing.

CHAPTER 54

FREELANCING AND STARTING A BUSINESS

When I was working a regular 9-to-5 job, I'd often fantasize about starting my own business—working for myself.

I'd think about **how nice it would be to be a freelancer and not have a boss.**

I'd daydream about traveling the world, working whatever hours I pleased, and making hoards of money from lucrative contracts.

Then I'd snap to reality as I realized I had no idea how to go about making something like this happen.

I mean, **how do you actually become a freelancer and work for yourself?**

How do you start a business?

I assumed what you had to do was bid on government contracts, and if you put together a strong enough proposal and got one of the contracts, bam!, you were a freelancer and you could run your own business.

I went far as to register for a DUNS number, which is like a social security number for a business, but that's about as far as I got.

I looked at some government contracts that I could submit proposals for, decided it was too difficult, and gave up.

I didn't really revisit the idea again until what I was wishing for sort of magically happened.

About a year after I created my Simple Programmer blog, I started getting some unsolicited offers to actually do some freelancing work.

People would email me and ask me if I could do a certain kind of work and what my hourly rate was.

With glee, I rubbed my hands together and cautiously typed "$50 an hour" as if I was pulling a fast one.

My offers were pretty quickly accepted and I ended up doing quite a bit of freelance work at what, at the time, I thought was a high hourly rate.

Later on, **I doubled that rate to $100 an hour and then to $200 and then $300** (https://simpleprogrammer.com/cg54-bill), **and now my minimum consulting fee is $500 an hour** (https://simpleprogrammer.com/cg54-coaching), **or $5,000 a day.**

But it wasn't easy to get there, and **I found out that many of my fantasies about what it would be like to be my own boss as a freelancer weren't quite what I had imagined**, to say the least.

I've definitely learned some important lessons along the way.

In this chapter, I'll share those lessons with you and give you some practical advice on how to start freelancing—if that's what you want to do—or even to start any kind of business in this modern era of the entrepreneur programmer.

ARE YOU SURE YOU REALLY WANT TO DO THIS?

The first question you should ask yourself is if you are sure whether or not you really want to embark upon this path.

Don't get me wrong; I want you to become an entrepreneur of sorts.

I want you to eventually stop working for "the man" and find your path to freedom.

But **freedom is not for everyone** (https://simpleprogrammer.com/cg54-freedom).

Most people can't actually handle freedom when they get it, and even more people aren't willing to pay the price it demands—and it ain't cheap.

Like I mentioned earlier, there is the dream of starting your own business and becoming a freelancer or some other kind of entrepreneur, and there is the reality.

The reality is that it is going to take a large amount of work to even get to the point where the dream is a reality.

You are going to have to be willing to put in long hours after you've already put in a full day's worth of work at your regular job.

You are going to have to **do things that make you uncomfortable** (https://simpleprogrammer.com /cg54-softskills).

You are going to have to **face rejection.**

In many cases you are going to have to **take large risks.**

Regular employment offers you a steady paycheck and certainty; freelancing and entrepreneurial efforts do not.

You could work for a client for weeks or months and not get paid.

You could spends months or even years creating a product and it could bomb.

This very book I'm spending months on writing, could turn out to be a complete failure.

And there are no halfway measures here.

If you don't "play full out," as one of my mentors, Tony Robbins, says at all of his seminars, you are not likely to succeed.

And if you do succeed on "leaving the nest" or regular employment, are you actually ready to handle that level of freedom in your life?

Before you say "of course," take a careful moment to think about it, because in actuality, most people are not.

It's easy to get up in the morning, drive to work, sit at your desk, and work from 9 til 5 when you "have to," because you'll be fired if you don't.

It's much more difficult to get up in the morning, walk to your office and decide to work, when you could be playing Xbox, watching TV, going for walk, or doing a multitude of other things with your freedom.

Some people just can't handle that much freedom.

The first two times I tried to become an entrepreneur, I couldn't handle it.

That much freedom crushed me.

I spent a large amount of time playing online poker, leveling up my Lore-Master on Lord of the Rings Online, and just generally goofing off.

Now, I'm focused. I'm disciplined.

I've learned that I have to create rules for myself (https://simpleprogrammer.com/cg54-rules) and follow them if I don't want to follow someone else's rules.

It's a difficult lesson.

All of this isn't to discourage you, but to push you off to one side of the knife's edge.

You may read this section and say, "Hell no, I'll pass!"

Or you may read this section, be even more inspired and **double your resolve to get free** (https://simpleprogrammer.com/cg54-levels).

Whichever path you choose is up to you, but don't say you haven't been warned.

WHAT IS FREELANCING?

Freelancing is pretty simple: it's when you aren't employed by anyone, but instead work for hire.

It's kind of like being a mercenary, except you aren't fighting other armies and crushing revolutions. Instead you are writing code and perhaps slaying a few dragons that lurk therein.

I further define freelancing here to mean that you have more than one client.

If you just are a contractor working for one client who isn't technically your boss, I call that consulting or contracting, not freelancing.

Nothing wrong with that, but it's much more like full-time employment then an entrepreneurial activity like the kind of freelancing I'm defining here.

A true freelancer works for multiple clients, although not necessarily simultaneously, and has to manage the overhead of finding clients, creating contracts, and running a real business.

HOW TO GET STARTED

This was the question I could never figure out the answer to.

When I was an employee, the idea of becoming a freelancer and getting clients to hire me to work on their projects seemed too foreign to me.

Working for someone else for too long sort of makes you like a lion in the zoo.

You expect to go to a certain place and be fed each day.

You've got a nice, comfortable enclosure you can walk around in and you know what the boundaries are.

You've "forgotten" how to get and kill your own food.

You've "forgotten" how to hunt for it.

Or, if you were born in captivity, you've never known how to do those things at all.

You just have this faint and barely discernible repressed instinct that sometimes whispers, "Hunt… kill."

How do you connect with that animal instinct and learn to feed yourself?

Well, there is a hard way and there is an easy way.

The hard way is to get out there, polish your sales skills, put on your anti-rejection armor and pound the pavement.

Start by going through all your social circles to find any connections you have or any connections of connections who might be interested in your service.

Start with a fairly low hourly rate and a "satisfaction or your money back" guarantee.

Contact everyone you can who either might be slightly interested in your services or might know someone who is, and let them know that you are in business and what specific benefits you can provide to someone who hires you.

Try to be as specific as possible.

Be specific in the kind of clients you are looking for and the specific services you can provide.

Only don't talk about what you can do in terms of services.

Talk about what you can do in terms of results.

Don't talk about how you can program C# code for someone and you know SQL.

Talk about how you can save them time and money by automating business processes and making existing software more efficient and cost-effective to maintain.

Talk about how you can get them more customers with a highly-optimized and performant web page that will set them apart from their competition.

Once you've exhausted the list of people you are connected to, you have to start prospecting on your own.

You might want to purchase a list of small businesses in your area through a service like the one Experian offers (https://simpleprogrammer.com/cg54-experian).

You could also hire someone to compile a list of small businesses in your area or just do the research yourself.

Get on the phone, send emails, and keep refining your pitch.

It's a numbers game to get clients this way, but if you are determined and persistent enough, you'll eventually crack this nut.

Once you have serviced enough clients and made sure they are happy, you can start to build up some word of mouth and referral business, which will make future business come much easier.

Along the same lines, you can talk to other freelancers you know and offer to take on any clients they don't have the capacity to handle, if they will refer them to you. Perhaps offer a referral fee.

While I don't recommend it, you can also get some experience and possibly land some long-term clients by using a service like Upwork or advertising your services in Craigslist. Just know the competition will be fierce and your hourly rate will likely have to be low.

DIDN'T YOU SAY THERE WAS AN EASY WAY?

So, yeah. That's the hard way.

I actually never got any clients the hard way.

I never figured out how to do it the hard way until years later—now it's obvious to me.

But, oh yes, the easy way. That's what you wanted, right?

If you've been paying attention to the other chapters in this section, you may have already guessed the "easy" way.

Get clients to come to you.

And how do you do that, you may ask?

This is where **building that reputation, specializing and creating that blog** come into play.

You see, there is a large amount of overhead in prospecting clients yourself.

It's much better if you can use what is known as "inbound marketing" to get potential clients, or leads, to come to you.

And you can do that by being the kind of person that people find or hear of and specifically seek out.

Now, this "easy" way can actually be more difficult in the short term.

It takes a large amount of effort and work and time to build up a reputation.

It's not easy to create a blog, write posts, speak on podcasts, and do other things to build up your personal brand.

But if you focus on doing these things while you are working at your regular job—and you start early on—when you are ready to jump into the world of freelancing, it will be easy because **your customers will already be coming to you.**

Not only will they come to you, but they'll be willing to pay you more money.

When you solicit someone else and try to get them to use your services, you aren't exactly in the best negotiating position.

But if someone comes to you and asks you specifically to do some work for them, you can sort of name your price.

This is the way I ended up doing freelancing work.

Like I said, I never did figure out how to drum up work the hard way.

Instead, as my blog started to get popular and my reputation in the software development industry started to grow, I started to get more and more email from potential clients wanting to specifically work with me.

In fact, I started to get so much business that I had to raise my rates again and again, until they reached what I considered an unimaginable number and that's where they rest today.

That reminds me, we should talk about rates...

HOW TO SET YOUR RATES

There is quite a bit of advice floating around out there on how to set your rates as a freelancer.

One of the most common pieces of advice today is to double your rate and keep doubling it, or at least keep increasing it, until potential clients start to say "no."

This is decent advice if you are already fairly well established, but if you are starting out it's horrible advice, because all you are going to get are nos.

In fact, **I'd recommend starting out at a very low, even close-to-free rate**, with a money-back guarantee so that you can gain some experience, get your first clients more easily, and understand what your true overhead and costs will be.

HEY JOHN

If I offer a money-back guarantee don't I run the risk of being ripped off by my customer?

No, and here's why:

If you don't deliver what you promised your customer, aren't they going to ask for their money back anyway? And aren't you going to have to give it back to them?

Think about it.

If you hire someone to do a job for you and they don't do the job or they don't do a satisfactory job, aren't you very likely to ask for—perhaps even demand—your money back; maybe even sue them?

So, if you are going to go into business at all, you are pretty much by default offering a money-back guarantee. You might as well make it explicit and gain the benefits of the additional clients you'll get just by making that offer.

But, I can understand that you might still not be convinced—I should put my "money where my mouth is," so to speak.

Well, I do.

For instance, if you aren't happy with this book, ship it back to me and I'll give you your money back.

Not only that, but just about every product I sell has a full one-year-unconditional money-back guarantee.

And these are on mostly digital products that you can easily download and then ask for your money back.

> Do people rip me off?
>
> Sure they do, but many more people buy who would have not otherwise bought, simply because of the guarantee.
>
> So, yes, occasionally someone may try to rip you off if you offer a money-back guarantee, but it's unlikely and the amount of additional business you'll get by having the guarantee will more than make up for it.
>
> Besides, you can always screen your clients and choose who to work with, and, like I said, aren't you going to have to give their money back anyway if you don't perform?
>
> Don't you think that would be the right thing to do, regardless of a guarantee?

Now, if you are having no trouble getting your first clients because you've done things the "easy way" and they are coming to you, you might want to just start off with the doubling your rate advice.

But if you are like most freelancers who are starting out and you've chosen to do things the hard way, or you didn't really choose but that's where you are, **I'd highly advise you not worry about making money at all, at least at first.**

I interviewed software-developer-turned-entrepreneur and freelancer Marcus Blankenship about how he "got free" (https://simpleprogrammer.com/cg54-marcus) from the corporate world. He talked about how, for his first few freelancing jobs, he charged a ridiculously low amount and it took him way longer than expected, so he ended up actually working for less than minimum wage.

Marcus said it was actually the best decision he ever made, because **even though that job effectively cost him money, it gained him valuable experience**, confidence, and true understanding of what freelancing would be like.

So, without beating a dead horse too much, I'll just say be willing to work cheaply at first and the money will come—trust me.

Now, if you are somewhat experienced and you are trying to determine what your rate should be, the answer is "higher."

I don't agree that you necessarily have to double your rates, but it's not a bad idea to try it and see what happens.

708 || THE COMPLETE SOFTWARE DEVELOPERS CAREER GUIDE

I doubled my rates from $50 to $100 and no one blinked an eye.

I jumped up to $200 and then $300 an hour and I finally started to get "nos" at $300, but I was still getting plenty of "yeses" as well.

Even when I jumped my rates up to $500 an hour—where they sit now—I still get takers. (Although usually not for programming tasks now, more for coaching and overall architecture consulting.)

Part of the reason why I was able to raise my rates so much—actually 90 percent or more of the reason—is because **my branding and reputation increased.**

You might not be able to increase your rate to that ridiculously high of a level, but if you are experienced and you have business right now, I can almost guarantee you that you can increase your rates.

But what should the actual rate be?

My simple answer is: **whatever the market will bear.**

Pricing on non-tangibles is entirely subjective.

I've known highly-paid programming consultants who billed corporate clients at $350 an hour while they sat around and did nothing, while other contractors on that same team did 90 percent of the work and billed out at $50 an hour or less.

So, while skill is important, it is a minor factor in determining rate.

The client will be the most important factor and reputation will be the second-most important factor.

You want to find the clients who are willing to pay the higher rates, and you'll find those clients and attract them mainly based on your reputation.

Your skills will help build your reputation, and they'll also make sure you don't get fired from the job you have, or have to give the money back.

One thing you may want to consider is **to move away from hourly pricing completely** and instead focus on what is known as value-based pricing.

Value-based pricing is where you price your services not on an hourly rate, but on an expected outcome for the client and what that outcome will be worth to your client.

Suppose I have a client who has a large ecommerce website and they want someone to build a module on it that will automate the processing of t-shirts, which they currently have to process manually.

I could determine how much that new system would save them in money, and then I could work out an offer to them based on that outcome.

Perhaps it will save that company a million dollars a year.

In that case, I could offer to do the job for $50,000, or even $100,000.

Maybe it only takes me 80 hours worth of work and **so I can actually make $625 to $1250 an hour.**

This would be a price no one would ever agree to pay when priced as an hourly rate, but when you look at it in terms of value-based pricing, it is a pretty good deal.

You can also price your services at a daily rate using a similar approach.

Most of the time if someone wants to hire me for some work, the minimum time I will allow someone to book me for is one day.

Then I price my daily rate at $5,000 a day or my weekly rate at $20,000 a week.

I've already taken up more space in this book talking about pricing, than I intended, so I'll stop here, but I recommend *Million Dollar Consulting* (https://simpleprogrammer.com/cg54-million) by Alan Weiss as an introduction to the topic. You can also check out an interview we did on Entreprogrammers, Episode 56, with Wes Higbee (https://simpleprogrammer.com/cg54-wes), where we talk about value-based pricing in depth.

STARTING A BUSINESS

Now let's shift slightly from freelancing to the general idea of starting a business, which incorporates freelancing.

Starting a business is easy; you just hang up a sign and say "open for business," and you are "in business."

Ok, maybe it's not quite that easy—there are a few legal hurdles you have to jump through depending on where you live—but for the most part it's really not all that difficult.

What is difficult is creating a profitable business, and maintaining that business and everything associated with operating a successful business.

As a software developer, you are in a great position to become an entrepreneur and start your own business.

You could be a freelancer, but you can also form a startup by creating an app or service that you sell.

Or, you can do what I do: produce content and teach what you know.

You have an advantage in that today it's much simpler to create a business online, especially if you know your way around the technology involved, and you've got more than a leg up on most people there.

Also, **one of the most profitable businesses to be in is that of software.**

Software businesses deliver a product that has almost no overhead, aside from the initial cost of creating the software, and that cost is greatly reduced if you can do it yourself.

(Oh, and before you start your business, read this book first, *The E-Myth Revisited* (https://simpleprogrammer.com/cg54-myth) by Michael Gerber. Trust me on this one.)

DON'T TRY TO GET IT PERFECT

Let's be honest, **most businesses fail.**

In fact, many fledgling business owners spend more time actually setting up their business, getting all the legal entities straightened out, creating that perfect logo, getting accounting software setup, and a bunch of other unnecessary stuff than they do actually operating the business.

What I mean by this, is that **many software developers who start their own business waste a huge amount of effort, time and money on things that don't really matter**, and they end up not having the energy to actually make the business itself successful.

My advice is: don't do that.

Assume the business is probably going to fail and then think about the smallest amount of work or overhead you can incur in getting it started.

I'm not a lawyer and this isn't legal advice, so don't sue me if you run into trouble, **but my non-professional opinion on this subject is to not even worry about legal entities, accounting, or anything else concerning your new business, until you are actually making a non-trivial amount of money** and can be pretty certain you will still be running the business a year from now.

The reason is simple and twofold: you want to exert as much of your energy as possible towards the things that really matter the most when you are first starting out, in order to give your new business the highest chance of success. And if you do fail or close shop, everything you've done that didn't make you money will be a complete waste, so you want to minimize that as much as possible.

It's really easy to get caught up in all those little details.

It's really easy to spend weeks and thousands of dollars working on a perfect logo or having your new website designed.

It's really easy to get sucked into the complex world of business law and tax accounting and worry about all of these little details.

So, avoid as much of them as possible for as long as possible.

Don't get me wrong.

I'm not suggesting you be careless and never address these important issues.

Not setting up proper accounting or the right legal entities for your business will eventually bite you in the ass—HARD—but it's best to know if your business is actually going to have chance of surviving—and to give it the best shot of doing so—before worrying about or investing in those things.

Plus, once you are making money with your business, these difficult matters become much easier to handle because you can hire professional help to get through them instead of having to try to figure it all out yourself.

DON'T QUIT YOUR JOB

One huge mistake many wannabe entrepreneurs make is to save up a bunch of money and quit their job so they can start their business (https://simpleprogrammer.com/cg54-quit).

It seems like a good plan, but it's a horrible one that often ends in disaster.

I don't know about you, but I don't like doing things with a gun to my head.

I don't perform as well.

Having six months or a year's worth of savings as a runway to get your business started and support yourself is a pretty big gun.

In fact, **the pressure can be crushing.**

When you have that kind of pressure on you, and you've never done something like this before, you are much more likely to sit in Starbucks all day procrastinating than actually getting any real work done.

Also, when you suddenly go from working a regular 9-to-5 job to having a bunch of freedom and sole responsibility for your own schedule, it is very easy to choke. Believe me, I've done it twice before.

So, **my suggestion is to not quit your job, at least not right away.**

Instead, **start whatever business you are going to start on the side, as a side business, while keeping your full-time employment.**

There are quite a few reasons I recommend taking this approach other than that whole gun-to-your-head thing—which is a pretty good reason in itself.

Another major reason for taking this approach is that you need to start getting accustomed to what it is like to be an entrepreneur, starting your own business.

And guess what it's like?

Well, it's surprisingly a lot like working a full-time job all day and then working four to six more hours on top of that—oh, and working weekends as well.

Believe me, if you aren't able to handle the sacrifice of working nights and weekends on top of a full-time job, you aren't going to cut it as an entrepreneur. You just aren't.

Better to find out now, while you still have that "cushy" job and haven't borrowed money from your friends and family or taken out a second mortgage on your house.

I'm not saying this to be mean.

Really, I'm not.

I just know, from experience, that **this shit is hard** and that you better be prepared for it.

Believe me, like I said, I've failed twice because I was not up to the task.

I actually quit my job twice.

It wasn't fun.

So, my best advice for you is to **start that business on the side.**

Get it running.

It might take you two years or more of working two jobs.

But at some point your side job will make you enough income that you can quit your regular job and make it your full-time job.

Notice I didn't say it will replace your income—that's not likely with a business you are running part time.

Instead, quit your job when your side income provides you just enough income for you to live on, which will likely be considerably less than you make at your full-time job.

Just another one of those sacrifices involved in becoming an entrepreneur.

BUILD AN AUDIENCE FIRST

I've mentioned this in various forms so far in this book, especially in regards to marketing yourself and building a reputation, but I want to spell it out here, because it's even more important that you do this if you are starting a business where you are selling something online.

Before you even start to create a product, or even think about charging money or finding customers, build an audience first.

Now, you don't have to take this advice.

There are plenty of businesses that were highly successful by building the product and then finding the audience, but I think it's a whole lot easier if you do it the other way around.

Many entrepreneurs have a great idea and then even build a great product from that idea.

So they have this shiny, awesome software that is perfect for solving someone's problems, but how do they find those someones and convince them to buy it?

They spend money on marketing to sell their product, tell everyone they meet about it, do everything they can to get customers, but more often than not, they run out of money and end up failing, all while having a perfectly great product.

It's difficult to get anyone to buy something from you without a relationship.

Consider the alternative.

At Simple Programmer, I have a pretty large audience of software developers.

At the time of writing this book, there are about 70,000 software developers on my email list, another 100,000 subscribed to my YouTube channel, and around 30,000 to 50,000 who visit one of my sites or properties each day.

If I decide to create a new product, I've got hundreds, if not thousands, of people ready to buy it immediately.

I don't have to go and hunt for customers.

My audience trusts me because I have a relationship with them.

They want me to produce things they can buy.

This makes the sale easy.

I also know what my audience wants and likes—another huge advantage.

Plus, **I can create multiple products and sell them to that same audience, rather than create one product, try to find customers for it, and have to start over if I want to create another product in the future.**

Consider this book: if you bought it, how did you end up buying it?

There is a pretty good chance you bought it because you saw one of my YouTube videos (https://simpleprogrammer.com/cg54-youtube), read a blog post I wrote, heard a podcast I was on or even read my earlier book.

Building an audience gives you a huge advantage.

It almost guarantees your success.

Yes, it takes extra effort.

Yes, it takes time and you don't make much money while you are building your audience.

And, yes, you have to create a large amount of free content.

But once you have an audience, you have a business which is not dependent on a single product and one that you can possibly tap into for the rest of your life.

LEARN HOW TO SELL

I can't think of one successful entrepreneur who isn't also a successful salesperson.

In fact, even if you never become an entrepreneur and never decide to start your own business, your salesmanship skills will likely be the limiting factor to your success in life.

We are always selling.

Everyone sells.

Some people just suck at it.

Whether you are trying to convince: your kids to go to bed without a hassle, your boss to give you a raise, or your coworkers that your way of doing things is the best way, you are selling.

Selling yourself, selling your ideas… and if you are an entrepreneur, selling your product. (Although, one might argue that the main thing an entrepreneur of any sort does is sell themselves and their vision for the world.)

Selling is difficult, though.

Not just because the techniques are difficult and non-obvious, but because **selling requires you to face one of the greatest fears in life: rejection.**

To sell is to face rejection.

But face rejection you must—especially if you want to be an entrepreneur.

So you are going to have to, as they say, suck it up, buttercup.

Fortunately, **sales is not that difficult to learn.**

There are plenty of books on the subject.

I'd recommend checking out anything by Grant Cardone, especially *Sell or Be Sold* (https://simpleprogrammer.com/cg54-sell).

You should also look into books on copywriting since selling online really is the same thing as copywriting.

I'd suggest starting with the books at Copy Hackers (https://simpleprogrammer.com /cg54-copy) for acquiring this skillset.

And one tried-and-true way to get good at sales is to just do it.

Get a part-time job doing phone sales or going door-to-door.

Don't worry about the money, get some real experience selling to people and facing rejection head on.

But, whatever you do, don't try to avoid mastering this skill.

You can't outsource sales if you are running a business.

You can hire a sales team, but you must be the master salesman first.

GET HELP

Simple Programmer would not exist today if it were not for Josh Earl, Derick Bailey, and Charles Max Wood.

These guys are also known as the Entreprogrammers (https://simpleprogrammer.com /cg54-entre).

They are part of a mastermind group I started a few years ago, which we made into a weekly video podcast.

What is a mastermind group?

It's basically **a group of people with different skillsets and businesses, but like-minded in their goals, who meet together on a regular interval to help each other succeed.**

Being an entrepreneur is difficult.

As the old man from Zelda says, "It's dangerous to go alone!"

You need to have some support—it's critical.

It doesn't have to be a mastermind group like mine, but you really need to have someone in your corner, encouraging you and cheering you on, because there are going to be plenty of times when you are going to want to just give up.

Like I said, these guys saved my business, because without them, not only would I have likely given up, but I wouldn't have got that cross-pollination of ideas which was so critical for Simple Programmer to grow and thrive.

Life as an entrepreneur is a rollercoaster.

One day you are on top of the world, the next day everything and everyone sucks.

Make sure you have some support so you can weather the storm.

IT'S DIFFICULT, BUT IT'S WORTH IT

I know I've painted a scary picture of entrepreneurship and starting your own business in this chapter—that was intentional.

I want you to know how hard it is going to be if you go down this path, so that you aren't unpleasantly surprised when the yellow brick road to Emerald City goes through some scary forests.

But **I also want you to know that being an entrepreneur is awesome!**

There is no better feeling in the world than knowing that your world is yours; that your life belongs to you; that you have made it on your own.

Every morning I wake up and get to decide what I am going to do that day.

Yes, I have a schedule.

Yes, I follow routines and have responsibilities.

But I've chosen them and they are up to me to decide.

I am literally the master of my fate and it feels good, man—damn good.

I get to decide how much money I am going to make.

I get to take a trip to Europe with my family for three months and still get paid and still be able to work.

Most importantly though, **I get to know that I've built something meaningful that positively impacts the lives of others.**

So even though the path is difficult, if you are up for it, I'd encourage you to join me on this wonderful journey.

CHAPTER 55

CAREER PATHS

Ding!

You have gained a level.

You are now a level 12 Web Developer.

You have unlocked a new JavaScript framework (https://simpleprogrammer.com/cg55 -javascript).

There are many career paths you can choose as a software developer.

And—just like a video game—there are paths within paths.

Where you ultimately end up in your software development career will be determined by the particular paths you choose.

Choose the wrong path and you'll end up a Kobold writing COBOL for the rest of your life.

Choose the right path and you just might become a white wizard or architect, living in your ivory tower and bestowing edicts from on high.

Ok, maybe it's not quite like that.

But **your career path choices do make a difference** (https://simpleprogrammer.com/cg55-paths); **they really do matter.**

Too many beginner programmers never take the time to consider what their actual career paths are and to deliberately choose which path and which guild they want to join.

Instead, they just stand on the sideroads shouting, "looking for group," and join any band of adventurers to come their way who will have them.

This chapter is all about making a conscious choice about which career path you want to pursue as a software developer, and that begins with enumerating your options.

THE THREE TYPES OF SOFTWARE DEVELOPERS

I classify software developers, at the highest level, into three broad categories.

You are probably not used to thinking about software developers and software development in terms of these three categories, because you might only really consider the largest of the three, where most software developers fall.

But, if we want to look at an exhaustive list of the software development career paths, we've got to start here.

With that said, here are the three broad categories of software developers:

- Career developers (most common)
- Freelancers (hired guns)
- Entreprogrammers (https://simpleprogrammer.com/cg55-entre) (programmer/entrepreneur hybrids)

Let's talk about each briefly.

First, we have the career developers.

In fact, most of this book is focused on career developers. And it's who we are going to be mostly focusing on in this chapter.

The reason is simple: most programmers either are, or at some point in their career were or will be, career developers.

A career developer, according to my definition, is a software developer who has a regular job working for someone else and getting a regular paycheck.

Most career developers want to work for a company they like, get promoted within that company, perhaps switch companies from time to time, make a good salary, and then perhaps retire some day.

Nothing wrong with this path. Like I said, it's the default.

Next up, we have the freelancer.

We talked about what a freelancer is in the last chapter, so I won't rehash it too much here.

Essentially, a freelancer is a software developer who works on their own, not owing allegiance to any particular company, instead choosing to operate as a hired gun and doing work for whatever client they choose to work for.

We won't cover that career path in this chapter, since we already talked about it earlier, and the freelancing career path really deserves its own book.

Finally we've got the kind of software developer who is most near and dear to my heart, since I am one of them, the entreprogrammer, or the software developer entrepreneur, developerneur if you will.

This career path is different than being a freelancer, because instead of using your software development skills to do work for someone else, you use them to create your own product or offering and sell that product or offering directly to clients.

This could be writing your own application that you sell, creating training videos or tutorials, blogging, writing, heck, even making music about your craft, and somehow making enough money from all that to put some macaroni and cheese on the dinner table each night.

We're not going to talk about that career path in this chapter, since, again, we really need a whole book to discuss how to be an entreprogrammer and we touched on the basics in the last chapter.

CAREER DEVELOPER OPTIONS

What follows next is what I think are the broad specializations you can pick as a software developer.

Note: This is not the same thing as the specializations I talked about in the chapter, Generalist vs. Specialist. The specializations in this chapter are far too broad.

Think of these specializations, which we will call options in order to limit confusion, as **very high-level career paths** you can choose to go down, in a technical sense, as a software developer.

To be clear, these options are not exclusive to career developers. Any kind of developer is going to have to choose one of these career paths.

You can pick multiple paths—you can "dual class"—but you should at least pick one.

WEB DEVELOPMENT

This is probably the largest class of software developers today.

Most software developers are web developers, or at least do some web development work.

As a web developer, you… well, make web applications. Surprise!

As a web developer, you can work on the front-end and make things pretty, you can work on the back-end and make things… work, or you can work on both and be an amazing, magical sort of web development unicorn—especially if you have some web design chops as well.

Typically web developers who can do it all, perhaps with the exception of web design, are called "full stack developers" since they develop on the full stack of web development technologies: front-end, middleware, back-end. (User interface, business logic, database.)

MOBILE

Apps man, apps is where it's at!

There is an app for that, you know.

Today, more and more software developers are choosing to become mobile developers, developing mobile applications for phones, tablets, even app-enabled TVs or wearable devices.

App development provides some exciting opportunities as a software developer, because more and more apps are coming out each year.

Just about every company needs a mobile app nowadays—and maybe even more than one.

DESKTOP

Software developers often write me to ask if desktop software development still exists.

I find this fantastical, because most of the time they typed that email from a computer running a desktop program—granted, it's usually a web browser, but it's still a DESKTOP program.

In fact, how do you write your code and compile it?

Most of us use desktop based IDEs, although cloud IDEs are getting more and more popular.

Ok, fine! I'll admit it, it's not looking good for desktop developers.

Are you happy? I said it.

But, in reality, I think there will always be at least some need for software developers who write applications that run directly on the PC.

I could be wrong, but at least for now, this is a viable career choice, just not a highly popular one.

VIDEO GAMES

Yes, I know you want to be a video game developer.

Yes, I do, too.

That's why I got into software development.

But instead of actually becoming a video game developer, I started programming printers, wrote a bunch of web applications, made some mobile apps, did a bunch of other things, and ended up writing books that drip with sarcasm and making a bunch of YouTube videos about how to pick up girls as a software developer.

Life is not always what you expect.

But, in all seriousness, this is a viable career option. It's just a difficult one with lots of competition, long hours working on video games, and well, I guess that's all the downside I can think of.

Damn, I should have gone down this route.

Go down this path—do it!

EMBEDDED SYSTEMS

Ok, this doesn't sound very lucrative or cool, but trust me, it is.

I was once an embedded systems developer making... printers!

YES! Printers!

Say it with me.

Say it with excitement!

EMBEDDED SYSTEMS ROCK!

You rock, baby!

Ok, it's not glamorous, but guess what, the refrigerator that just made that ice in the glass you are drinking out of... it's got brains in it.

Everything has brains in it nowadays.

And someone's got to write those brains.

And that someone could be YOU.

Embedded systems developers work on mostly real-time operating systems (https://simpleprogrammer.com/cg55-embedded), which run inside of electronics, hence the name *embedded* systems—clever, I know.

It's a good career choice, because it's in high demand and it requires specialized skillsets, which are highly valuable.

Some of the most difficult work I've ever done as a software developer has involved trouble-shooting really hairy timing issues on embedded systems' programs.

DATA SCIENCE

This one is a fairly new career path, but is appearing to be one of the most lucrative ones.

What exactly does a data scientist do?

No one really knows... I think it has something to do with "big data."

In all seriousness though, data science is a huge and fast-growing area that software developers can go into, especially if they want to make the big bucks.

A data scientist utilizes skills and technologies from several different fields to take large amounts of data, make sense of it, and draw conclusions and predictions.

Data scientists often utilize their programming skills to write custom programs to extract, manipulate and reorganize data in order to represent it in a digestible way.

With the ever-growing amount of data, data science definitely holds some interesting possibilities.

TOOLS AND ENTERPRISE

Many software developers don't actually create software that is commercially published and sold or used inside a product that is commercially sold. Instead, they create tools to be used within an organization or internal applications.

I actually find tools development to be extremely interesting and rewarding, because when you build an effective tool that helps your team or another team do their job better, the effect can be very noticeable.

Enterprise development can be very challenging and requires a unique set of abilities and knowledge since enterprise developers often have to have a deep understanding of the organization and the political factions which shape how software is crafted.

CLOUD

Cloud development is also a fairly new field, but also rapidly growing as more and more applications move to the cloud and a distributed model.

Most cloud applications are also web applications, but they don't necessarily have to be.

Cloud developers need to understand how the cloud works, especially in regards to scalability and availability.

With cloud IDEs, you can even be a cloud developer developing in the cloud.

AUTOMATION

It's a pretty amazing feeling when you watch an automated test you wrote run and automatically fill out fields in an application, click buttons, navigate around the app, and verify the results.

Test automation is fun.

I love it.

Not only is it fun, but it's rapidly expanding and in very high demand.

There is a serious lack of talented software developers who understand the proper way to create automation frameworks (https://simpleprogrammer.com/cg55-selenium) and write automated tests to test other software.

A software developer who focuses on test automation builds tools for automating the testing of applications and writes automated tests to execute and verify functionality.

Test automation can be extremely challenging and complex because it essentially requires you to write an application to test another application.

But, like I said, I think it's pretty fun.

ADVANCING BEYOND THE GLASS CEILING

In general, you'll find that even though you've picked a specific class of software developer to become—or perhaps more than one—you'll eventually hit what is known as the "glass ceiling."

This glass ceiling is the practical limit on how far you can advance or how much you can get paid as a software developer.

It doesn't matter how good you are, there is a point where you reach the top and you can't really advance any further.

But, there are ways around—or through—this glass ceiling.

First, you can choose to stop working for someone else.

As a freelancer your glass ceiling is much higher, although there is still a practical limit on how much you can make as a freelancer since **you still have to trade hours for dollars.**

As an entrepreneur, it's completely uncapped, but you could also make zero dollars or negative dollars.

Either of those choices are viable paths that can take you through that glass ceiling.

If you want to stay a career developer, you can invest heavily in your personal brand and marketing yourself, and you may be able to find a company which will pay you significantly more than average just because of your reputation.

In fact, I specifically created my "How to Market Yourself as a Software Developer" (https://simpleprogrammer.com/cg55-marketyourself) course to help you learn how to do this.

But, there is another way…

You can look for a large corporation to join and go down either a management or technical track.

MANAGEMENT OR TECHNICAL?

Most smaller or medium-sized companies have a practical limit on upward mobility.

As a software developer, you just can't get any higher than the highest level they have, which might not be that high at all.

But **at large corporations like Microsoft, Apple, IBM, Google, Facebook, HP, and others, the ceilings can be much higher.**

These kinds of companies often want the very best technical people available, so they create special technical tracks to incorporate them.

Usually these kinds of large companies either have a technical or a management track for advancement.

You'll have to choose if you want to go down the management road and leave behind your coding skills, or the technical track and keep on coding until they tell you you just can't code no more.

If you choose the management track, you might advance your career by becoming a developer manager, and then perhaps a section manager or project manager, and then work your way all the way up into executive level positions like a director of development, or even the chief technology officer (CTO).

HEY JOHN

Can anyone do the management track or do you need to be a "people" person?

Regardless of which path you choose, you need to be a people person.

Really, I mean that. You definitely should focus on your people skills if you want to be successful in your career.

This book doesn't focus on people skills as much, but read my other book, *Soft Skills: The Software Developer's Life Manual*, or Dale Carnegie's timeless classic, *How to Win Friends and Influence People*, if you feel like you could use a little work in this area.

As far as management, I would say that the biggest issue you are going to face is not whether you can be the kind of "people" person who can handle a managerial job, but rather whether you can be the kind of technical person who can live with not doing technical work.

Every time I have been put into any kind of managerial position, my biggest issue was always that I wanted to be writing the code and working in the technology.

Most software developers go into the profession because they like solving technical problems—not just to make a shit tonne of money.

So, really you should be asking yourself, can you handle not writing code for the rest of your career?

If you choose the technical track, you might go from senior developer to architect and then to a fellow or senior fellow.

Each organization is going to have its own specialized tracks for technical and non-technical advancement, so the titles and positions are going to vary greatly.

But if you reach that glass ceiling and you want to keep on advancing, you'll have to make a choice to either pursue the technical or management track.

In fact, if you are not at a large corporation that offers an advanced technical track, you might not even have a choice.

Going into management may be your only choice for advancement—well, either that or going out on your own.

ALWAYS BE THINKING ABOUT WHERE YOU ARE HEADING

Really, the point of this chapter is to get you to give some serious thought to where you are heading and to deliberately steer your career.

If you want to advance in your career, you need to know in what direction you are going.

So think carefully first about what kind of software developer you want to be.

Do you want to be a career developer forever?

If so, what kind?

A web developer? Mobile? Cloud?

And, to what end?

Do you want to eventually become an architect?

Do you just want to code and do cool stuff and not worry about advancing past a certain point?

Do you want to rise as high as you can?

If so, you'd better start looking for companies that have high-level technical tracks.

Perhaps you want to get into management eventually, or maybe you to become a CTO, or even CEO.

Or maybe you want to be a career developer earlier on in your career, and then transition to becoming a freelancer or even an entrepreneur.

Whatever you decide to do, it's important you make a decision and have a plan.

You can always change the plan later—you don't have to commit forever to a path once you pick it—but, you should always have at least some plan, otherwise you'll be aimlessly drifting in your career.

CHAPTER 56

JOB STABILITY AND SECURITY

Repeat after me:

There is no such thing as job security.

There is no such thing as job security.

Even in Japan, where for a long time it was generally understood that once you started working for a company, you worked for that company for life, those ways are coming to an end.

Yes, I know your parents told you everything would be okay if you to go to school, get good grades, become a college graduate, and find a good job with a good company.

Well, it's not ok!

Everything isn't going to be ok.

The world may have worked that way in the past, but it certainly doesn't now.

You can "do everything right" and not even get a job at all.

There is no such thing as seniority.

There is no such thing as entitlement.

There is no such thing as "paying your dues," at least not in terms of having some employer owe you something because you did it.

So, get the idea of job security and stability out of your head right now.

Get comfortable with being uncomfortable.

Get comfortable with facing the unknown and trading your expectations for adaptation, and paradoxically, that job security and stability you are seeking will come to you.

Just in a different way than you expect.

IT'S UNSTABLE, AND THAT'S OK

You might be thinking everything I said above was to shock you a little bit and now I'm actually going to tell you that it is going to be alright and it is all going to be ok.

I'm not.

It's not.

And that IS ok.

The world will never be like it was.

Regardless of what any political candidate says, the "jobs" are not coming back.

They are gone forever and how we work has changed and continues to change.

You just can't expect to get a job with a company and stay there for 20 or 30 years until you get a retirement or pension anymore.

There is too much disruption.

The rate of change is too damn fast.

Take a look at Blackberry.

Blackberry was the king of the mobile market.

No one saw them going anywhere and then BOOM, overnight they were circling the drain.

So, even if you had a great job as a software developer at Blackberry and you had been there for years, you suddenly found yourself in a place where you didn't quite feel that stable anymore.

The truth is, you never were.

And wherever you are now, or wherever you are hoping to be, you are not stable there either.

It's just the nature of the current work environment, and it goes both ways.

These days employers can't count on their employees being there forever, either.

It used to be a black mark on your resume to have worked for multiple companies in a fairly short timespan. Now it's the norm.

The sooner you realize this, the better off you'll be, because it greatly affects the choices you make.

Think about it.

If you are looking for a job and expect to be working at whatever company hires you for the next 20 years of your life, you are very likely to make a different decision than if you assume you might only be there for a few years at the most.

Too many software developers are acting like it's still the 1970s. It's not.

Too many software developers are picking jobs at "stable" companies instead of taking better, "riskier" opportunities, because they think that a big behemoth of a company can't go down as fast as a startup. WRONG.

Accept that the current business world, especially where technology is concerned, is inherently unstable.

Do you have an "oh shit" plan, a playbook you can start executing immediately if your boss walks in tomorrow and hands you a pink slip? You can download an "in case of emergency, break glass" emergency job hunt toolkit right here (https://simpleprogrammer.com /career-guide-toolkit). Knowing exactly what you'd do in this situation will remove the fear and give you confidence that you can handle anything that comes at you.

Stop trying to find stability; instead, work on making yourself more robust and adaptable so that you are always employable.

JOB SECURITY DOESN'T COME FROM HOARDING KNOWLEDGE

We'll get back to talking about stability in a bit, but before we do, I want to take a moment to tackle job security, because some of the things people do to try and achieve job security are ass-backwards and pretty damn lame, if you ask me.

One of the worst things that many software developers do when trying to be more secure is hoard knowledge.

Instead of openly sharing what they are learning, and teaching other people how to do their jobs so life will still go on if they get hit by a bus, they do the opposite.

They **purposely convolute things** and try to make sure they are the only person who knows how the build system works or how to work on this hairy part of the architecture.

They are trying to create an environment where if they do get hit by a bus, the world would basically end.

Well, well, I got news for you.

It doesn't matter how important you think you are, or what "secrets" you know, the world does go on.

Your guts are cleaned off the grill of the bus, someone else gets hired to do your job, and everyone else puts together the pieces to finally figure out how you did what you did.

And when they do, they realize that what you were doing wasn't all that important after all—they could have gotten rid of you a long time ago (and they probably should have, asshole).

Don't do this.

This is NOT the way to create job security.

It's just going to piss people off and make you less valuable, not only to your current company, but to any other company.

You could have been spending all that time and effort learning new things (https://simpleprogrammer.com/cg56-learning), teaching other people what you learned and improving your own skills, but instead you wasted it, trying to hold onto something you can't hold onto anyway.

Perhaps you could have mild success at this technique and temporarily hold a company hostage, but **eventually, they'll pull off the duct tape, kick their feet through a loose floorboard, and go running down the street.**

You can't stop progress.

INSTEAD, DO THE OPPOSITE

Ironically, **you can achieve the highest level of job security by purposely trying to make yourself unnecessary.**

I know it seems counterproductive and I know that many well-meaning elders may have given you the advice to not give away all your secrets or you won't be needed anymore.

But, it turns out that **the most valuable employees any company can have are the ones who make their own jobs unnecessary** by automating as much of it as possible and training other employees to be able to do what they can do.

And yes, if you make your job unnecessary, you won't keep that job, but you won't get fired either.

You'll get promoted.

That's where real job security lies—being so valuable that everything you touch turns to gold, so you just keep being put in charge of more and more things to touch.

You see, **as a lone software developer working for a company, you can only do so much.**

You can be a very good coder, but you are going to have some real limits on what you can accomplish in a day.

But if you can help your fellow software developers accomplish more, or you can automate parts of your job so that you don't have to manually do them anymore, **you are using the power of leverage to become way more effective than any single employee** working on their own.

The more you share what you know, the more valuable you become, and that is the only true form of job security that exists today.

REPLACE STABILITY WITH ABILITY

Ultimately, job stability and security is best achieved not by securing that perfect job with that stable company and holding the company hostage with critical secrets about how to do your job that only you know, but rather **by becoming more valuable by both accumulating knowledge and sharing it freely.**

Instead of trying to play political games to secure your position and betting on the right horse of stability, **how about setting yourself up so that you don't need job security or stability?**

Why not consider the strategy of **increasing your own abilities to the point where you can easily get a new job whenever you want**, instead of putting your hopes into one company or one job at a particular company?

Become so valuable that companies will be clamoring to hire you and suddenly job security and stability seems like a silly notion.

This is the better strategy, because this strategy relies on what you can control—you—instead of on external factors you cannot control.

And, like I said before, times have changed.

Today, there is only an illusion of job security and stability.

So, it's a much more profitable and intelligent strategy to become self-reliant (https://simpleprogrammer.com/cg56-mindset) by increasing your ability than to count on any kind of security or stability in any job.

CREATE YOUR OWN SAFETY NET

One of the best ways to never have to worry about job security or stability again is to create your own safety net of three to six months of living expenses saved up for a rainy day.

I am constantly amazed how many software developers, and people in general, live paycheck to paycheck.

It just doesn't make any sense and there is no excuse for it.

If you are living paycheck to paycheck, you are putting yourself in what I call a "squeeze" situation (https://simpleprogrammer.com/cg56-squeeze), where if one thing goes wrong in your life, financially it can set off a cascade of problems until your whole life can self-destruct right before your eyes.

If you are relying on your next paycheck to pay your rent and other bills, of course you are going to be overly concerned about job security and stability, because losing your job is going to have drastic effects on your life.

But if you've got a nice savings cushion of a few months of living expenses, you don't necessarily want to lose your job, but if you do, it's not a huge deal because you have plenty of time to find another one—a better one.

Now when I say this, most people agree.

They nod their heads and say "Yeah, that makes sense."

But then they tell me that they wish they could save a few months of living expenses, but **they just can't right now.**

They tell me some sob story about the bills they have or how they are barely making enough to get by as it is and that once they get that raise or they pay off that car, then they'll start saving and building their safety net.

Bullshit!

I don't care how little or how much you make, **there is no reason why you can't start putting away at least 10 percent of your income into a reserve account today**—TODAY!

If you think you can't afford it, you are living far beyond your means.

Perhaps you need to get a smaller house or an older car.

Perhaps you need to stop eating out five times a week and stop going out to the movies.

Perhaps you don't need that expensive data plan on your cell phone. Heck, maybe you can do without a cell phone completely for a while.

Cut out cable, pack your lunch, downsize your car, your house, **do whatever it takes to get to the point where you can save at least 10 percent of what you are earning** so you can start building that reserve.

If you start now, you can have three months worth of living expenses saved up in a couple of years.

Then you'll never have to worry about job security again.

Won't that feel great?

Isn't that worth a small sacrifice?

For the past 10 years, I've always had at least a year's worth of reserves saved up.

Do you know the power you have when you have a year's worth of living expenses in your bank account?

You can literally tell your boss to f-off and not care, because you've got enough runway to spend a whole year looking for another job. (Not that this is recommended.)

It feels great.

Plus, you never have to balance a checkbook again.

I can't remember the last time I had to balance my checkbook.

And it's not because I'm rich and have a ton of money. It's because **I make sure that I always live far below my means** so that I will never be put into a squeeze situation.

Even when I made far less than I do now, I still had plenty of reserves saved up and didn't worry about losing my job or balancing my checkbook.

One of the best books on this subject, which I highly recommend, is called *The Richest Man in Babylon* (https://simpleprogrammer.com/cg56-babylon).

I highly recommend you read that book and commit to living by its principles.

HEY JOHN

I love what you're saying but I can't get my spouse onboard. They are out of control with spending. Help!

This is a tough one.

Unfortunately, there isn't really an easy or one-size-fits-all solution, but here is some general advice.

First of all, recognize that you can't control other people and what they do—even your spouse—but, you can control what you do.

So, even though your spouse may be sabotaging your efforts to get your spending under control, you can still exercise principled restraint and frugality, which will at least make some impact and will also serve as an example.

Often leading by example is the best way to get someone to do something.

If you start acting wiser with monetary decisions and start being more frugal, there is a good chance your spouse will eventually start to develop some of the same habits—not guaranteed, but worth a try.

Secondly, make sure you've communicated clearly to your spouse exactly what kind of financial changes you'd like to make and why.

Try to do it in a non-judgmental way, but be very clear about what you want and talk in terms of what you intend to do, not in terms of what you are requiring your spouse to do.

Ask the question, "how can we achieve this goal together?" in order to create buy-in and the feeling of a joint effort.

Finally, recognize you are ultimately in charge of your own life.

If you have a spouse that isn't willing to cooperate at all with your financial plans, you might want to reevaluate whether you want to spend the rest of your life living paycheck-to-paycheck.

I'm not suggesting you get a divorce if your spouse insists on buying Gucci handbags or the latest tech gadget, but you might want to think carefully about what you will and will not allow in your life and how important it is to you.

You may need to set clear boundaries and say that you will not allow your financial future to be jeopardized and make it very clear in what ways you feel that the actions of your spouse are doing so and then take appropriate action.

Remember, in life you always have three choices for any given situation:

1. Accept it
2. Change it
3. Remove yourself from it

If you can't accept it or change it, you may have to remove yourself from it.

EMBRACING UNCERTAINTY

I'll end this chapter with one final nail in the job-security-and-stability coffin: **embrace, instead of avoid, uncertainty.**

Last year, I went to one of Tony Robbins' most famous seminars called Date With Destiny (https://simpleprogrammer.com/cg56-tony).

It's an extensive six-day program where you basically deconstruct and then reconstruct yourself and your life based on the values that you want to live your life by.

It's a life-changing event—I highly recommend it.

Anyway, at this seminar, he said something that was extremely powerful, fundamentally altering the way I look at life and changing my whole outlook on stability and certainty.

*"The quality of your life is in direct proportion to the amount
of uncertainty you can comfortably live with."*
(https://simpleprogrammer.com/cg56-uncertainty)

You see, up until that point in my life I was chasing certainty, security and stability.

I was trying to build up an impenetrable fortress around my life, my finances, and my future.

I was trying to make it so nothing bad could possibly happen to me.

I wanted to nail down every floorboard, make my ship unsinkable.

I spent a great deal of my life trying to achieve this goal.

But, I realized by doing this, I **was actually decreasing the overall quality of my life.**

Not only was I decreasing my overall life quality, but I was also trying to achieve an impossible goal.

No matter how much money you have, or how good your job is, or how much you've tried to protect and hold on to what you have, there is always some risk.

There is always some chance that whatever you have could be taken away from you.

When you do everything in your power to prevent that from happening, you suck the joy right out of life.

Instead, I've found that by actually embracing uncertainty, paradoxically, like Tony said, the quality of my life dramatically improved.

When I made that pivot in my own life, all of a sudden I wasn't as stressed out.

I still work hard and I still try to make wise decisions, but I do what I can and then I leave the rest up to fate.

I can't control fate and I don't even bother trying.

Life is much more enjoyable when you don't try to control things you have no control over and you are willing to accept whatever comes your way—it's also more exciting.

My final piece of advice for you would be to **embrace uncertainty**. (A good book on this subject is Mark Manson's *The Subtle Art of Not Giving a Fuck* (https://simpleprogrammer.com /cg56-subtle).)

Yes, it's a good idea to increase your abilities so that you can find a new job much more easily.

Yes, it's a great idea to make yourself more valuable at your current position by sharing all the knowledge you can instead of hoarding it.

Yes, it's a fantastic idea to build your own safety net so that no matter what happens to you financially you can weather the storm.

But, you can do all that and still be taken by what one of my favorite authors, Nicholas Taleb, calls a black swan event, and lose it all.

So, why not embrace uncertainty and just accept it as a natural part of life?

CHAPTER 57

TRAINING AND CERTIFICATIONS

I don't know about you, but **I don't like wasting my time. Or my money.** Or both.

And there are certainly plenty of ways to waste your time and your money.

Take playing World of Warcraft, for instance.

I wasted plenty of time and money doing that, although I guess not all that much money—more the time, really.

I've also wasted plenty of money.

Early in my real estate investment days, I made a $10,000 down payment on some fourplexes that were supposed to be constructed later that year.

My real estate agent warned me, my lender warned me, the title company said the builder wasn't "reputable."

But did I listen?

No.

The good news is, I did get to claim a $10,000 loss of bad debt on my next year's tax return.

Anyway, even though this chapter might appear to be about how stupid I am (plenty), it's actually not about that at all. It's about training and certifications.

Yes, really.

You see, **you can spend—and waste—plenty of time and money on training and certifications and get nothing for it, or you can make wise investments and get the biggest bang for your buck.**

But the path is not always clear.

So, let's make it a little more clear, shall we?

ARE CERTIFICATIONS WORTH IT?

The first question most software developers inevitably ask is whether or not certifications are "worth it." (https://simpleprogrammer.com/cg57-certification)

As in, **is it worth spending my money and my time to get a certification?**

Well, as any good consultant or lawyer likes to say, "it depends."

It depends on what you hope to get out of a certification.

If you hope to actually learn something useful that is going to make you much better at your job and cause everyone who sees the new set of initials after your name on your resume to worship you and offer you a job where you can name your price, then no.

No, it's not worth it.

I've gotten plenty of certifications in my career and I can tell you that in getting them, I didn't really learn anything useful.

Sure, I temporarily memorized the exact syntax for some obscure ASP.NET library call.

And sure, I got some pretty wide-breadth knowledge about the different technologies and tools I got certified in, but it was nothing I couldn't have learned just as easily on my own without studying for a certification.

I also found that **having certifications didn't really make my job search any easier.**

In some ways it made it a bit more difficult at interviews, because the interviewer would automatically take an aggressive stance and ask if I thought my certifications meant I actually know something, or would tell me about how **they think certifications are bullshit.**

Haha, that's a fun situation to be in.... just smile and nod.

Let them get all that misdirected anger out.

It's not your fault their parents never really loved them.

Anyway, that's not to say that certifications are all bad and completely worthless.

I'm just saying that a certification on it's own doesn't mean all that much; it's not going to make a huge difference in your career.

WELL THEN, WHY WOULD YOU GET A CERTIFICATION THEN, JOHNNY BOY?

Good question.

I'm glad you asked... youie... you.

Although a certification is not necessarily going to get you a great job alone, it can be an enhancement, especially if you are applying for a job with a consulting company.

Many consulting companies who happen to be official Microsoft solution providers require the software developers they hire to either have Microsoft certifications or to get them shortly after being hired.

In this case, already having a certification—or more than one—is going to make it easier to get a job with one of these companies.

A certification can also help you when you don't have a large amount of experience and/or a college degree.

It might not convince someone that you are an expert, but it will indicate that you at least know what you are doing and have spent the time and follow through it takes to actually complete a certification.

A certification can also **help you look like more of an expert in your niche or specialty** if it's directly related to that specialty.

And if you are already employed, a certification is a good way to show that you are making progress towards self-improvement and in your overall skills, so it could help you get a promotion.

At one point in my career I was stuck and finding it difficult to climb up the corporate ladder because my work wasn't challenging and I wasn't being given the opportunity to work on anything more challenging due to my level in the organization.

I decided to start getting as many Microsoft certifications as I could.

I ended up getting six Microsoft certifications that year and getting my MSCD (https://simpleprogrammer.com/cg57-mcsd) and MSDBA credentials.

When review time came around, **I had a really good argument for a raise and promotion** into to a higher-level position.

I didn't learn a huge amount from getting the certifications, but I demonstrated grit and determination, and that is what made the difference.

HOW TO GET A CERTIFICATION

I've completed many certifications in my software development career, and I can tell you that getting a certification is all about one thing and one thing only: **learning how to take that particular certification test.**

In order to get a certification, at least all the ones I know of, you must study the test, not the material itself. (https://simpleprogrammer.com/cg57-pass)

This is one of the flaws of certifications and why they aren't taken as seriously as you might think.

Once you've passed a certification, you realize quickly that **the exam was really only testing you on your ability to take that particular exam**, not really based on what you know.

(I know some people aren't going to like that I'm saying this—and I admit there may be some certification tests I have not taken, which do overcome this drawback.)

I do realize that the people who create the certification exams don't try to make it this way on purpose, but it's very difficult to test someone on their programming ability or knowledge in a particular area in some kind of standardized test.

Regardless of why, the reality is that if you want pass a certification, you need to specifically study for taking that certification exam.

All the prep books are not going to help you nearly as much as studying the actual practice questions for the exam.

I've found the Transcender practice exams (https://simpleprogrammer.com/cg57-transcender) to be the best ones for practicing most certification exams.

Their questions seem to be very close to the actual questions that will be asked on the exam.

Don't get me wrong, **I'm not saying just study for the exam by only taking practice exams.**

You should also study the actual material and content that the exam is supposed to be testing you on, perhaps even read an exam prep book.

But the majority of your ability to pass the exam will likely come from taking practice exams with software like Transcender (https://simpleprogrammer.com/cg57-transcender).

Also, don't be afraid to take the exam as soon as you think you are ready.

So what if you fail?

For most certifications, you can just try again at a much reduced fee or even for free and you'll learn about what you need to study.

WHAT ABOUT TRAINING?

While certifications are typically not useful for actually increasing your knowledge or skills in a meaningful way, training is more of a mixed bag.

There is good training and there is bad training.

Good training can **accelerate your learning** a lot, **helping you learn a new skill** or master one much faster than you can on your own.

But **bad training is just a waste of time and money**—and can even be detrimental if you are being taught the wrong concepts.

The most valuable training is the kind of training where you are able to assimilate a large amount of information or experience into a much shorter period of time than you would spend studying on your own.

You really want to look for the kind of training that offers you something more than what you can easily do on your own.

For example, suppose you were trying to learn a new programming language.

If you could go to a training where an expert in that language was able to condense the most important concepts you needed to know down to a three-day course, it would probably be very valuable, since this wouldn't likely be something that you could very easily do on your own.

You would also benefit from the immersive experience of working with that programming language for three days straight uninterrupted.

So, **look for trainings that are going to provide you shortcuts for learning.**

When I give training (https://simpleprogrammer.com/cg57-pluralsight), I always try to teach three things:

1. How to quickly get started.
2. The big picture and overview of what the technology can do.
3. The 20 percent you need to know to handle 80 percent of what you'll do with that technology.

The idea is to accelerate students in the areas where they would likely struggle the most on their own.

It can be difficult to know how to get started, so having someone show you how is valuable and can save you time.

Likewise, when you are starting with a technology, it's difficult to know the full scope of that technology and those unknown unknowns—what you don't know that you don't know.

By giving a broad overview of a topic and revealing the scope of the technology, a large amount of time is saved by converting unknown unknowns into known unknowns, which are much more Googleable if you get stuck.

Finally, by teaching the 20 percent that gives you 80 percent of the benefit of the technology, it saves a huge amount of time, because as a beginner, it's difficult to know what is important.

And don't forgot to look outside the realm of software development for training that can help develop you in other areas of your life.

I've made personal investments in training/seminars from Tony Robbins, internet marketing, fitness, business, and other areas of my life. I have found it to be immensely valuable—both on a personal and professional level.

WHAT KINDS OF TRAINING ARE AVAILABLE?

Typically, training can be broken up into two categories: online or live/instructor-led training. And of course, there are hybrid versions of these.

There is a huge amount of online training available at an extremely low cost.

It's really amazing how much quality training is available online today, and how cheap it is.

For just about anything you want to learn, you can find training online.

I'm a bit biased, since I created 55 courses for the company, but **I highly, highly recommend all software developers get a subscription to Pluralsight** (https://simpleprogrammer.com /cg57-pluralsight)**.**

In my mind, **it's one of the best possible investments you can make in your software development career** because of the huge number of available courses on every technical topic and programming language you can think of, and the cost is extremely low.

Other places to get online training are: TreeHouse, Lynda, Udacity, Udemy, and many others.

I offer my own online training with some of my more specialized courses like:

* "How to Market Yourself as a Software Developer" (https://simpleprogrammer.com/cg57-marketyourself)
* "10 Steps to Learn Anything Quickly" (https://simpleprogrammer.com/cg57-10steps)
* "Simple Real Estate Investing for Software Developers" (https://simpleprogrammer.com/cg57-realestate)

- "10 Ways to Make Money With Your Blog"
  (https://simpleprogrammer.com/cg57-money)

And you can of course find plenty of good, **free training on sites like YouTube.**

You can also find plenty of the traditional live training, but it's usually a little more expensive and takes more time, since you actually have to show up at a physical location.

Still though, **I don't think live training will ever go away, because it is so valuable.**

Live training offers you **a more interactive experience** and lets you communicate with the trainer, as well as others who are participating in that training.

One of the best ways to learn is to have a feedback loop where you can ask questions and get immediate answers; live training usually supports this kind of mechanism.

And while you often have to travel for live training, **that full immersion can be extremely valuable** for learning a subject rapidly since you are less likely to be distracted—you've got nowhere else to go.

I went to Tony Robbins' Date With Destiny seminar (https://simpleprogrammer.com/cg57-tony) and it's a fully immersive experience.

For six days you are in the seminar hall for around 14 to 16 hours each day.

You really only have time to sleep—and you get little of that.

But it's an amazing experience because it is so immersive.

You can get a large amount of the same information and exercises from Tony's book *Awaken the Giant Within* (https://simpleprogrammer.com/cg57-awaken), but it's a much more valuable experience when you attend the seminar because you are forced to dedicate six full days of your life to working on yourself and actually doing the exercises.

So, I'm a big proponent of live training if only because **it forces you to focus and immerse yourself in what you are trying to learn.**

You can usually find live training offered on a large number of subjects and often companies bring in trainers to teach a specific topic.

Also, many conferences offer workshops before or after the conference in which some of the speakers will offer some kind of training on the subjects they are experts in.

MAKING THE MOST OF TRAINING

Attending training is not enough.

Just because you sat in the same room with someone who's an expert on the topic and you got a little certificate that says you are "certified" or attended, doesn't mean you actually learned anything or improved your skills in any meaningful way.

If you want to get the most out of any training, you have to do what Tony Robbins calls "playing full out."

That means that when you go to a training event or participate in some kind of training, you shouldn't just listen and do the exercises or activities that appeal to you, but instead, you should give it your best and participate as much as possible.

Turn off your cell phone, don't check your email, don't try to work on "emergency work stuff" while you are at the training.

If you can't devote some serious time to your personal development, don't bother with the training in the first place because it will just be a waste of time and money.

You get out of training what you put into it.

So, the first rule is to **be selective in the training you attend and pursue.**

Make sure it's actually good and valuable training that is worth your time.

Don't just go to a training because it's offered to you, and don't just attend training because it's free, heavily discounted, or you feel like you should be "doing something valuable."

Instead, be selective and vet out training before you even participate in it.

Next, **plan ahead.**

Clear your schedule.

Make arrangements so that you will not and cannot be interrupted during the training, so that you can actually get the most out of it.

Yes, shit happens, but if I'm at training or doing something important, I make sure that no one can get a hold of me when it does.

You are not as important as you think you are. Someone else can handle it—trust me.

Finally, when you actually attend the training, like I said before, **play full out.**

HEY JOHN

Why do you keep plugging Tony Robbins and talking about Tony Robbins all the time? Are you drinking the kool-aid?

Hah, I get it, I get it.

It might seem that I'm a huge Tony Robbins fanboy and that I have some hidden agenda in plugging his content and training; perhaps that I'm getting some kind of huge kickback for doing so, or that I've joined some kind of Tony Robbins cult.

First off, I'm not getting paid to promote Tony Robbins (at least not at the time of writing this chapter)—although I suppose I should be looking into a referral program.

So, there isn't really a financial incentive.

Secondly, although I'm a fan of what Tony Robbins says, and his books and programs have been very impactful in my life, it doesn't mean I'm 100% on board with everything he says—for example, I don't agree with much of his health and fitness advice.

But, I do find what he says to be extremely helpful and useful for most people—myself included.

So, that's why I talk about him and recommend him.

> I don't have very many people in my life who I would consider to be true mentors, but Tony Robbins is certainly one of them.
>
> But, just like any person, he has his faults, he's not 100% correct all the time and you shouldn't follow him blindly.

GETTING YOUR EMPLOYER TO PAY FOR TRAINING

Training can be expensive.

For example, **that Tony Robbins Date With Destiny seminar I attended was about $5,000 a ticket**, plus I had to pay for travel and accommodations.

So, it might be a good idea to figure out a way to get your employer to pay for you to attend training.

(Although I'd argue that even if your employer refuses, you should be willing to pay money out of your own pocket to invest in yourself.)

How though, do you get your employer to pay for your training?

Simple. **You make it into an investment that will yield a good return.**

This starts with vetting the training to make sure that it is actually valuable.

Online training, like Pluralsight (https://simpleprogrammer.com/cg57-pluralsight), should be a no brainer.

Every employer should pay for their software developers to have access to Pluralsight (https://simpleprogrammer.com/cg57-pluralsight)**.**

It's very easy to demonstrate the return on investment, since access is extremely low cost.

Just show your boss how much time you save by having quick access to training on just about any technical topic you want, versus you having to hunt for information, possibly buy books and read them, or figure it out on your own.

You could also contrast it to live, in-person training, and show how much cheaper it is to just buy a Pluralsight subscription.

HEY JOHN

Umm, how about Pluralsight; any financial incentive there or kool-aid drinking going on?

Well, yes, this is the case and there is a bit of both.

Ok, well not so much the kool-aid drinking, but definitely a financial incentive.

I do get paid for Pluralsight referrals... I know *gasp*.

And I have also created courses for Pluralsight, so if you go to Pluralsight and watch my courses, I do get an increase on the percentage of royalties from those courses.

But, even with a bunch of Pluralsight referrals and you watching my Pluralsight courses, it's really not going to move the needle much in terms of my income.

Honestly, the real reason I plug Pluralsight so much in this book is just because of what a ridiculous deal it is for high-quality training. I really think every software developer should have a subscription, because it's such a great investment in your career.

It's really difficult to convey just how valuable it is to have all of this on-demand training for almost any technical topic you can think of.

So, yes, I am slightly biased, and if you are opposed to me making money from promoting Pluralsight or still think that's my sole motivation, go ahead and sign up without using my affiliate link—just go directly to the Pluralsight website—and don't watch any of my courses.

Really, I wouldn't want you to miss out on something that is so valuable to your career just because you might not trust me.

But **if you are trying to get your employer to pay for the more expensive live training, and the travel that goes with it, you might have to be a little more strategic.**

You might want to offer to take copious notes during the training and share what you learn with the rest of your team. This way you can take the cost of the training and divide it by the number of software developers on your team, which should be a much more palpable number.

You can also talk about the expected results and outcomes that you anticipate the training will produce in the company or business.

Remember **there are three ways for a business to make more money** (https://simpleprogrammer.com/cg57-hiring):

1. Increase the number of customers.
2. Increase the value from each customer.
3. Reduce the cost to deliver and support the product or service to the customer.

How can the training do one of those three things, or perhaps all of them?

You might also ask if there is a training budget; if not, ask if you can have a training budget each year.

Some companies already have training budgets set up, and some larger corporations have a policy of paying for a certain number of trainings per employee per year.

Finally, see if you can get the training to come to you.

See if your employer will pay for training for your whole team by hiring on-site training.

In this case, travel costs are reduced and you can get personalized hands-on training and perhaps hire the trainer for an extra day of consulting.

I often make myself available for this kind of training, so if you are interested, **you could ask your employer to hire me to come to your office** to give training directly to your team.

BECOMING A TRAINER

Speaking of training, have you ever considered being the one who gives it?

If you are an experienced software developer, especially if you have expertise in a specific area, you may be able to advance your career and make some decent money by becoming a trainer.

There are always companies looking to hire outside consultants and trainers to come and give their software development teams training.

Like I said, I give this kind of training, and I charge around $10,000 a day for it.

This seems like a large amount, but if you have a team of 10 software developers, that's about $1,000 a person for training, which is a bargain for personalized, hands-on training, if you ask me—I'm biased, of course.

You can also **offer to do workshops at conferences**, especially if you have a popular topic that you can give hands-on training about. (Although in that case, you'll probably be splitting your fee with the conference organizers.)

Even though online training is all the rave these days, there are still plenty of companies who specialize in providing in-person training.

They are often looking for new trainers, and in many cases will even give you the material to do the training.

So, if you have a knack for teaching and have some specialized skills, you might want to actually consider giving some training yourself.

IT'S ALL ABOUT WHAT YOU PUT INTO IT

Well, that just about sums up all I've got to say for now about certifications and training, but I want to leave you with one important point.

It's all about what you put into it.

Certifications and training are not valuable by themselves, just like a college education isn't necessarily valuable.

Like many things in life, it's about what you put into it that counts—that effort is what determines the value you get out of it.

You can't get muscles by just going to the gym and sitting on a bench while chatting to your friends, or by making various poses in front of the mirror—although, I knew plenty of people who try.

The same goes for your software development career.

So, go out there, pick up some dumbbells, pump some iron, and play full out!

CHAPTER 58

SIDE PROJECTS

I don't know a single software developer who hasn't thought of starting a side project.

I, myself, have had many different side projects throughout my career.

Well, I should be more clear by saying that I *started* many side projects throughout my career.

To be honest, **most of them didn't get finished.**

To be honest, most them didn't really get started.

You see, there is a huge difference between a dream and a goal.

A dream is something you chase and a goal is something you do (https://simpleprogrammer.com /cg58-goals)—something you make happen.

I used to be a dreamer.

I used to chase ideas… dreams.

I've always been involved in some side project, but **I haven't always been committed** (https:// simpleprogrammer.com/cg58-half).

In fact, I can trace my life and career back to a single moment in time where things drastically changed—a single inflection point.

That inflection point was one of the first side projects I actually finished.

I wanted to learn Android development and to create an Android application, so I decided to make an app called PaceMaker, which I eventually renamed to "Run Faster" due to a trademark dispute. (Long story.)

HEY JOHN

I like long stories. That's why I picked up this MASSIVE book.

Ok, well you asked for it.

So, initially I created my Android app—and later an iOS version—called PaceMaker.

I didn't do any research on trademarks or the name, because I really didn't think about it and didn't think it was a big deal.

The app was designed to tell you if your running pace was too fast or too slow based on your target pace. It would tell you either "speed up" or "slow down," based on if you were too fast or too slow.

Initially the app sold pretty well. I got a mention in Shape magazine early on and that sold a bunch of copies of the app, but eventually things dried up and I'd sell perhaps 4-5 copies of the app per week.

(I actually still make about $30-$50 a month from the app and haven't updated it in years.)

Well, one day, I got an email from a company that makes DJing software called "Pace-Maker." (https://simpleprogrammer.com/cg58-pacemaker)

They had the Trademark on the name PaceMaker and asked me to change the name of my app.

I wasn't sure of all the legal repercussions of saying "no," and whether they had a case or not since my app was a running app and theirs was in the music industry, but I decided that the smartest thing I could possibly do would be to ask them for some compensation for going through the trouble of changing the name of my application and giving them the email address, Twitter account, etc for the name PaceMaker.

You might think "no way they would pay you for a name they already have a legal right to," but you'd be wrong.

I won't go into the exact details of the negotiation here, but let's just say that I arrived at a price that made it well worth my time to make a quick name change in the app store and change the password on the PaceMaker Gmail account.

Anyway, I worked on this side project, just as I had worked on many other unfinished side projects, until I got bored with it and decided to quit.

But then, something happened.

Instead of quitting, **I dug in my heels.**

I said to myself, "John, you are going to finish this app and put it into the Android app store. It doesn't matter how long it takes, but you are going to work on this app at least an hour each day, until it's done."

That was the moment everything changed.

That was the moment I became a finisher (https://simpleprogrammer.com/cg58-finisher).

Finishing that one side project led to opportunities upon opportunities and other side projects, which eventually took me to where I never thought I'd be today; writing a book, making videos, owning my own company, and essentially being retired.

Fifteen or so years of my previous work experience didn't make as much of a difference in my career and life as the one, small side project that I finally finished.

That side project is still in the Google Play store today. In fact, there is an iOS version as well.

I haven't updated it in years, but it still makes me just a little bit of money each month and reminds me of just how important a little side project was to my career.

YOU SHOULD ALWAYS HAVE A SIDE PROJECT

One of the best ways to advance your career as a software developer, bar none, is through side projects.

I've already told you my story of how that little Android app made all the difference in my life and career, but even the smaller, unfinished side projects I started before "Run Faster" helped me enhance my software development skills, learn new technologies, and sometimes even make a little bit of extra cash.

One of my earliest side projects was a Palm Pilot application I called MaLi (Magic the Gathering Life Counter).

It was written in C and I ended up selling it for around $5 on my website at ssmoimo.com.

Using the power of the WayBack Machine, you can actually see the website I created (https://simpleprogrammer.com/cg58-old) and even download an old version of MaLi.

I learned quite a bit doing that side project.

I learned a bit of graphic design using PhotoShop to create my logo and the images for the website.

I learned how to create an animated GIF.

I learned some web design skills.

I had to learn a little bit of Perl so I could create a CGI script to handle PayPal payments and automatically send someone a registration code to unlock the registered version of the app.

I even had to learn how to implement a primitive copy protection and registration system, and how to conduct basic ecommerce on the web.

Now, **I didn't make a large amount of money, but I developed a wide range of skills that helped me greatly advance my career.**

Most importantly, **I developed confidence** in my ability as a programmer.

I had created my own application and figured out how to sell it online—and I did it all on my own.

That's the power of a side project: you learn new skills, practice your existing skills, are challenged in new ways and develop confidence in your abilities.

One six-month side project has the potential to gain you the experience it might take you years to get just working your 9-to-5.

Not only that, but each side project is like a small lottery ticket.

Each one has the chance of having a large amount of economic success, especially as you grow and learn.

That's why I advise all software developers who really want to advance their careers to always be working on some kind of a side project.

PICKING A SIDE PROJECT

So maybe I've convinced you that you should start a side project, but you might be wondering what kind or how to pick one.

It's easy to get stuck trying to figure out that perfect idea and end up never doing anything.

Remember how we talked about the difference between a dream and a goal?

To make something a goal, it needs to be concrete (https://simpleprogrammer.com/cg58 -thegoal).

You need to figure out what you are going to do and start doing it.

I'd highly advise you to start out with something very small (https://simpleprogrammer.com /cg58-small).

Start with a very simple side project that you know you can easily complete.

Perhaps even something that will only take you a few weeks or a month at the most.

The reason why you should pick something small first is that **most people get pretty good at lying to themselves.**

They get so used to breaking their own promises and commitments to themselves that they lose the ability to trust themselves.

And they break their promises because they try to tackle projects or life changes that are too large and too much of a commitment.

They get in over their head, which causes them to fail or give up, and then they create this pattern where they continuously let themselves down, because they've lost the ability to trust themselves.

Maybe you are trapped in that pattern right now. I've certainly been at times in my life.

The best way to break out of this cycle is to make small commitments and follow through with them. (We'll talk more about the power of being a finisher a little later in this chapter.)

So, start with a very small, non-ambitious side project.

Something you know you can do and can complete.

In fact, **I usually advise most software developers to make their first side project a clone of something that already exists.**

When I was first learning game programming, I didn't try to create the masterpiece of a game I had in my mind that would take three years to build. Instead, I made a very simple Pong clone.

Don't worry about copying; it's not the same as plagiarizing.

In case you haven't noticed, the app store is full of games and apps that are pretty much copies of other ones. They just aren't exact copies, and your copy won't be, either.

Your project becomes much easier and has a much higher chance of success if you aren't trying to design software and build it at the same time.

Start by building software, and later, when you are more experienced with completing side projects and trust yourself more, you can work on designing something new and building it.

Once you've gotten a few of these smaller and easier side projects done, and have cemented your trust in yourself, it might be time to pick something more ambitious, but I would still limit my ambitions to a project which can be completed, or at least the first version shipped, in under three months.

You can always create future versions and build onto a side project over time—perhaps even make it your full-time gig, like I did—but you want to get it done and out there as soon as possible so you can gain the benefits from it, test out the idea, and not have it drag on for years.

MAKE THE SIDE PROJECT SERVE AT LEAST TWO PURPOSES

I'm a big fan of multi-purposing.

Multitasking sucks, it's difficult to do, and it ends up making you less productive overall.

(There are of course some exceptions to this.)

But multi-purposing, on the other hand, is where it's at.

It's the bee's knees.

What is multi-purposing, you ask?

It's exactly what it sounds like: you take one thing—a side project in this case—and you have it accomplish more than one purpose.

Take this book, for instance.

I'm writing this book in many small, blog post-sized chapters: why?

Well, it started out with me wanting to maintain a writing habit of writing at least 1,000 words a day.

Rather than just write random stuff, I thought, *hmm, I should write a book*.

But a book takes a long time, isn't usually very profitable, and you don't get any benefit until you finish it—(if you do) and actually sell it.

So, I thought, how can I multi-purpose this even more?

Then I realized that I could take each chapter of the book and write it as a blog post on my blog first, then when I was done, I could make a book out of all the chapters.

I also thought this would be a great way to increase email signups on my blog.

So...

This "book side project"—and it is a side project since I'm only working on it an hour each day—serves the following purposes:

1. Maintains habit of writing 1,000 words a day
2. Results in a completed book
3. Generates additional company revenue when I sell the book
4. Creates blog content
5. Increases email signups

In my mind, that's pretty good.

I'm getting quite a few benefits out of writing this book and I've structured it in a way that fulfills multiple purposes.

But that's not all. I can multi-purpose it further by:

- Selling an eBook version
- Selling a print version
- Selling an audio version
- Making some videos and selling a premium packaged version with all the above
- Using chapters to create YouTube content

So when you pick a project to work on, even a small one:

Think about how you can multi-purpose that project in as many ways as possible.

Perhaps with your side project you can combine multiples of these purposes together:

- Learn a new programming language
- Learn a new framework
- Practice an existing skill or master it
- Create an app to solve some problem you have
- Create an app to solve someone else's problem
- Create an additional income source
- Use it for your interview portfolio
- Use it for blog content
- Use creating the app for video content

- Use the project to mentor someone
- Use the project to be mentored
- Increase your self-discipline
- Try out a new time-management technique
- Make new friends
- Learn about an industry you are interested in
- Complete a college or university assignment
- More...

GETTING STARTED

Before you start coding away—or doing whatever you are doing—it's important to plan out what you are going to do and define what the end goal is.

Oftentimes, projects aren't completed because they are missing three essential things:

1. A goal or "finished" criteria
2. A deadline
3. A system or set interval to work on the project

You need all three of these things to be successful.

Start with defining your end goal.

What is the criteria you will use to say that the project is finished, or at least shippable?

Define the **minimum** feature set or criteria which will define the successful completion of your project.

The scope can increase later and you can create new projects to build new functionality into your existing projects, but make sure that you have an initial scope that will determine when this particular project is "done."

Next, **set a deadline.**

Be aggressive, but not too aggressive.

Pick a deadline that you know you can accomplish, and give yourself a little buffer, but not too much.

If you give yourself too much buffer, you'll procrastinate.

Having a deadline will create urgency and help you take yourself more seriously.

When I said I was going to complete this book by the end of this year, I had something to shoot for and commit to.

I couldn't procrastinate and put things off, because I had a deadline that not only held myself accountable, but...

I also told the world.

Finally, **you need a system and a schedule** for actually working on the side project and making progress.

I talk about how I use various systems, including a quota system, in my book *Soft Skills: The Software Developer's Life Manual* (https://simpleprogrammer.com/cg58-lifemanual), in the section on productivity.

So I won't go into the details here, but make sure you have some kind of system in place that will do the following things:

- Define clearly how much time you will commit to spending on the project each day or week
- Define when you will spend that time (put it on your calendar)
- Define the process you will use to track the work and what needs to be done

Good systems are the key to success.

This book had a system.

Every successful project I've ever undertaken had a system in place for getting it done.

BE CONSISTENT

Speaking of systems, let's talk about one of the most important things you can do to actually complete and benefit from your side project: be consistent (https://simpleprogrammer.com /cg58-consistency).

This means that you don't work on the side project only when you feel like it, because there will be plenty of times you don't.

It means you create a schedule for working on the side project and, come hell or high water, you stick to that schedule.

Any measure of true success I have enjoyed in my life has come from consistency.

I'm in shape and look good because I'm consistent in my diet and workout program.

(If you are wondering, I eat one meal a day, run 40 miles a week, and lift weights three times per week.)

I don't miss a day—and I mean that.

I'm consistent in the writing of this book, of writing blog posts, of making YouTube videos, of just about anything I want to accomplish in life.

It's all those small things that add up.

You build a wall by laying one perfect brick every single day.

Consistency is the key.

If you want to finish your side project, learn to be consistent.

HEY JOHN

You said you basically never miss a day. How is that possible? Don't things come up that throw off your perfect schedule?

One of the main reasons why I never miss a day is because I plan ahead.

If I know something is coming up that absolutely will prevent me from doing my workout, recording my YouTube videos, writing a chapter in my book, or whatever else I have planned at my normally scheduled time, I already have a replacement time committed in my calendar.

Whenever I travel—which is pretty frequently—I always plan ahead what my workout plan will be.

What gym will I go to work out at and at what time on what days?

Where will I go to run and when?

How will I get my YouTube videos recorded?

It's great to have a schedule, and just having one is going to really help you to be consistent, but you also have to plan ahead for when your schedule is interrupted.

BE A FINISHER

And you want to be a finisher... trust me.

My life completely changed when I became a finisher (https://simpleprogrammer.com /cg58-finisher).

It's really easy to start things and not finish them.

I've got a yellow belt in my closet, some old soccer cleats, a guitar, surfboard, and more.

I call it the closest of broken dreams, and we all have one.

We've all started things that we didn't see through to the end.

We've all begun projects with the greatest of hopes, only to end up quitting after a few weeks or even days.

Stop doing that right now!

Resolve today to become a finisher!

Decide that no matter the project, no matter how much you hate it, once you start something, you will finish it, even if it kills you.

It's that attitude that shifted my life around.

Now, I never start something unless I intend to finish it.

And even if I don't feel like finishing something, I do it anyway.

I would have never written my first book, shipped 55 Pluralsight courses (https://simple programmer.com/cg58-pluralsight), made multiple products, obtained 6-pack abs, or done really much of anything if I had not decided one day to adopt this attitude for life.

That doesn't mean every project I put my hands on turns to gold, but I'll tell you what, they all get DONE.

HEY JOHN

How do I handle getting "stuck" in a project? When I don't know what to do next or how to solve a problem?

For the most part you just push on—even when you know your solution or your answer isn't optimal.

It's tough, believe me. I tend to be a perfectionist, but perfect is the enemy of good.

If I let myself get "stuck" because I didn't know what to write or I couldn't find the perfect sentence, you wouldn't be reading this book right now.

The trade off is that some parts of this book won't be as great as I'd like them to be.

But, the book will be finished and shipped.

Getting 99% done with a project, but not shipping it has 0% value.

It's almost always better to push through and forge ahead rather than to allow yourself to get stuck and caught up in the problem you are trying to solve because you are trying to solve it perfectly.

Oftentimes, you have to just go forward with a best guess and perhaps a hope and a prayer.

Sometimes you'll be wrong, but you are guaranteed to miss 100% of the swings you don't take.

So, if you are feeling stuck, the first thing you should do is evaluate whether or not you are really "stuck" or if you are just waiting for a perfect solution.

If you still feel "stuck" and don't know what to do, just try to think of the next smallest possible step and take it—even if it doesn't feel right.

Can't solve a problem, ask for help and then skip it and move on.

Not all problems have to be solved anyway.

Sometimes you just take a best guess and accept the consequences, knowing that something is almost always better than nothing.

MAKING MONEY FROM YOUR SIDE PROJECT

Let's wrap up this chapter by talking about how you—yes, you—can actually make some money on your side project.

First of all, I recommend that on any side project you undertake, you find some way to make money from it, even if it's not a large amount.

Charge 99 cents for it if you must, but put it in the app store.

Make the app available for free, but put some ads in it.

Make the web app have a trial and a paid version.

At least put a donation button up, for goodness sake!

Try to come up with some way you are going to be able to monetize the project from the start.

If you are creating a blog—although, I suppose the same concept would apply to many endeavors—check out my short course on "10 Ways to Make Money From Your Blog" (https://simpleprogrammer.com/cg58-money), for some ideas.

Now that I've said that, let's be realistic.

You are not going to make a ton of money from your side project.

Yes, I know you think it's awesome, and it probably is, but just don't expect to make a large deal of money from it, at least not at first.

In time, you may be able to make some good money, but at first just try to figure out a way that you can make some kind of money.

If you work on multiple side projects, a little bit of money here and there can add up greatly over time through different income streams.

The important thing is to think about this upfront.

You are not Twitter or some ridiculously-funded startup who can try to get users and then worry about figuring out how to actually make money from them.

GET CRACKING!

Alright, so hopefully you have a good idea by now of what to do and what not to do in terms of starting a side project.

And hopefully you are inspired to start one.

Like I said, I think all software developers should always have some side project going.

Just remember to **start small, commit, and finish** and you'll be fine.

You always want to make sure you get a real benefit—and hopefully more than one—out of any side project you are going to devote your free time to.

Good luck and Godspeed!

CHAPTER 59

BEST BOOKS TO READ

It's no secret **I love books.**

When I am out running my 40 miles a week, it's study hall time for me.

I spend a good eight hours a week reading books—or rather, listening to the audio versions (https://simpleprogrammer.com/cg59-audible) when I'm running or driving.

In a year, I'll easily go through more than 50 books.

A huge amount of the success I've been able to achieve in life is directly attributable to the books I've read.

I've never had any real mentors.

When I wanted to learn how to invest in real estate (https://simpleprogrammer.com /cg59-realestate), there was no one to show me the ropes.

I had to figure it out myself and books helped.

When I first wanted to learn how to program, once again, I didn't have a real mentor.

I didn't know any programmers—I was just a kid.

So, I turned to books.

When I wanted to advance my career as a software developer, again, no one to turn to, so more books.

Start a business—books.

Stock trade options—books.

Improve my life, my discipline, self-esteem, willpower—get in shape?

Books, books, books, and more books.

(Also plenty of failing, but getting back up again (https://simpleprogrammer.com/cg59-bad).)

Perhaps you, like me, don't have access to a real-life mentor who can guide you on the path of programming and life?

Hopefully this book has helped to serve that purpose, but the journey hasn't ended. It never does.

That's why I've decided to wrap up this book by giving you a list of **some of my favorite books** so you can create your own virtual mentors.

It's tempting for me to list hundreds of books, but to save some space, I've trimmed the list down to what I think are the best of the best.

However, if you'd like to download a complete list of my all-time most influential books, broken down by topics, you can get it right here (https://simpleprogrammer.com/career-guide-toolkit).

I hope you enjoy.

WRITING GOOD CODE

As a software developer, you should be especially interested in writing good code, since that is one of the most foundational things software developers do.

Here are some of the best books I've found on the topic that greatly influenced me in my career and directly improved the quality of the code I wrote.

Code Complete: A Practical Handbook of Software Construction, Second Edition
(https://simpleprogrammer.com/cg59-complete)

This is a foundational and pivotal book on writing good, clean, understandable code that clearly communicates what the code does without the need for excessive comments.

It has fundamentally changed the way I think about writing code and creating software.

It talks about how to debug code, create quality software, and many other topics every software developer should understand.

The book is a little dated as far as methodologies go, but is still a must-read book for every serious software developer.

Clean Code: A Handbook of Agile Software Craftsmanship
(https://simpleprogrammer.com/cg59-clean)

This is one of my all-time favorite books, written by one of my favorite mentors in the software development industry, Bob Martin (Uncle Bob).

This book teaches you how to write clean, highly understandable code and to refactor existing code by example.

It is full of principles and best practices that are timeless in nature and greatly aid the understanding of code written in any programming language.

While Code Complete is a bit dated in terms of methodology, Clean Code makes up for it by presenting an Agile way of crafting and maintaining software.

Agile Software Development, Principles, Patterns, and Practices
(https://simpleprogrammer.com/cg59-agile)

Another book by Uncle Bob, but this one focuses more on object-oriented programming.

It covers a wide range of topics from Agile methodology and how to use it, to object oriented design principles, to design patterns and more—all with excellent examples.

WHAT YOU NEED TO KNOW

There are many things you need to know as a software developer. I've covered the basics of them throughout this book, but the following books will give you a more in-depth understanding and round out a few areas we didn't discuss:

Design Patterns: Elements of Reusable Object-Oriented Software
(https://simpleprogrammer.com/cg59-design)

This book is a classic, but it's still relevant today, as you'll commonly see design patterns in code you are maintaining, or you'll recognize some of these patterns in code you are writing.

Every software developer should at least understand the basic, classic design patterns presented in this book.

Testing Computer Software
(https://simpleprogrammer.com/cg59-testing)

Another classic book, but an essential one for understanding software testing and what it is all about.

This book covers the basics of what every software developer should know about testing and test methodology.

Introduction to Algorithms
(https://simpleprogrammer.com/cg59-algorithms)

Not an easy book by any means—requires some math—but it is one of the best books on the modern algorithms commonly used in software development today.

Every software developer should be familiar with these algorithms.

Patterns of Enterprise Application Architecture
(https://simpleprogrammer.com/cg59-patterns)

This book covers just about everything you should know about writing large-scale, robust applications.

Although the focus is on enterprise applications, many of the principles and patterns apply to any kind of large-scale software application.

WORKING WITH EXISTING CODE

One of the most frequent things you'll be doing as a software developer is working with and maintaining code you didn't write, i.e. legacy code.

Fortunately, there are some pretty good books on the subject.

Refactoring: Improving the Design of Existing Code
(https://simpleprogrammer.com/cg59-refactor)

One essential skill in working with legacy code is refactoring.

Refactoring is changing the structure of the code without changing its functionality.

This book covers just about every major refactoring pattern you need to know.

Now, most of these refactorings don't have to be done manually any more, since they are baked into modern IDEs, but this book will teach you what they are and how to implement them when you have to.

Working Effectively With Legacy Code
(https://simpleprogrammer.com/cg59-legacy)

This is considered one of the best overall books for learning how to deal with and maintain legacy code.

It covers just about every topic you can think of in dealing with legacy systems, including safely refactoring, identifying where to make code changes, dealing with systems that aren't object-oriented, and much, much more.

I highly recommend every software developer read this book—more than once.

Refactoring to Patterns
(https://simpleprogrammer.com/cg59-refactorpatterns)

One of the best ways to clean up legacy code through refactoring is to simplify it, especially if it is a mess.

This book shows you exactly, step-by-step, how you can take existing code and refactor it using common design patterns found in software development.

This doesn't mean you should refactor every bit of code into design patterns, or forcefully implement overly-complex design patterns when a simpler solution will do, but there are definitely plenty of times where the content of this book will come in handy.

DEVELOPING YOURSELF AS A DEVELOPER

Being a good software developer involves more than just writing good code and being technically competent.

Various soft skills are also very important to your success as a code monkey.

The following books will help you grow and develop as a developer in more than just technical skills.

Soft Skills: The Software Developer's Life Manual
(https://simpleprogrammer.com/cg59-lifemanual)

Of course I have to include my book here, as I specifically wrote it to fill the need for a comprehensive book about developing soft skills as a software developer.

In this book, I cover everything from your career, to marketing yourself, learning, productivity, finances, health and fitness, and even mastering the mental game and mindset.

I think every software developer should read this book—but I'm a bit biased.

The Pragmatic Programmer: From Journeyman to Master
(https://simpleprogrammer.com/cg59-pragmatic)

Based on the wisdom of a couple of very experienced software developers, this is an extremely popular programming book all about how to advance your career as a software developer..

It's funny, it's entertaining, it's real stories about real difficult situations in software development.

The Passionate Programmer: Creating a Remarkable Career in Software Development
(https://simpleprogrammer.com/cg59-passionate)

This book is chock-full of practical advice about your career as a software developer and the inevitable struggles you'll face.

It's about learning how to increase your skills, changing your attitude, staying motivated, and keeping that passion alive, and of course, about advancing your career.

DEVELOPING YOURSELF AS A HUMAN BEING

Ok, this is where it gets tough for me to narrow things down.

I have a TON of books on this subject, since it's my mission in life to develop myself and help others achieve their own personal growth, but I'm picking the best of the best and the ones I think will especially help software developers.

I'm limiting myself to these three. Ok, four (I can't resist).

How To Win Friends & Influence People
(https://simpleprogrammer.com/cg59-influence)

Start with this book.

It's one of the best books of all time about interacting with others. Don't let the title or the age of the book fool you.

This is a classic book frequently on the top book list of many successful people.

I honestly read this book at least once a year, sometimes twice.

I can't say enough good things about this book—it changed my life.

As a Man Thinketh
(https://simpleprogrammer.com/cg59-thinketh)

This is a short book, and another old one, but extremely potent.

The mindset presented in this book is the mindset required to achieve success in life.

It's all about focusing on your thoughts and how you choose to perceive the world, which ultimately determines what your life and world is like and what it will become.

Maximum Achievement: Strategies and Skills That Will Unlock Your Hidden Powers to Succeed
(https://simpleprogrammer.com/cg59-max)

If I had to pick one personal development book, and only one, this would be it.

Why?

It's packed with many concepts, which are sourced from classical books on the subject and they are explained in a way that is concise and clear. It has plenty of exercises for you to actually do to make real, positive changes in your life.

This book covers a wide range of personal development topics, and gives you a huge "bang for your buck" in terms of what can be offered in a single book.

How to Fail at Almost Everything and Still Win Big: Kind of the Story of My Life
(https://simpleprogrammer.com/cg59-fail)

This final book choice was difficult.

There are still so many good personal development books out there, but I picked this one because the author is none other than Scott Adams—yes, that's right, the creator of Dilbert.

But he's so much more than that.

This book lays out a philosophy of life that can't help but make you a champion.

I never expected such wisdom from the creator of a cartoon about a pointy-haired boss, but this book delivers.

(If you really want to see how deep Scott Adams can go—and you really want to bake your brain— check out God's Debris (https://simpleprogrammer.com/cg59-debris). Don't say I didn't warn you, though.)

I'll stop here, but I could write a whole book on what books to read for personal development and growth.

GOING DEEP

Sometimes as a software developer it's fun and enlightening to go deep.

What do I mean by going deep?

I mean blasting through abstractions and dissecting things to understand how they really work.

Sure, we don't need to know how CPUs work and the underlying details of operating systems to do our normal jobs, but gosh darn it, it's fun to dig into those details. Sometimes.

So, if you want to go deep, I've got a few book recommendations for you that will take you to the depth you desire and fulfill that childlike curiosity we all have.

Code: The Hidden Language of Computer Hardware and Software
(https://simpleprogrammer.com/cg59-hidden)

This book filled in so many of my knowledge gaps around computer hardware, low-level computer science and computer architecture concepts.

The best part is, it does it in a fun, entertaining and easy-to-digest way—at least mostly easy to digest.

I highly recommend that every software developer read this book, not because you need to know what is in this book, but because you'll have so much fun learning what is in this book.

Plus, you'll understand computers and code in a way that you couldn't imagine.

Structure and Interpretation of Computer Programs
(https://simpleprogrammer.com/cg59-structure)

This is a difficult book about programming—especially if you go through the book and do all the exercises.

But I think you'll find the experience rewarding and it's likely to change the way you think about and approach programming, especially if you've never been introduced to functional programming concepts.

Cracking the Coding Interview: 150 Programming Questions and Solutions
(https://simpleprogrammer.com/cg59-cracking)

If you want to get a job at a company like Microsoft or Google, this is required reading.

If you want to be able to pass a whiteboard interview where you have to code up a solution to some algorithm problem, this is required reading.

This book pretty much covers everything you need to know about solving the difficult, computer science, algorithm-type programs that are often asked during coding interviews.

It covers the fundamental types of algorithms and data structures, gives you practice problems, and sets you up for success.

If you want to go deep with learning how to solve algorithm-type coding problems, this is your book.

The Art of Computer Programming
(https://simpleprogrammer.com/cg59-art)

Can I really recommend a book series I've never read?

Sure can.

This four-volume set was on my list of "someday to read" books, but I never got around to it.

Why?

Because reading these books is a huge undertaking.

These books go through, in depth and in detail, computer science algorithms—and not the easy stuff.

If you really, really want to go deep with algorithms, and you are prepared for some heavy math, go for it.

Let me know how it goes. I wish you luck.

Compilers: Principles, Techniques, and Tools (Second Edition)
(https://simpleprogrammer.com/cg59-compilers)

This book is known as the dragon book—and for good reason.

It goes down deep into places where the dragons live; in the realm of compilers and operating systems.

Some of the information might be a bit dated, but if you are really interested in how compilers work and perhaps want to write your own, take a crack at this book.

ENTERTAINING AND FUN

You might think that going deep into algorithms or compilers is both fun and entertaining, and while I agree, in part, I have to admit that not every software developer thinks so.

So, what I will present to you here are books that I feel are especially fun and entertaining to most software developers.

Your mileage may vary.

Gödel, Escher, Bach: An Eternal Golden Braid
(https://simpleprogrammer.com/cg59-golden)

The first time I heard about this book, it was someone saying they wished they could read it again for the first time.

That was enough to get me to buy and read this book, and I was not disappointed.

It's not a computer science or programming book, but it has many programming-related concepts and delves deeply into the paradoxical, contradiction-heavy realm of logic.

Magic 2.0 Series
(https://simpleprogrammer.com/cg59-magic)

I don't read much fiction, but these books appealed to me because they combine D&D kind of elements with computer hacking and time travel.

Oh, and they are very funny.

Again, I'm not a huge fiction reader, but as a programmer, I really enjoyed these books, so I'm recommending them here.

The Martian
(https://simpleprogrammer.com/cg59-martian)

Like I said, I don't read many fiction books, but I read this one because it was written by a programmer, I like space, and so many people kept talking about it.

I was not disappointed.

Fantastically funny, thrilling, and intellectually stimulating book.

Pretty much loved every moment of it.

Snow Crash
(https://simpleprogrammer.com/cg59-snow)

Yes, I'm recommending another book I haven't read—yet.

But I promise I just added it to my Amazon wish list and I'll be reading it soon.

As far as fiction programming books go, this is probably the most highly recommended book.

So, I felt I would be doing you a disservice if I didn't recommend it here.

Like I said, I haven't read it myself, but I plan to.

(Update: I did read it, but it wasn't my cup of tea. Still, so many developers do like and recommend it that I'm leaving it in this list.)

PERSEVERANCE AND MOTIVATION

There is no real substitute in life for getting your ass kicked.

It's through adversity that we learn to overcome and grow stronger.

Life will kick you in the ass.

Life will be hard and cruel at times.

You are going to lose your motivation.

You are going to want to quit and give up.

The following books will help you in those times.

The Obstacle is the Way
(https://simpleprogrammer.com/cg59-obstacle)

This book is the first book that really introduced me to the stoic philosophy I hold so central to my life today.

This book is about how the bad things that happen to you can be used to make you strong and help you find the right path instead of defeating you.

Most of these lessons come right out of stoic philosophy; they are told using historical stories that demonstrate the principle.

The 10x Rule
(https://simpleprogrammer.com/cg59-tenx)

The author of this book, Grant Cardone, quickly became one of the greatest role models in my life after I read this book and the next one, also his.

This book is all about how you probably need to set your goals 10x higher, and how it will probably take 10x more effort to achieve them than what you think.

It's about how you can, and should, take massive action to achieve success in life.

This book will kick you in the ass—I promise.

Be Obsessed or be Average
(https://simpleprogrammer.com/cg59-average)

Hey, so do the people around you say that you are "obsessed" and that what you are doing isn't healthy because you are working too hard?

This book gives you permission to politely "give them the finger" and keep on blazing your trail.

It's all about harnessing the power of obsession to get where you want to go.

It also talks quite a bit about the people who will try to bring you down and how to deal with them.

The War of Art
(https://simpleprogrammer.com/cg59-war)

I've read this book at least a dozen times—it's that good.

It's all about sitting down to do the work and realizing that it will always be difficult; you'll often feel unmotivated, but as a professional, you do it anyway.

This book helped me develop the work ethic to write my first book, and that work ethic has continued to help me write this book.

This book is all about fighting and overcoming the resistance that we all face in life whenever we try to improve ourselves in any way.

Plus, it's written so poetically that it's a pleasure to read.

READ ON, MY FRIEND...

Well there you have it; those books should keep you busy for a while.

If you get through all the books on this list, I guarantee your life will be drastically improved.

But the journey shouldn't stop there.

I challenge you to make reading a daily habit, if it isn't already.

There are so many more good books out there. It was quite difficult to narrow all my favorites down to make this list.

Here are a few final tips to help you on your journey.

Make sure you spend your time reading good books.

Always look for books that are highly recommended.

Always have a list of books that you want to read next so that you aren't stuck "looking for a good book."

Utilize audio if you can.

When you are running, walking, lifting weights, driving in the car, or doing some other activity where you can easily listen to an audiobook, do it.

Invest in getting an Audible.com subscription (https://simpleprogrammer.com/cg59-audible) and don't be afraid to buy extra credits.

Finally, **put what you learn into action.**

Knowledge without action is worthless.

Don't just read the books, do what they say.

Think about how you can apply what you are learning to your own life.

And, maybe... someday... write your own book.

CHAPTER 60

PARTING WORDS

Well, I can't believe we've made it here.

I say "we" because **if you've joined me through the 200,000 or so words in this book, you deserve some credit as well.**

So give yourself a pat on the back, knowing that most people buy a book and never even crack it open; even a majority of the ones who do, don't make it much further than the first chapter.

But, before you congratulate yourself too much, I want to remind you that there is a huge difference between "reading" and "doing."

Whenever I sign copies of my first book, *Soft Skills: The Software Developer's Life Manual* (https://simpleprogrammer.com/cg60-lifemanual), I almost always write, "Take Action."

When people ask why I write that instead of something more endearing like, "Joe, you rock! Keep being awesome!", I tell them that a book is merely words on a page without action.

So that's what I would encourage you to do: go out there and "take action."

I've done the best I can.

I've given you as much knowledge as I have about software development and how to be successful as a software developer, but I can only do so much.

I can only take it so far.

The rest is up to you.

So, I challenge you—I implore you—**don't let this be just another book you read.**

The excuse of not knowing what to do is not one you can hold onto any longer.

You know what to do now.

If you need to get started as a software developer, you know how.

You know what skills you need to have, you know how to pick a programming language, and how to get started learning.

You know how to choose whether or not to go to college, a boot camp, or learn on your own.

And if you need to find that first job, or get a new job, you know how to do that now as well.

You know about internships and getting a job with or without experience.

You know how to create a good software development resume, how to interview and negotiate a salary or raise, and even how to leave a job or switch into one mid-career from another vocation.

And although I couldn't give you every single detail of everything you need to know as a software developer, you know the basics, from the types of development, to testing and QA, to methodologies, source control, best practices, debugging and more.

You know how to work as a developer and to improve your working environment by choosing to be provocative instead of blaming life or circumstances.

You know how to deal with your coworkers and your boss, how to balance your life, work on a team, present and sell your ideas—even how to dress.

You know how to get that promotion, how to deal with the people who will try to take you down, and how to eventually lead them.

Finally, you know how to take things to the next level—how to advance your career.

You know what it takes to build a reputation and the value of it.

You know how to network and how to build your skills, how to specialize, to create a blog, and get your name out there.

You know your options, what career paths and choices you can make, whether it be climbing the corporate ladder or going out on your own as a freelancer.

So lack of knowledge—for you, at least—is not an excuse.

There is a big difference between knowing what to do and knowing how it will turn out.

None of us know how it will turn out, so we have to take the knowledge we have, do our best to apply it, and then trust the process (https://simpleprogrammer.com/cg60-trust), knowing that there will be some failures along the way, but as long as we get back up and try again, as long as we do not give up, we'll eventually succeed.

So, it's up to you now, to take action, to change your life, to choose to succeed.

You can read this book and say, "Oh, that was nice. Lots of good advice in there." And that can be the end of it. Or, you can look at this book as the turning point in your life.

The point where you finally say, "I've had enough. I want something better. I want something more. I want to be something more."

I encourage you to do the latter.

It's those short and fleeting moments in life, when we convert our wishes and aspirations into resolve, that make all the difference.

This is your moment now.

This is your chance.

There are only so many points in life where someone is whispering in your ear, telling you, "Make something happen. Do it. Do it now!"

So, plant your flag.

Set a new standard.

Set a course for your career, for your life, in the direction you want to go.

Resolve today—in this very moment—to take action.

A FINAL FAVOR TO ASK

Before I let you go, I have a favor I would like to ask of you, if it's not too much trouble.

First of all, whatever you do, spread the love—share the knowledge.

If you benefit in any way from this book, pass on that benefit to someone else who could use it.

I'd, of course, be thrilled if you decided to gift them a copy of this book, or my other book if you think they would benefit from that more. Make a real difference in someone's life.

I wrote this book to make a difference.

So if it made a difference to you, all I ask is that you be part of—in some small way or large—making a difference in someone else's life.

All those little differences add up to make this world a much better place.

But it begins with you taking action and then showing someone else how to do the same.

With that said, I sincerely thank you for reading this book.

I wish you the best and greatest success in your career as a software developer—and in life.

Even if no one else believes in you.

Even if YOU don't believe in you, I do.

So go out there and conquer the world!

P.S. Come visit me on the web to continue the journey at https://simpleprogrammer.com *and* https://youtube.com/simpleprogrammer.

OVERWHELMED BY THE NON-STOP FLOOD OF NEW TOOLS AND TECHNOLOGIES IN SOFTWARE DEVELOPMENT?

The most important survival skill any software developer can have is **knowing how to LEARN efficiently.**

In "10 Steps to Learn Anything Quickly", John Sonmez shares his system for stripping a subject down to the bare essentials that give you a **productive, working knowledge** of the topic in the **shortest time possible.**

You'll discover:

- How to harness your natural creativity and curiosity for better, faster learning (with zero frustration and overwhelm).
- The reason why including a mandatory "play time" in your study sessions can rocket you up the learning curve faster than you thought possible—even though you feel like you're just goofing off.
- A reliable heuristic for knowing what to read—and what to ignore. That's right: Dumping that massive stack of unread books and deleting your Instapaper queue will actually make you a faster learner. (This will free you from "Amazon reading list guilt" forever.)
- How to chart your own course for learning a new topic. This will free you from the soft tyranny of book authors and trainers who think they know the best way for you to learn.
- The 3 critical questions you must answer when you start learning anything new. (Don't waste weeks wandering around lost and confused. These questions will point you in the right direction, every time.)
- How to learn more by learning less. (This is critical to eliminating overwhelm—and actually putting what you're learning into practice.)

Save $20 Today!

Just visit:
https://simpleprogrammer.com/cg-10-steps

WHY YOU DIDN'T GET THE JOB

Fact: The Best Jobs Rarely Go to the Most Talented,
Knowledgeable Developer

In his early years as a developer, John Sonmez struggled to earn respect and move his career ahead.

Why didn't employers didn't seem to value his deep technical knowledge?

Eventually he realized that when it comes to landing a great job, your coding skills will only take you so far... And the way to create real, life-changing opportunities for yourself is to first give value to OTHERS.

In **"How to Market Yourself as a Software Developer"**, John shares the details of this unusual approach—the same techniques that helped him become a highly paid, highly sought-after senior developer and software consultant.

* Landing the job you've always wanted—solving challenging problems, pushing yourself to develop your technical skills, and working with people who share your passion for the craft of software development
* Earning a raise of 20%, 50% or even as much as 300% over the coming months and years
* Building a reliable feeder system for 4- and 5-figure freelancing and consulting work
* Earning more respect from your team and manager and a voice in making critical decisions
* Creating your own "safety net" of career opportunities so you never have to worry about where your next paycheck will come from—this is TRUE security

Get $100 Off Today!

Go to:
https://simpleprogrammer.com/cg-developer-marketing

87257148R00439

Made in the USA
Lexington, KY
21 April 2018